CHILDREN OF SEPARATION

An Annotated Bibliography For Professionals

by

Greta W. Stanton

THE SCARECROW PRESS, INC.
METUCHEN, N.J., & LONDON
1994

British Library Cataloguing-in-Publication data available

Library of Congress Cataloging-in-Publication Data

Stanton, Greta W.
Children of separation : an annotated bibliography for professionals / by Greta W. Stanton.
p. cm.
Includes index.
ISBN 0-8108-2695-X (acid-free paper)
1. Parent and child—United States—Bibliography. 2. Family life education—United States—Bibliography. 3. Children of divorced parents—United States—Bibliography. 4. Stepfamilies—United States—Bibliography. 5. Single-parent family—United States—Bibliography. 6. Children, Adopted—United States—Bibliography. 7. Foster parents—United States—Bibliography. I. Title.
Z7164.M2S73 1994
[HQ755.8]
306.874—dc20 93-43575

Manufactured in the United States of America

Printed on acid-free paper

TABLE OF CONTENTS

INTRODUCTION

The last ten years have seen a plethora of attention to the rising number of remarriages, especially due to divorce, in the U.S. and elsewhere, both in popular and professional literature. A number of bibliographies on the subject of stepfamilies have also begun to appear, many of which deal with some aspects of raising children in remarried families. However, children of the divorced, divorcing, the single-parent family (never married, divorced or widowed), and the remarried (alias "stepfamily") need focal attention due to the unique crisis aspects of their lives. Complexities in these families are perceived as arising from lack of clear role expectations on the part of adult marital partners, their extended families, and therefore the children themselves, as well as from community expectations and prejudices. Special attention needs to be paid to the impact on women and minorities. Vulnerability to legal and economic problems, a threat to social stability and to our cherished notions of family living, presents special challenges.

Preparation for family separation and for remarriage and/or helping processes for coping on the part of all family members are viewed as a continuum from the breakup of a marriage, to two single-parent households, to remarriage.

Foster Care and Adoption

The analogies to the lives of children in foster care and in adoptive homes need to be considered. These children, too, need to mourn losses and adapt to non-nuclear family life-styles. The special effects of multiple-parental models on the child's perception of his/her roots and identity, on the ability to form new bonds, and last but not least, the power of the law and the traditional perceptions of family living seem to be areas of vulnerability which all children of separation have in common.

Helping Efforts

The concept of prevention and of early-case entry through "non-therapy" channels of outreach, consultation to self-help groups, family-life education and brief, reality-focused counseling are beginning to be emphasized as relatively new foci for professionals. Interventions require a sophisticated ability to assess (diagnose) and work with adults and children, individually and in groups, on the level of crisis counseling, and family-life education as well as providing stimulus to self-help groups. Skills in the development of community contact with family networks and community support systems are required. Programs providing help for these new ''problems-in-living'' are coming into being and a body of empirical knowledge and research is slowly developing.

Reason for Bibliography

The author (in her role as a teacher of graduate students in social work) developed a course and formulated a study approach to the needs and experiences of children who are raised in non-nuclear families, either by single parents or serial parents, thus relating to more than two biological parents over their growing years. The approach represents an outgrowth of many years as a practitioner and teacher of child werlfare, and the study, practice, and teaching of the more recent phenomenon of living in stepfamilies. Last but not least, the author's last 25 years as a stepmother provided a testing ground for principles learned earlier which have been incorporated into further professional endeavors.

Why a Bibliography?

As a professional and a teacher of professionals, I have been concerned with the ever-increasing volume of research and clinical literature, both in books and journal articles, with which students and practitioners in the helping professions as well as in more theoretical research areas need to become familiar. Since these are generally focused on one of the particular problem categories, e.g. stepfamilies, or children in foster care, it was felt that a resource book focusing on an identification of the commonalities in the experiences of children living in these families, as well as an emphasis on emerging and re-emerging preventive approaches, may provide a beginning effort at integrating some of the developing professional literature.

We have focused on the similarities of living in multiparenting situations, on the development of children, and the possible intra- and interpersonal problems, both in terms of currently known research efforts, and the validity of short-term crisis-oriented interventions based on multiple theoretical orientations. We are aware of the limitations and need for further efforts in distinguishing differences such as remarriage and stepparenting after the death of a parent rather than after divorce, foster care in wartime, and amicable adoptions, all of which have more social sanctions than the situations which we were able to study.

To complete this project, the published clinical and research literature from approximately 1965 through July 1988 was searched under the subject headings of Blended Families, Second Marriages, Remarried Families, Stepfamilies, Reconstituted Families, Foster and Adoptive Families; also, Law, Loss, and Identity as related to these families. Regret is expressed for any overlooked material. I started by collecting books and articles on stepfamilies and wound up expanding the subject. Since then, especially in the last two years, much more bibliographic material has appeared, which is included here wherever it dealt with one of the major subjects of concentration, the four core problems, family typology, and the nature of the remedial process. Since most papers and dissertations reviewed were involved either with research, or with counseling/therapy, or both, no effort has been made to separate the two as distinct categories. However, the renewed professional efforts at family life education and at prevention have been lifted out for special attention.

Since this is a resource book, I have attempted as much as possible to suspend my critical evaluation of what was cited. My professional opinion and/or bias are reflected in my selection of materials but not in my summarizations. To the extent possible, though with necessary abbreviating efforts, the original authors' conceptualizations have been retained. Since this is intended as a general resource book to stimulate further research efforts, we have omitted details of test materials and specific professional and/or research language, wherever possible.

Organization of Annotations

In classifying the material, I have divided the reading into four basic sections, with a number of subsections in each: Central Issues, Types and Categories of Families, Interventions, and Children. In view of the mass of popular literature available in other places, this book has been confined to the literature available on specific issues in professional books and journals. The children's section provides both fiction and non-fiction, to be read by children, read to children, and read by parents and children together. The annotations marked DHHS were obtained from the U.S. Department of Health and Human Services publication *Helping Youth and Families of Separation, Divorce, and Remarriage. A Program Manual*—now out of print. Many of those were credited to Parents Without Partners (PWP) and AIR, organizations which had first found and annotated them. These are to be considered more as an undifferentiated listing for further research and suggested further analysis.

Acknowledgments

Most of the research for this book was done in Alexander Library of Rutgers University. Without the advice and help of Mr. Ed Pason, the Library's Professional School bibliographer, the collection of material would have been a much more arduous task. I am indebted to Ms. Jean Coyne for the assignment of space in the library, and to all of the library staff for their patient, helpful attitude. Special appreciation goes to Mr. Ralph Moreno and Ms. Linda Langshied for their helpful organization of the Roars abstracts.

Acknowledgment and thanks are extended to the personnel of the following abstracting services, which granted me permission to cite or to draw on their abstracts, found through the Roars Computer Service, for my own abstracts: Dissertation Abstracts International, Psychinfo Database, Sociological Abstracts Data Base, ERIC, Social Work Abstracts, NCFR, The Stepfamily Association of America, and Dr. Ellen Gruber are herewith thanked for their permission to be included. Government publications and journals provided additional resources.

It should be noted that in line with the permission granted by various organizations, we have indicated the source of information by designations such as ERIC, SAA (Stepfamily Association of America), Gruber, DAI, Psychinfo, etc. When quotes are used ("___"), we have cited a verbatim version of our source. Otherwise, the sources are given credit; the citations are ours alone.

Special thanks are due to the many professional friends and colleagues who have contributed their wisdom, their considerable knowledge, and their encouragement and support concerning the worthwhileness of this endeavor. Professor Naomi Golan, Drs. Emily and John Visher, Dr. Clifford Sager, and Ms. Holly Brown, the early researchers on transitions and stepfamilies, were very inspiring. My warm appreciation goes to Dr. Silvia H. Abramsky, and Professor Marilyn Lieberman, friends and professional advisers. Thanks also go to Mrs. Beatrice Saunders who helped me and other Rutgers School of Social Work faculty to become somewhat more knowledgeable about publications. Mrs. Harriet Fink, Manager of Computer Services at the Rutgers School of Social Work, was instrumental in bringing this collection into shape by advising me and teaching my computer assistant, Ms. Linda Savage, the specific skills needed. A warm note of appreciation goes to my many students, who in their required bibliographies in the courses I have taught for the last eight years have contributed very much by their diligent research into the areas of my endeavor and who have permitted me to use their contributions. Equally appreciated is the Rutgers University School of Social Work's former Dean, Prof. Harold W. Demone, Jr., who urged me to continue the research for this publication despite serious personal hardships which had delayed its completion.

I. CENTRAL ISSUES

Loss

1. Abarbanel, A., 1979, "Shared Parenting After Separation and Divorce: A Study of Joint Custody", *American Journal of Orthopsychiatry,* Vol. 42, No. 2, pp. 320–329

   Intensive study of four families with joint custody, which works under some conditions.

2. Ahrons, C.R., 1979, "The Coparental Divorce: Preliminary Research Findings and Policy Implications", In A. Milne (ed), *Joint Custody: A Handbook for Judges, Lawyers, and Counselors.* Portland, OR: Association of Family Conciliation Courts

   Describes the post-divorce parental and nonparental relationships reported by 41 divorced joint-custody parents. While continuing to relate in some nonparental areas, the data suggest, these parents nonetheless have emotionally terminated their spousal relationships and tended to establish child-centered coparenting relationships postdivorce. The author argues that social policy must support this coparenting relationship following divorce and suggests that for some families, joint custody is one way to provide this social support.(SAA)

3. Berman, L.C. & R.K. Bufferd, 1986, "Family Treatment to Address Loss in Adoptive Families", *Social Casework,* Vol. 67, No. 1, pp. 3–11

   All partners in the adoptive triangle experience serious losses, usually without an opportunity to mourn them adequately. This article explores the major issues for the various participants and develops a treatment approach based on family systems theory in which adopted children and their adoptive families are seen together to deal with these issues. The article also points out the pitfalls about seeing only the child or only the parent(s). Case examples are given.

4. Bermann, E., 1973, *Scapegoat—The Impact of Death-Fear on an American Family,* The University of Michigan Press, Ann Arbor

An in-depth anthropological study of a family whose father anticipates death. Developmental impacts on individual family members as well as societal influences and interactions are documented and reviewed. Scapegoating as a protective family defense is explored and qualifications for the scapegoat candidate arc given.

5. Bowen, M., 1978, ''Family Reaction to Death'', *Family Therapy in Clinical Practice,* J. Aronson, New York

   A discussion of open versus closed emotional systems and factors that affect family's reaction to death. Closed system hinders adaptation.

6. Bowlby, J., 1973, *Separation Anxiety and Anger,* Basic Books, New York

   Academic compilation of anxiety upon separation throughout the species. Fear in its multitude of ramifications is examined. Individual human differences in susceptibility to fear, pathologies, and normal childhood phases are explored in depth. Excellent resource for persons working with children.

7. Bowlby, J., 1980, *Attachment and Loss,* Basic Books, New York

   Theoretically sound observations put forth new concepts of attachment behavior versus dependency. This normalized approach continues throughout sections on adult mourning as differentiated from childhood mourning. Disorders are addressed as well as normal life-cycle variations in response to death. A major contribution to the field.

8. Bowlby, J. & C.M. Parkes, 1970, ''Separation and Loss Within the Family'', In Anthony, E.J. and C. Koopernik, eds, *The Child In His Family,* Wiley Interscience, New York

   Important chapter addressing grieving process in both adults and children. Authors differentiate between attachment and dependency: normalizing attachment to a loved one, therefore normalizing the grieving process itself. They offer professionals guidelines for supporting the bereaved in a non-intrusive therapeutic manner.

9. Bugen, L.A., 1977, ''Human Grief: A Model for Prediction and Intervention'', *American Journal of Orthopsychiatry,* Vol. 47, pp. 196–206.

   ''Bugen presents a model to facilitate both the prediction and understanding of grief reactions. He proposes that pivotal is the centrality or peripherality of the relationship, combined with whether the mourner believes that the death was preventable or unpreventable. Where the bereaved stands in relation to these issues will determine the intensity and the length of the grieving process. It follows that intervention suggested by the model may then be used to help the individual move from a belief in preventability to the belief in unpreventability and/or to help the individual make the relationships shift from centrality to peripherality. Bugen includes case illustrations to demonstrate his model. Although the use of the model is suggested for grief in response to death, it may also be helpful for use with clients following divorce."(SAA)

10. Bumpass, L., 1984, "Some Characteristics of Children's Second Families", *American Journal of Sociology,* November, pp. 608–623

    What children go through as they lose their family of origin and gain a new family experience. Helps the professional begin to "rethink the conceptualization of the family in sociological research."

11. Draughon, M., 1975, "Stepmother's Model of Identification in Relation to Mourning in the Child", *Psychological Reports,* Vol. 36, pp. 183–189

    Lack of role definition and the conflict-filled nature of the stepmother role is addressed. Three role models, the primary mother, other mother and friend are proposed. Friend model is recommended when biological mother is alive physically or psychologically to allow the mourning process to continue. Primary mother model is suggested upon demise of biological mother. Other-mother model is not recommended under any circumstances.

12. Edelstein, S., 1981, "When Foster Children Leave: Helping Foster Parents to Grieve", *Child Welfare,* Vol. 60, No. 7, pp. 467–473

    "The theory of grief is related to the realities of loss and separation for foster parents. Obstacles to the healthy resolution of grief include ambivalent relationships with the lost child and natural parent, important reality demands on the foster parent, the foster parent's lack of social supports for grieving, and a personality based on avoiding feelings of loss and dependence. To help foster parents through the fear of loss, loss itself, and the grieving process, social workers should be direct and honest with those parents regarding the anticipated duration of the placement and should provide supportive relationships with the parents even after the child has left. Agencies should provide foster parents with sources of gratification to help them through the difficult times, and foster parents' child welfare workers should be given education about loss and the grieving process. Self-help groups for foster parents could assist foster parents through normal grief reactions. Finally, there must be definite time limits on how long a child can remain in the limbo of foster care.'' (SWAB)

13. Elbow, M., 1987, ''The Memory Book: Facilitating Terminations With Children'', *Social Casework,* Vol. 68, No. 3, pp. 180–183

    Termination of the professional relationship is fraught with feelings of loss and separation. The author points out the importance of addressing these issues, particularly with children, for whom the loss of a worker is more of a real loss than for adults in similar situations. Children in treatment who have experienced previous separations are particularly vulnerable. This article discusses the use of a ''memory book'' to review the worker-child relationship as a tool to facilitate termination, allow residual and actual feelings to surface, and then conclude with more positive evaluations of the gains and the remaining memories, which both worker and child will take with them.

14. Elizur, E. & M. Kaffman, 1983, ''Factors Influencing the Severity of Childhood Bereavement Reactions'', *American Journal of Orthopsychiatry,* Vol. 53, No. 4, pp. 668–676

    25 pre-adolescent Kibbutz children who lost their fathers during the October 1973 war were studied in an effort to assess the contribution of the child's family and circumstantial variables to the intense emotional disturbance exhibited by half of the group. The degree of vulnerability and the severity of the bereavement process seemed to be related not only to the child's idiosyncratic reaction to the trauma but to pre-traumatic conditions, the mother's response, and the availability of a supportive and stable family and environment.

15. Fausel, D.F., 1986, ''Loss After Divorce: Helping Children Grieve'', *Journal of Independent Social Work,* Vol. 1, No. 1, pp. 39–47

    ''Based on secondary sources and the author's experiences with divorced families, this paper suggests ways the social work practitioner can help the child or the parents assist the child in dealing with the loss of his first family and his single-parent family through divorce.'' (NCFR)

16. Fraiberg, S., 1962, ''A Therapeutic Approach to Reactive Ego Disturbances in Children in Placement'', *American Journal of Orthopsychiatry,* Vol. 32, pp. 10–31

    The author, a renowned psychoanalytic clinical social worker, gives an early example of 3 cases in which what was then considered short-term treatment of about one year's duration can help latency-age boys who had been placed in an institutional setting by a parent. The treatment focused on the assumption that the separation blocked or interrupted the child's capacity to form new object relationships, because of the trauma of the interrupted relationship to primary love objects. Two successful cases and one unsuccessful one are reported, increasing the diagnostic understanding of the age of the child at which separation occurs, and differentiating the treatment of a child in which early attachment had not taken place. The paper shows the possibility of group treatment, then in its early stages, along with individual treatment, or even the beginning of considering group treatment by itself, to help overcome traumatic experiences of separation. It is also noteworthy that the scene was not a treatment institution, nor were there trained personnel available with the exception of the author who acted also as consultant to personnel, and who integrated the treatment process.

17. Furman, E., 1974, *A Child's Parent Dies: Studies in Bereavement,* Yale University Press, New Haven, CT

The author states in her preface that this book is "the outcome of many years of cooperative work of a group of child analysts in Cleveland." Case reports, illustrative samples support the research which reportedly started on a small sample of 23 children who were seen over a period of 15 years in intensive psychoanalytic treatment along with their parents, or were treated through treatment of the parents. This was the beginning of the study. As the child analysts shared and pooled their knowledge, a three-year study of all the available data was undertaken. The question of bereavement and mourning, how to help bereaved children, differences in relation to object loss and mourning in adults and children, some effects of the loss of a parent on the child's personality development, depression and apathy, and relating this work to other studies of mourning are concepts in the chapters written by a variety of authors. A foreword by Anna Freud introduces the book.

18. Gelcer, E., 1983, "Mourning is a Family Affair", *Family Process,* Vol. 22, pp. 500–516

Presents an interactional, systemic view of mourning. Focuses on how non-resolution of mourning permits a ghost to become an integral member of the family system. Examples of stepfamilies with a "ghost" are cited.

19. Golan, N., 1981, *Passing Through Transitions, A Guide For Practitioners,* Free Press, New York

At home in two countries, the U.S. and Israel, the author uses her rich bi-cultural experiences to examine the developmental stages of the life cycle. Having worked in the field of Crisis theory previous to this book, the author examines recent theory and research on the individual and family life cycles, and a variety of more recent treatment approaches, especially crisis intervention and short term treatment. She defines "normal problems of normal people", categorizes nine specific transitional areas, and suggests ways of assessing and intervening during such life cycle stages. "Separation, Divorce, and Remarriage" and "Untimely Widowhood, Grief and Bereavement" are two of these chapters. An ecological perspective and rich case examples permeate the book.

20. Herman, S., 1974, "Divorce: A Grief Process", *Perspectives in Psychiatric Care,* pp. 108–112

    An early paper on the dynamics of divorce describes the crisis phases which family members pass through. It is felt that the mental health approach to grief provides an appropriate framework from which both professionals and those who influence the portrayal of divorce in the media can profit. Nursing intervention along those lines is especially highlighted.

21. Hetherington, E., 1972, "Girls without Fathers", *Psychology Today,* Vol. 6, No. 2, pp. 47–52.

    "Girls who grow up without fathers often display inappropriate behavior in relation to males. Early separation causes more difficulty than separation after age 5. Differences in girls' behavior may relate to differences in maternal behavior."(SAA)

22. Jensen, G. & J. Wallace, 1967, "Family Mourning Process", *Family Process,* Vol. 6, pp. 55–76

    Sees mourning as a family crisis which is reacted to by all family members and affects family interactions. Illustrates how mourning can be managed therapeutically as a family process.

23. Kaplan, L., 1979, "A Matter of Loss: Living On, Surviving Sadness", *School Counselor,* Vol. 26, pp. 229–235

    The author describes the loss program: A student group, how it got started, what it hoped to accomplish, and its mix of structured activities and free discussion leading to self-disclosure. A staff seminar parallelled the loss program. Measures for evaluating the program were built in. It was felt that this was an important program at a high school level, that a larger number of meetings might be more beneficial than what had originally been structured in, that more teacher support was hoped for (only 10% of the school's teachers actually referred students), but that the staff members involved with the grieving students had the opportunity for broader and deeper understanding of the multifaceted readjustment needed after a loss.

24. Kleinman, J., Rosenberg, E. & M. Whiteside, 1979, "Common Developmental Tasks in Forming Reconstituted Families", *Journal of Marital and Family Therapy,* Vol. 5, No. 2, pp. 79–86

    Developmental tasks common to the formation of a reconstituted family are described. Mourning of losses and achieving separateness from the original nuclear family represents the first stage of adoption. Learning new members, stabilizing marital relationship, and defining new parent-child roles, plus dealing with sexual tensions follow as subsequent steps. Relinquishing hopes to return to the original family needs continuous observation.

25. Knight, M., 1985, "Termination Visits in Closed Adoptions", *Child Welfare,* Vol. 64, No. 1, pp. 37–45

    A final contact is recommended by the author, to allow both child and parent some reaction to the separation, to decrease the child's sense of guilt and responsibility for the separation, to diminish the realm of fantasy, and to leave the road open for new bonding. It is emphasized that this must be "a process rather than an event" and that the worker's influence on both parent and visit are crucial. Some of the more negative factors are cited but seem outweighed by the positives, according to the author's experience.

26. Kohn, J.B. & W.K. Kohn, 1978, "My Children's Grief", In *The Widower,* Beacon Press, Boston

    Actual case reports of family members' reactions to death help us understand where communications break down and the grieving process becomes stunted. Sensitive guidelines for helping children cope with grief are offered. Underlying feelings children often experience in reaction to death and how to help children through this period are also outlined in a practical way.

27. LeShan, E., 1976, *Learning To Say Good-by,* Stepfamily Association of America, Towson, Md.

    Written for the whole family, this frank discussion of mourning opens the way to genuine communication between youngsters and adults. Offers a practical strategy, based on life experiences, to provide comfort and hope while dealing with the grief and bewilderment that follows a parent's death.

28. Lifton, R.J., 1979, *The Broken Connection: On Death and the Continuity of Life,* Simon and Schuster, New York

An academic work based on evolving psychoanalytic theories. Section on psychiatric boundaries addresses emotional reactions to death from a theoretical perspective. Widespread death resulting from nuclear war and psychological impact on culture is related to spiritual imagery. Only significance of book is massive references made in author's attempt to piece together concepts.

29. Lindemann, E., 1965, ''Symptomatology and Management of Acute Grief'' in *Crisis Intervention,* Family Service Association, New York

Conceptualizes grief as a crisis. Defines grieving syndrome and grief work. Describes morbid reactions resulting from unresolved mourning.

30. Mayfield, J. & J. Nell, 1983, ''Group Treatment for Children in Substitute Care'', *Social Casework,* Vol. 64, No. 10, pp. 579–584

The separation of children is usually neglected in the stresses of the actual processes, and even when children seem to have adjusted, there is much underlying trauma which has not been addressed, frequently aggravated by multiple subsequent placements. This author uses four basic models which were originally developed as ''survival roles'' by children of alcoholics and applies these same general roles or defense mechanisms to children of separation, from neglectful or abusive backgrounds. The lost child, who appears withdrawn, has low self-worth and is a high suicidal risk during adolescence; the clown, who survives by charm but denies emotional pain; the troublemaker, who is probably scapegoated and, as semi-delinquent, experiences many replacements; and the achiever, who appears unaffected but has built a wall around himself, and is at high risk for emotional breakdowns. A structured eight-week program called ''Sunday's Child'' was developed in order to enhance the self-esteem, learn to trust, assist in alleviating guilt feelings, learn responsible decision making. Differences in biological families as well as some of the issues of being in substitute care were especially emphasized. The results seemed to corroborate that this is a viable approach for helping children come to terms with their past even after considerable time has passed since their first separation. However, early attempts at similar interventive steps are highly recommended.

31. Millen, L., & S. Roll, 1985, ''Solomon's Mothers: A Special Case of Pathological Bereavement,'' *American Journal of Orthopsychiatry,* July, Vol. 55, No. 3, pp. 411–418

    ''Illustrates ways in which the bereavement process was distorted and delayed in 22 females seen in psychotherapy who had earlier given up a child for adoption. It is concluded that the experience of a mother relinquishing her child is similar to pathological mourning and includes feelings of intense loss, enduring panic, and unresolved anger; episodes of searching for the lost child in waking life or in dreams; and a sense of incompleteness. Steps are outlined that can be taken to reduce the intensity of such pathological mourning.'' (APA)

32. Palombo, J., 1981, ''Parent Loss and Childhood Bereavement: Some Theoretical Considerations'', *Journal of Clinical Social Work,* Vol. 9, No. 1

    Critical review of the major psychoanalytic positions on the impact of parent's loss during childhood. By reviewing the theoretical positions of authors on this subject, the writer concludes that no one approach can sufficiently explain the complexity of the impact of a parent's death on a child. A multivariant approach is suggested to generate hypothesis and begin systematic data collection.

33. Paul, N. & G. Gosser, 1965, ''Operational Mourning and its Role in Conjoint Family Therapy'', *Community Mental Health Journal,* Vol. I, No. 4, pp. 339–345

    A discussion of the ''fixated family equilibrium'' that results from unresolved mourning. Description of techniques of operational mourning which involves family in belated mourning process and leads to emergence of individuation.

34. Ramos, S., 1975, *Teaching Your Child to Cope with Crisis:* How to Help Your Child Deal with Death, Divorce, Surgery, Being Adopted, Moving, Alcoholic Parents, Sick Parents, Leaving Home, and Other Major Worries, David McKay, New York

    This book is intended to assist parents in dealing effectively with child-rearing problems, to anticipate and avert crises, and to utilize life stresses and even tragedies to strengthen the child's emotional growth. Chapter titled ''Children, I'm Getting Married'' discusses child's typical reactions when the resident parent remarries and typical reactions of stepparents and stepchildren.

35. Robinson, B.W. & W.W. McVey Jr., 1985, "The Relative Contributions of Death and Divorce to Marital Dissolution in Canada and the United States", *Journal of Comparative Family Studies,* Vol. 16, No. 1, pp. 93–109

In view of some similarity of trends in divorce and marriage rates in these two countries over the past 60 years (except for divergent rates in marriage patterns beginning in the mid-seventies) and building on existing research, the authors attempt to develop understanding of the changes which have occurred in these two countries. The nature of the research, which spans a considerable time period is carefully described, and certain patterns are discernable. In the U.S. the overall marriage dissolution rate did not substantially change from 1860–1970, but the relative contribution of death and divorce to marital dissolution changed, although death still dissolved more marriages than divorce, with somewhat similar results in Canada, though not viewed over as long a period. Subdata show other similarities and are substantiated with research data. It is predicted that children in Canada will soon show similar trends as in the U.S., i.e. are more likely to live in single-parent families, and death may not strike until children are grown, in terms of general longevity patterns. In view of divorce trends, however, the median duration of marriages ending in divorce was 10.0 years in 1982. Remarriage became a significant element in the lives of children. The authors progress to the assumption that the available statistical changes in families would lead one to inevitable questions about the viability of our traditional "family life cycle construct". The necessity for developing alternate descriptive constructs is pointed out.

36. Rowling, L., 1982, Children and Loss: Part 1—A Teacher's View: The Child in the Single-Parent & Blended Family. Part 2—Helping Children Cope With Loss Unit for Child Studies, Selected papers #25, New South Wales University, Kensington (Australia), School of Education.

"In two parts, this paper discusses areas in family disruption, describes children's experiences of loss, and suggests strategies for helping children cope with such experiences." (ERIC)

37. Rudolph, M., 1978, *Should the Children Know? Encounters With Death in the Lives of Children,* Shocken Books, New York

Alternatives, such as writing about feelings, for children unable to cry provided within a real-life context. Short chapters, well written in story-like themes convey actual how-to-relate-to-death concepts to children. Author uses different levels of loss (e.g. moving or death of a pet), to help adults incorporate ideas of loss into a child's cognitive framework.

38. Rustin, S., 1980, ''The Legacy is Loss'', In Quaitman, W., ed., ''Holocaust Survivors: Psychological and Social Sequelae. A Special Issue of the Journal of Contemporary Psychotherapy'', Vol. 11, No. 1, pp. 32–43

Discontinuity and loss are identified as central issues in dealing with Holocaust survivors' offspring (''second generation survivors''). Therapists are cautioned to consider a great number of variables in their assessment of their young clients' parents, and to choose their treatment roles with great flexibility. Survivors' groups were found to be helpful. Therapists are cautioned to guard against countertransference issues.

39. Rutter, M., 1971, ''Parent Child Separation: Psychological Effects on Children'', *Journal of Child Psychiatry and Psychology,* Vol. 12, pp. 233–260

The author, a well-known British child psychiatrist, does a careful comparison of the effects of divorce and death on children. His review was based on studies in which the effects of permanent separation were manifested in subsequent delinquent behavior. For boys whose parents were separated or divorced, the delinquency rates were almost double as compared to two biological-parent households. The implication that the discord and friction associated with separation and divorce rather than the parent absence cause higher delinquency rates seems appropriate. Extended grief of a parent surviving the death of the other parent, the personality of the parent, the effect on girls are some variables which were not considered. However, the author raises many potential questions for further research into the hypothesis that permanent loss through death may be less traumatic than continued partial and repeated losses in separation and divorce situations.

40. Sager, C.J., 1980, ''Remarriage Revisited'', *Family and Child Mental Health Journal,* Vol. 6, No. 1, pp. 19–33

The strong point is made that the stepfamily, also termed remarried, reconstituted, or blended (abbreviated ''Rem'') is quite different from the biological or nuclear family unit. The various differences are outlined. Clinical and research studies of remarried families are described and reviewed.

The review is divided into children of divorce and the experience of parental loss; the remarried couple; and stepparents and stepchildren, as three distinct target groups.

41. Segal, R.M., 1984, "Helping Children Express Grief Through Symbolic Communication", *Social Casework,* Vol. 65, No. 10, pp. 590–599

Artistic modes of expression such as music, art, body movement are used to express grief as the major problem of loss, symbolically, and thus aid the child's coping with trauma and concomitant stresses. Studies on communication processes of children are reviewed, to emphasize the need to find a non-verbal, i.e. symbolic way of communicating the intense feelings surrounding the trauma of separation and death. Therapists need familiarity with the principles and practice to use this mode as an ancillary tool to open communication for more effective use of more traditional forms of therapy.

42. Simon, A.W., 1964, *The Stepchild in the Family: A View of Children in Remarriage,* Odyssey Press, New York

A professional journalist's review and personal experience of the problems of stepchildren. An early comprehensive book on the problems of bereavement and divorce, especially as they affect children. It is considered a classic.

43. Simos, B.G., 1979, *A Time to Grieve,* Family Service Association of America, New York

The author, a clinical social worker, gives credit to family, colleagues, and clients for having taught her over the years to view the grief process as an important series of stages which people have to master to deal with normal losses successfully, and even to grow through the process. Gaps in scientific and professional knowledge are identified and new sources of knowledge are uncovered, whether conflicting or in harmony with her own conceptualizations. A wide range of human experiences which can be considered losses are first identified. Then normal grief is described with some of the complexities, especially the controversy about the duration of the grief process. The earlier chapters study the major components of the grief process with examples from practice and with suggestions for the practitioner. The final chapters deal with the more complex nuances and differential assessments of grief, whether normal or pathological, with practice material providing the underpinning for professional guidelines.

44. Sugar, M., 1970, "Children in Divorce", *Pediatrics,* October, Vol. 46, No. 4, pp. 588–595

One of few articles written by a pediatrician, which draws attention to some of the literature on separation. He likens the divorce to the experience of the death of a parent, describes some of the most common reactions of both parent and child during separation and divorce. He urges attention to the fact that even parents upset by the events in their own lives can be helped to work preventively with their children, when they are given help by a neutral professional.

45. Thomas, C.B., 1967, "The Resolution of Object Loss Following Foster Home Placement.", Smith College Studies in Social Work, Vol. XXXVII, pp. 163–234

Investigated the process through which children respond to object loss initiated by placement as it relates to efforts in establishing new relationships within the foster family. Thirty-five foster children were selected based on no previous placement and continuation in placement for no more than eighteen months (between ages of seven and twelve). Case records and interviews with foster parents provided data. Questions asked of foster parents to provide evidence of presence or absence of grief process were described in detail. Author suggests specific information concerning the grief process should be shared with foster parents to promote understanding and acceptance of children's reaction to placement.

46. Tomko, B., 1983, "Mourning the Dissolution of the Dream", *Social Work,* Vol. 28, No. 5, pp. 391–392

Author emphasizes the significance of fantasied losses as critical to a successful mourning process. People's unspoken hopes and dreams are validated as real losses and demonstrated as a useful therapeutic intervention. Author's awareness of this hidden (unaddressed) process adds to a more complete means of treatment.

47. Walker, C.W., 1974, "Separation and Object Loss: The Plight of the Foster Child", *Childhood Deprivation,* Thomas, Springfield, Ill.

The author explores the stages, feelings, experiences and defenses used in coping with the trauma of separation. It is imperative that the worker and foster parents know the facts about prior relationships in order to help resolve the effects of this trauma. It is further imperative that both the child's biological family and foster family be included in treatment.

48. Wallerstein, J.S. & J.B. Kelly, 1974, "The Effects of Parental Divorce: Experiences of the Preschool Child", *Journal of the American Academy of Child Psychiatry,* Vol. 14, No. 2, pp. 600–616

Research data on the response of 34 preschool children to their parents' separation through divorce was obtained by four to six interviews with individual family members over a period of six weeks, with a follow-up one year later. The school system was also used to obtain information about the children. The findings indicated that separation triggered regression, bewilderment, aggression, and need in the two-and-a-half and three-and-a-quarter-year-old group, guilt, diminished self-esteem, and depression in the three-and-three-quarter to four-and-three-quarter-year-olds, while five to six-year-olds were able to go through the separation experience without noticeable developmental interruption or regression. However, 55% of all children had regressed psychologically one year later, and the mother (resident parent)-child relationship had deteriorated, and father-child relationship had improved. At follow-up, 63% of the girls and 27% of the boys had deteriorated.

49. Wallerstein, J.S. & J.B. Kelly, 1986, "The Effects of Parental Divorce: Experiences of the Child in Early Latency", *American Journal of Orthopsychiatry,* Vol. 46, No. 1, pp. 20–42

This is a partial report on the authors' research on the impact of divorce on children. Criteria of age-appropriate developmental tasks are used as a base. The children showed deep suffering and longing for their absent fathers, with little help for their hurt, since their ego structures could not tolerate such intense pain and grief. Feelings of loss and deprivation, fears about the very existence of the family and its future were expressed by loyalty conflicts, reconciliation fantasies, and possessiveness. At follow-up, one year later, the nature of the post-divorce family structure had strong bearing on the outcome. Twenty-three percent of the children were worse, manifested by sadness, resignation toward the divorce, and strong reconciliation wishes.

50. Wallerstein, J.S. & J.B. Kelly, 1976, "The Effects of Parental Divorce: Experiences of the Child in Later Latency", *American Journal of Orthopsychiatry,* Vol. 46, No. 2, pp. 256–269

Report on part of a larger study, this one concentrating on 9 to 10-year-olds (later latency), at the time of parental divorce and one year later. These children seemed to function more on age-appropriate levels. They seemed to struggle actively to master their experience by denial and avoidance activities, thus appearing courageous, and containing their grief, while functioning well. Anger continued to exist, but was quite consciously expressed by temper tantrums and/or demanding, dictatorial attitudes and identification with the non-resident fathers. There were not infrequently cases of poor school performance, somatic symptoms, fears, and loneliness. At one year follow-up, fifty percent of the children were significantly worse and one third remained enraged with either one of the parents. Low self-esteem, depression, peer and school difficulties were observed.

51. Warmbrod, M.E.T., 1986, ''Counseling Bereaved Children: Stages in the Process'', *Social Casework,* Vol. 67, No. 6, pp. 351–358

This article focuses specifically on the counselor's activities in assisting child and parent through the three stages of grief. The time of death, memories of the deceased, and present and future arrangements and plans are considered in some detail.

Identity

52. Anderson, J.O., 1982, The Effects of Stepfather/Stepchild Interaction on Stepfamily Adjustment, Dissertation Abstracts International, Vol. 43/04-A, page 1306

''Each year in the United States one-half million adults become stepparents, and one million children become part of a stepfamily. However, few studies have explored the dynamics of stepparent families. The purpose of the present study was to examine specific aspects of stepfamily adjustment relative to the stepfather's interaction with his family. The aspects of interaction which were hypothesized to be related to mother and father stepfamily satisfaction and child self-esteem were the stepfather's communication, supportive interaction, and time spent with a target child, and the amount of emotional support he received from his wife for his involvement in disciplining a target child. One hundred and ten middle-class, white stepfamilies participated in the study. A stepfather, mother, and target child in each family filled out an extensive questionnaire, and multiple regression was used to test the hypotheses. Three variables were found to be significant predictors of stepfather satisfaction in stepfamilies. They were the stepfather's communication with a target child, the time he spent with a target child, and the support he received from his wife for his involvement in disciplining the target child. These were related in a positive way to his stepfamily satisfaction. The only significant predictor of mother satisfaction identified in the present study was her support of the stepfather's discipline of the target child. A positive relationship was found to exist between her support of the stepfather's discipline and her stepfamily satisfaction. The target child's self-esteem was predicted by the stepfather's supportive interaction with the child and a positive relationship was found between supportive interaction and self-esteem.''(DAI)

53. Backhaus, K.A., 1984, ''Life Books: Tool for Working with Children in Placement'', *Social Work,* Vol. 29, No. 6, pp. 551–554
''Interviewed 15 social workers to examine the use of Life Books for children in substitute family care. Results indicated the project was valuable in helping children integrate past and present experiences and develop a sense of identity.'' (ERIC)

54. Barocas, H.A. & C.B. Barocas, 1980, ''Separation-Individuation Conflicts in Children of Holocaust Survivors'', In Quaitman, W., ed., ''Holocaust Survivors: Psychological and Social Sequelae. A Special Issue of the Journal of Contemporary Psychotherapy'', Human Sciences Press, New York, Vol. 11, No. 1, pp. 6–14
The ''conspiracy of silence'' which did not permit survivors to experience sufficient mourning affected the depth of their experiences with their children whose reactive inability to separate and individuate is identified by the authors. More recent openness and ability to bear witness have led to such adaptive solutions as the formation of self-help groups and Holocaust courses, which have had mediating effects according to the authors.

55. Berg, B. & R. Kelly, 1979, ''The Measurement of Self Esteem in Children from Broken, Rejected and Accepted Families'', *Journal of Divorce,* Vol. 2, pp. 363–369
Since clinical findings generally suggest that children of divorce are prone to develop problems, particularly in the area of self-esteem, the authors examined three groups of children, those with divorced parents, those from intact but rejected families (unhappy families), and those from ''accepted families.'' Children with divorced families, contrary to clinical expectations, were not found to have lower self-esteem than those of accepted-intact families. Children from intact-rejected families evidenced levels of self-esteem significantly lower than those of the two other groups. (N-57)

56. Beste, H.M. & R.G. Richardson, 1981, ''Developing a Life Story Book Program for Foster Children'', *Child Welfare,* Vol. 60, No. 8, pp. 529–534
''The Life Story Book provides foster children with a way to understand events of their past life and present circumstances and to build their identities. Children in the uncertainties of foster care need the continuity and clarity that a Life Story Book can provide.

Realizing the positive benefits of Life Story Books, a community services agency began a program to encourage the construction of Life Story Books for each foster child. The idea was proposed to the administration by a foster parent-staff advisory committee. The proposal included the benefits and anticipated cost. It was approved rapidly by the administration. A workshop was planned to disseminate the ideas and information quickly to foster parents and social workers. The workshop was presented frequently. The accompanying publicity campaign is discussed.'' (SWAB)

57. Colon, F., 1978, ''Family Ties and Child Placement'', *Family Process,* Vol. 17

Colon hypothesizes that persons who experience unresolved severed relationships are emotionally ''at-risk.'' He focuses on the child's early experiences relating to his biological roots and connectedness to his family and shows how this will affect how he feels about himself later in life.

58. Colon, F. , 1973, ''In Search of One's Past: An Identity Trip'', *Family Process,* Vol. 12, pp. 429–438

Colon, a former foster child, expressed his deeply felt personal need to explore his biological past. His investigation takes the form of a journey to Puerto Rico where he reintroduces himself to his biological father and extended family. Colon expresses to the reader the extreme joy and inner sense of personal fulfillment this journey produced for him. It is the author's purpose to demonstrate the need of all human beings for contact with their biological roots, not only for himself as a family therapist.

59. Cordell, A., Cicely, N. & V. Krymow, 1985, ''Group Counseling for Children Adopted at Older Ages'', *Child Welfare,* Vol. 64, pp. 113–124

The high-risk nature of later adoptions and the vulnerability of adolescents to stresses, as well as the experience from other studies showing that adoptees feel they do not get sufficient information from adoptive parents, led to an agency experiment. The format consisted of counseling-group sessions for teens and pre-teens, culminating in an overnight retreat for these children as well as for a group of children who were being prepared for adoption, so that the adoptees were in the role of consultant to the newcomers. The program is described in detail. It was started by a group of adoptive mothers who became the coordinators of the program and worked with two professionals in the agency. Concurrent meetings were held with the parents of the participating adoptees. It can be inferred that the meetings enhanced the children's self-concept and opened up future channels of communication, especially with peers who have had similar experiences.

60. DiGiulio, J., 1979, "The 'Search': Providing Continued Service for Adoptive Parents", *Child Welfare,* Vol. 58
This article deals with one agency's ideas for a program that will lessen the fears raised in adoptive parents by the current controversy over sealed records. The author deals with issues concerning the adoptees, whose search for biological parents proved to be generally effective.

61. Erikson, E.H., 1959, "Identity and the Life Cycle", *Psychological Issues,* Vol. 1, No. 1
In a psychoanalytic framework, Erikson describes the stage of identity formation as a natural happening in one's life cycle.

62. Erikson, E.H., 1968, *Identity: Youth and Crisis,* W.W. Norton and Co., Inc., New York
Identity formation is viewed as a normative and necessary process in human development. He offers case histories of individuals who have experienced identity confusion.

63. Fisher, A., 1974, *The Search for Anna Fisher,* Fawcett Crest, New York
Anna Fisher's book describes her 20-year search for her biological parents. It is a deeply emotional book that allows the reader to put herself into the adoptee's life and actually feel the dilemma and multitude of feelings adoptees go through in order to answer the question, "Who am I?"

64. Freedman, J., 1977, "An Adoptee in Search of Identity", *Social Work,* Vol. 22, No. 3, pp. 227–228
The author describes his advocacy efforts at helping a returning Vietnam veteran to discover his family of origin. Through discussion with legal and social service organizations in different states as well as with ALMA chapters (Adoptee's Liberty Movement Association) the client was allowed to inspect his court records. A reunion with the biological mother took place, preceded by her revealing the facts of his existence to her current family without apparent traumatic effects. Attempts at reunion with the biological father were under way, and the adoptive parents' sensitivity to their son's need for the search enhanced their relationship. The implication is strong that

the successful search greatly enhanced the client's sense of his identity.

65. Gil, E. & K. Bogart, 1982, "An Exploratory Study of Self-Esteem and Quality of Care of 100 Children in Foster Care", *Children and Youth Services Review,* Vol. 4, pp. 351–363

Children's self-perceptions were studied with regard to their placement situations, and their career aspirations and hopes for the future. 100 children, ages 8–18, 50 living in foster families and 50 living in group homes were both interviewed and given a questionnaire. The authors designed a questionnaire touching on a number of variables in the children's lives, attempting to get their feelings. Findings indicate as most important the children's need to understand the circumstances leading to their need for foster home or foster care placement in order to come to terms with their life situations.

66. Grossman, M., Shea, J. & G. Adams, 1980, "Effects of Parental Divorce During Early Childhood on Ego Development and Identity Formation of College Students", *Journal of Divorce,* Vol. 3, pp. 263–272

This study assesses the level of ego development and achievement of identity in 294 college students from nuclear, divorced, and divorced-remarried families. Contrary to popular assumptions, divorce was not predictive of lower scores. Actually males from divorced families had higher ego-identity achievement scores than either males from nuclear families or females from both nuclear and divorced families. No evidence was available that remarriage (stepfamily living) may lessen the negative consequences of divorce on college students' development. "(c) APA"

67. Gwynne, E.M., 1984, Self-Regard, Parent Perceptions, and Family Representations of Latency-Age Foster and Biological Children of Foster Parents, Dissertation Abstracts International, Vol 45/03-B, page 1016

"The study had as its primary aim the investigation of the self-regard, perceptions of mother, and family representations of latency-age foster children as compared to those of same age and ethnic group in biological children of foster parents. A secondary purpose was the exploration within the foster group of hypothesized relationships between placement variables and performance on the socio-emotional measures. Self-concept was assessed on the Piers-Harris Children's Self-Concept Scale and the Child Scale of the Family Perception Inventory. A scale of family representations on the Children's Apperception Test was developed for the study and yielded reliability and validity data. As predicted, foster children demonstrated significantly lower self-regard than biological children; the family membership effect on self-esteem was bounded by the measurement instrument and the child's ethnic membership. Placement variables were ruled out as confounding factors in the derivation of ethnic differences in self-concept. The comparison (biological) group perceived mother and represented family relationships significantly more favorably than did the foster children. While the foster and biological children manifested highly significant differences in the valence of family content, the groups were equivalent in the frequency with which family inter-relationships were invoked. Both groups evidenced high degrees of relationship between perceptions of self and (foster) mother. Unlike foster children, biological children displayed moderately high convergence of self-concept and family representations. The within-group analyses of the foster sample yielded few significant correlations between the developmental-placement variables and the socio-emotional measures. The investigation empirically corroborates theoretical suppositions and clinical reports in the literature. The findings are discussed in terms of their theoretical relevance, particularly with regard to object relations and social perception. Directions for future research to clarify certain theoretical and practical issues are suggested. In general, the present findings point to the detrimental, complexly determined effects of the foster care experience on children's self-image and parent and family perceptions, as well as to the apparent psychological resiliency tempering the socio-emotional sequelae of separation.''(DAI)

68. Hartman, A., 1984, *Working With Adoptive Families Beyond Placement,* Child Welfare League of America, Inc., New York

This book provides a post placement plan designed for practitioners to aid the adoptive family in dealing more effectively with feelings surrounding placement. Hartman discusses a model for providing services to all members of the adoptive family throughout the development phases of the adopted child's life cycle for the child's and family's better understanding.

69. Hoffman, N., 1981, Factors Related to the Foster Child's Sense of Interpersonal Security, Dissertation Abstracts International, Vol 42/09-A, page 3901

''Foster children are at substantially greater risk for social-emotional maladjustment problems when compared to their nonfoster care peers. There is evidence suggesting that underlying this greater vulnerability is an impaired sense of security in interpersonal attachments and relationships. The nature of foster care itself has inherent elements potentially harmful to the child's sense of interpersonal security. Yet, these potentially negative effects are not equally realized in all foster children. The problem addressed in this study was 'What are the factors that explain the differences in foster children's sense of interpersonal security?' Sense of security was defined as a subjective feeling state of an individual, comprised of two components—the child's perceptions of others as responsive, available agents of protection, nurturance, and support, and the child's self-perceptions of his or her own attachability and acceptability. It was measured by the attachment-individualization balance of the Separation Anxiety Test Method (SATM), and by Factor 1 (Acceptance-Rejection) and Factor 2 (Psychological Autonomy-Psychological Control) of the 56-item revision of the Children's Report of Parental Behavior Inventory (CRPBI).

Thirteen factors were selected as independent variables and were placed under the general categories of entry into foster care, composition of foster homes, experience in foster care, and demographic variables. Information concerning these variables was obtained from foster parents and Department of Social Services' caseworkers. The subjects were seventy-two foster children (50% male, 50% female, 81% black, 19% white) ages 11–14, who volunteered to be part of the study. The findings did not support the hypothesis that children placed because of neglect, abuse, or abandonment feel less secure than those placed for other reasons. In fact, these children were generally found to feel more secure. The findings did support the hypothesis that the younger the child when placed, the more secure the child feels. The following factors were also found related to greater sense of security on one or more of the dependent measures: placement with natural siblings, longer time in same foster home, greater continuity of current caseworker, and more regular and frequent church attendance with the foster family. Unexpectedly, greater number of placements was also associated with a healthier sense of security as measured by the SATM. White children and girls were found to feel more secure than black children and boys, respectively. In general, the findings suggest that current stability factors may be more important to the foster child's sense of security than are his or her past experiences in foster care. The implications of the research findings for attachment theory were discussed. It was also suggested that the findings may be useful for early identification of high-risk youngsters in foster care as well as for placement and service planning.'' (DAI)

70. Horns, V. & G. Abbott, 1985, ''A Comparison of Concepts of Self and Parents Among Elementary School Children in Intact, Single Parent, and Blended Families'', *Annual Meeting of the Mid-South Education Researcher's Association*

''Three types of family structures can be identified: (1) intact families with children living with both natural parents; (2) single-parent families with children living with one natural parent; and (3) blended families with children living with one natural parent and one step parent. A study was conducted to examine the differences in children's self-concepts and their concepts of the adults they live with in relation to family structure. Gender and grade differences were also examined. Participants (N=404) were students in grades 2–5 with approximately equal numbers of girls and boys, all of middle to high socioeconomic status. The Personal Attribute Inventory for Children, consisting of 24 negative and 24 positive descriptors from which subjects choose 15 words that best describe a designated person or group, was used to assess interpersonal and intrapersonal evaluations. Few differences on self-concept and concepts of parents were found. No statistically significant differences related to gender or grade were found. Specific feelings reported were different, with children of single parents evaluating themselves as less calm and less complaining but more afraid and nicer than other children. Children from intact families rated themselves as calmer, healthier, stronger, and wiser than other children. It is suggested that further research should examine the relationship between children's self-concept and the level of conflict in their families.'' (ERIC)

71. Howard, M., 1975, ''I Take After Somebody; I Have Relatives; I Possess a Real Name'', *Psychology Today,* December, pp. 33–37

Traces an adoptee's personal search for her natural parents. Finding out her mother's name and background was sufficient for her in terms of feeling a sense of background and identity.

72. Image Associates, ''The Scrapbook Experience—Building a Child's Identity'', Image Associates, Santa Barbara, CA

''The process by which a foster child develops a sense of identity by making an autobiographical scrapbook is illustrated in this sixteen-minute film. The child is guided by a social worker who encourages the child to think about his past and express his feelings. The film is primarily intended for use as a training tool for social workers who help children deal with past life experiences. It may also be useful with foster and adoptive parents in demonstrating the value of preserving mementos and photographs from the child's past. Foster children may also potentially benefit from viewing the film by being stimulated to share their own feelings and experiences.'' (NCFR)

73. Juroe, D. & B. Juroe, 1975, *Successful Stepparenting: Loving and Understanding Stepchildren,* Fleming H. Revel Company, Tarrytown, New York

When a stepchild fears abandonment or needs attention he/she will regress to a time when he/she felt more secure. Youths of all ages, including adolescents, can regress in some manner such as bedwetting, infantile behavior, becoming a ''loner,'' shutting out relationships. These defense mechanisms are heightened when a stepparent comes into the picture. For many adolescents, presumed replacement of a lost parent can create considerable difficulty. The authors provide guidelines and explanations to the stepfamily for solving problems that occur within this type of family system. It is important for the stepchild to spend time with the ''lost'' biological parent. This will help to regain personal identity and provide positive reinforcement to feel more secure again.

74. Kaplan, H. & A. Pokorny, 1971, ''Self Derogation and Childhood Broken Home'', *Journal of Marriage and the Family,* Vol. 33, pp. 328–337

500 adults constituted the sample in a survey research study about their feelings and the results were analyzed to determine the particular characteristics of their ''broken home'' situation, with reference to age at breakup, reason for breakup, resultant living arrangements, e.g. remarriage and subject's age at remarriage. Results are given for subgroups such as race, sex, and societal class as well as for the total group. The data clarify that it is not the breakup per se which results in self-derogation but rather the idiosyncratic features of the break-up, a finding which concurs with larger-scale studies. No significant differences were found for the total group from subjects in nuclear families. However, when cause of break-up and age at break-up were considered as well as age of remarriage, a statistically significant differentiation occurred. The relevance of the sex of the absent parent (and therefore the resident parent) to self-derogation differed with the subject's race, sex, and social class. The negative effects of divorce and death on self-esteem seemed to be relatively undifferentiated. Increasingly refined definitions of the circumstances and conditions surrounding family break-up are suggested for better understanding of the reasons for the process which generates self-derogation.

75. Kowal, K. & K. Schilling, 1985, ''Adoption Through the Eyes of Adult Adoptees'', *American Journal of Orthopsychiatry,* Vol. 55, No. 3, pp. 354–362

This research study presents the results of a survey of 100 adopted adults who went to the adoption agency to search for information and/or biological relative. The perspective of the search was compared with data from the clinical literature and with recommendations in adoption practice which were prevalent a generation ago. Other research findings are reported on as a background. The results show that adoptees who come to adoption agencies are a priori a self-selected group. However, the findings do have implications for practice: Fantasies about biological parents are present in a non-clinical sample of the population, and cannot be assumed to be uncommon without further study. There seems to be a different salience for male and female adoptees to search. Adults who enter a search in the majority are not looking for a surrogate family or for contact, but find the search important in an existential sense to enhance their knowledge and sense of identity. As a result of the study, the authors suggest adolescence and pregnancy/childbirth as appropriate life-cycle stages to offer post-adoption services.

76. Lifton, B.J., 1975, *Twice Born: Memoirs of an Adopted Daughter,* McGraw-Hill, New York

As a journalist and a playwright, the author uses her considerable writing skills and her intense emotional experiences, both while growing up as an adopted child and later in her search for her biological parents, to lead the reader through the identity conflicts of the adopted child, especially fostered by the taboo of secrecy about adoption which is both legally required and societally more acceptable.

77. Lutz, P., 1983, ''The Stepfamily: An Adolescent Perspective'', *Family Relations,* Vol. 32, pp. 367–375

A study involving 103 adolescents aged 12 to 18 living in stepfamilies. Found divided loyalties and discipline to be the most stressful areas in stepfamily living. Experiencing one biological parent talking negatively about the other received the highest stress rate with all respondents. Discipline is very stressful for all adolescents because they are seeking autonomy. Other perceived areas of stress were cited, such as divided loyalty. Prevention of developmental problems by knowledgeable professionals is emphasized to maintain a sense of roots and identity.

78. McDermott, V.A., 1987, "Life Planning Services: Helping Older Placed Children With Their Identity", *Child & Adolescent Social Work Journal,* Vol. 4, No. 3–4, pp. 245–263

The author describes a time-limited intensive approach for working with children who are or have been in the foster care system and who are about to go out on their own. Since 1983, 175 youngsters have participated in this program, which was found to have an enormous impact on their own sense of self and clarification of a sense of personal identity. Group meetings form the nucleus of activities with the youngsters. However, an enormous amount of professional and staff work goes into the uncovering of any kind of material that can elucidate the origins of the child, and make connections between the past, the recent past, and the present. Both the child welfare system and the court system have been reminded that a child's need for family does not end at age 18. Existing family connections have been strengthened, alternatives have been explored and new avenues found to help the youngster integrate his family connections, and get a better sense of self.

79. McFadden, E.J., 1984, *Emotional Development: Fostering the Child's Identity,* Eastern Michigan University Institute for the Study of Children and Families, East Lansing, MI.

" 'Emotional Development: Fostering the Child's Identity' is a manual for use in training families providing service to foster children. Consisting of information to be covered in eight class sessions and numerous appendices providing supplementary material, this instructor's manual contains instructor's materials and participants' course content. Instruction focuses on stages of development; developmental dimensions and developmental lag; emotional development; understanding children's behavior; handling behavior to build self esteem; the child's family and ethnic heritage; the fantasy family and heroes; and the foster family's role in assisting development. Lists of suggested readings for foster parents and instructors are provided." (ERIC)

80. Noble, J. & W. Noble, 1977, *How to Live With Other People's Children,* Hawthorne Books, Inc., New York

Some common experiences among stepparents who had never been around children of their own as well as a child's conflicting identity which would keep him or her at arm's length and hostile toward the stepparent. Implications for practice may be helpful in neutralizing and normalizing stressful situations in stepfamilies where one of the parents had never been a parent before and might be assuming the role too quickly.

81. Pardeck, J.T., 1984, ''Multiple Placement of Children in Foster Family Care: An Empirical Analysis'', *Social Work,* Vol. 29, No. 6, pp. 506–509

The author examines the relationship between factors related to the foster child him/herself, the biological family, the placement agency's caseworker, and the number of placements by examining data from a large national study. Older children after three years of placement are more likely to move, and initially identified problems of the child may continue to be the cause of multiple placements. Parents' problems seem to have less of an impact than expected, but turnover of the caseworker was found to have a statistically significant relationship with multiple placements. The author indicates in his conclusions the importance of his findings of the presence of good continuous relationships with foster families and advocates a middle road between the two extremes of surrender for adoption and return to the biological parents, i.e. the viability of permanent long-term foster care, since the foster parents do become the psychological parents of the child, thus providing him or her with more of a sense of identity.

82. Parish, J.G. & T.S. Parish, 1983, ''Children's Self-Concepts as Related to Family Structure and Family Concepts'', *Adolescence,* Vol. 18, No. 71, pp. 649–658

''A total of 426 children from intact, divorced, and reconstituted families responded to two forms of the Personal Attribute Inventory for Children (PAIC) in an attempt to evaluate their families and themselves. Considering each of the adjectives on PAIC separately, the study found that choice of a particular adjective when describing oneself, for example, self-concept, was related to family structure in 46 instances and was related to family concept in 29 instances, with a significant interaction found in 13 instances. These findings are useful to parents, counselors, educators, and other helping professionals who seek to better understand the needs of children from various family situations.'' (SWAB)

83. No entry.

84. No entry.

85. Parish, T.S. & J.C. Taylor, 1979, ''The Impact of Divorce and Subsequent Father Absence on Children's and Adolescents' Self-

Concepts'', *Journal of Youth and Adolescence,* Vol. 8, No. 4, pp. 427–432

This study examined the self-concepts of 204 male and 202 female students in grades 3–8. Those in single parent families of divorce demonstrated significantly lower self-concepts (44 subjects). 15 subjects whose mothers had remarried possessed somewhat lower self-concepts than the 347 students from nuclear families, to which they were compared, but the difference was not found to be significant. The findings held for both sexes and all grade levels. ''(c)APA''

86. Parish, T.S. & J.W. Dostal, 1980, ''Relationships Between Evaluations of Self and Parents by Children from Intact and Divorced Families'', *Journal of Psychology,* Vol. 104, No. 1, pp. 35–38

639 students in 5th and 6th grade in 14 school districts from one state completed questionnaires with reference to themselves, their mothers, fathers, and when applicable, stepfathers. Hypothesis, as in previous study held. Those in intact families were found to have self-concepts significantly related to evaluations of biological fathers and mothers, those in stepfamilies after divorce were correlated with evaluations of mothers and stepfathers but not of biological fathers, those whose biological parents had been divorced less than two years had self-concepts strongly correlated to those of biological mothers, but also of both biological and stepfathers. ''(c)APA''

87. Parish, T.S. & T.F. Copeland, 1979, ''The Relationship Between Self-Concepts and Evaluations of Parents and Stepfathers'', *Journal of Psychology,* Vol. 101, No. 1, pp. 135–138

206 student volunteers were tested with relation to their self-concepts. Subjects from nuclear families were found to have self-concepts which were significantly related to their evaluation of their fathers and mothers. Those from stepfamilies with absent biological fathers showed self-concepts which were significantly correlated with their evaluations of their mothers and stepfathers but not of their biological fathers, as had been hypothesized. ''(c)APA''

88. Raschke, H. & V. Raschke, 1979, ''Family Conflict and Children's Self-concepts: A Comparison of Intact and Single-Parent Families'', *Journal of Marriage and the Family,* Vol. 41, No. 2

289 children in third, sixth, and eighth grade were the subjects in collecting information with reference to self-concept and family structure; and to family conflict with respect to family structure. No significant differences were found in children from intact, single-parent, step or any other type of family structure as far as the self-concept was concerned. However, the self-concept scores were significantly lower for children who reported higher levels of family conflict.

89. Rest, E. & K. Watson, 1984, "Growing Up in Foster Care", *Child Welfare,* Vol. 63, No. 4, pp. 291–306

This study was designed to assess program results in a multiple service inner-city child welfare agency. It was to locate and describe a group of young adults reared within the agency program, and to learn how they viewed themselves and their experience in the agency. The findings are consistent with previous ones, indicating that former foster children seem to manage their lives well, but that they saw themselves differently from other adults, remained acutely sensitive to their former status as foster children and view this as a contemporary issue. Parental rejection and pain from loss of family persists into adulthood regardless of the circumstances under which placement took place and of the therapeutic efforts attempted by the agency. Their greatest anxiety centered around the knowledge and feeling about the circumstances of their placement, and difficulty in dealing with losses. Agency efforts did not have the expected results of lessening the trauma. The recommendation appears to be in the direction of a reality-oriented approach which de-emphasizes the traditional community sentiment and emphasizes the child's need and ability to master and take control of his/her own life.

90. Sorich, C. & R. Siebert, 1979, *Toward Humanizing Adoption,* Child Welfare League of America, New York

This article discusses the benefits of exploring alternatives to the traditional closed adoption placement. It explores open adoption, and the sharing of a meaningful relationship between adoptive parents and biological parents, in order to provide adopted children with continuity and a sense of identity.

91. Sorosky, A.D., et al, 1975, "Identity Conflicts in Adoptees", *American Journal of Orthopsychiatry,* January

Authors emphasize the genealogical concerns of the adopted adolescent and describes him as "at risk" for the development of identity problems in late adolescence and young adulthood. During this time feelings about adoption resurge and questions about the past increase.

92. Sprey-Wessing, T. & P. Portz, 1982, "Some Aspects of Identity Problems in Foster Families", *Journal of Comparative Family Studies,* Vol. 13
    104 German foster parents were the subjects of this study. The authors hypothesize that foster children, unlike adopted children, cannot take on the role of biological child; this leads to role confusion, since the maturational process of children involves the integration of ego functions into their personality which is dependent on the healthy establishment of identity. The authors further hypothesize that insecurity with reference to status problems, loyalty conflict, and anxiety about the total loss of biological parents lead to identity confusion in the foster child. They also point to an identity confusion in the foster parents as parents based on these ambiguous situations engendered by decision making, tenuous relationships with agency and biological parents, and possible class differences between foster and biological parents. A further purpose of the study was to determine motivation for foster parenthood. "(c) APA"

93. Stein, L.M. & J.L. Hoopes, 1985, "Identity Formation in the Adopted Adolescent", *Child Welfare,* Vol. 64
    The authors highlight some of the difficulties which adopted adolescents experience in terms of the complexity of their status. However, they successfully dispel some myths which the literature on the subject has emphasized with reference to the pervasiveness of identity problems in this population. On the contrary, the authors' answer to the question whether adoptees are negatively affected by their adoptive status is a decisive "no." Contrary to theoretical expectations, a comparison of adopted versus non-adopted adolescents along the dimensions of identity formation reveal no significant differences. Of all the variables considered, the findings indicated that the quality of family relationships was most predictive of positive identity formation of all groups, and that the presence or absence of non-adopted siblings failed to show any impact. The limitation of the sample to white middle-class children adopted before age 2 needs to be considered. A study of search behavior seemed to relate somewhat to total adjustment and/or lack of family coherence. Differences in appearance seemed to have a bearing on the need to search. However, continuity and openness of communication about adoption appeared to be of major significance. Implications for practice and future research are outlined.

94. Triseliotis, J., 1984, ''Identity and Security in Adoption and Long-Term Fostering'', *Early Child Development and Care,* Vol. 15, No. 2–3, pp. 149–170

The author, a well-known British authority on issues of adoption, draws in this article on information from a larger study in which people who grew up in adoption were contrasted with those who grew up in long-term foster care situations (average 11 years with the same foster family). At the time of interview the 44 adoptees were mostly in their mid-twenties, and the 40 in the foster care group were in their early twenties. Both groups but particularly those in foster care came from very disadvantaged biological families. The author describes the development of a sense of personal identity and some of the questions asked to elicit this kind of information. Social functioning, competence and behaviors are further considered. Conclusions are summarized to indicate that undoubtedly adoptees who grew up to feel more secure had more complete identification with their adoptive families, while in the long-term foster care group the legal ambiguities, anxieties about permanence, and welfare stigma contributed to their less strong sense of identity. The author concludes with some important concerns that long-term foster care not be considered too negatively, but suggests some more positive ways of using this form of placement along with better continuity with biological families who have some bonds with their children. The alternative of more flexible adoption and foster care is highlighted as a need for the future.

95. Weinstein, E.A., 1960, *The Self Image of the Foster Child,* Russell Sage, New York

An early research study on children in foster care, in which the author examines the children's self-concepts in relation to a number of variables such as they exist in biological families, foster families and social agencies with which they come in contact, and whose personnel is responsible for the interaction of the child with the biological and foster parents and their relatives. An unexpected outcome of the research was the finding that there was a strong correlation between the children's sense of self and the existence and continuity of contact with the biological family even in instances in which the children had been placed and were living in quasi-adoptive or absorptive homes.

96. White, S., 1976, *Human Development in Today's World,* Little, Brown and Co., Boston

The fifth stage of Erikson's stages of the life cycle is "ego identity vs. role confusion." Erikson believes that the new interpersonal dimensions which emerge during this period of adolescence relate to a sense of ego identity (Who am I?). Role confusion is a negative sense of not knowing "who I am or where I belong." When a person cannot attain a sense of personal identity because of an unfortunate childhood or unusual social circumstance, confusion of roles occurs, fragmenting the adolescent's ego identity. It is necessary for practice with clients, especially the stepfamily with adolescents, to have knowledge and understanding of the identity issues during this phase of development.

97. Williams, M.B., 1984, "Family Dissolution: An Issue for the Schools", *Children Today,* Vol. 13, No. 4, pp. 24,25,27–29

The author explicates some of the findings in young children of separation and divorce to emphasize the importance of early intervention in order to deal with the identity confusion in young children. Group programs under the auspices of the school are recommended on the basis of the author's own experience in conducting, with a student as a co-leader, 40-minute group meetings with several small groups (4–6) of kindergarten children who live in single-parent families. Sessions with the children, joint sessions with the separated parents on parent- child issues are described, as is some work with a stepparent. It is felt that mediation efforts in the school can be of considerable help to both children and parents.

Bonding

98. Cherlin, A., 1977, "The Effect of Children on Marital Dissolution", *Demography,* Vol. 14, pp. 265–272

The author examines whether the presence of children affects separation and divorce, using data from the first four years of the National Longitudinal Survey of Labor Market Experience in Women aged 30 to 44. The data showed that only when there were children of preschool age were they a deterrent, since at that time the child-care investment is at its peak. The authors suggest that children do not prevent marital disruption because they add to parental bonding but only because early child-care may be too time-consuming and too expensive for one partner to manage alone.

99. Foster, H. & D. Freed, 1981, ''Grandparents' Visitation: Vagaries and Vicissitudes'', *Journal of Divorce,* Vol. 5, pp. 79–100
 The authors examine attitudes and ambiguities in the law concerning visitation of grandparents in divorce, and adoption cases. The ''best interest of the child'' doctrine is given some attention both in its positive and negative aspects. The law seems to be more positive toward grandparents who have custody claims, when there was parental neglect. Only 32 states have laws concerning permission for grandparents and relatives to visit. The weight of animosity of the parties as against the emotional bonds of the feuding adults to the child is one of the important issues pointed out for further consideration. The other major issue is the discontinuance of old ties in the case of adoption. It is pointed out that total discontinuity seems to be the opposite of the child's best interest; if needed there were ties before the event of divorce, stepfamily formation, or adoption as the case may be.

100. Guidubaldi, J., Cleminshaw, H., Perry, J., Nastasi, B. & J. Lightel, 1986, ''The Role of Selected Family Environment Factors in Children's Post-Divorce Adjustment'', *Family Relations,* Vol. 35, pp. 141–151
 This article extends previous reports of a nationwide study of the impact of divorce on children, examining current and longitudinal correlations with reference to the impact on home environment. A sample of 341 children was studied. Age and sex show important differences in functioning in the children of divorced and nuclear families; corroborating features of other studies are reported on. Important guidelines for professionals are highlighted; parent education is of great significance, especially in reference to authoritative features of child rearing. Heavy emphasis should be placed on the enhancement of parenting skills of both the resident and non-resident parent, and on maintaining good parent-child relationships with both parents. Involving the absent parent in professional contacts and educating the resident parent about the potential benefits of this to the child are aspects mentioned as important therapeutic strategies.

101. Hess, R. & K. Camara, 1979, ''Post-Divorce Family Relationships as Mediating Factors in the Consequences of Divorce for Children'', *Journal of Social Issues,* Vol. 5, pp. 79–96
 The effects of divorce on child behavior (stress signals, aggression, peer relations, school functioning) were examined through two-fold research, one by comparing children in intact and in divorced families, thc other, which proved ultimately more

important, an analysis of family processes and their relevance to child behavior. The family processes were the affective relationship between the parents, the affective relationship between the child and each parent separately, and in divorced families the amount of contact between the child and the non-custodial parent. The results are clear that the post-divorce relationships affect children much more than the divorce itself; the continuing relationship with the non-custodial parent (father) is as important as that of the custodial parent. Disruption of both primary bonds affects the child's emotional and cognitive processes. It is recommended that more attention be given to relationship variables rather than comparative studies and there are serious implications for now-existing (adversary) legal practices, agency policies, and treatment activities.

102. Hetherington, E., 1979, ''Divorce: A Child's Perspective'', *American Psychologist,* Vol. 34, pp. 851–858

A landmark paper focusing on the child's perspective in divorce. The author attempts to combat the popular professional and societal view of the single-parent family as a pathological one, and reviews instead the transitional phases through which the child passes when parents divorce, and some of the subsequent pitfalls and potentials. A conflict-ridden nuclear family is perceived as the most harmful. Thus divorce is potentially remedial. However, the transition is difficult, and the attitude and the supports available to children during the transitional years are more important than the divorced family status itself. The changing circumstances upon remarriage, and the potential for corrective emotional experiences, as well as the importance of extended family and community supports are described. Research evidence for the differential experiences depending upon the developmental phase of the child is cited and examples are given.

103. Huntington, D., 1982, ''Attachment, Loss, and Divorce'', *Therapy With Remarried Families,* Aspen Systems Corporation, Rockville, MD, pp. 19–29

The author gives an update of recent theories of attachment and then applies a reconsideration of attachment to the bonding processes of all children, and details the importance of this understanding to children of divorce. The crucial importance of extended family, even early peer group attachments, different functioning of parental role models, and the total context of familial and societal support systems needs to be considered. The strong point is made that parents (adults) are allowed to love many people while children are reared to love and trust only two people, their biological parents. This must change in order to adjust to the reality in the lives of children of divorce.

104. Joliff, D., 1984, "The Effects of Parental Remarriage on the Development of the Young Child", *Early Child Development and Care,* Vol. 13, No. 3–4, pp. 321–333

This paper presents a literature review of contemporary writers in this field. It concludes that children of remarriage may experience considerable adjustment challenges, but insignificant long-range developmental effects. It appears that the quality of family life is more relevant to child development than family structure. Children of divorce and remarriage show the least significant effects under age 8, the most in adolescence. Though the bonds between stepparent and child are not as strong as biological bonds, they can be very meaningful.

105. Kraft, A. D. et al, 1985, "Some Theoretical Considerations on Confidential Adoptions: III. The Adopted Child", *Child and Adolescent Social Work Journal,* Fall, 2(3) 139–153

"In all cases of newborn adoption in which placement is made directly into the permanent adoptive home, the adoptive parents become the psychological parents for that child. While adopted children do have separate psychological and genetic parents, the capacity for intimacy, identity and a cohesive sense of self develops through the consistent empathic attachment between the adoptive parents and the child. The adopted child's development through infancy, preoedipal, oedipal, latency, and adolescence is outlined, focusing on the child's intrapsychic tasks at each developmental phase. Ways in which development is different for the adopted child are discussed, and it is suggested that open adoptions have the risk of serious interference at each developmental phase. Confidential adoptions appear to provide the child with psychological protection for the unfolding of development. The crucial aspects of the intrapsychic difference for an adoptive child experiencing an open or confidential adoption are outlined." (APA)

106. Kirk, H.D., 1964, *Shared Fate: A Theory of Adoption and Mental Health,* The Free Press of Glencoe, London

A seminal work, in which the author puts forth a theoretical formulation of adoptive relationships. He reviewed available studies on the topic as well as the thinking and practice which were prevalent in adoption agencies. Early thoughts on the process of bonding in adoptive families are particularly noteworthy. This is the basis on which the author's further studies were built.

107. Lawder, E.A., Poulin, J.E. & R.G. Andrews, 1986, "A Study of 185 Foster Children 5 Years After Placement", *Child Welfare,* Vol. 65, No. 3, pp. 241–251

"A study of 185 children, five years after their placement in foster care, examined those variables that affect the length of time in placement, as well as the final disposition of cases. It found that of these children, 113 were discharged to members of their biological families, 29 were adopted, and 33 were still in foster care after five years, six were transferred to other agencies, and four were classified as 'other.' Thus, almost 77 percent of the children who were placed in foster care did not remain in care for a long period of time. Eighty-two of the 113 children who returned to their biological families did so within one year's time. The strongest predictor of whether a child returned to the biological family or remained in foster care was the frequency of visitation by family members. A significant relationship emerged between the dispositional status of the child and placement because of neglect, family crisis, parental mental health problems, parental age, and the number of behavioral problems of the child. Overall, these predictor variables accounted for 0.49 percent of the variance in the children's status after five years." (SWAB)

108. Maluccio, A. & P. Sinanoglu, eds., 1981, *The Challenge of Partnership: Working With Parents of Children in Foster Care,* Child Welfare League of America, New York

This is a collection of papers presented under a grant of the Children's Bureau at the University of Connecticut School of Social Work. The focus is on the untapped resources of biological parents. Preface, foreword, and the first paper which identify issues and trends in the literature, quickly identify the fact that parents are rarely, if ever, offered the kinds of continuous help that would enable them to function as a true physical or emotional resource to their children and more efforts—though also not enough—are invested in substitute arrangements. The papers offered give both a theoretical/research and "hands on" view of the child-placement process, both foster home and institutional care, and discuss means of continuity between biological parents and their children through the process to avoid the proverbial "drift" and insure maximum bonding despite separation experiences.

109. Meyer, C., 1985, "A Feminist Perspective on Foster Family Care: A Redefinition of the Categories", *Child Welfare,* Vol. 64, No. 3, pp. 249–258

The author uses the feminist perspective to demystify mothering. It helps to differentiate the notions of parenting functions in many areas of caring for children, not to be automatically characterized as mother love. A separate analysis of mothering and parenting opens new possibilities to redefine foster parenthood as a social service, instead of a "pretend" biological family. This would clarify the role relationship of foster mother to agency worker, increase accountability of service, and free clinical workers' skills where and when needed.

110. Pink, J.E. & K.S. Wampler, 1985, "Problem Areas in Stepfamilies: Cohesion, Adaptability, and the Stepfather-Adolescent Relationship", *Family Relations,* Vol. 34, No. 3, pp. 327–335

Twenty-eight stepfamilies were compared with twenty-eight nuclear families with reference to family functioning and the (step)father-adolescent relationship. Mother, (step)father, and adolescent ratings were obtained. Quality of the mother-adolescent relationship and marital satisfaction did not differ by family type, but, as anticipated, all ratings revealed lower family cohesion and adaptability, and less quality in the male parent-adolescent relationship in stepfamilies. Length of remarriage, amount and quality of contact with the absent biological father and adolescent gender were not related to stepfamily functioning. However, contrary to expectation, a high amount of contact with the biological father was more positive than either a moderate or low amount, in terms of the regard of the stepfather toward the adolescent. Some of the implications include the authors' suggestions for deliberate nurturing and bonding activities at the beginning of the step-relationship, and any activities aiming at "unconditionality." Attempts to fashion stepfamilies in the mold of nuclear families are felt to be misdirected. Counselors and educators should be helped to recognize and direct their clients in the direction of the issue of greater distancing (perhaps especially between stepfathers and stepdaughters) to provide functionality.

111. Poulin, J.E., 1985, "Long Term Foster Care, Natural Family Attachment and Loyalty Conflict", *Journal of Social Service Research,* Vol. 9, No. 1, pp. 17–29

"A study assessed the influence of the involvement of the natural family on the adjustment of foster children who had been in care two or more years and whose goals for placement were continued foster care. Findings revealed that about half the children were visited by their natural families fairly regularly, almost one third had strong psychological attachments to their families of origin, and about one quarter experienced conflicted feelings of loyalty between their foster families and natural families. The strongest predictor of such feelings was attachment to the natural family. In addition, visiting influenced conflicted feelings of loyalty indirectly through its effect on attachment.'' (SWAB)

112. Stanton, G.W., 1981, ''Child in Stepfamily: Extended Family Bliss or Nuclear Family Nightmare?'', APHA Social Work Section, Los Angeles, CA (Unpublished paper)

The author discusses the child's need to grieve losses and to clarify both biological and psychological continuity, before new bonding can take place. Professionals and educators are reminded of the impact which absent biological parents have on the child, even in successful stepfamily systems. The importance of clear understanding and continuity of biological ties to the establishment of a postive sense is stressed. Analogy is drawn to children in foster care, adoption, and those living with extended family members.

113. Triseliotis, J. , 1983, ''Identity and Security in Adoption and Long-Term Fostering'', *Adoption and Fostering,* Vol. 7, No. 1, pp. 22–31

''A study compared adoptees with foster children in relation to such issues as identity, security, and a sense of belonging. Forty-four adoptees and 40 foster children in their early and middle twenties participated in interviews. The adoptees were placed with their adoptive parents when aged 3–7, and those in foster care were placed with their foster parents when aged between a few months and 9 years. The foster children had spent an average of 11 years with the same foster parents. Findings revealed that compared with adoptees, foster children were less secure and less confident about their capacity to cope with life. Adoptees identified with their adopted families more than foster children identifed with their foster families. Despite strong psychological bonds between the majority of foster children and their foster parents, the ambiguous nature of the arrangement seemed to have a qualitative impact on the sense of identity among these children. Implications of these findings for long-term foster care are discussed.'' (SWAB)

114. Ward, M., 1981, ''Parental Bonding in Older Child Adoptions'', *Child Welfare,* Vol. 60, No. 1, pp. 24–34

Examines various factors in an attempt to isolate those belonging exclusively to the birth situation and those that may be used to enhance bonding of the parent to the older adopted child.

Legal Issues

115. Andrews, R.G., 1978, ''Adoption: Legal Resolution or Legal Fraud?'', *Family Process,* Vol. 17, September

Adoption, presumably a binding contract, is under attack, especially from adult adoptees seeking their ''roots'' who claim that social agencies, courts, and last but not least, the interpretations of law and policies by adoptive families have led to secrecy, and a feeling of stigma, differentness, and being cut off on the part of adoptees. The author makes a good case of the pros and cons of the ''open record'' controversy currently being fought state by state and also in the Supreme Court. The author considers the ''search'' of adoptees a ''developmental crisis.''

116. Atwell, A., Moore, U. & C. Nowell, 1982, ''The Role of Stepparents in Child Custody Disputes'', *Bulletin of the American Academy of Psychology and the Law,* Vol. 10, pp. 211–217

This article deals with the roles of stepparents in custody conflicts. A stepparent who has not had biological children often presents a more positive influence. It is also emphasized that compatibility between biological parents and stepparents in general lifestyle and child-rearing practices and some sharing in the development of new roles are important contributors to positive relationships. The absence of some of these leave children with loyalty conflicts and resulting symptoms of depression or acting out.

117. Barsky, M., 1984, ''Strategies and Techniques of Divorce Mediation'', *Social Casework,* Vol. 65

This article describes ''macro'' strategies to guide mediation in a general way, e.g. the use of the physical environment, an awareness of self, teaching the mediation process, identification of patterns, power relationships; real and symbolic issues, and the management of the mediation process. ''Macro'' techniques are specific interventions which reduce conflict, improve communication, and clarify the fields of agreement; they consist of encounters that foster the carrying out of each of the mediators' long-range strategies.

118. Benedek, R. & E. Benedek , 1977, ''Postdivorce Visitation'', *Journal of Child Psychiatry,* Vol. 16, pp. 256–270

This article is written from the point of view of the children's rights to both parents. Therefore an awareness of the child's need for continuity with both parents through visiting arrangements is emphasized. It is suggested that the courts take cognizance of these important concepts and discontinue the usual pattern of locating sole rights and power with the custodial parent. Individual consideration of family dynamics are suggested to develop individual solutions. Parents, agencies, courts, and private therapists are alerted to the potential for conflict which can be played out in this arena, and are reminded not to locate authority for these decisions solely in court-mandated solutions but to examine and re-examine the situations in which families find themselves. The therapeutic establishment in its various locations is seen as an important locus for enlightened interventions.

119. Benedek, R.S. & E.P. Benedek, 1979, ''The Child's Preference in Michigan Custody Disputes'', *The American Journal of Family Therapy,* Vol. 7, No. 4, pp. 37–43

Two lawyers discuss the relative merits of the provision in the Michigan law which requires the court to consider the child's preference. Some problems encountered in implementation include lack of specification re: the child's age, the question of who is to interview and/or evaluate the child. Although this is considered an enlightened law, it is felt by the authors that trial judges do not seem willing or able to implement it. It is suggested that ''behavioral scientists'' of unspecified professional background be the ones to interview, assess, and evaluate, rather than members of the legal profession.

120. Berger, B.R., Sudhakar, M. & V. Roebuck, 1988, ''Child Custody and Relitigation: Trends in a Rural Setting'', *American Journal of Orthopsychiatry,* Vol. 58, No. 4, pp. 604–607

884 divorce cases were examined in a rural North Carolina County with regard to the types of child custody decision made, and the rates of post-divorce litigation were examined for each type of custody. It was surprising that joint legal custody (available for 15 years in this country) was only used in 2.3% of all cases, in contrast to recent national figures. However, caution must be used in interpreting these data, since 29% did not ask for custody adjudication at the time of the divorce. Some, perhaps most, of these might have been joint custody type settlements. However, in comparing the figures as to the rates of relitigation, the two types

of custody do not favor formal joint custody over exclusive custody of one. Parental preference for settlement outside of court, may, according to the authors, reflect a fear that the legal decisions may add uncertainties in guessing at the future needs of children.

121. Berkowitz, B., 1970, ''Legal Incidents of Today's 'Step' Relationship: Cinderella Revisited'', *Family Law Quarterly,* Vol. 4, pp. 209–229

This is an early article dealing with the legal rights and obligations of stepfathers to children brought into and living in their households. The legal and factual assumptions of responsibilities are based on the premise that men marrying women with children are ready to assume custodial, in loco parentis, and legal responsibilities for them. The article discusses the controversial interpretations of both laws and statutory mandates and provisions. Differences in laws and legal interpretations in a number of states are cited, and the author concludes with the hope for legal reform, on the premise of the greater security of the child if the mother's new husband in whose household she lives will assume major financial responsibilities.

122. Bernstein, B., 1982, ''Understanding Joint Custody Issues'', *Social Casework,* Vol. 63

This article discusses the custody of children as a paramount social and family crisis. The creation of good feelings between divorced parents clearly is a prime objective for mental health professionals. Identifying the objective introduced the question of why custody could not be settled by joint custody agreements in which enlightened couples, encouraged and assisted by caring, competent mental health counselors and attorneys, would be responsible for parenting skills needed to rear their children cooperatively.

123. Bernstein, B. & B. Haberman, 1981, ''Lawyers and Counselors as an Interdisciplinary Team: Problem Awareness in the Blended Family'', *Child Welfare,* Vol. 60, pp. 211–218

The authors suggest that the complexities of remarriage and stepfamily living warrant a premarital agreement as a protection to both children and marital partners. Counseling to help with problems of the family in formation is suggested as a separate issue, but it is felt that given some legal protection, the counseling problems are not too different from some of those occurring in nuclear families.

124. Bernstein, B. & S. Collins, 1985, "Remarriage Counseling: Lawyer and Therapist's Help with the Second Time Around", *Family Relations,* Vol. 34, pp. 387–391

The authors summarize problems specific to remarriage with the help of current literature. They focus on the appropriateness of a counselor-therapist to involve a lawyer in helping with issues of remarriage. Options and limitations currently in the law are outlined, and such instruments as premarital agreement, inventories, estate planning, postmarital partition, antenuptial agreements are discussed. The need for competence and skills from both professionals is emphasized.

125. Chasin, R. and H. Grunebaum, 1981, "A Model for Evaluation in Child Custody Disputes", *The American Journal of Family Therapy,* Vol. 9, No. 3, pp. 43–49

The authors, two MD's and clinical professors who have been involved in child custody decisions, describe their philosophy and the process in which they engage. They subscribe first and foremost to the belief that the professional should maintain a neutral position and should work with both parents and their attorneys' agreement in their involvement. They further describe how they help parents prepare the children for a personal interview, as well as the actual process and procedure which they follow in the evaluation. The emphasis in these authors' conceptualization is on continuity with both parents, and an emphasis in which the child should experience as little loss as possible. Sample agreements are included in the paper.

126. Chesler, P., 1987, *Mothers On Trial, The Battle for Children and Custody,* The Seal Press, Seattle, WA

The author, a psychologist, who has many times been a speaker, witness, or consultant on child custody issues, raises many questions about the ambiguities and abuses of legal situations in contemporary society. She gives evidence of the victimization of children, and mothers in particular. Her questions are well formulated and often provocative, always stimulating thought and further inquiry. Poverty, violence, custodial and non-custodial mothers, politics about custody of the fetus, reproductive rights of husbands, unwed fathers, sperm donors, and of women are some of the challenging foci of the twenty-two chapters of this book.

127. Coogler, O.J., 1978, *Structured Mediation in Divorce Settlement,* Lexington Books, D.C. Heath Company, Lexington, MA.

Description of structured mediation: including definition, goals and procedures for arranging custody, support, budgets, tax considerations, and marital settlement agreement.

128. Crosbie-Burnett, M., 1987, ''Impact of Joint Versus Maternal Legal Custody, Sex and Age of Adolescent, and Family Structure Complexity on Adolescents in Remarried Families.'', *Annual Convention of the American Psychological Association,* New York

''No published research has investigated the impact of joint custody on the adjustment of children of divorce who become stepchildren. This research examined the differential effects of joint versus maternal custody, structural complexity (presence or absence of stepfather's children from a prior marriage), and sex and age of the adolescent on adolescent outcomes in stepfamilies. The volunteer sample consisted of wives, husbands, and oldest or only adolescents in 84 white, middle-class stepfather families. Each family member independently completed a questionnaire in the family's home. Findings revealed that adolescents in joint custody and simple stepfamilies reported more happiness and more inclusion than did those in joint custody and complex stepfamilies. Joint custody families with older adolescents and with boys reported the most role ambiguity (disagreement about the stepfather's role in the family). Structural complexity affected loyalty conflicts only for younger adolescents, who reported less loyalty conflicts in complex stepfamilies. Boys were reported to have greater well-being than girls regardless of custody arrangement.'' (ERIC)

129. Derdeyn, A. & E. Scott, 1984, ''Joint Custody: A Critical Analysis and Appraisal'', *American Journal of Orthopsychiatry,* Vol. 34, pp. 199–209

The authors, a psychiatrist and a lawyer, combine their expertise in this review article. Joint custody has gained rapid acceptance, is now in the statutes of over half of the states and is becoming the legally preferred custody arrangement. It eases the burden of the courts and there is some notion that it benefits all members of divorced families. However, the research results are mixed. Children do gain from maintaining a relationship with both parents; however, some of the assumptions that joint custody is the best or the only way to achieve this are not corroborated. The arguments such as father's traditional rights to custody or mother's traditionally established quality as the custodial parent are no longer valid, and ''the best interest'' theory holds biased perceptions which must be more thoroughly examined. The authors claim a marked disparity between the power and groundswell of the joint custody movement, and the lack of sufficient evidence that joint custody can fulfill what is expected of it.

130. Ernst, T. & R. Altis, 1981, "Joint Custody and Co-Parenting: Not By Law, but By Love", *Child Welfare,* Vol. 60, pp. 669–677
The authors review relevant literature, give indications and counter-indications and generally advocate these options, emphasizing the role of social workers in the areas of practice, research, and social action.

131. Festinger, T.B., 1976, "The Impact of the New York Court Review of Children in Foster Care: A Follow-Up Report", *Child Welfare,* Vol. LV, Sept/Oct, pp. 515–544
In response to criticism of the increasing number of children in foster care, the New York Social Services Law was enacted to review children who had been in care for two years. This study explores how effective the law has been and ways it can function more effectively. The 235 cases that had entered care in 1970 and were reviewed by courts were the focus of the study. Findings demonstrate that court review hastened movement of children out of foster care.

132. Festinger, T.B., 1975, "The New York Court Review of Children in Foster Care", *Child Welfare,* Vol. LIV, April, pp. 211–245
This study was developed to address three questions regarding the Pisani Law (effective mid-1971) which "requires agencies charged with care and guardians of foster children to petition the Family Court to review status of all children voluntarily placed continuously for 24 months." Sample includes 427 children placed in 1970. Data in the study related to answering the three following questions: (1) What factors are related to court's determination that a child should be continued in foster care, discharged, freed, or placed for adoption? (2) To what extent does the court agree with agencies' recommendations as to what is in the child's best interest? (3) Does the Family Court have any impact on moving children out of foster care? Descriptions and discussion included.

133. Foster, H. & D. Freed, 1981, "Grandparents' Visitation: Vagaries and Vicissitudes", *Journal of Divorce,* Vol. 5, pp. 79–100
The authors examine attitudes and ambiguities in the law concerning visitation of grandparents in divorce, and adoption

cases. The "best interest of the child" doctrine is given some attention both in its positive and negative aspects. The law seems to be more positive toward grandparents who have custody claims, when there was parental neglect. Only 32 states have laws concerning permission for grandparents and relatives to visit. The weight of animosity of the parties as against the emotional bonds of the feuding adults to the child is one of the important issues pointed out for further consideration. The other major issue is the discontinuance of old ties in the case of adoption. It is pointed out that total discontinuity seems to be the opposite of the child's best interest; if needed there were ties before the event of divorce, stepfamily formation, or adoption as the case may be.

134. Fox, W.F., 1979, "Anonymity in the Adoption Process: The Legal Aspects", *Social Thought,* Fall, pp. 43–52

A concise, yet informative article clearly explaining the legal process as it relates to adoption. More specifically, it explains the adoption process, the sealed record statutes, the constitutional and non-constitutional aspects of adoption and a proposal for change.

135. Gardner, R.A., 1982, *Family Evaluation in Child Custody Litigation,* Creative Therapeutics, Creskill, New Jersey

The author is a well-known child psychiatrist and psychoanalyst who has written several best-selling books about children of divorce and children in stepfamilies. In this book he develops guidelines for child custody evaluations based on his long and rich experience in having been called to court as an expert. He views the various problems both from the available literature and from the mental health and legal perspectives. There are several appendices, offering sample custody evaluations, parents' questionnaires, and guidelines for a contract before an expert accepts a child custody evaluation case.

136. Gill, M. & C. Amodeo, 1983, "Social Work and Law in a Foster Care/Adoption Program", *Child Welfare,* Vol. 62, pp. 455–467

This article deals with the need for cooperation between social workers and lawyers in situations in which children who are not (yet) free for adoption are placed with foster families who have made a commitment for permanence prior to the placement. The intention of reducing the number of foster home placements is outlined. Guidelines for the identification of children appropriate for such placements are offered. The balance of the legal rights of biological parents, and the attachment between child and foster parents (psychological parents) is considered by the authors.

137. Goldsmith, M.A., 1978, ''AFDC Eligibility and the Federal Stepparent Regulation'', *Texas Law Review,* Vol. 56, No. 1, pp. 79–100

This paper focuses on the recurring problem of the negative effect which a stepparent's presence has on AFDC eligibility of the biological parent's children. A provocative and challenging presentation, first of the historical background of the states' AFDC programs, with their original moralistic interpretation of family need, the Social Security Act's presumably temporary contribution to the states' programs, and continuing lack of clarity with reference to eligibility. The author also describes with the support of several legal cases the problem by which the inexact legal definition of the term ''parent'' at this time can seriously deprive children of the Aid for Dependent Children (AFDC) support, since it is up to the states to interpret the legal definitions in their own way. The author warns that even the rigid interpretation of absence or presence of a biological father has deprived children of contact with their fathers, a source of serious problem in this program. The implicit warning is not to carry this further by either inexact or overzealous interpretations of a stepparent's legal responsibilities. This ''note'' is written for lawyers, thus legal language predominates. However, the social implications of this paper are quite far-reaching.

138. Goldstein, J. A. Freud & Solnit, A. J. 1973, *Beyond the Best Interest of the Child,* Free Press Paperback, New York, London

A psychoanalyst of considerable renown, a pediatrician, and a lawyer combined their expertise to do a critical examination of what happens to children in the court system. They review historical context and the ''best interest of the child'' doctrine and suggest that a child's best interest is rarely served under the circumstances created by legal constraints and interpretations, and by social agencies and their relationships to the court system. The book gained a great deal of popularity and was very influential in obtaining some court reform. A significant contribution is the differentiation of biological and psychological parenting, and a departure from some common assumptions. While the authors' critique of existing conditions is scathing and seemingly quite justified, their solutions are based on the psychological belief systems of their day.

139. Greif, J. & S. Simring, 1982, ''Remarriage and Joint Custody'', *Conciliation Courts Review,* Vol. 20, pp. 9–14

The authors address the difficulties arising generally in divorced families with visiting arrangements and continued contact of children with both biological parents. They generally think that joint custody arrangements can benefit these situations. They especially address the effect of the new structural arrangements when one of the divorced partners (especially the custodial parent) remarries. They posit that joint custody can contribute positively to the remediation of the natural stresses and strains arising in stepfamily living. Prior to developing a systematic study, the authors share their clinical observations. The sense of loss the child experiences upon the parent's remarriage, the effect of the child's presence on the couple bonding, the possibly diminished role of the nonresident parent may all be positively influenced by the existence of shared custody arrangements. Problems and constraints are also examined.

140. Greif, J.B., 1979, ''Fathers, Children, and Joint Custody'', *American Journal of Orthopsychiatry,* Vol. 49, No. 2, pp. 311–317

''Survey of 40 middle-class divorced fathers. Those with joint custody more likely than those with visitation rights to continue high involvement with and influence on children's development.''(SAA)

141. Gross, M., 1984, ''Custody Conflicts Between Foster and Birth Parents in Pennsylvania'', *Social Work,* Vol. 29, pp. 510–515

The author reviews the development of legal decisions related to foster care and traces recent history of custody conflicts between foster parents and birth parents in Pennsylvania as significant in portraying the relationship of the courts to social agencies. The seemingly neutral position of agency staffs as representing both foster and biological family is in sharp contrast to the adversary position of the courts. Legal position and changes in the standards, e.g. a more flexible interpretation of the ''best interest of the child,'' as well as the significant cessation of the ''tender year doctrine'' which automatically made the mother the most logical custodian are discussed. Visitation as a right or as the child's need for continuity is debated. The question of the child's bonding to a psychological parent seems to be rejected by the court. The author sees the court's ''either or'' position of foster parents versus birth parents as unfortunate.

142. Hare-Mustin, R.T., 1982, ''China's Marriage Law: A Model for Family Responsibility and Relationships'', *Family Process,* Vol. 21, No. 4, pp. 477–481

A brief commentary accompanies the presentation of the

contrast between the 1950 and 1981 marriage law in China. The responsibilities of spouses, parents, siblings, grandparents to each other are clearly defined. Equality and the rights of women, children, and the aged are emphasized in the 1981 law. Divorce, adoption, remarriage, and the rights of stepchildren are clearly defined, and the inference that some if not all provide a model seems justified.

143. Harper, P., 1984, ''Children in Stepfamilies: Their Legal and Family Status. Institute of Family Studies Policy Background Paper No. 4'', *Institute of Family Studies,* Melbourne

''One of the features of Australian society during the past 25 years, from the late 1950's to the early 1980's, has been the changing nature of the family. Significant changes have occurred in family formation and breakdown; in family composition and structures; in family relationships; and in the status, rights, and obligations of family members. This paper (1) outlines some of these changes, directing particular attention toward implications for stepfamilies; (2) examines the arrangements some families have made, especially by using adoption, to clarify and establish the legal status and family relationships of children and stepparents; (3) outlines the options available in establishing legal status and family relationships in stepfamilies; and (4) recommends changes to legislation to overcome existing problems and provide a more appropriate means of establishing legal status and clarifying relationships within stepfamilies. It is proposed that stepparents be enabled to seek guardianship or custody rights but that adoption of stepchildren be abolished.'' (ERIC)

144. Haskins, R., Schwartz, J., Akin, J. & A. Dobelstein, 1985, ''How Much Child Support Can Fathers Pay?'', *Policy Studies Journal,* Vol. 14, pp. 201–222

On the basis of various empirical studies (which indicate that custodial mothers and children are much worse off after separation and divorce, many living in poverty and more, while above the poverty line, living below the median pre-divorce family income), the authors question the poor results of the 1974 federal-state program of Child Support enforcement. Using income data, census bureau data, for their analysis, they attempted to establish fair figures which absent fathers should pay in child support. Their conclusions indicate that absent fathers could pay about 3.6 times as much as they actually did pay in 1984. They concluded therefore that the financial security of custodial mothers and their children could be substantially increased by a vigorous enforcement of the Child Support Enforcement legislation. It is clearly pointed out that the major part of such resources would go to children of fathers in the highest income brackets; thus improvement in the nation's system of collection would not benefit the welfare system to any substantial degree. It would nevertheless contribute meaningfully to the rearing of a substantial number of the nation's children.

145. Horowitz, A. & C. Burchardt, 1984, ''Procedures for Court Consultations on Child Custody Issues'', *Social Casework,* Vol. 65, pp. 259–266

The authors develop and discuss six variables for decision making if a determination and/or a change of custody recommendation is required. They illustrate this graphically in a figure which depicts a ''Decision Tree for Differential Custody Recommendations.'' Based on the success or lack of success of historical requirements and their assessment of the Goldstein et al concept of psychological parent, they address such issues as joint custody as their first preference, assessment of parental continuity, parenting capacity, child's preference and its pros and cons, and their own best judgment based on practice experience.

146. Ihinger-Tallman, M., 1985, ''Perspectives on Change of Custody Among Step-Siblings'', *Annual Conference of the National Council on Family Relations,* Dallas

''In an attempt to understand perceptions of custody arrangements from the perspective of children with a focus on sibling and stepsibling relationships, exploratory research was conducted. Lengthy, unstructured interviews were conducted with 12 college students who ranged in age from 18 to 37. Data were gathered on family communication and affection patterns, authority or power relations, coalition formation, cohesiveness and solidarity, and the development of trust and commitment. Several of the subjects had experienced a custody shift, most often occurring because the father sought and won custody. A common reaction to parental divorce was a drawing together of the sibling group. Factors affecting stepsibling relations were: (1) differential treatment; (2) strained relations between stepsiblings while visiting the second home; and (3) differential treatment of ''own'' children versus stepchildren. Shared experiences, respect, and general liking served as a basis for stepsibling closeness. Subjects' family lives exhibited disruption. Negative feelings were more likely to be directed towards stepparents than toward step-siblings.'' (ERIC)

147. Jenkins, S., 1978, "Children of Divorce", *Children Today,* March/April, Vol. 7, #2, pp. 16–20

In view of the very high divorce rate, the high remarriage rate and the rising percentages of divorce involving young children in the U.S., the author selects four areas for special attention: economic problems and child support; custody issues and court involvement; emotional problems and intervention, including peer group support; and kinship patterns in step-relationships and the stepfamily. Solutions for economic problems need to be worked out in general policy areas for the population at large, such as income maintenance, jobs, day care, etc. This could avoid stigmatizing a large segment of the population. Custody decisions are continuing to be based on state laws, though the 1968 Uniform Child Custody Jurisdiction Act which was instituted to curb child snatchings is gaining in some states. Empirical research is missing as a base for decision making. While substantial literature on divorce and its psychological effect has been generated, the adjustment of children seems to be measured against the adjustment of well-functioning children in intact families. The Kelly-Wallerstein study is cited as an important contemporary research effort. The controversial aspects of the "Best Interest of the Child" concept are discussed, as are the pros and cons of court-mandated counseling. The unique position of the stepfamily is further considered. Legal problems, custody issues, and special problems in stepfamilies are cited to consider special types of help, e.g. peer groups, as well as professional counseling for children in these families.

148. Johnston, J., Campbell, L. & M. Tall, 1955, "Impasse to the Resolution of Custody and Visitation Disputes", *American Journal of Orthopsychiatry,* Vol. 55, pp. 112–129

The authors present a typology of (post) divorce situations in which litigation and prolonged debates go on about custody and visitation issues. The study is based on an examination in depth of 80 feuding families of multiethnic and mixed economic class, which, despite court intervention and mediation could not resolve their differences. The authors developed the notion of a "divorce transition impasse" along several systems levels (e.g. external-social, interactional, intrapsychic) along with the outward personal and community representations of such conflicts. Specific intervention goals are suggested on the basis of a phase-specific assessment, which invalidates the stated conflictual issues over visiting and custody. A realistic focus on the children plus an accepting but mildly confronting approach to the parents' predominantly personal issues will help to unblock the impasse and lead to more focused strategic interventions.

149. Jones, M., 1978, ''Stopping Foster Care Drift: A Review of Legislation and Special Programs'', *Child Welfare,* Vol. LVII, pp, 571–579

This article reviews legislation addressing the lengthy foster-care stays. Legislation from New York, Virginia, Ohio and New Jersey is mentioned. In addition, special projects addressing this issue are also alluded to.

150. Kargman, M.W., 1983, ''Stepchild Support Obligations of Stepparents'', *Family Relations,* Vol. 32, pp. 231–238

The legal responsibilities of support by stepparents for stepchildren during remarriage is discussed. Implications for the impact of the divorce upon child support, visitation and custody after divorce from the remarriage are presented. Court cases and laws relevant to stepchild support obligations of stepparents are reviewed. The article cites recently enacted legislative updates (as of 2/12/80) for twenty-one states. (Gruber)

151. Khan, A., 1981, ''Adoption by Parent and Stepparent'', *Family Law,* Vol. 11, No. 3, pp. 73–74

This article, written in England, deals with the legal and social aspects of adoption by stepparents living with one of the child's biological parents (which was considered detrimental by the helping profession but applications are very much on the increase). It is felt that the court is called upon to deal with very complex psychological issues. A significant though not conclusive factor to be considered is the child's own wish and feelings, depending on age. Recollection of the biological parent (father) is another important issue, as is being cut off from the biological father's family. A Court of Appeals Review of a case that is cited here was considered a landmark decision, which may vary in its application or may not be an example for further such decisions.

152. Koopman, E.J. & E.J. Hunt, 1988, ''Child Custody Mediation: An Interdisciplinary Synthesis'', *American Journal of Orthopsychiatry,* Vol. 58, No. 3, pp. 379–386

The authors review current and recent literature on divorce and child custody mediation paralleling the changes in divorce and family law. They relate their recommendations for an interdisciplinary understanding and collaboration to their understanding of child development in post-divorce families, and how this could be best achieved by blending the accumulated knowledge of legal, child development, and conflict-resolution principles.

153. Kornhaber, A., 1983, ''The Vital Connection—The 1983 Grandparents Are Coming of Age in America'', *Children Today,* July-August 1983

The author discusses the unique contribution which grandparents can and do make to the lives of their grandchildren. The Foundation for Grandparenting, a nonprofit organization, is mentioned with varied tasks, such as research, creating programs, educating the public, etc. A legal attempt has been made to propose grandparents' visitation rights. A proposition called a Uniform Grandparents Visitation Law was proposed and unanimously approved by the U.S. House of Representatives in 1983. The author speaks for the enhancement of family relationships and depth in family bonding with positive help from grandparents.

154. Levin, J., 1974, ''Stepparents and Guardians'', *New Law Journal,* May, pp. 507–509

The ambiguous legal status of a stepparent with reference to his/her rights and responsibilities are reviewed. A case is cited where only formal rights through adoption would have been recognized upon the biological parent's death. Wardship procedures in court can be used by stepparents to assume legal rights for guardianship. However, rights to custody by unrelated parental caretakers may be viewed controversially in the court system. Local authorities have discretionary powers, which could be questioned in legal proceedings initiated by a stepparent. In spite of the few, if any, rights of a stepparent, he may still find himself liable for financial support, and if in possession of custody have the duty to educate and to protect the child. Legal guardianship may or may not protect the relationship's rights. A proposed Children's Bill, if passed, is presumed to bring greater clarity into these confused legal aspects and their interpretations, as far as stepparents are concerned.

155. Lyon, E., Silverman, M., Howe, G. & J. Bishop, 1985, ''Stages of Divorce: Implications for Service Delivery'', *Social Casework,* Vol. 66, No. 5, pp. 259–267

A three-stage model (pre-separation decision making; litigation-reconstructuring; recovery post-dissolution stages) is studied in terms of the adults' and children's perceptions, and their use of legal and other support systems. All respondents in the study (adults) had attended divorce-education groups in a family service agency over a thirty-two month period. Questionnaires and interviews were used. The different reactions in the three different stages were addressed, and the perceptions and feelings of the participants were described. Their perceptions of their children's feelings were also described. In spite of the respondents' participation in various forms of help processes plus the divorce-education groups, conflicts, especially over visitation, continued for nearly half the group. The data suggest differential needs during the various phases, and recommend professional sensitivity, with different forms of intervention. Early mediation and counseling programs are suggested, as well as organized support groups. Lawyers seemed to concur, since much of their time with clients seemed to be spent on non-legal issues.

156. Maidment, S., 1976, "The Step Relationship and Its Legal Status", *Anglo-American Law Review,* Vol. 5, pp. 259–283

The legal status of a stepparent is examined in its many ramifications. The formal legal processes are presented, i.e. adoption, custodianship, guardianship, and wardship. The article deals with the legal processes now operating in the courts and examines some alternatives. There are specified reasons when a stepparent (assumed to be the stepfather in all situations cited) could easily assume the "in loco parentis" role on a legal basis, while in most cases he assumes this role "de facto." A 1972 committee which forms the basis for much of what is reported here saw that a stepparent could clearly acquire legal rights short of adoption. However, adoption is not normally proposed as a solution. The Children's Act of 1975 has created "the worst of worlds for the stepparent," since it did not create procedures for stepparents who marry divorced parents. Half-orphaned or illegitimate children fare better as far as the possibility to adopt them goes. However, in very many instances, stepfathers assume parental duties by their de facto relationship, on a voluntary basis. The writer concludes that the legal position of the stepparent is indeed precarious. It seems that liabilities are required rather than legal rights and sanctions. Since a stepparent is neither a parent nor a relative, his consent is not required where a legal guardian's consent usually is. On the other hand, he is frequently required to support his stepchildren in some Welfare policies. This author raises a lot of very sound questions pointing up legal inconsistencies, hoping for an interpretation which favors the welfare of the child rather than parents' legal rights.

157. Meriam, A.S., 1960, *The Stepfather in the Family,* University of Chicago Press, Chicago, IL

A study for social caseworkers which presents the legal position of the stepfather. Specific cases are considered through the years 1739 to 1939, which show the handling of the question of obligation by the courts, the nature of the problems which have necessitated litigation and the judgment of the courts in their solution.

158. Mnookin, R. & L. Kornhauser, 1979, ''Bargaining in the Shadow of Law: The Case of Divorce'', *Yale Law Journal,* Vol. 88, p. 950

Brief description of impact of present adversarial legal system on divorce-settlement negotiations. Authors suggest an alternative way of thinking about the role of law at the time of divorce. They describe the mediation process in regard to child and spouse support, custody and visitation rights and arrangements.

159. Noble, D., 1983, ''Custody Contest: How to Divide and Reassemble a Child'', *Social Casework,* Vol. 64, No. 7, pp. 406–413

The author refers to the custody battle as a favorite competitive game and defines four stages. Continued splitting is much harder to adjust to than a short crisis, and the so-called facts in the situation turn out to be more in the nature of emotional statements. Even the tremendous costliness has negative impact on the lives of the children who will eventually miss out on some of the costly aspects of life such as large orthodontia bills or college education. The conditional nature of legal judgments contributes negatively to the stability in children's lives, biased attorneys and judges add their parts, child snatching, and involved legal countermeasures all add up to enormous problems in children's lives. Some more recent and seemingly more humane ways of approaching the problem, e.g. visitation rights and joint custody, are discussed. The sad fact of the drawbacks of any arrangement is emphasized, but it is stressed that knowledge of the legal aspects, of rights and responsibilities on the part of the professionals who are often used as middlemen, could go a long way, and there is an implied plea for the neutrality of the professional, to use him/herself more decisively to develop policies which will be responsive to the true needs of the children and therefore their families.

160. Noble, D.N. & C.E. Palmer, 1984, ''The Painful Phenomenon of Child Snatching'', *Social Casework,* Vol. 65, No. 6

The emotions and possible motivations involved in the increasing incidents of child snatching are examined. Legal attempts at control are analyzed, and a case example is cited, to illustrate the author's points. The obscurity of existing laws and the great variety in legal statutes as well as their interpretation are shown to aggravate the personal trauma of all participants, as well as demonstrate the enormous legal cost and lengthy process. It is recommended that social workers be on the alert to the increase of this phenomenon and try to forestall it by early encouragement of feuding parents to obtain temporary custody, rather than wait for final legal decisions, explore custody options and be cognizant of early danger signals. Support of social and legal changes should be part of social workers' child and family advocacy.

161. Oxtoby, M., 1985, ''The New Adoption Legislation: Medico-social-legal Views'', *Adoption and Fostering,* Vol. 9, No. 4, pp. 46–51.

''Discusses the new adoption legislation that became effective in England and Wales on May 27, 1984. The issues raised by participants in three related seminars include the role of medical advisors, practice issues, collection and use of medical information, freeing, communication, confidentiality, consents, putative/natural fathers, wardship, adoption allowances, court reports, change of name, adoption panels, direct placement, and rights of access.''(''APA'')

162. Proch, K. & J. Howard, 1984, ''Parental Visiting in Foster Care: Law and Practice'', *Child Welfare,* Vol. 63, No. 2, pp. 139–147

The authors examine and critique the legal basis for using visitation or lack of visitation as a major criterion in the reunification with parents or the termination of parental rights. They review some of the existing provisions at state and federal levels and contrast them with some model acts. Recommendations for statutory reform and changes in child welfare practice are made.

163. Pruhs, A., Paulsen, M. & W. Tysseling, 1984, ''Divorce Mediation: The Politics of Integrating Clinicians'', *Social Casework,* Vol. 65, No. 9, pp. 532–540

A process of divorce mediation is described, which has the potential of providing an avenue of cooperative conflict resolution and custody resolution counseling, without taking over the functions of the legal system. The experiences of a mediation service in one agency are cited, to suggest that some trauma for children can be mitigated through this service. The process is clearly outlined, the advantages to cooperating with the legal system are highlighted, and the cost benefits both in preventing long drawn-out battles and later mental health costs are touched upon.

164. Ramsay, S., 1986, "Stepparent Support of Stepchildren: The Changing Legal Context and the Need for Empirical Policy Research", *Family Relations,* Vol. 35, No. 3, pp. 363–369
The author reviews federal and state laws on the issue of stepparents' financial support, outlining areas in which social science research can contribute to policy development. Changes are expected as stepparents' roles become more formally recognized and they are identified as an important resource for children. Issues are identified, e.g. the proportion of liability between biological and stepparent in terms of their respective roles; visitation and contact with children and its relation to financial responsibility; liability of stepparent after divorce of the remarriage; stepparents' responsibility for child support as defined by welfare laws or beyond. Policies both in this country and in England are cited to show some of the available data as well as to point to possible areas of inquiry about this important legal subject which in its implementation is fraught with emotions.

165. Roman, R. & W. Haddad, 1978, *The Disposable Parent: The Case for Joint Custody,* Holt, Rinehart and Winston, New York
This book explores relatively new alternatives to parenting in the divorced family. It rejects theories that the mother should generally be given custody on the grounds that such ideas enshrine or enslave women. The primary message is that parenting responsibilities should be shared, no matter who is awarded custody. (DHHS)

166. Rosen, R., 1979, "Some Crucial Issues Concerning Children of Divorce", *Journal of Divorce,* Vol. 3, No. 1
This paper considers two crucial aspects of the post-divorce situation affecting children—custody and visitation arrangements. The effects these factors have on the adjustment of children are described and analyzed.

167. Saffrady, W., 1973, "The Effects of Childhood Bereavement and Parental Remarriage in Sixteenth Century England: The Case of Thomas Moore.", *History of Childhood Quarterly,* Vol. 1, No. 2, pp. 310–336.
"Fascinating study of the effects on Thomas Moore of the death of his mother and the subsequent remarriages of his father.

Moore's emotional reactions are analyzed as to (1) pathological reactions to early object loss that persisted in later life, (2)developmental consequences of early object loss; (3) the impact of changes in the family structure produced by his father's remarriages. The effects of parental loss and remarriage on 16th century children generally are discussed and it is concluded that however prevalent death may have been 16th century children were no more successful in escapings its effects than children of today.''(SAA)

168. Schindler, R., 1985, ''Court Orders and Custody Evaluations in Israel'', *Child Welfare,* Vol. 63, No. 4, pp. 383–393

Sixty-two court orders were examined covering 1979 to 1982. Professional social workers were responsible for writing custody recommendations after three to six interviews with the family. Seven categories of concern were identified, which enter into custody judgments: continuity, emotional welfare, support systems, children's wishes, parental agreement, caretaking, and child abuse. In all cases in which visiting rights were granted to the non-custodial parent, the family was always seen together; the children were involved in discussions in a majority of cases.

169. Seltzer, M.M. & L.M. Bloksberg, 1987, ''Permanency Planning and Its Effect on Foster Children: A Review of the Literature'', *Social Work,* Vol. 32, No. 1, pp. 65–68

''Review of quantitative outcome research on permanency planning for foster children examines extent to which permanency planning resulted in higher rate of placement of children into presumably permanent homes; presumably permanent placement did not result in return of children to foster care; and children whose placements were guided by permanency planning adjusted better than children whose placements were not.'' (ERIC)

170. Victor, I. & A. Winkler, 1977, *Fathers and Custody,* Hawthorne Books, New York

The experience of the father as both custodial and visiting parent is described. The positive benefits of both father/child relationships are explored. The book lists a number of resources, and includes information about legal problems and support groups. (DHHS)

171. Weitzman, L.J., 1974, ''Legal Regulation of Marriage: Tradition and Change'', *California Law Review,* Vol. 62, No. 4, pp. 1169–1213

172. Woolley, P., 1979, *The Custody Handbook,* Summit Books; New York

This practical guide for divorcing parents offers current information about how custody battles can be avoided. Views of traditional custody arrangements by mothers and fathers are included. Although the author is an advocate of joint custody, the book is appropriate for parents interested in other custody arrangements as well. (DHHS)

II. TYPES OF FAMILIES

Stepfamily

173. Ahrons, C. & M. Bowman, 1981, ''When Children From Divorced Families Are Hospitalized: Issues for the Staff'', *Health and Social Work,* Vol. 6, pp. 21–28

The article identified major issues for social workers and other hospital personnel to consider when working with hospitalized children whose parents are divorced. (SAA)

174. Albrecht, S., et al, 1983, *Remarriage,* Greenwood Press, Westport, Conn.

Remarried couples are vulnerable to numerous problems such as trying to make two families one, as well as the problems inherent in marriage itself. Comparisons have also been made between divorced, non-divorced, remarried and first and later marriages as to the level of satisfaction. A greater focus on the varying factors in a remarriage need to be considered when comparing first-marriage satisfaction to remarried satisfaction. The scope needs to be broadened for future studies on remarriage to include: age of the couple, age of the children, non-custodial children, and the problems that are associated with a divorce.

175. Aldous, J., 1974, ''The Making of Family Roles and Family Change'', *Family Coordinator,* Vol. 23, pp. 231–235

The author discusses the concept of roles as a vehicle to analyze family change. Implications for understanding problems specific to various family combinations, including live-in and remarried couples, are explored. Practitioners can aid the process.

176. Amato, P.R., 1987, ''Family Processes in One-Parent, Stepparent, and Intact Families: The Child's Point of View'', *Journal of Marriage and the Family,* Vol. 49, No. 2, pp. 327–337

''Examined effects of divorce and remarriage on adjustment and development of children. Elementary school children (N=170) reported on processes in mother-custody one-parent, mother-custody stepparent, and intact two-parent families. Children reported similar levels of support and punishment from mothers, regardless of family type. Discusses varying levels of father and stepfather involvement.'' (ERIC)

177. Amato, P.R. & G. Ochiltree, 1987, ''Child and Adolescent Competence in Intact, One-Parent, and Stepfamilies: An Australian Study'', *Journal of Divorce,* Vol. 10, No. 3–4, pp. 75–96

''Five measures of competence-reading ability, everyday life skills, self-esteem, social competence, and impulse control were investigated among children and adolescents from intact two-parent families, one-parent families, and stepfamilies in Australia. Interviews were conducted with 195 students aged 8–10 and 207 students aged 14–17 randomly selected from 57 secondary schools in Victoria in 1982/83; their parents were interviewed separately at home. Controlling for socioeconomic status, students in one-parent families were similar to those in two-parent ones, while those in stepfamilies scored lower on reading ability, impulse control, and self-esteem. Children in intact two-parent families scored lower on everyday skills performance than did their counterparts in the other family types. It is concluded that children in single-parent homes are not disadvantaged in the development of competence, while those in stepfamilies may experience some problems.'' (Sociological Abstracts)

178. Ambler, J., Pollack, S., Bohannan, P., Perlman, J., & K. Pasley, 1985, *Bibliography of Literature on Remarriage and Stepfamilies,* Stepfamily Association of America, Towson, MD

Update of previous bibliographies (see Bohannan).

179. Anderson, J.O. , 1982, The Effects of Stepfather/Stepchild Interaction on Stepfamily Adjustment, Dissertation Abstracts International, Vol. 43/04-A, page 1306

''Each year in the United States one-half million adults become stepparents, and one million children become part of a stepfamily. However, few studies have explored the dynamics of stepparent families. The purpose of the present study was to examine specific aspects of stepfamily adjustment relative to the stepfather's interaction with his family. The aspects of interaction which were hypothesized to be related to mother and father stepfamily satisfaction and child self-esteem were the stepfather's communication, supportive interaction, and time spent with a target child, and the amount of emotional support he received from his wife for his involvement in disciplining a target child. One hundred and ten middle-class, white stepfamilies participated in the study. A stepfather, mother, and target child in each family filled out an extensive questionnaire, and multiple regression was used to test thc hypotheses. Three variables were found to be significant predictors of stepfather satisfaction in stepfamilies. They were the stepfather's communication with a target child, the time he spent with a target child, and the support he received from his wife for his involvement in disciplining the target child. These were related in a positive way to his stepfamily satisfaction. The only significant predictor of mother satisfaction identified in the present study was her support of the stepfather's discipline of the target child. A positive relationship was found to exist between her support of the stepfather's discipline and her stepfamily satisfaction. The target child's self-esteem was predicted by the stepfather's supportive interaction with the child and a positive relationship was found between supportive interaction and self-esteem."(DAI)

180. Anderson, J.W., 1983, *Teen is a Four Letter Word,* Betterway Publishers, Whitehall, VA

The author provides thoughtful guidance on dealing with the important stages of teen life. Offers counsel on discipline, dating hours, schoolwork, car use, etc.; also on problems that may result from sexual activity and drug and alcohol abuse.

181. Anderson, J.Z., 1983, Interaction and Relationship Patterns in Functional and Dysfunctional Intact Families and Stepfamilies., Dissertation Abstracts International, Vol. 44/04-B, page 1225

"The purpose of this study was to investigate relationship and interaction patterns in stepfamilies and intact families. The study was designed to identify key variables which distinguish intact from stepfamilies as well as functional from dysfunctional stepfamilies. A 2x2 factorial design was used to examine the four family groups: functional and dysfunctional intact and stepfamilies. Sixty-three family triads consisting of mother, father, and child whose age ranged from 11–17 years were studied. Five instruments were used: (1) Family Concept Inventory; (2) Locke-Wallace Marital Adjustment Test; (3) Family Relations Test; (4) Family Interaction Task; and (5) a background questionnaire. Results indicated that intact and stepfamilies differ in a number of important ways including: (1) functional stepfamilies have a strong marital bond but significantly less involvement between stepparent and stepchild as compared to intact parent-child relationships; (2) there is a virtual absence of parent-child coalitions in functional intact families, while functional stepfamilies have a pattern of significantly stronger biological parent-child coalitions; (3) dysfunctional stepfamilies have significantly better marital relationships than dysfunctional intact families. Significant differences were also found between functional and dysfunctional stepfamiilies including (1) dysfunctional stepfamilies demonstrate extremely stronger biological parent-child coalitions and more exclusion of stepparent from family than functional stepfamilies; (2) functional stepfamilies have greater positive involvement between stepchild and stepfather and more effective decision-making skills than dysfunctional stepfamilies. Results were discussed in terms of suppositions about family functioning from family systems theory as well as other research in the stepfamily literature. Clinical implications for working with stepfamilies are presented, particularly the idea that functional stepfamilies should be used as the bases of evaluation rather than the traditional intact family model.(DAI)

182. Auerbach, L. & M. Whiteside, 1978, ''Can the Daughter of My Father's New Wife Be My Sister?'', *Journal of Divorce,* Vol. 1, pp. 271–283

Family therapy interviews with four families are used to outline structural changes in the process of integration of families in remarriage following divorce. Emphasis is on the spouse subsystem: the stepparent, stepchild, and the relationship to family members outside of stepfamily residence.

183. Bachrach, C., 1983, ''Children in Families: Characteristics of Biological, Step, and Adopted Children'', *Journal of Marriage and the Family,* Vol. 45, pp. 171–179

58,542 children were compared in terms of different living arrangements: with both biological parents, with one biological parent and one stepparent; with biological mother only; with adoptive parent(s). Results indicate similarity in the lives of children with two parents, biological or step, but differences in several aspects when living in a single-parent family, with poverty being the most outstanding difference, especially when the mother never married. Adopted children were more economically advantaged than others.

184. Baker, P.W., 1982, A Study of Family Interaction Variables in Remarried and Intact Families., Dissertation Abstracts International, Vol.44/-3-B, page 905

''This study was designed to explore the interactional similarities and differences between remarried and intact families and their members. A review of the literature on family interaction variables and the formation process of remarried families indicated that remarried families have a complex organization structure and undergo complicated and stressful processes of reforming themselves into new family units. Two general study questions were addressed: (a) Are there meaningful interactional differences between remarried and intact families? (b) Do the remarried families appear to be functioning as well as the intact families? Six dependent variables were investigated: dyadic psychological space, whole family psychological space, cohesion, family incongruence, stress, and family interaction with the environment. Twenty-eight three-member family units from middle or upper-middle socioeconomic levels were selected for this study. Subjects were interviewed in their homes, and collected data were analyzed by analysis of variance. Study findings indicate that remarried families appeared to perform similarly to intact families in many ways. The family psychological space variable results indicated that children in remarried families used more symbolic psychological space in placing themselves with family members. The implications are that these children use the larger spacing patterns, perhaps to reduce tensions between themselves and other family members. Both study groups described similar levels of feelings of cohesion, indicating no significant differences in emotional support for family members. Remarried families had higher incongruence scores than the intact families. Remarried mothers had the highest disagreement scores, implying that they may be closer to the emotional struggles of the family and see the family social environment more clearly. Remarried families experienced higher stress levels than the intacts, perhaps reflecting the complex set of tasks involved in reforming a family. There was no difference in the interactions of the study groups with relatives or others outside the nuclear family. In both groups, family members interacted more frequently inside the home than out. All study participants indicated a high frequency of interactions around attending church and church events, recreation, and household maintenance duties. In spite of their differences, remarried and intact families shared numerous interactional similarities. Overall levels of functioning in the two study groups were similar. Recommendations are made for future research.'' (DAI)

185. Bank, S.P. & M.D. Kahn, 1982, *The Sibling Bond,* Basic Books, New York

Eight years of research into the sibling bond are described and some conclusions are suggested. The authors focus on the little-researched relationship among siblings throughout their lifetime. Twin research and psychoanalytic views on sibling rivalry, as well as family systems, birth order research, and sociological studies were considered along with clinical observations in the authors' own practice. Trends toward greater freedom and separateness as well as trends toward greater interdependence are studied. The meaning of continued access and contact to the development of the sibling bond and to the development of a sense of sibling and/or family identity are considered. Some guidelines are developed for therapists, to help them focus more on siblings and to help them develop individualization along with greater bonding and caring.

186. Baptiste, D.A., 1983, "Family Therapy With Reconstituted Families: A Crisis-Induction Approach", *American Journal of Family Therapy,* Vol. 11, No. 4, pp. 5–15

"A crisis-based therapeutic approach for overcoming resistance in reconstituted families conceptualizes crises as potentially growth enhancing. Therapeutically induced crisis is presented as a means through which therapists might purposefully disequilibrate families in which resistance is high, and subsequently redirect them to meaningful change. Implications, contradictions, and caveats of the approach are discussed, and a case study illustrates the application of the approach in treating a reconstituted family." (SWAB)

187. Baptiste, D.A., 1987, "Psychotherapy With Gay/Lesbian Couples & Their Children in 'Stepfamilies': A Challenge for Marriage & Family Therapists", *Journal of Homosexuality,* Vol. 14, 1/2

"As increasing numbers of gay/lesbian parents and their children enter into stepfamily-like relationships with a gay partner, they are beginning to seek therapy for difficulties peculiar to step-family living involving two same-sex partners. This paper focuses on the difficulties experienced by gay parents and children in a step-relationship, and seeks to sensitize mental health professionals to issues specific to intervention with such families. Effective therapy with these families requires that therapists be sensitive to their personal biases and prejudices with regard to gay men and women in general and as parents, and be aware that such attitudes can intrude and negatively affect the therapeutic process and its outcomes. Guidelines for therapy are offered." (NCFR)

188. Barlow, K.H., 1987, "Family Stress Factors Across Three Family Types", Dissertation Abstracts International, Vol. 48/08-A, p. 1983

"This study investigated the difference in stress levels of stress factors according to the structure or type of family. The relatedness of the ranking of stress factors within and across three family types and the relationship between level of stress and number of years in current family type were also examined. The Family Stress Questionnaire, developed for this study, was administered to caretaker parents representing 108 families who had been in counseling for one month or less. There were 91 females and 17 males ranging between the ages of 21 and 60 with a mean age of 36. Three family types were represented: divorced, step, and intact. Amount of time in the current family type ranged from .5 years to 37 years. Findings indicated that family structure did significantly affect the level of stress among family types. Factors stressful at the 2.00 level for all family types were Understanding, Discipline, Pseudo-mutuality, and Unrealistic Expectations; for the divorced family type were Living With One Part of Your Family, Sexuality and Money; for the stepfamily type were Biological Family Living Elsewhere, and Family Constellation. Understanding was stressful for all family types, but was significantly more stressful for the stepfamily. Regardless of family structure, seven of nine factors considered stressful were similarly ranked. The length of time spent in a family type was not related to level of stress. Important aspects of this study were using three family types, using families seeking counseling as the subjects, and investigating numerous stress factors across family types. These research techniques avoided the limitations of previous research which investigated only one family type, thus isolating special stress issues for a certain family type where those special issues actually might not differentiate among family types. Also, considering numerous stress factors at one time, rather than only a few factors, indicated relative levels of stress as well as absolute stresses that families are likely to experience. Targeting families who had sought counseling should give counselors a more realistic view of clients and their problems." (DAI)

189. Bergquist, B., 1984, "The Remarried Family: An Annotated Bibliography, 1979–1982", *Family Process,* Vol. 23, pp. 107–119

The author examined and abstracted 48 articles in the literature to provide a reference source for professional and other interested individuals. Six sections divide into demography/legal issues; remarriage as a transition; remarriage formation: restructuring relationships; children in remarried families; treatment issues; and how-to books.

190. Berman, C., 1982, *What Am I Doing in a Stepfamily?,* Lyle Stuart, Secaucus, NJ
An illustrated book that answers young children's questions, including the most important question, "Where do I belong?" (SAA)

191. Berman, C., 1981, *Making It as a Stepparent: New Roles/New Rules,* Bantam Books, New York
The author, who has for years been connected with public education, particularly in the adoption field, used her knowledge as one of the early writers on the stepfamily. She interviewed several hundred remarried couples and their children and quickly became one of the people who were able to combine personal and professional experiences. She touches base with significant areas of stepfamily living, including such areas as choice of geographic location of the new home, various combinations of "blended" families, money, sex, extended family relations, remarriage after widowhood; the seeking of professional help and support groups are further interesting areas.

192. Berman, E., 1980, *The New-Fashioned Parent: How to Make Your Family Style Work,* Prentice-Hall, Englewood Cliffs, NJ
"This book provides guidelines for traditional families, stepfamilies and single-parent families." (SAA)

193. Bernard, J., 1971, *Remarriage: A Study of Marriage,* 2nd Ed., Russell and Russell, New York
"This volume is a classic. Bernard, using mass census data, individual case material, and questionnaires, filled in by informants who were closely connected with 2,009 remarriage people who fail in one marriage after another; if one takes a sample of remarried people at any one time, most are as successful in their remarriages as are those in their first marriages. In her data, Bernard differentiates between the previous marital status of the spouses, the presence or absence of children by the previous marriages, and the relative significance of the first and subsequent marriages, based on whether they ended in death or divorce. She suggests that first marriages can be seen as an apprenticeship for remarriage and that remarriage couples bring with them higher motivation, a willingness to work things out, greater age and maturity, and a different set of environmental conditions than existed at the time of the first marriage. Bernard explored such variables associated with reported success in remarriage as age, time between remarriage, education, custody arrangements, the

attitudes of the ex-spouses, inlaws, and the children; and she presents a thorough discussion of the problems of adjustment in remarriage both for a couple without children, and for families with stepchildren. The limitation of her study is that her sample population is neither random nor representative of the remarriage population and it is conducted only at one point in time. Her study, however, is recommended as a source for information on remarriage issues and the wealth of data and good case examples provide a framework for looking at remarriage families, which is helpful in clinical work.'' (SAA)

194. Bernard, J., 1973, *The Future of Marriage,* Bantam Books, New York

``Explores the future of marriage, using predictions based on historical trends, projections based on statistical curves and ``prophecy'' based on human wishes and desires. Presents evidence to demonstrate her thesis that there are two marriages: his and hers, and that the man's is good for him physically, socially and psychologically while the woman's is devastating for her, and can be destructive of her personality. Recommends and advocates many changes, including an upgrading of the status of women, shared roles, alternative living arrangements and many other options. Bernard ends with an affirmation that marriage does have a future, though it may not take the form we know today.'' (SAA)

195. Bernstein, B. & B. Haberman , 1981, ``Lawyer and Counselors as an Interdisciplinary Team: Problem Awareness in the Blended Family'', *Child Welfare,* Vol. 60, pp. 211–218

The authors suggest that the complexities of remarriage and stepfamily living warrant a premarital agreement as a protection to both children and marital partners. Counseling to help with problems of the family in formation is suggested as a separate issue, but it is felt that given some legal protection, the counseling problems are not too different from some of those occurring in nuclear families.

196. Bilber, H. & D. Meredith, 1974, *Father Power,* David McKay, New York

Deals with psychological perspectives addressed to father or stepfather. Chapter entitled ``The Stepfather'' gives an introduction to the complex process of becoming a stepfather. Notes potential problems with biological father, effect of child's age on developing relationship, feelings, and attitudes of stepfather, mother, and children toward the new relationship. Advises the need to make changes in routine and activities slowly. (E & N)

197. Bitterman, C.M., 1968, "The Multi-Marriage Family", *Social Casework,* Vol. 49, pp. 218–224.

In an article based on clinical experience and addressed to caseworkers, the author points out some special needs of lower socioeconomic clients. The one-parent, low-income family may have a great need for a new father as provider or a new mother as nurturer. Discusses patterns of remarriage and special problem areas, including unresolved anger and grief, economics, former spouse, social, cultural, religious differences, and adolescents' special concerns. The adaptation of children and the implications of multimarriage and stepfamilies for casework practice are discussed. (E & N)

198. Bohannan, P., 1983, untitled, Stepfamily Association of America, Towson, MD

A partially annotated bibliography of books and articles, also listing dissertations pertaining to stepfamilies.

199. Bohannan, P. & J. Perlman, 1984, *Stepfamilies, A Bibliography,* Stepfamily Association of America, Baltimore, MD

Update of the 1983 bibliography. Updated at regular intervals.

200. Bohannan, P.J., 1975, "Stepfathers and the Mental Health of Their Children", Final Report, La Jolla Western Behavioral Sciences Institute, La Jolla, CA

"The effects of stepfathers on the mental health of their children were studied with the purpose of: 1. Determining the demographic facts of the proportion of stepfather households in the country; 2. increasing the understanding of the stepfather role and its impact; 3. discovering what points in the social structure of stepfamilies have different developmental tasks than do those of natural parent families. The most significant finding was that stepchildren view themselves as happy as natural children and were as successful and achieving as natural children." (SAA)

201. Bowerman, C. & D. Irish, 1962, "Some Relationships of Stepchildren to Their Parents", *Marriage and Family Living,* Vol. 24, pp. 113–121

Study in which questionnaires were given to junior and senior high school students in three states in 1953 and 1960 of whom 2145 were stepchildren. Scales were used to measure the adjustment and orientation of children to each of their parents. An analysis was given of the adjustments of children living with (1) both biological parents; (2) with stepfather and biological mother and (3) stepmother and biological father. Findings were that in all aspects, stepfamilies were more likely to have stress, ambivalence and low cohesiveness. Reactions of adolescents indicated that stepmothers have more difficulties than do stepfathers. Stepdaughters generally manifested more extreme reactions than stepsons. The presence of stepparents in the home also affected the adjustment of children to their biological parents.

202. Bradley, B., *Where Do I Belong?,* 1985, Harper & Row, New York

Discussion of the difficult feelings elicited when a family breaks up and changes; how to handle holidays and vacations, new rules, new roles, the ''wicked stepmother'' myth and much more.

203. Brand, E., 1985, The Interdependencies of Intrafamilial Dyads: Marital Quality and Parent-Child Relationships (Stepfamilies, Remarriage, Stepparenting), Dissertation Abstracts International, Vol. 46/08-B, page 2797

''This multimethod-multisource study examined the interdependencies of husband-wife and stepfather-stepchild relationships during the first two years, or adjustment phase, of the remarriage. Qualitative dimensions of both dyads were assessed by rating scales and self-report questionnaires and behavioral measures (i.e. behavioral coding of videotaped interaction tasks) in twenty stepfather families with 9–12-year-old stepsons and twenty stepfather families with 9–12-year-old stepdaughters. Families were recruited from Marriage License Records and data were collected in 3 1/2-hour home visits. One major hypothesis was tested: Husband-wife relationships are positively related to stepfather-stepson relationships, but negatively related (or unrelated) to positive dimensions of stepfather-stepdaughter relationships. Overall, qualitative dimensions of marital and parental dyads were positively correlated for stepfather perceptions of and behaviors toward both stepsons and stepdaughters but uncorrelated, or negatively correlated, for stepchild perceptions of and behaviors toward stepfathers. Consistent with research on husband-wife and parent-child relationships in nuclear families, more positiveness in the marital relationship (higher proportions of positive communications and greater perceived marital quality) was associated with greater stepfather positiveness (both perceptions and behaviors) toward both stepsons and stepdaughters. Moreover, when both custodial biological mothers and stepfathers evaluated the marital relationship more positively, stepfathers tended to perceive more love from both stepdaughters and stepsons. Stepfathers also communicated more positively to stepdaughters and stepsons to the extent their wives communicated more positively to them in the marital relationship. Only custodial mothers' marital quality was related to stepchildren's perceptions of and behaviors toward stepfathers. Greater marital satisfaction of biological mothers was associated with less stepdaughter and stepson positiveness towards stepfathers. Implications of the differential salience of the marital relationship for stepfathers and stepchildren are discussed. Recommendations for future research are presented.'' (DAI)

204. Brand, E. & G.W. Clingimpeel, 1987, ''Interdependencies of Marital and Stepparent-Stepchild Research Findings and Clinical Implications'', *Family Relations,* Vol. 36, No. 2, pp. 140–145

''Examined interdependencies of marital and stepparent-stepchild relationships and children's psychological adjustment in 62 stepfamilies. In stepmother families, higher marital quality was associated with more positive stepmother-stepson relationships and better stepson adjustment, but less positive stepmother-stepdaughter relationships and poorer stepdaughter adjustment. In stepfather families, stepfathers with better marriages were more positive toward stepchildren of both sexes.'' (ERIC)

205. Breen, D.T., 1987, Changing Family Structures: An Intervention Study in the Schools, Dissertation Abstracts International, Vol. 48/12-A, p. 3050

''Sixty-seven nuclear, 19 single-parent, 18 stepfamily children (40 females and 65 males) in the 5th grade in a rural Midwestern community, along with their teachers and counselors participated in an intervention focusing on the dynamics of nuclear, single-parent, and stepfamilies. The students were assessed using the following questionnaires: Harter's Self-Perception Profile for Children, Reynold's Child Depression Scale, a sociogram, identification of moral problems, the Attitudes Toward Family Scale, and the Devereux Elementary School Behavior Rating Scale II. T tests, chi-squares, repeated measures analyses of variance, and McNemar tests of dichotomous change produced the following major findings: (1) Before the intervention: (a) compared to nuclear family children, non-traditional family children were not popular with nuclear family children; self-reported lower behavioral conduct scores; were afraid of being abandoned; did not feel like they were ''regular'' and ''real'' families; were not happy with their families as they were; and described more family-related moral problems. (b) Teachers reported having lower behavioral and social expectations for non-traditional family children. (2) After the intervention: (a) Non-traditional family children reported feeling better about their physical appearance. (b) More non-traditional family children reported their families were not ''regular'' and ''real'' families. (c) More nuclear family children felt like they could tell the teacher if they were sad or mad about something at home. (d) More non-traditional family children reported that they liked talking with their teacher. (e) More nuclear family children felt the counselor understood their families. (f) The teachers' perceptions were that non-traditional family children had good work organization; little irrelevant thinking and talking; but, needed direction in work; were socially withdrawn; had failure anxiety; blamed others; were negative and aggressive; had lower peer cooperation; and achieved low academically compared to the average.'' (DAI)

206. Brice, J.R., 1985, Living in Stepfamilies: Perceived Obstacles, Depression, and Anxiety (Remarriage, Marriage Reconstituted), Dissertation Abstracts International, Vol. 47/02-B, page 779

''This research study focused on the stepparent in the remarried family. Because they have been the most beleaguered and defamed family members, the author wanted to know how they perceived themselves and if they regarded themselves as being more stressed than parents. The following research questions were addressed: (1) What factors do stepparents perceive as obstacles to the smooth functioning of their families? (2) Are stepparents more depressed than their non-step counterparts? (3) Are stepparents more anxious than parents? (4) Are they more likely to become anxious in reponse to situational stress than their non-step counterparts? (5) Are stepparents better able to adapt to changes than their non-step counterparts? (6) Do parents perceive their families as more cohesive than stepparents? (7) Do stepparents and parents differ in terms of how they would like their families to be?

Results revealed that: (1) Stepparents were not found to be clinically depressed or anxious and (2) they were not significantly different from the control group on these two dimensions. (3) There was a sex effect with regard to depression, such that males, regardless of parental status, scored significantly lower on depression inventory than females. (4) The two groups did not differ significantly on the variable cohesion but the difference in their scores approached statistical significance on adaption. The parents perceived their families as significantly more adaptive than stepparents. (5) There were no differences in terms of how the groups would ideally like their families to be. A factor analysis of the stepparent questionnaire revealed seven factors: harmony, marital issues, triangulation, rivalry with ex-spouse, stepparents exclusion, spousal support, and visitation. In summary, the study tentatively identified seven obstacles to smooth functioning in stepfamilies. Further work on subscale reliability and validity is needed. The results of the second part of the study confirmed the notion that although stepparents are stressed by the changes their families undergo, they are not clinically depressed or anxious and they do not differ from other parents in regard to those two variables.'' (DAI)

207. Brown, J.K., 1984, Stepmothering in Stepmother and Combination Families: The Strains and Satisfactions of Making the Role of Stepmother, Dissertation Abstracts International, Vol. 45/07-A, page 2254

''The purposes of this study were to explore what stepmothers perceive as the most difficult and the most satisfying aspects of stepmothering, to identify some of the methods stepmothers have utilized to cope with felt difficulties; and to examine how a given set of variables correlate with the level of difficulty a stepmother experiences in the stepmother role. Participants were 51 volunteers who had been stepmothers in combination or stepmother families for at least one year. Data was collected utilizing a questionnaire and an interview. The questionnaire is composed of two main sections: (1) background information and (2) a rating scale and one close-ended question. Stepwise multiple regression/correlation analysis was used to analyze the quantitative data. Notes were taken during each interview. Preliminary Data Analysis Sheets were completed after the interviews, and were utilized to analyze qualitative data. The results of this study indicated that stepmothers in combination-only families have less difficulty with the role than stepmothers in other types of stepfamilies. Stepmothers employed full-time experience less difficulty in the stepmother role than do stepmothers employed part-time and unemployed stepmothers. The longer one is a stepmother the less difficult the role becomes. The interviews revealed that stepmothers in this study perceive the following aspects of stepmothering to be the most difficult: relating to the biological mother of one's stepchildren; being a stepmother without being a biological mother; handling feelings toward stepchildren; handling with one's husband discipline of stepchildren and biological children from a previous marriage while maintaining fair treatment of both sets of children. Most of the stepmothers identified numerous satisfactions with the stepmother role and reported various creative coping strategies they had developed to address the difficult aspects of the stepmother role. This exploratory research explicitly and specifically addresses the issues of stepmother and combination families. The findings provide a beginning step in understanding the complexities of making the role of stepmother.'' (DAI)

208. Brown, K., 1987, ''Stepmothering: Myth and Realities'', *Affilia,* Vol. 2, No. 4, pp. 34–45

The author reports on an exploratory study of 51 stepmothers regarding their role perceptions, their satisfactions and problems with regard to the development of family unity. Contemporary theories such as role theory and family systems theory are employed to objectivify the study. The author concludes that women can develop successfully into the role of stepmother and the Cinderella myth can be dispelled, provided sufficient objective information is provided.

209. Bryan Jr., S.H., 1983, An Investigation of Helping Professionals' Attitudes Toward Stepparents and Stepchildren, Dissertation Abstracts International, Vol. 44/12-B, page 3975

''This study investigated attitudes of helping professionals toward stepparents and stepchildren. An assessment instrument (First Impressions Semantic Differential, FISD) measuring attitudes toward stepfamily members was developed as part of this investigation. Helping professionals (N=378) responded to a parent and a child presented within a stimulus paragraph describing a family varying in family status (stepfamily, intact nuclear family), sex of parent and sex of child.

The results of the multivariate and univariate analyses of variance, based on the FISD scores indicated that: (1) There was a significant difference on certain factors of the FISD in helping professionals' perceptions of stepparents' nuclear families, with stepparents and stepchildren as compared to parents and children in intact nuclear families, with stepparents and stepchildren being viewed in a more negative direction. (2) There was a significant difference between experienced and inexperienced helping professionals' perceptions of stepparents/stepchildren and parents/children from intact nuclear families. Inexperienced helping professionals viewed members of intact nuclear families more positively than stepfamily members and experienced helping professionals did not differentiate between intact nuclear and stepfamily members in their perceptions. (3) Having been a stepparent or stepchild did not make a significant difference in the subject's perceptions. It was concluded that a stereotype of stepfamilies similar to that prevailing in society is shared by inexperienced helping professionals.''(DAI)

210. Bryan, H. , 1985, ''Counselors' Perceptions of Stepparents and Stepchildren'', *Journal of Counseling Psychology,* Vol. 32, No. 2, pp. 279–282

This is a report on a study which investigated the attitudes of helping professionals toward stepfamilies. 256 female and 119 male counselors were given brief vignettes of an adult and an adolescent. Both adults and children who were described as stepparent or stepchild were evaluated less positively and viewed as less well adjusted than their counterpart from a nuclear family. However, experienced counselors did not view stepfamilies as different from nuclear families. The possible implications of this are discussed, although it is pointed out that in general the helping establishment reflects similar stereotypes. More exposure and more research are recommended.

211. Bryan, L.A., Ganong, L.H. & M. Coleman, 1986, ''Person Perception: Family Structure as a Cure For Stereotyping'', *Journal of Marriage and the Family,* Vol. 48, No. 1, pp. 169–174

This study compared perceptions of adults and children in stepfamilies to those of children and adults living in other family structures (e.g. nuclear families continuing together, widowed, divorced, or never-married parents). 236 male and 460 female college students provided the universe. The general finding supports the notion that family structure is one basis by which stereotypes are formed. However, the authors discuss some of their findings in detail, including questions about the results, and a number of suggestions for further research.

212. Bryan, L.R., 1983, Family Structure Stereotypes: Perceptions of Stepfamilies, Dissertation Abstracts International, Vol. 44/12-A, page 3827

''The major purpose of this study was to investigate attitudes and perceptions toward parents and children from different family structures--stepfamilies, intact nuclear, divorced, widowed, and never married. Exploring attitudes and perceptions toward stepparents and stepchildren was the specific purpose of the study. A pilot study, utilizing data from 268 college students, was conducted for the purpose of developing an instrument (First Impressions Questionnaire) designed to measure perceptions of individuals varying in family structure. By employing item analysis and factor analysis, the First Impressions Questionnaire (FIQ). consisting of 68 semantic differential scales, was reduced to 40 scales. After a second data collection, data from 422 females and 106 males were subjected to factor analysis which produced six factors (dependent measures). The factors were named Evaluative, Satisfaction/ Sccurity, Potency, Activity, Familiarity, and Stability. Independent variables were family structure, sex of subject, sex of parent, and sex of child.

The general finding of this study was that students differentiate (stereotype) on the basis of family structure. Subjects responded to stepparents and stepchildren less positively than to parents and children in intact nuclear families. Stepparents and parents of single-parent families were viewed similarly, yet consistently less positively than parents of intact nuclear families. Stepchildren were viewed less positively than children from all other family structures on five of the six dependent measures. Stepchildren were rated less positively than their repective parent. Students responded differentially to male and female family roles. Daughters and mothers from all family structures were seen generally more positively than sons and fathers. In general, males assigned a less positive rating to both parents and children than did females. Students may have the belief that the intact nuclear family is the standard of comparison for all other families. Negative stereotypes of stepparents and stepchildren exist especially in comparison to individuals in intact nuclear families. Stepparents and stepchildren and parents, and children of single-parent families (divorced, widowed, and never married) are perceived less positively than parents and children of intact nuclear families. Negative stereotypes of children exist when compared to adults.''(DAI)

213. Buehler, C., Hogan, M.J., Robinson, B. & R.J. Levy, 1986, ''Remarriage Following Divorce: Stressors and Well-Being of Custodial and Noncustodial Parents'', *Journal of Family Issues,* Vol. 7, No. 4, pp. 405–420

''A study examined the relationships between (1) remarriage status and former spouses' divorce-related stressors and (2) remarriage status and former spouses' current well-being. Divorce-related stressors were classified as economic, housing, legal, parent-child, or former spouse. Self-esteem, parenting satisfaction, and economic well-being were used to measure current well-being. A sample of 125 former couples (250 individuals) was divided into four remarriage groups: (1) neither former spouse had remarried; (2) only the husband had remarried; (3) only the wife had remarried; and (4) both had remarried. Multivariate analysis of variance indicated that divorce-related stressors, self-esteem, and parenting satisfaction were not related to remarriage status, whereas economic well-being was related. These findings are discussed, and the relationship between the divorce and remarriage transitions is explored.'' (SWAB)

214. Burns, C., 1988, *Stepmotherhood: How to Survive Without Feeling Frustrated, Left Out, or Wicked,* Random House, New York

Based on research, consultation, and interviews, this book covers the range of experiences stepmothers face: ex-wives, visitation schedules, discipline, guilt, and the unhappiness that can be found. Done with humor and understanding of the role of stepmother. Unique section on custodial stepmothers and problem stepchildren.

215. Campbell, M.E., 1985, ''Parenting Children from a Different Culture'', Annual Parenting Symposium, Chicago, IL

''Available research in the area of transracial adoptions is surveyed, emphasizing the programs and services which could be developed based on this accumulated knowledge. It is argued that, because of the implications for the growing number of lives involved, the area of cross cultural adoptive placements needs further research, thoughtful program development, and careful consideration by both the professionals in the field and the adoptive families. Issues discussed include children's self concept, racial identity, social adjustment, adoptive family life, identity formation, and age at time of adoption, particularly in relation to black and minority group children. Recommendations are made for helping adoptive families adjust to the cross culturally adopted child.'' (ERIC)

216. Canfield, D.G., 1982, Cross Sex Parent-Child Relationships in Stepparent Families, Dissertation Abstracts International, Vol. 43/09-A, page 3125

''The purpose of the study was to investigate the relationship of the sex of the stepparent and stepchild as a factor in establishing positive stepfamily relationships. The sample included 25 volunteer stepfathers, 20 volunteer stepmothers, and their 96 stepchildren. All families had at least one boy and one girl stepchild, between the ages of 11 and 18, living at home. The Itkin (1952) questionnaires were used. The stepparents' questionnaire was titled ''Stepparents Judgment Regarding a Particular Child'' and the stepchildren's questionnaire was titled ''Attitudes Towards Stepparents'' (Stepmother Form M and Stepfather Form F). A demographic questionnaire developed by the investigator was also used. Data was analyzed by computing an analysis of covariance on the difference between the parent's score and the children's score and the demographic variables were the covariates. An analysis of variance was used to determine the mean differences in the groups and a Student Neuman Keuls was computed to locate the individual group mean differences. The results indicated that both stepmothers and stepfathers developed more positive relationships with their sons than their daughters and the longer the stepparents were married the more positive their stepparent-stepchild relationships were.'' (DAI)

217. Capaldi, F. & B. McCrae, 1979, *Stepfamilies: A Cooperative Responsibility,* Viewpoints Vision Books, New York

''Written by family therapists who specialize in working with stepfamilies, this book considers remarriage and stepfamilies. It aims to assist stepparents and stepchildren to gain a better understanding of problems that confront them, and helps to guide them toward successful solutions.'' (SAA)

218. Catton Jr., W., 1969, ''What's in a Name? A Study of Role Inertia'', *Journal of Marriage and the Family,* Vol. 31, pp. 15–18

A hypothetical role transition experience was created for 186 undergraduates. Each subject was confronted with a hypothetical marriage of a widowed parent to a classmate. There was strong resistance to applying parental role to a stepparent with whom the subjects had already established a peer relationship. The resistance to addressing the classmate as ''mom'' or ''dad'' prevailed even when seen as a norm violation. The pre-established relation inhibited transition to a filial one. It simulated a continuation of the pre-established non-erotic relationship that inhibits incest. There was similar resistance to applying parental position labels to in-laws. The author suggests that such resistance to role transitions are not conducive to family integration.

219. Chapman, M., 1977, ''Father Absence, Stepfathers, and the Cognitive Performance of College Students'', *Child Development,* Vol. 48, pp. 1155–1158

Evaluation of father absence and stepfather presence on cognitive performance of 96 college students. Results support earlier findings of lower SAT scores in father-absent males but indicate that stepfather presence had an attenuating effect. Possible reasons for finding no such effects in females are discussed. ''(c) APA''

220. Cherlin, A., 1981, *Marriage, Divorce, Remarriage: Changing Patterns in the Postwar U.S.,* Harvard University Press, Cambridge, MA

The author views trends in remarriage, marriage, and divorce through research in these fields since the end of World War II. Data are both presented and analyzed to determine reasons for the changes which have taken place.

221. Cherlin, A., 1978, ''Remarriage as an Incomplete Institution'', *American Journal of Sociology,* November, pp. 634–50.

''The higher divorce rate for remarriages after divorce than for first marriages, it is argued, is due to the incomplete institutionalization of remarriages after divorce in the U.S. Persons who are remarried after divorce and have children from previous marriages face problems unlike those encountered in first marriages. The institution of the family provides no standard solutions to many of these problems, with the result that the unity of families of remarriages after divorce becomes precarious. The incomplete institutionalization of remarriages shows us, by way of contrast, that family unity in first marriages is supported by effective institutional controls, despite claims that the institutional nature of family life has eroded in the 20th century. Some suggestions for future research on remarriage and on the institutionalization of married life are presented.'' (SAA)

222. Cherlin, A. & J. McCarthy, 1985, ''Remarried Couple Households: Data From the June 1980 Current Population Survey'', *Journal of Marriage and Family,* Vol. 47, No. 1, pp. 23–30

''Remarried couple households consist of married couples in which one or both of the spouses has been divorced. To tabulate information about these households, a study drew on data from the June 1980 Current Population Survey. Findings revealed that in one out of five households maintained by a married couple, one or both of the spouses had been divorced. In addition, these households were classified further by the existence and current living arrangements of children from previous marriages. Stepparents and stepchildren were present in about 2.3 million of these households.'' (SWAB)

223. Cline, D. & J. Westman, 1971, ''The Impact of Divorce on the Family'', *Child Psychiatry and Human Development,* Vol. 2, pp. 78–83

Examines post-divorce interactions in 105 cases. In two years 52% of divorced families had hostile interactions requiring court intervention, 31% repeated interactions with 2 to 10 interventions. Most common reasons for court actions were money and children. Several patterns emerged: (a) hostile interaction over parenting roles, (b) continued conflict between divorced spouses not involving children, (c) perpetuation of interaction between parents by the children. (SAA)

224. Clingempeel, W.G., 1980, Quasi-Kin Relationships and Marital Quality in Stepfather Families, Dissertation Abstracts International, Vol. 42/04-B, page 1599

"Remarriages after divorce which include children from a previous marriage are afflicted with higher divorce rates than first marriages. Cherlin (1978) hypothesized that the greater instability of these remarriages stems from the absence of societal role prescriptions to regulate steprelationships and interactions with quasi-kin (former spouses of the remarried couple). Employing a multimethod assessment of marital quality (including two self report and two behavioral measures) rather than divorce rates, the current study tested three predictions derived from Cherlin's 'Incomplete Institution' hypothesis: (1) divorced-remarried couples where both spouses have children from a previous marriage will exhibit lower marital quality than couples where only one spouse has children from a previous marriage. (2) the greater the frequency of interaction with quasi-kin, the lower the marital quality of divorced-remarried persons; and (3) divorced-remarried women will reveal significantly lower marital quality than divorced-remarried men. Stepparent couples from two structural types of stepfamilies differing only in terms of whether the husband was a noncustodial parent (complex stepfamilies) and did not have children from the previous marriage (simple stepfamilies) participated in this research. In both types the wife had custody of at least one minor child from the previous marriage. Fifty-four persons (27 couples) from complex stepfamilies and twenty-six persons (13 couples) from simple stepfamilies were recruited from the marriage License Records of six cities. Simple and complex stepfamilies did not differ on annual income, number of custodial children, length of current and previous marriages, and time between marriages. The total frequency of contact with quasi-kin in the last six months was assessed for each participant and three frequencies of contact groups (High, Moderate, & Low) were formed based on the upper, middle, and lower 33% of total contact scores. A 2 x 2 x 3 (sex of respondent by type of stepfamily by frequency of contact with quasi-kin) multivariate analysis of variance revealed two significant effects--a main effect for type of stepfamily and frequency of contact with quasi-kin. Contrary to the prediction, women did not differ from men on the marital quality measures. As predicted, persons in complex stepfamilies registered lower marital quality than persons in simple stepfamilies. In examining the significant main effect of frequency of quasi-kin contacts, post hoc Hotelling T('2)s revealed that, instead of a linear and negatively correlated relationship, the Moderate group exhibited better marital quality than either the High or Low groups (which did not differ). Role strain and "permeability of boundaries" concepts were used to interpret these findings. Directions for future research were also proposed." (DAI)

225. Clingempeel, W.G., Brand, E., & R. Ievoli, 1984, "Stepparent-Stepchild Relationships in Stepmother and Stepfather Families: A Multimethod Study", *Family Relations,* Vol. 33, pp. 465–473

Previous literature on the subject precedes a description of this study which analyzed the results of 3 1/2-hour home visit interviews with 16 stepmother and 16 stepfather families, half of which had a male and half a female child between the ages of 9 and 12. Self reports from stepparent and stepchildren revealed love and higher scores on detachment dimensions in the stepparent-stepdaugher relationship. Behavioral measures indicated less positive verbal behavior and greater negative problem-solving behavior than did boys (toward the stepparent). The stepparents did not differ in their responses to girls and boys.

226. Coleman, M., Ganong, L. & R. Gingrich, 1985, "Stepfamily Strengths: A Review of Popular Literature", *Family Relations,* Vol. 34, No. 4, pp. 583–589

The authors, who have been involved in stepfamily work and research, wrote this paper to review the popular literature, which had been proliferating within the last ten years; they identified self-help books, magazines, and adolescent fiction as to content which identified family strength. 243 pieces of literature in all were reviewed. Though potential strengths were identified in all three types of literature examined, the major emphasis was found to be on the problems of stepfamilies. The details of the review reveal interesting sub-data. Perhaps the most specific contribution found was the notion that the literature emphasized problem-solving skills. Adolescent fiction, written from the child's point of view was found to be more geared to situations where a parent had died, thus perhaps atypical, since most of the stepfamily literature written deals with children of divorce. However, it was found to be more contructive to problem-solving than the general notions seen in the adult self-help literature. The authors point the review in the direction of less problematic aspects of stepfamily life which they recommend for greater attention.

227. Collins Jr., L.E., 1981, A Study of Locus of Control in Children of Intact, Single Parent, and Reconstituted Families, Dissertation Abstracts International, Vol. 42/07-B, page 3030

''*Purpose*. The purpose of this study was threefold: (1) to determine if a relationship could be identified between the experience of parental divorce and remarriage and the alteration of locus of control as a generalized expectancy, (2) to determine if a difference in academic and social functioning could be observed between groups of children who have experienced parental divorce and remarriage and those who have remained in intact fmailies, and (3) to determine if a relationship could be identified between the generalized expectancy of locus of control and the observations of academic and social functioning.

Methods and Procedures. A modification of the post-test only control group design was used for this investigation. The subjects were 180 sixth, seventh, and eighth grade students enrolled in three suburban middle schools. They were selected using a stratification technique based on sex, and whether they lived in intact families, single parent families, or reconstituted families.

The subjects were administered the Children's Nowicki Strickland Internal-External scale of locus of control (CNSIE) and the Teachers Observation checklist of academic performance, classroom behavior, interpersonal relations with peers, and level of general adjustment (TO). The demographic data was gathered with the Family Structure Questionnaire. In order to test the assumptions of relationships between (1) Parental divorce and remarriage and an alteration of the generalized expectancy of locus of control, (2) parental divorce and remarriage and teacher-observed differences in academic and social functioning and (3) the generalized expectancy of locus of control and the teacher observations of academic and social functioning, five criterion measures were analyzed using a multivariate analysis of variance with the type of family structure as the independent variable. For those Multivariate Analyses of Variance in which a significant F was obtained, a one-way analysis of variance with Scheffe's Procedure was employed as a post hoc analysis to determine the source of the differences. *Results*. The results of the multivariate analysis of variance indicated non-significant differences on the Children's Nowicki Strickland Internal-External scale of locus of control (CNSIE) among the family structure groups, between the sexes, and the interaction between family structure and sex. Significant differences were found in the Teacher Observation (TO) of academic performance, classroom behavior, and interpersonal relations with peers and with sexual differences. The children from intact families were rated better in three of the four areas than were the children of single parents and reconstituted families. On academic performance the difference was significant between the intact family group and both of the other two groups. On classroom behavior the difference was significant between the intact family group and the reconstituted family group. On interpersonal relations the difference was significant between the intact family group and the single-parent group. On the level of general adjustment there were no significant differences among the family structure groups. Female subjects received significantly better ratings than the male subjects on all four TO oberservations. Therefore, all research hypotheses on the CNSIE were rejected. Some of the research hypotheses on the Teachers' Observations in relation to family structure were accepted and some were rejected. The research hypotheses were accepted on the Teacher's Observations as they pertained to sex.

Conclusions. From the data analysis, it was concluded that either there were no significant alterations of locus of control because of parental divorce and remarriage or that the CNSIE was not sensitive to differences in generalized expectancy of locus of control among the three groups of students. Results of the analysis suggested two possible conclusions: (1) The teachers were sensitive to differences between those who had experienced parental divorce and those who had not or, (2) The teachers were biased in favor of children of intact families and girls regardless of the family structure.'' (DAI)

228. Colvin, B.K., 1981, Adolescent Perceptions of Intrafamilial Stress in Stepfamilies, Dissertation Abstracts International, Vol. 42/11-B, page 4557

``One purpose of this study was to measure and compare adolescent perceptions of intrafamilial stress for 1698 natural-parent, 283 stepfather, and 77 stepmother families. The Index of Family Relations scale was used to measure the level of intrafamilial stress in family member relationships. Results of the one-way analysis of variance show that while adolescents in stepfather families report significantly more intrafamilial stress than adolescents in natural-parent families, adolescents in stepmother families report the highest degree of stress. These results indicate that one-third of the adolescents in stepfather families and approximately one-half of the adolescents in stepmother families report clinically significant family member relationship problems. On the other hand, two-thirds of the adolescents in stepfather families and approximately one-half of the adolescents in stepmother families perceived no clinically significant problems in their intrafamilial relationships. A second purpose was to examine the relationship between adolescent perceptions of intrafamilial stress in stepfamilies (n=360) and: (A) quality of the marital relationship (QMR); (B) quality of the mother-child relationship (QMCR); (C) quality of the father-child relationship (QFCR); (D) length of time the stepfamily has lived together; (E) presence or absence of a common child of the remarried couple; (F) type of termination of the previous marriage; (G) stepchild's religion; (H) stepchild's age; (I) stepchild's sex; (J) stepparent's age; and (K) stepparent's sex.

The results of the regression analysis indicate that the QMR, the QMCR, and the QFCR (i.e. variables which were indicators of relationship dynamics) were excellent predictors of adolescent perceptions of intrafamilial stress in stepfamilies. The remaining eight demographic variables were non-significant. These results indicate that if researchers want information on family member relationship problems, it seems imperative to focus on variables which are related to relationship processes rather than single-factor demographic characteristics." (DAI)

229. Corsica, J.S., 1980, The Relationship of Changes in Family Structure to the Academic Performance and School Behavior of Adolescents From a Middle Class, Surburban High School, Dissertation Abstracts International, Vol. 41/06-A, page 2508

"The current investigation provides information regarding the impact of change in family structure on the adolescent high school student. The family structures of interest in the study are: (1) the intact family, (2) the father-absent family, and (3) the reconstituted family. Family systems theory provides the theoretical base for the study. The family system, ruptured by the loss of the father, must learn new ways to carry on family business. Family confusion regarding roles and responsibilities is almost always present during the difficult task of family reconstruction. Remarriage families must survive two traumatic adjustment periods (1) adjustment to the loss of the original parents, and (2) adjustment to the introduction of the stepparent into the existing family unit. It was the author's contention that children from single-parent families, experiencing father-absence, undergo sufficient stress and developmental disruption to perform less well academically and behaviorally in school than adolescents from intact families. Similar effects were predicted for adolescents from families where remarriage had occurred. The above assumptions led to the development of nine research hypotheses. The hypotheses stated that differences exist among (1) intact families, (2) father-absent families, and (3) reconstituted families on family relationship and process variables. Further, differences exist among the three comparison groups on measures of school achievement and social behavior. Subjects in the study were selected from the population of Penfield High School. This high school serves a town in surburban Rochester, New York, defined by socio-economic determinants as middle to upper-middle class. Sampling included boys and girls from grades nine, ten, eleven, and twelve representing the three family structures of interest. The final number of students participating in the study was 94. Of the 94 subjects in the study, 32 represented father-absent families, 18 represented reconstituted families and 44 represented intact families. Selection of students according to SES, IQ, sex, age, grade, and presence of older male siblings, helped to keep the group homogenous. The instruments used in the study were the Family Environment Scale by Rudolph Moss, the Structural Family Interaction Patterns Questionnaire by Linda Perosa and the Otis Lennon Mental Abilities Test by Arthur Otis and Roger Lennon. The first two measures provided comparison data on family relationship and process variables. The Otis Lennon Mental Ability Test provided an assessment of intelligence. In addition, the study included measures of grade point average, school absence, school tardiness, use of guidance services, willingness to do assignments, school suspensions, and numbers of mental health referrals.

With the exception of one test analysis measuring the effect of father visitation on students in the father-absent sample, all analyses were of a 3 x 2 x 2 (Family x Sex x Grade) factorial analysis of variance design. Cell equality was statistically obtained by the method of unweighted means. The analyses resulted in 13 significant main effects and nine significant interaction effects providing considerable support for the research hypotheses. Reconstituted families tended to be rigidly organized, with less freedom of expression and family closeness than in the other two groups. In addition, the reconstituted family sample recorded the poorest performance on school-related variables. The father-absent sample showed the weakest control and parent management and the greatest amounts of conflict. As in the reconstituted sample, the father-absent group performed far less well on school-related variables than the intact family sample. There are sufficient hypotheses generating data in this study to warrant future investigations directed toward establishing causal relationships.'' (DAI)

230. Craven, L., 1982, *Step-Families: New Patterns of Harmony,* Julian Messner, New York

The book is directed towards members of stepfamilies (especially teenagers) to help them gain a clearer perspective of the problems that arise from the formation of a new family unit. Having struggled through her own difficulties of stepparenting, coupled with her professional experience working with stepfamilies, the author offers a contemporary picture of the stepfamily. Issues with which stepfamilies are confronted are presented; case samples exemplify how some stepfamilies have learned to cope with their problems. It is a useful guide for professionals and lay people alike.

231. Crosbie-Burnett, M.A.D., 1983, Assessment of Stepfamily Adjustment, Dissertation Abstracts International, Vol.44/09-B, page 2890

"The stepfamily is an emerging family form in the Western world. The higher divorce rate for remarrieds with stepchildren suggests that the structure of stepfamilies causes stresses in family functioning that intact families do not experience. The purpose of the present research is threefold: the development of an instrument designed to assess descriptive information about the impact of remarriage on adults' and children's lives, and the testing of hypotheses. The self-reported behaviors, cognitions, emotions, and background information of the individual family members in 87 upper-middle class Caucasian mother-stepfather households with one or two adolescent children were assessed via a paper-and-pencil questionnaire which was personally administered in the subjects' homes. The volunteer subjects were located through clinician contacts, stepfamily organizations, responses to newspaper articles, and personal referrals from families already in the study. The three forms of the questionnaire (wife, husband, and youth) consisted of psychologically-oriented questions which were combined to form 17 component scales and 3 dependent measure scales. Estimates of the instruments' reliability and validity yielded generally satisfactory results. Descriptive statistics and a series of multiple regressions and analyses of covariance produced the following major findings: (1) The remarriage of the custodial mother or the non-custodial father tends to decrease the amount of visitation between minor children and the non-custodial father. (2) Approximately half of the financial support of stepchildren is assumed by stepfathers in this sample. (3) Families reporting high cohesion were those in which family members respected the emotional ties between children and non-custodial fathers. (4) Families in which the adults had more leadership power than the older child reported more happiness than families in which the older child reported more leadership position. (5) The satisfaction with the stepparent-stepchild relationships was more highly associated with family happiness than was the marital relationship. (6) One-adolescent families with one or more additional children born into the remarriage reported less happiness than the other family structures.''(DAI)

232. Crosbie-Burnett, M.A.D., 1984, ''The Centrality of the Step Relationship: A Challenge to Family Theory and Practice'', *Family Relations,* Vol. 33, pp. 459–463

This article challenges the traditional view of family theory and practice that the marital relationship is at the center of healthy family functioning. A questionnaire was given to 87 upper-middle-class white mother-stepfather households with one or two adolescents. Family relationships, family happiness, and step-relationship among family members were more highly associated with family happiness than the marital relationship. Implications for theory and practice are discussed.

233. Crosbie-Burnett, M.A.D., 1983, *The Impact of Remarriage on Labor Force Participation, Divorce Decree Modification, Visitation, Ex-Spousal Relationship, and Extended Family Reorganization,* Paper presented at the Annual Meeting of the National Council on Family Relations

Although 41 percent of all marriages are remarriages for one or both partners, little is known about the impact of this change in marital status on various aspects of family life. To assess the linkage between the remarriage household and the labor force, the legal system, visitation with non-custodial parents and grandparents, relations between new couples and ex-spouses, and relations with the extended family, questionnaire data were gathered from adult and adolescent family members in 87 white-stepfather households in which the mother's natural children resided. Results showed that men's participation in the labor force increased after remarriage, while women's decreased. Custody and visitation were renegotiated at the time of remarriage, with actual visitation consistently less than the amount legally agreed upon both before and after remarriage. Men and women both reported more friendly than hostile relationships with ex-spouses after remarriage, and that relationships with parents had improved. (A series of tables presenting the survey data is appended.) (JAC)

234. Cuddeby, G.W., 1984, The Effects of Stepparent Education on Perceived Family Cohesion, Organization, and Conflict (Remarriage), Dissertation Abstracts International, Vol.45/04-A, page 1072

"This study investigated the effectiveness of a stepparent education program and a follow-up self practice package on stepparent dyad's knowledge of stepfamily issues and their perceived family cohesion, control, and organization. The program included discussion of stepfamily issues, communication training, conflict resolution, and parenting skills improvement. Twenty-four stepparent couple volunteers were assigned to either experimental or control groups for four weekly, 2-hour meetings. To be eligible for participation in the study, there had to be at least one stepparent and one stepchild currently living in the home. All subjects were administered the Stepfamily Knowledge Instrument and the Family Environment Scale with the experimental group being retested after a four-week follow-up period. A multivariate analysis showed significant results for the program. The primary source of variation proved to be the knowledge variable with the experimental group also showing improvement in all other categories. Follow-up results revealed continued improvement on the conflict and organization variables."(DAI)

235. Currier, C., 1982, *Learning to Step Together,* Stepfamily Association of America, Baltimore, MD

A leaders manual for educators and mental health practitioners leading courses or workshops for couples in stepfamilies. Complete with handouts.

236. Curtis, S.S., 1983, Stepfamily Patterns: Authority, Responsibility, and Roles Reported by Parents and Stepparents, Dissertation Abstracts International, Vol. 45/03-A, page 962

"The exploratory examination of stepfamily patterns employs symbolic interaction as the theory. Sixty (30 couples) white, middle class, stepfamily adults, with at least one child from the previous marriage living with them, participated in in-depth, tape recorded interviews (2 1/2 hours each) using a non-scheduled, structured interview format. Questions were on topics of authority, responbility and bonding, and the difference between parent and stepparent roles. Questions came from theory, literature, and researcher's experience with stepfamilies.

Men and women responded to stepfamily issues differently. Mothers desired to share authority and stepfathers felt they had a right to this authority. Fathers tended to rely on stepmothers to provide child with daily care and nurturing; stepmothers saw child as responsible for own care, and father as nurturer. Stepfathers tended to want more involvement with family, while stepmothers tended to see parent as most responsible. Mothers tended to expect less from husbands, while fathers tended to expect more from wives. Three major findings are described. (1) Sex role stereotypes appeared to be the primary influence. Families rejected the nuclear family model as unrealistic, but didn't reject the stereotypes which come from this model. (2) The stepfamily experience may be different for the children of fathers versus the children of mothers. The mothers' sharing of authority resulted in more change in rules and expectations for the mothers' children and more problems for these children. The reliance on the stepmother for care and nurturing of the fathers' children may result in less attention to these needs and hence insufficient care for these children. Finally, (3) there appeared to be three different family forms for the mother-stepfather families: two conflict groups and one conflict-free group. The two conflict groups were marked by stepfather demand for change for the child. One group had troubled children and mothers who withdrew from these children; the other group had neither troubled children nor mothers who withdrew. The third group was marked by need for each other on the part of the stepparent or child. This third group was relatively conflict free and resembled nuclear families.''(DAI)

237. Dahl, A.S., et al, 1987, ''Life In Remarriage Families'', *Social Work,* Vol. 32, No. 1, pp. 40–44

''In preliminary findings from research interviews with non-clinical remarriage families who were not receiving treatment, both marital satisfaction and children's adjustment were described in primarily positive terms, especially after the first few years. Families reported that the process of managing complexitites, uncertainties, and mixed feelings can help achieve cohesion in remarriage families.'' (ERIC)

238. Daly, M. & M. Wilson, 1985, ''Child Abuse and Other Risks of Not Living With Both Parents'', *Ethology and Sociobiology,* Vol. 6, pp. 197–210

A well-researched, comprehensive study in a midsized Canadian city to quantify various risk factors in the lives of children as a result of the status of the person functioning in loco parentis. Telephone interviews of randomly selected families were compared with available data on families of child abuse victims, runaways, and juvenile offenders to arrive at data on victimization according to age and household types. Both abuse and police apprehension were found to be least likely for children living with both biological parents. Abuse risk was significantly higher for children living with one biological and one stepparent than for children living with a single parent. Other variables examined such as household composition, socioeconomic status, family size, and maternal age, were all considered predictors of abuse risk but differed little or not at all in terms of family type. It was concluded that stepparenthood by itself constitutes a risk factor for child abuse.

239. Day, R. & W. Mackey, 1981, ''Re-Divorce Following Remarriage: A Re-Evaluation'', *Journal of Divorce,* Vol. 4, pp. 39–47

The authors indicate the difference in the outlook of family researchers over the last 30 years, but admonish that there are still some popular myths about the instability of second marriages which influence current research. They suggest that a more accurate view is in order and attempt to provide it by analyzing and updating previous data. It is suggested that the traditional family form is not in as much decline as might be suspected, that ''most people stay married,'' and that 68% of those who divorce have either one child or none and most remarry. They suggest that more attention be paid to those who remarry, to the stability of those remarriages, and to those who re-divorce, and to the stability of those marriages. A re-examination, they suggest, would reveal that only a few re-divorce many times, most divorces are of the very young (under 24), most divorced people (especially men) remarry and stay married, and two-third of all divorces involve only zero to one child.

240. Deighan, M.E., 1980, ''Towards Collaboration in Foster Care: A Training Guide'', State University of New York, Albany, School of Social Welfare

''The curriculum presented in this training guide is seen as the foundation upon which the child welfare system can build collaboration in foster care. The first training module focuses on the significance of the parent-child relationship and the impact of separation on this relationship. It presents a general framework for understanding dysfunctional family patterns and intervention techniques. The second module concentrates on the balance between the personal and professional roles of foster families, the therapeutic skills of foster families, and the need to include foster families in the treatment team. The third and fourth modules concern the training and supervision of foster families. The last module emphasizes the importance of the preplacement and termination stages within the framework of permanency planning. Each presentation begins with a rationale explaining why the training was developed. The purpose for each training module is then described along with specific behavioral objectives and anticipated behavioral changes. The session outline next provides time frames and an explanation of the process of the training session. Materials for training, such as sample lectures, experiential exercises, and handouts for participants, appear at the end of each module. Most of the modules suggest alternative strategies for training.'' (ERIC)

241. Deutsch, H., 1973, *The Psychology of Women: a Psychoanalytic Interpretation, Vol.2, Motherhood,* Bantam, New York

''Deutsch includes a chapter on stepmothers and likens their situation to adoptive mothers. She outlines the myth of the wicked stepmother and was one of the first to advocate an understanding not only of the mother's psyche but also of the whole environment involved. The various psychic patternings and motivations of the stepmother are similarly outlined. Deutsch uses one long case history of a family with a stepmother, stepchild, and a new mutual child to detail the expected outcome in such a situation both for male and female stepchildren.'' (SAA)

242. Draughon, M., 1975, ''Stepmother's Model of Identification in Relation to Mourning in the Child'', *Psychological Reports,* Vol. 36, pp. 183–189

Three models of identification are proposed for the stepmother, to clarify and ease her interactions with her stepchildren: the roles of primary mother, other mother, and friend. Selection of these roles is made on the basis of the child's mourning stage. If the mourning is incomplete and his/her mother is still psychologically alive, the role of friend is recommended. If the child's mourning is complete and the mother is psychologically dead, the stepmother's role of primary mother is suggested. The model of other mother is not recommended at all.

243. Duberman, L., 1974, *Marriage and its Alternatives,* Praeger Publishers, New York

Discusses some demographic factors in remarriage, the choice of a second mate, common problems, and the adjustment to children. It does not yet include data from the research reported in *The Reconstituted Family* by the same author, published in 1975.(E&W)

244. Duberman, L., 1975, *The Reconstituted Family: A Study of Remarried Couples and Their Children,* Nelson-Hall, Chicago

Explains the dynamics of the stepfamily, its possible effects on society, and the societal influences upon it. The author bases her findings on a systematic study of 89 families in Cuyahoga County, Ohio, and on personal experience as a member of a stepfamily. Her conclusions offer guidelines for effective action and a broad view of how second families cope with the difficult process of consolidating steprelations.(E&W)

245. Duberman, L., 1973, ''Step-kin Relationships'', *Journal of Marriage and the Family,* Vol. 35, pp. 283–292

The author discusses dyadic relationships in stepfamilies, and comparisons are made between step-siblings' relationships and sibling relations. A random sample of parents who remarried was drawn. A Parent-Child Relationship Score was obtained through self and investigator ratings. Social factors influencing differing scores were investigated. Younger women were found to be more likely to have excellent relations. Protestant stepparents and those whose previous marriages ended by death rather than divorce scored higher. Tentative findings for intrastep-sibling relations seemed to indicate relations are better when they live in the same household, and when the couple has a child together. The author stresses continued studies to provide a broader understanding of the socialization process.

246. Einstein, E., 1982, *Stepfamilies: Living, Loving and Learning,* Dutton, New York

''This well-researched book chronicles the developmental passages of the stepfamily, exploring its complex internal and external relationships. The book won a National Media Award from the American Psychological Association.'' (SAA)

247. Engebretson, J., 1982, ''Stepmothers as First-Time Parents, Their Needs and Problems'', *Pediatric Nursing,* Nov/Dec

The author defines mothers having their first parenting experience with stepchildren as a group with special needs and recommends that they be considered as much in crisis as new mothers. Nurses must get involved and expose the ''bad stepmother'' myth and other problems such as the expectation of instant love. The nurse, it is felt, can help the stepmother deal realistically with her expectations, frustrations, and anger as well as advise her about disciplining techniques and child development. Interventions are quite detailed and some literature is recommended. The article takes in the major problems of stepparenthood and is prevention oriented. Unfortunately it is not specified where and how nurses meet these stepfamilies, nor how first-time stepmothers differ from stepmothers who have had biological children before.

248. Espinoza, R. & Y. Neuman, 1979, *Stepparenting,* D.H.E.W.

This monograph delves into research of the special problems of stepfamilies and finds that research studies of stepfamilies were only at this point beginning to appear in greater numbers. Stepfamilies themselves tended to keep a low profile and very often were made to feel uncomfortable and outside of the culturally defined norms of the concept of family. Stepfamilies tended not to disclose their problems. Their response to workshops and lectures was minimal. This government-sponsored early research document is a very scholarly presentation of existing studies and cites the major areas of difference in stepfamily living and some suggestions for programs to service agencies. A helpful bibliography was added.

249. Fancett, C.S., 1984, Predictors of Adolescent Stepchildren's Satisfaction With Their Stepparents, Dissertation Abstracts International, Vol.45/05-B, p. 1573

''Previous studies on stepfamily satisfaction have primarily employed the stepparent and natural parent as respondents. Studies with stepchildren have focused on cognitive development and school achievement while studies with stepparents have addressed personal stress and relationship issues. The present study examined how adolescent stepchildren's relationships with their stepparents were influenced by communication, perception of shared stress with the stepparent, and the complexity of the stepfamily system. The author developed a stepparent-satisfaction questionnaire to assess these variables. The Cornell Medical Index and the Two-Factor Index of Social Position were also used to supplement the questionnaire. Sixty stepchildren, ages 12–19, completed a structured one-hour interview. Seventy-four percent of the variance in the model was predicted by six of the questionnaire items: (a) whether the stepchild perceived the stepparent to be interested in what she or he had to say; (b) whether the custodial parent's and stepparent's religion was the same; (c) how often the stepchild and stepparent talked with each other; (d) whether the stepchild perceived that she or he, the stepparent, or both had adjusted the most to the stepfamily; (e) the stepchild's perception of the custodial parent and stepparent's relationship; and (f) how the stepchild felt about family finances compared to how the billpayer in the family felt. Several areas mentioned in the literature as important stresses were not significant in predicting satisfaction: (a) differences in reactions to discipline; (b) contact with the noncustodial parent; (c) adoption orientation: and (d) the presence of half-siblings in the present marriage. Reasons for these findings were discussed. Recommendations for interventions and further research were made with an emphasis upon the role that empathy and perception of shared stress play in the adjustment of teenage stepchildren to their stepparents. The orientation is taken that stepchildren and stepparent can learn more about each other's stresses through open communication.''(DAI)

250. Fast, I. & A. Cain, 1966, ''The Stepparent Role: Potential for Disturbances in Family Functioning'', *American Journal of Orthopsychiatry,* Vol. 36, pp. 435–491

Fifty case records of stepfamilies were examined to review the social role of stepparents. Difficulties in developing stable patterns of feeling, thinking, and acting toward their stepchildren are discussed in terms of contradictory pressures to act as parent, non-parent and stepparent. The sharing of role functions with the non-resident parent is not clearly established in society. Weakened social mores (e.g., the incest taboo) and the absence of role-learning opportunities are discussed. Implications for treatment are considered.

251. Fausel, D., 1981, ''Social Work Practice With Reconstituted Families'', *Annual Meeting of N.A.S.W. Professional Symposium*

252. Felker, E., 1981, *Raising Other People's Kids: Successful Child-rearing in the Restructured Family,* William B. Eerdmans, Grand Rapids, MI

''Addressed to people raising children who are not biologically their own: stepchildren, adopted children or foster children. The author, an experienced foster parent, refers to these families as ''restructured'' or ''functional'' families. Chapters dealing with bringing the child into the family and the child experiencing new value systems are practical and informative.'' (SAA)

253. Filinson, R., 1986, ''Relationships in Stepfamilies: An Examination of Alliances'', *Journal of Comparative Family Studies,* Vol. 17, pp. 43–61

Objective of this study was to compare stepfamilies with non-stepfamilies in Scotland and to examine if similar or dissimilar family alliances occur. An alliance is described as the separation of the (step)family into separate cliques or groups, along blood kinship lines, and further to designate any set of preferences among family members above all others. A never-married person's marriage, though technically not a remarriage, was included, since many out-of-wedlock children spend much of their lives in stepfamilies. Data was obtained from a study of the family lives of children born illegitimately and raised by their biological mothers in Great Britain, aiming at a very homogeneous group. A small sample population was women aged 18–21 who gave birth in 1970, 1975, 1978. The number of legitimate children was approximately triple that of the ones born illegitimately. Interviews took place in 1980/81 when the oldest (target) child was 2,5, or 10 years old. The stepparent usually was a man, entering as a stepfather to the resident child and producing half siblings (''stepsiblings'') with the resident biological mother. Alliances were defined as neutral (not disruptive), and disruptive (offensive and defensive) alliances. The author describes in detail what the findings were on these three. She concludes that a range of relationships were found in both step- and non-step families. However, it was not felt that the disruptive alliances could be defined as idiosyncratic to stepfamilies. Asymmetrical relationships were not felt to be signs of family problems, since they were found in non-stepfamilies as well. Concealment of the step status in the cases of children in whose lives the stepfathers entered early is perceived as a positive factor which needs more exploration. Willingness to adopt and absence of problems generally found in the external circumstances (e.g. financial problems, competing biological parents, outsiders' views) are given as possible reasons for the difference from problems pointed out in the general stepfamily literature. A more differentiated study of different types of stepfamilies is suggested.

254. Fine, M.A., 1986, ''Perceptions of Stepparents: Variation in Stereotypes as a Function of Current Family Structure'', *Journal of Marriage and the Family,* Vol. 48, No. 3, pp. 537–543

This study explores a sample of college students as to their perceptions of stepfamilies versus biological families and whether there is a relationship of this perception and the kind of family in which the rater lives. Three groups of students were raters, 90 from intact nuclear families, 55 from single-parent families, and 30 from stepfamilies. The results supported the notion that increased exposure to stepfamilies decreases negative stereotypes of stepmothers, through increasing sensitivity and familiarity with the challenges of stepfamily living.

255. Fine, M.A., Donnelly, B.W., & P. Voyanoff, 1986, ''Adjustment and Satisfaction of Parents: A Comparison of Intact, Single-Parent, and Stepparent Families'', *Journal of Family Issues,* Vol. 7, No. 4, pp. 391–404

''A study compared the relative adjustment and satisfaction of three different groups of parents. An in-depth telephone interview assessing a number of dimensions of well-being (anxiety, depression, child problems, marital satisfaction, and family satisfaction) was administered to 154 parents from intact families, 28 single parents, and 28 remarried parents. Results indicated that single parents were significantly less satisfied and less well adjusted than their counterparts from first marriages and remarriages, but there were no differences on any dimensions between the latter two groups. These findings are discussed with reference to existing literature, and suggestions for future research are made.'' (SWAB)

256. Fishman, B., 1983, ''The Economic Behavior of Stepfamilies'', *Family Relations,* Vol. 32, pp. 359–366

Two economic patterns are described: ''common pot'' pooling of all family resources and ''two pot'' couples, separating individual resources for personal use or for biological children only. Results indicate that common pot economy tends to unify the stepfamily. It is also suggested that money management be used as a therapeutic strategy to help remarried couples express commitment to each other and to the partner's children.

257. Fowler, R., 1981, ''Efficacious Factors for Facilitating the Emotional Adjustment of Children in Remarriage'', *Psychology, A Quarterly Journal of Human Behavior,* Vol 18, pp. 50–53

''Four factors have been identified in this literature as crucial to facilitate the emotional adjustments of a child in remarriage: (1) the pre-marriage adjustment of the child; (2) the age of the child at the time of remarriage; (3) the stepparent-stepchild relationship; and (4) the presence of stepsiblings. A dual-focused, dual phasic preventative program was presented.'' (Gruber)

258. Furstenberg Jr., F.F., 1981, ''Conjugal Succession in the American Kinship System'', Unpublished article

An analysis of current data on the non-traditional family form, in which ''many if not most children'' will spend some time during their growing years. The difference between previously prevalent stepfamilies, in which following the death of a parent, parents were replaced rather than augmented and the current pattern in which ex-spouses need to relate to each other with regard to child-rearing issues is pointed out. The existence of continuing relationships to extended family, e.g. grandparents, is further highlighted. A widening of the concept of parenthood is cited as a successful way by which some families cope. The effect of enlarging the child's kinship network as a result of remarriage is positively cited.

259. Furstenberg Jr., F. & G. Spanier, 1981, "The Risk of Dissolution In Remarriage: An Examination of Cherlin's Hypothesis of Incomplete Institutionalization", American Sociological Association meeting

260. Furstenberg Jr., F. & G. Spanier, 1984, *Recycling the Family: Remarriage After Divorce,* Sage Publications, Inc., Beverly Hills, CA.

A compilation of previously written articles on the subject, with two introductory chapters added, this book attempts to assess the changes in family relations and expectations, on the basis of a longitudinal study carried out in the late seventies, in one county in Pennsylvania. The authors identified a number of popular concepts which they believe have been eroded as divorce and remarriage have become more prevalent. The process of change from first marriage through divorce and remarriage both on a personal and cultural level are examined and some hypotheses are formulated. Areas for further research are outlined, especially in the realm of the complicated life situations for children and their coping reactions.

261. Furstenberg, F. & C.W. Nord, 1985, "Parenting Apart: Patterns of Childrearing After Marital Disruption", *Journal of Marriage and the Family,* Vol. 47, No. 4, pp. 893–904

"Divorce and remarriage have become prominent features of American life. Nowadays many parents divide their attention and resources among two or more families, and children frequently grow up with multiple parents. Using a nationally representative household sample of children, the authors describe relations among parents, stepparents, and children after separation and divorce. The results suggest that most children have little contact with their non-resident parents, and what contact there is tends to be social rather than instrumental. Contrary to popular impressions, however, when the former spouse remains active in the child's life, stepfamily life—at least in the mother-stepfather families—does not seem to suffer." (NCFR)

262. Ganong, L. & M. Coleman, 1983, ''Stepparent: A Pejorative Term?'', *Psychological Reports,* Vol. 52, pp. 919–922

208 college students' responses were examined regarding their attitudes toward various semantically different descriptive terms. The concepts of ''stepmother'' and ''stepfather'' elicited more negative responses. The authors conclude that the prefix ''step'' appears to be pejorative, eliciting a more stereotyped, negative image, contradicting the beginning assumption that the pervasiveness of stepfamilies in our society may have reduced previous biases. The data appears to support the pejorative image engendered by the prefix ''step,'' and the notion that the current bias against both stepmothers and stepfathers seems quite strong.

263. Ganong, L.H. & M.M. Coleman, 1985, ''Stepchildren's Perceptions of Their Parents'', *Journal of Genetic Psychology,* Vol. 148, No. 1, pp. 5–17

126 unmarried high school and college students ages 15–22 who were enrolled in psychology, human development, and family living courses at their respective schools were chosen from a pool of 1225. There was some racial mixture, and some representation of medium-sized as well as urban communties. A previous questionnaire used in 1962 by Bowerman and Irish was included in the questions to determine if there had been changes in the steprelations in the past two to three decades. The conclusions indicated differences in the perceptions male and female stepchildren had of their stepparents. The stepdaughter-stepfather relationship seems to be less emotionally close than other dyads in the stepfamily. Stepchildren do not feel more distant from stepmothers than stepfathers. Stepchildren generally feel minimally moderately close to their stepparents. The length of family in residence, or family problems prior to the stepfamily do not affect family closeness. Discussions and suggestions for further research are included in the article.

264. Ganong, L.H. & M.M. Coleman, 1986, ''A Comparison of Clinical and Empirical Literature on Children in Stepfamilies'', *Journal of Marriage and the Family,* Vol. 48, No. 2, pp. 309–318

114 empirical studies and clinical references were reviewed and compared along several dimensions, e.g. theoretical approaches, types of families, and methodology. The attempt was to identify and sort what is known from empirical research and from clinical, applied work, and to establish congruence of the two types of research. Little congruence of foci was found and the authors discuss the implications of this lack of congruence. The classic

split between research and practice is felt to be detrimental, and greater interchange between the two is recommended to enhance and stimulate both research efforts and clinical practice.

265. Gardner, R., 1984, "Counseling Children in Stepfamilies", *Elementary School Guidance & Counseling*
"Focuses on some of the primary problems of stepchildren and the techniques that may be useful for the elementary school counselor. The author addresses the problems of the stepchildren, the stepmother, and the stepfather separately even though these distinctions may be somewhat artificial in that the problems often involve all concerned parties, including natural parents. Problem areas for stepchildren include hostility, anger inhibition, sibling rivalry, and loyalty conflicts. Although the potential exists for deep involvement and loving feelings from the outset on the part of the stepmother, some factors that may compromise the relationship are discussed. The stepfather's role is often less important, but he plays an active role when the natural father is either ineffective or absent." (c) APA

266. Gardner, R., 1982, *The Boys and Girls Book About Stepfamilies,* Bantam Books, New York
This is a straightforward approach intended to be read by children in stepfamilies. Dr. Gardner addresses and normalizes common concerns and worries of children, offering concrete advice and information on how to decrease fighting with stepsiblings, and on how to get along with stepparents. The child is encouraged to realize that his/her feelings are normal and is offered suggestions about what to do about anger. Stepfamily myths are exposed, i.e. "instant love." The book hopes to help children cope with the difficulties inherent in being members of a stepfamily.

267. Gilbert, S., 1975, *What's a Father For? A Father's Guide to the Pleasures and Problems of Parenthood With Advice From the Experts,* Parent's Magazine Press, New York
This book is based on interviews with fathers and experts, e.g. Benjamin Spock, Margaret Mead, Louise Bates Ames, and Eda LeShan, to find answers to questions all fathers ask. Chapters on part-time fathers, stepfathers, and double-time fathers are included.

268. Giles-Sims, J., 1984, "The Stepparent Role: Expectations, Behavior, and Sanctions", *Journal of Family Issues,* Vol. 5, pp. 116–130
Based on a previous study (Nye), the author explores the role of

biological parent and stepparent in remarried families with the specific foci outlined in the title of the paper. In-depth interviews were conducted with one of the partners in 99 families in which one or both had been previously married and children from the previous marriage were present. 311 children were included in this sample. On the basis of the author's findings she draws three tentative conclusions, which contain inconsistencies. Over half of the respondents expected stepparents to share child-rearing duties, yet stepparents generally do share less. Actually fewer than one-third shared in decision making. Stepparents are not likely to be sanctioned for refusing to bring up stepchildren, and their positive role is not as sanctioned as for biological parents. The findings point up discrepancies, confusing expectations, and unclear mandates. In general the stepfamily model differs significantly from the biological-nuclear family model. The authors discuss their opinion of whether this is problematic and in which way.

269. Glick P., 1976 ''A Demographer Looks at American Families'', *Journal of Marriage and the Family,* pp.15–26.

Presents data from census information collected since 1939, concerning American families. Analyzes and interprets patterns and trends in marriage, childbearing, divorce, remarriage, etc.

270. Glick, P., 1980, ''Remarriage: Some Recent Changes and Variations'', *Journal of Family Issues,* Vol. 1, No. 4, pp. 455–478

271. Glick, P. & A. Morton, 1977, ''Marrying, Divorcing, and Living Together Today'', *Population Bulletin,* Vol.32, No.5.

Presents the most up-to-date figures from the Census Bureau as analyzed by the authors. Documents changing U.S. patterns of marriage, divorce, and living arrangements in the mid-1970's which undoubtedly reflect changed attitudes toward conformity with traditional behavior.(E&W)

272. Glick, P. & A. Morton, 1973, ''Perspectives on the Recent Upturn in Divorce and Remarriage'', *Demography*

The cohort study shows that the upward trend in divorce is not ''phasing out'' yet, as it did after World War II. An analysis of nationwide data on birth cohorts from 1900 to 1954 demonstrates that early marriage has declined since the mid-1950's but leaves open the question as to whether lifelong singleness is becoming more prevalent.(E&W)

273. Glick, P.C., 1975, ''Some Recent Changes in American Families'', U.S. Government Printing Office

A report for public officials which is a revised version of an address by Dr. Paul C. Glick. It cites recent family statistics and analyzes their potential impact on public policy.(E&W)

274. Goetting, A., 1983, ''The Relative Strength of the Husband-Wife, and Parent-Child Dyads in Remarriage: A Test of the HSU Model'', *Journal of Comparative Family Studies,* Vol. 14, pp. 117–128

In 180 divorced and remarried families their adult members were asked to complete a questionaire regarding spouses consulting each other regarding activities with the children, and influencing each other in this way. The results indicate that in stepfamilies the maritial dyad dominates over the biological parent dyad with regard to child rearing. ''(c) APA''

275. Golan, N., 1981, *Passing Through Transitions,* Free Press, New York

Chapter 2—The Nature of Transitions and the Change Process—Discusses the transitional period and its stages which one passes through while experiencing a great loss. Chapter 1—Where Transitions are Met and Missed—Applies crisis theory modality as a means of intervention during normal life transitions. The author's normalizing approach to these life crises rests on the ready accessibility of those in crisis, combined with the reorganization skills of the helper (usually a social worker).

Chapters 9&10—Separation, Divorce and Remarriage and Untimely Widowhood Grief and Bereavement—includes the crucial period of recovery from loss as a prerequisite for successful coping and remarriage. The author outlines an ideal planning stage in which a client's fantasies and fears should be explored, then delineates outlines for new roles centered on nurturance and discipline for remarried couples where children are involved.

276. Goldmeier, J., 1980, ''Intervention in the Continuum from Divorce to Family Reconstitution'', *Social Casework,* Vol. 61, pp. 39–47

The author considers the movement from family breakup to remarriage a continuum, and develops some concepts for practice with particular emphasis on the need for an open-ended treatment contract, so that client-worker continuity can be maintained over a considerable time span, without having a continuous treatment process.

277. Goldstein, H., 1974, "Reconstituted Families: The Second Marriage and its Children", *Psychology Quarterly,* Vol. 48, pp. 433–440

The author begins with the premise that there are inevitable and special stresses in the integration of a remarried family system. Mistrust, fear of failure, and a sense of vulnerability are almost always present. Issues that add stress to the system's adaptive mechanisms, and their manifestation in the family are identified: Pseudomutuality, Parental Role Freeze, Displacement of the Child, Lowered Incest Taboo, Myth of the Dead Parent. It is implied that the therapists' task is to make these issues explicit for the whole family, and that open discussion of these special stresses will enable the family to integrate into a stable growth-permitting whole.

278. Goodman-Lezin, S., 1985, "The Remarried Family: Variables Affecting Adjustment to Stepmothering", *Annual Convention of the American Psychological Association*

"Despite the increase in the numbers of remarried families, little research has examined interpersonal relationships within these stepfamilies. Interpersonal and family systems variables which may contribute to stepmothers' satisfaction were examined in 65 part- and full-time stepmothers aged 22–27 and in 65 stepchildren aged 10–16. Eleven instruments were used to determine: (1) the extent to which the stepmother had achieved healthy differentiation from her family of origin; (2) marital satisfaction; (3) the amount of conflict existing between the biological parents; (4) the extent to which the biological father invested the stepmother with parental responsibilities; (5) the degree of other life stress experienced by the stepmother; (6) the amount of conflict in the stepmother-stepchild relationship as perceived by the stepchild; and (7) the stepchild's adjustment to the biological parents' divorce. Results of the multiple regression analyses revealed that the group of predictor variables was significantly related to both indices of adjustment, satisfaction with role, and general well-being. The extent to which the biological father invested the stepmother with parental responsibilities and thereby created a parental unit was the most powerful predictor of stepmother satisfaction. The amount of conflict in the stepmother-stepchild relationship also had a significant effect on satisfaction with the stepmother role. Specific aspects of differentiation from family of origin relating to autonomy, inter-generational boundary definition, and mutuality were found to play a salient role in stepmother's adjustment." (ERIC)

279. Gorman, T., 1983, *Stepfather,* Gentle Touch Press, Boulder, CO
Based on a compilation of interviews over a 10-year period, the author explores the role of stepfather. Wives, stepchildren, and stepfathers offer their stories in their own words, revealing that even less than perfect relationships can work.

280. Gray, J.M., 1986, An Exploratory Study of Family Reorganization and Behaviors at School (Stepchild, Second Grade, Stepfamily, Third Grade, Single-Parent), Dissertation Abstracts International, Vol. 47/06-A, page 2017
"This study was designed to explore behaviors at school of second- and third-grade children experiencing three different family lifestyles: the nuclear intact family, the single-parent family, and the remarried family. Teachers rated 548 students on 14 characteristics commonly considered by educators in evaluating children of this age. The teacher ratings were compared for each of the three groups noted. The chi-square test of independence was employed to determine if the distributions of scores rating school behaviors of children being reared in each of the three family lifestyles varied significantly. Teachers rated children being reared in the nuclear intact family as demonstrating more appropriate social-emotional development than children in single-parent and remarried families. This study also examined the more specific behaviors of peer relationships: adjustment to the world of school with its rules, regulations, and norms: and willingness to apply energies to learning. The data indicated that no significant difference exists between children in nuclear intact families and children in single-parent fmailies in either their adaption to school procedures or their desire to learn. In addition, children no longer living in their nuclear intact family, whether they were currently being reared in single-parent families or remarried families, exhibited no significant differences in their behaviors at school. Furthermore, the data suggest that children in these two groups do not behave significantly differently from each other in any of the three specific areas of peer interactions, adjustment to the school milieu, and motivation to learn. The data of this study suggest that both overall social-emotional development and specific behaviors at school are related to the phenomenon of family reorganization. These data indicate that children experiencing family reorganiza-

tion do not demonstrate the behaviors that are expected of children of this age at school.'' (DAI)

281. Green, M., 1976, *Fathering,* McGraw-Hill, New York
''Practical aspects of fathering in terms of (1) fathering children within the nuclear family, (2) fathering natural children separated from one parent by divorce, (3) assuming the role of stepfather, (4) father-son relationship, (5) father-daughter relationship. Conclusion: in light of women's liberation and changing roles of women, redefinition of father's role is needed.'' (SAA)

282. Greenberg, L.I., 1975, ''Therapeutic Grief Work With Children'', *Social Casework,* Vol. 56, No. 7, pp. 396–403
Describes the therapeutic techniques used to help children in three different case studies to work through their grief over the death of a parent.(SAA)

283. Griffin, S., et al, 1985, ''Stepfamilies: Awareness and Attitudes of Preschool Children'', *Early Child Development and Care,* Vol. 19, No. 4, pp. 277–290
''Attempted to determine whether a specific stepfamily curriculum would affect the stepfamily's awareness of preschool children. Although no changes were found in attitudes in either control or experimental groups, a significant increase was found in the experimental group's awareness.'' (ERIC)

284. Groff, M. & L. Hubble, 1984, ''A Comparison of Father-Daughter and Stepfather-Stepdaughter Incest'', *Criminal Justice & Behavior,* Vol. 11, pp. 461–475
''Compared the characteristics of father-daughter and stepfather-stepdaughter incest, using historical data, demographic information, and MMPI scores from 42 cases of child sexual abuse. Sixteen fathers and 26 stepfathers were convicted of the sexual abuse of 20 daughters and 27 stepdaughters. The same cases also were used to compare attributes of incest involving younger and older daughters/stepdaughters. Results show that there were no systematic differences across types of incest, either in terms of offender attributes or specific characteristics of the incestuous relationships. In general, all offender groups appeared to have a fairly adequate level of overall functioning.'' (c) APA

285. Gruber, E., 1986, *Stepfamilies: A Guide to the Sources and Resources,* Garland Publishing, Inc., New York and London
This is the most recently published bibliography book, which

includes a section on parents and one on children, as well as much needed sections on Audio-Visual Resources, Organizational Resources, and Newsletters.

286. Guidubaldi, J., Cleminshaw, H., Perry, J., & B. Natasi, 1984, Longitudinal Effects of Divorce on Children: A Report From the NASP-KSU Nationwide Study, American Psychological Association convention

287. Hafkin, N.F., 1981, Factors Affecting Satisfaction in the Stepfamily Couple, Dissertation Abstracts International, Vol. 42/05-A, page 1960

"This study was designed to assess the effectiveness of eight factors in predicting marital satisfaction in stepfamily couples. Based upon the demographic variables utilized in marital satisfaction research upon first-married couples, the following variables were selected: social position as determined by the Two-Factor Index of Social Position (Hollingshead, 1958), religion, frequency of religious activity, sex of stepparent, age of stepchildren, presence or absence of a child from the present relationship, relocation into home new to the relationship, and contact with the non-custodial biological parent.

Ninety remarried couples who had married during 1977 were chosen from the Marriage License Bureau in Montgomery County, Maryland, a suburb of Washington D.C. One-third of the sample were stepfather couples, one-third were stepmother couples, and the final third were couples in which both spouses were stepparents. Each couple had at least one child under the age of 18 in residence. Subjects were contacted by telephone and filled out questionnaires in their homes. The Dyadic Adjustment Scale (Spanier, 1976) was used to measure marital satisfaction and a demographic questionnaire secured data regarding the independent variables. It was hypothesized that a combination of the predictor variables would account for a significant proportion of the variance of the criterion variable (satisfaction). Results of a forward selection multiple regression analysis did not confirm this hypothesis. When individual multiple regression analyses were performed separately for the three groups, differences became apparent. Within the Stepfather group, the variables of being Jewish, presence of child from the present relationship, being Protestant, and frequency of religious activity were the most related to satisfaction. This combination of variables accounted for 27 percent of the variance and approached significance at the .05 level. In the Stepmother group, the variables of relocate, age of children (younger), being Jewish, being Prostestant, having no religion, and absence of a child from the present relationship predicted couple satisfaction at the .05 level of significance (R=.42). With the Stepmother-Stepfather group, social position and presence of a child from the present relationship significantly predicted satisfaction at the .01 level (R=.38).'' (DAI)

288. Haley, J., 1973, ''Strategic Therapy When a Child is Presented as the Problem'', *Journal of American Academy of Child Psychiatry,* Vol. 12, pp. 641–659

Haley examines the child-as-the-problem situation in the dysfunctional family. He identifies from a systems perspective why a child is often the focus of what actually is a family or marital problem. Discussions of approaches to treatment include 1) using the peripheral person, 2) breaking up the dyad with a task and 3) entering family through the parents' problems.

289. Halperin, S. & T. Smith, 1983, ''Differences in Stepchildren's Perceptions of Their Stepfathers and Natural Fathers: Implications for Family Therapy'', *Journal of Divorce,* Vol. 7, pp. 19–30

140 children, 70 aged 10–12 from stepfamilies and a control group of 70 children from nuclear families were compared as to their perceptions of their biological fathers and stepfathers respectively. Results showed that the stepchildren perceived both their biological and their stepfathers more negatively. However, the stepchildren's feelings toward biological and stepfathers did not show more positive or negative differentiation. The suggestion is made that the stepchild's greatest need is open acknowledgment and clarification in clinical treatment.

290. Halpern, H.M., 1982, A Family Systems Exploration of the Difficulties Encountered by Stepfamilies Attempting to Achieve Cohesiveness, Bryn Mawr Dissertation Affiliation

''This study examines the psychosocial functioning of reconstituted families or stepfamilies. Ten families were chosen from an initial sample of eighteen for observation for a period of four to six months. Data were gathered from an open-ended questionnaire, informal interviews, and extensive observation to derive specific as well as general conclusions about stepfamily functioning. Of particular interest were the following: (1) the nature of the differences between stepfamilies and original families; (2) the specific areas of conflict for reconstituted families; and (3) the homeostatic mechanisms used to achieve cohesiveness in the family. It was found that stepfamilies appear to differ from original families only in the quantity and complexity of their transactions, not in the actual nature of their familial dealings. Similarly, the specific areas of conflict around boundaries, loyalties, and roles reflected the extra pressures in these areas caused by a more extended cast of characters surrounding each stepfamily unit. These specific challenges to family cohesiveness are found to affect the marital dyad most profoundly. In stepfamilies whose marital coalitions were strongest, problems in other areas were resolved more readily than in families where the marriage was weak.'' (SWAB)

291. Handelman, L.S., 1982, ''The Concept of Remarriage Among Israeli War Widows'', *Journal of Comparative Family Studies,* Vol. 18, No. 3, pp. 361–373

This paper attempts to address two questions, one trying to define the complexities of remarriage, the other addressing the difference between first and second marriages. This is one of the few studies addressing remarriage after widowhood rather than after divorce. Some of the answers seem to be the much larger number of relationships within a family living under one roof but relating to many others perhaps not in the immediate proximity. Somewhat older age and perhaps concomitantly less flexibility was another reason frequently given. The author adds another factor, which impedes the decision to remarry stemming from the differences in the interpretation of the concept of remarriage itself. The universe consisted of 249 women widowed in the Six Day War (1967). They lived in towns and cities and ranged from age 19–47. 65 of these were interviewed. The discussions were tape-recorded and transcribed in their entirety.

292. Hanes, H.C., 1981, Perceptions of Family Concepts of Stepfather and Stepmother Stepfamily Dyads, Dissertation Abstracts International, Vol. 42/04-B, page 1586

''This study compared perceptions of family concepts among the two most common structural varieties of stepparent family dyads, that of natural mother and stepfather, and natural father and stepmother. Remarriage among men and women, who have children from a previous marriage, has become increasingly commonplace in our society. It is estimated that there are probably 25 million stepparents and that one out of six children is a stepchild; yet research on the stepfamily is limited and almost entirely of recent origin. Such research has generally compared the natural mother-stepfather stepfamily to that of the 'intact' family wherein both adults about are biological parents of the children.

Little is known about the perceptions of the natural parent in the stepfamily, or that of the structural variety of stepfamily consisting of natural father, his offspring from a former marriage, and stepmother.

Few resources are available for assessing differing perceptions of the natural parent-stepparent dyad as to their perceptions of family concepts. First-marriage family concepts are usually dependent only on experiences with the family of origin, whereas remarriages among couples with children of former marriages have three or more concepts of the family. The perceived effectiveness, satisfaction and congruence with their partner in the stepfamily may deter or enhance the integration of the stepfamily as a functioning unit. This study focused on an attempt to discover whether there are differences in perceptions of family concepts among stepfather and stepmother stepfamily dyads, and whether certain demographic variables contributed significantly to any differences. Subjects were 20 legally remarried couples, wherein either the natural father or the natural mother had a child or children of a former marriage aged 18 or younger residing in the stepfamily. Couples wherein each of the partners had a child or children from a former marriage residing in the stepfamily were excluded. Ten natural mother-stepfather couples and 10 natural father-stepmother couples from northeast Texas who volunteered to participate comprised the subjects of the study. The Family Concept Q-Sort which develops scores for family effectiveness, family satisfaction and family congruence, along with a demographic questionnaire were used as assessment instruments. Each couple completed two Q-Sorts each, one for their 'real' family and one for the 'ideal' family. Each participant completed the demographic questionnaire. All possible comparisons of natural mother, natural father, stepmother, stepfather and the stepfamily dyads were subjected to a one-factor multivariate analysis of covariance, using the subscales of effectiveness, satisfaction and congruence as dependent measures. Demographic variables were subjected to a stepwise multiple regression in process of defining which of these to include as the covariate set, with the result that only subjects' age, education, and number of sex of children resulting from the remarriage proved to be significant predictors and were used as the covariate set. Results of the analysis indicated there were no significant differences in perceptions of family concepts among any of the comparisons. It was concluded that findings of no significant differences among all possible comparisons of the stepparent stepfamily dyads may be an important implication. The study found that regardless of the number of prior family concepts held by a partner, or whether the natural mother or natural father was a custodial parent, the differences in perceptions of those individuals and that of the stepparent, whether stepmother or stepfather, were nonsignificant. Likewise, demographic variables failed to predict any significant differences in the dyads' perceptions of family concepts. Additional research comparing the two types of stepparent dyads with those of 'intact' family dyads, as well as research to include family concepts of the offspring is indicated.'' (DAI)

293. Harper, P., 1984, *Children in Stepfamilies: Their Legal and Family Status,* Institute of Family Studies Policy Background Paper No. 4, Institute of Family Studies, Melbourne

''One of the features of Australian society during the past 25 years, from the late 1950's to the early 1980's, has been the changing nature of the family. Significant changes have occurred in family formation and breakdown; in family composition and structures; in family relationships; and in the status, rights, and obligations of family members. This paper (1) outlines some of these changes, directing particular attention toward implication for stepfamilies; (2) examines the arrangements some families have made, especially by using adoption, to clarify and establish the legal status and family relationships of children and stepparents; (3) outlines the options available in establishing legal status and family relationships in stepfamilies; and (4) recommends changes to legislation to overcome existing problems and provide a more appropriate means of establishing legal status and clarifying relationships within stepfamilies. It is proposed that stepparents be enabled to seek guardianship or custody rights but that adoption of stepchildren be abolished.'' (ERIC)

294. Hartell-Lloyd, G.L., 1984, The Well-Functioning Stepfamily: Five Case Studies, Dissertation Abstracts International, Vol. 46/05-B, page 1686

''The major purpose of the study was to examine the commonalities of 'well-functioning' stepfamilies in an effort to generate hypotheses regarding the processes by which these families handle divorce and 'reconstitution.' Communication patterns, coping and problem solving strategies, as well as familial rules, roles, and discipline patterns were examined. Participants included five families where at least one partner had previously been married and brought a child or children from that marriage into their second marriage. Each member over the age of 5 years old submitted to an interview which lasted approximately one hour for each child and approximately three hours for each adult. It was found that the families who reported the least amount of conflict and the most satisfaction within their familial lives shared the following characteristics: (1) Parents maintained a "united front," were supportive of each other and shared in the decision-making process. (2) Parents made special efforts toward private time for themselves without the children. (3) All parents maintained that they had very good to excellent marriages, yet four out of five couples felt that there would be significantly less familial conflict without problems relating to stepchildren or ex-spouses. (4) Stepparents were perceived as 'friends' as opposed to 'parents' by children. (5) Children felt that their stepparents were 'good' for their natural parents. (6) Parents were on 'friendly terms' with ex-spouses. (7) Humor played an important role in the lives of the participants." (DAI)

295. Hayes, M., 1984, An Empirical Test of the Circumplex Model with Thirty Stepfamilies, Dissertation Abstracts International, Vol.45/03-A, page 963

"In the United States families comprised of one or both previously divorced partners are increasing in numbers, importance, and visibility. If the present trend continues, stepfamilies of this form could become the dominant family form in this country. If they are to be accepted by the general public as examples of the normal family, it should be possible to find normative assumptions about the cultural, structural and emotional characteristics of stepfamilies. Until recently, however, the divorced and remarried family as a significantly emerging pattern was neglected in the family literature. Information that was available about stepfamilies was often misinformation based on untested assumptions. In response to this information gap the present study addresses the question of whether or not cohesion (the degree of connection among family members) and adaptability (the change) are major organizing dimensions for stepfamilies as they are considered to be for families in general. This investigation assesses the relationship of cohesion, adaptability, duration of existence, structure and selected characteristics to the communication of stepfamily systems. Relationships among the major variables were studied using the Circumplex Model (Olson, 1979) modified by the addition of the two variables of duration of existence and structure, the Family Adaptability and Cohesion Evaluation Scale II (Faces II), an assessment tool based on the Model, and a background questionnaire. Thirty stepfamilies in the Southwestern United States voluntarily responded to mailed-out and mailed-back questionnaires during the Spring and Summer of 1983. The data collected was coded into machine-readable form. The influence of structure, duration, adaptability, and cohesion (summarized into family type) on stepfamily communication was assessed using analysis of variance. The results failed to support hypothesized relationships among the major variables of the model. It was recommended that additional investigations of stepfamilies be conducted to substantiate or disprove current assumptions regarding the dynamics of non-nuclear families.'' (DAI)

296. Heilpern, E., 1943, ''Psychological Problems of Stepchildren'', *Psychoanalytic Review,* Vol. 30, pp. 163–196
''Presents cases of remarriage families in which the sexual problems of the stepchildren—the Oedipus complex, efforts to replace a dead parent, and jealousy—are examined. This is one of the earliest studies which presented material on such issues.'' (SAA)

297. Herndon, A. & L. Combs, 1982, ''Stepfamilies as Patients'', *Journal of Family Practice,* Vol.15, No. 5, pp. 917–922
In view of the increase in the stepfamily population, the authors think it is important for family physicians to be aware of the special stepfamily characteristics which are not present in nuclear families: formation out of loss; previous history of only some family members, as well as previous parent-child bonds; bio-parent elsewhere; children as members of two households; and legal limitations of step-relationships. Recommendations for the training of residents and continued education for physicians are made. The article's special contribution is on the normalization of other-than-nuclear family patterns. (SAA)

298. Hobart, C., 1987, ''Parent-Child Relations in Remarried Families'', *Journal of Family Issues,* Vol. 8, No. 3, pp. 259–277
''Interviewed spouses from 232 remarried and 102 first-married families to examine relationships with categories of (step)children and effects of relationships on spousal relation. Found that shared children, wives' unshared children, and husbands' unshared children experienced qualitatively distinctive relationships with (step)parents, and these relationships had differing positive and negative effects on spousal relationships.'' (ERIC)

299. Howell, E.L., 1982, Evaluation of a Communication Skills Program with Stepfather-Adolescent-Mother Triads, Dissertation Abstracts International, Vol. 43/06-A, page 1837

''The purpose of this study was to evaluate a communication skills program called Families Living Effectively Together (FLET): the objective was to determine if FLET could alter significant behavior within the blended family. The central themes analyzed were altering parenting styles, enhancing family communication, improving marital adjustment, and reducing family stress. The 22 stepfamily respondents (132 subjects) who completed this quasi-experimental program were randomly assigned and classified as experimental, n=27; and control, n=17. The composition of each stepfamily included the female parent, the male stepparent and at least one adolescent child. Both the experimental and control-group families were given a pretest packet containing four paper-pencil instruments with instructions for completion at home. This procedure was repeated for the experimental and control posttest following the five-week training program. The test instruments were the Family Game, Parent-Adolescent Communication Inventory, Dyadic Adjustment Scale, and Behavior Profile Inventory. The data showed no statistical significance of improvement in the four areas under investigation. However, it can be inferred that most dysfunctional families tended to resist change, receive new parenting concepts slowly, and terminate self-growth activities prematurely, thus avoiding adequate closure on their dysfunction.'' (DAI)

300. Hunter, J. & N. Schumann, 1980, ''Chronic Reconstitution As a Family Style'', *Social Work,* Vol. 25, pp. 446–451

This article identifies and describes a process termed chronic reconstitution and emphasizes the normalcy of this process. The authors suggest after a review of the literature that it is seriously lacking consideration of alternative family lifestyles, yet they find there is a low level of commitment to maintaining any household over time, and attitudinal orientation which is opposed to the ''till death do us part'' notion. It is recommended that clinicians be more concerned about flexible definitions of contemporary norms and values, and see the potential for greater freedom and creativity in these lifestyles.

301. Hutchens, R., 1979, ''Welfare, Remarriage, and Marital Search'', *The American Economic Review,* Vol. 69, pp. 369–379

The staggering statistics of the 40% increase of female-headed households (from 1964–1974) with children under 18, and the doubling of the AFDC caseloads gave impetus to this research. By focusing on families without husbands, it was felt that the AFDC program might have increased marital separations and decreased chances for remarriage, however inadvertently. This article focuses on one aspect of these complex issues, the effect of AFDC transfers on the probability of remarriage for female heads of households with children. A number of important variables are researched and serious policy questions are raised, along with possible policy alternatives.

302. Hutchins-Cook, W.B., 1983, Parental Attributions for Adolescent Behavior in Intact and Step-Families, Dissertation Abstracts International, Vol. 44/04-B, page 1279

"The present research investigated the effect of family status (Intact vs. Stepfamily) on parental causal attributions for adolescent behavior. Weiner's theory of achievement motivation, which posits that attributions on the dimensions of Internality/Externality and Stability/Instability result in predictable affective states and behavioral response was extended to parent-adolescent relationships. Forty Intact married couples and 37 Stepfamily couples, whose family included an 11- and 15-year-old adolescent responded to the following: a Demographic questionnaire, which assessed parental age, income, education and marriage duration, the Family Environment Scale of which the Conflict subscale was of interest, and a Scenario Questionnaire which consisted of 20 short vignettes. The vignettes varied in the sex of scenario stimulus person and the good-deed, bad-deed nature of the scenario. Parental responses to the Scenario Questionnaire were made on a 5-point scale to the following causal attributions: Adolescent trait (Internal-Stable), Parent trait (Internal-Stable), Adolescent stage (Internal-Unstable), Family status (Internal-Unstable), Societal (External-Stable), and Luck (External-Unstable). In addition a Favorability and Unfavorability index were formed by combining attributions considered theoretically to be favorable or unfavorable to the adolescent or parent. Data analysis revealed significant effect of scenario type (good-deed vs. bad-deed) on parental attributions and a significant sex of scenario stimulus person effect on attibutional choice. The results did not reveal differences in attributional choice as a function of family status. In contrast to the correlational analyses which indicated a positive relationship between parent-perceived conflict and marriage duration for Intact parents but not for Stepparents, the relationship between conflict and attributional choice existed for Stepfamily parents but not Intact parents. A regression analysis indicated that the Favorability Index could be predicted by parent education for female adolescent scenarios. The Unfavorability index was predicted by parent education for male adolescent scenarios. The limitations and implications of the findings as well as direction for future research in the area of parental attributions were discussed.'' (DAI)

303. Ievoli, R.J., 1983, The Quality of Stepparent-Stepchild Relationships in Simple and Complex Stepfather Families, Dissertation Abstracts International, Vol. 44/01-B, page 311

''This research examined two factors which may influence the quality of stepfather-stepchild relationships: (1) sex of the stepchild, and (2) whether the stepfather is a noncustodial parent or has no biological children from a previous marriage. Relationships between stepfather and stepchild were examined in a total of 40 stepfather families. Target children were between 8 and 12 years of age. Nineteen complex stepfather families (both spouses had children from a previous marriage but only the wife had custody) and 21 simple stepfather families (only the wife had children from a previous marriage) were assessed on a variety of measures of the quality of the stepfather-stepchild relationship. Eight of the complex stepfather families had girls as target children, and 11 had boys. Of the simple stepfather families, the target child was a boy in nine families and a girl in 12 families. Dependent measures included independent assessments of the stepfather, stepchild, and custodial mother. As predicted, stepfathers in complex stepfather families exhibited poorer quality relationships with their stepchildren than did stepfathers in simple stepfather families. Contrary to prediction, girls and boys did not differ in the quality of their relationships with stepfathers. Results are discussed in terms of the loyalty conflicts which may be experienced by stepfathers in complex stepfamilies, and possible confounds are noted.'' (DAI)

304. Jackson, J.A., 1981, ''Helping Troubled Teenagers in Blended and Single-Parent Families'', *Social Work Papers,* Vol. 16, Spring, pp. 43–52

''As divorces multiply, increasing numbers of single-parent and blended (non-traditional) families are seeking help from clinical social workers. The troubled children and adults in these families present special themes and life complexities which demand that the clinician develop a clear framework for therapy. Systems, communication, and learning theories are the base of the intense, directive, and often brief therapy described. Family therapy is conceptualized as a point of view rather than a method of treatment. The focus of change is interrupting dysfunctional interactional patterns; as new forms develop within the family, individuals have different subjective experiences. Stages of therapy and positive reframing are basic to family systems work; the adaptations of these fundamentals as well as the use of outside resources are described. Form and progression of therapy are presented, together with some aspects of strategy and intervention applicable to work with single-parent and blended families. Brief case material illustrates the use of this model of therapy." (SWAB)

305. James, M., 1974, *What Do You Do With Them Now That You've Got Them?,* Addison-Wesley, Reading, MA.
The chapter titled "Stepparents Step Carefully" discusses the transactional analysis approach to being a good stepparent, using: question, explanation, anecdotal format, developing a new parent ego state, discipline, in-laws, ex-spouses, home emotional climate. Familiarity with transactional analysis is hopeful.

306. Jenkins, R., 1968, "The Varieties of Children's Behavioral Problems and Family Dynamics", *American Journal of Psychiatry,* Vol. 124, pp. 1440–1445
Describes three groups of children with clinical symptoms separated by computer clustering of these symptoms. Overanxious children are likely to have anxious, infantilizing mother. A critical, deprecative, punitive, inconsistent mother or stepmother is typical for the unsocialized child. Socialized delinquents are likely to come from large families characterized by parental neglect and total delegation of parental responsibilities. Parental pathology is typically more paternal than maternal, and frequently includes an alcoholic father or stepfather.

307. Jensen, L.C. & J.M. Jensen, 1981, *Stepping Into Stepparenting: A Practical Guide,* R&E Research Associates, Inc., Palo Alto, CA
A step by step descriptive book on "getting there from here" with practical hints for stepparents, especially stepfathers. Realistic perceptions and goals for the newly formed stepfamily are perceived as essential; personal experiences, psychological research, and practice wisdom are used to compile the data presented.

308. Johnson, H., 1980, "Working With Stepfamilies: Principles of Practice", *Social Work,* Vol. 25, pp. 304–308
Johnson discusses common characteristics of stepfamilies: their complexity, variability, unclear expectations, losses and gains, questions of turf, and suggests there are some positive, beneficial elements in stepfamilies. Principles for practice are drawn, in particular, the need to understand the sociological and economic

basis for the breakup of nuclear families to reduce the tendency toward later development of pathology. It is emphasized that groups can be very helpful, especially in prevention.

309. Jones, S.M., 1978, ''Divorce and Remarriage: a New Beginning, a New Set of Problems'', *Journal of Divorce,* Vol. 2, No. 2, pp. 217–227.

''Current trends, practices and problems of remarriage; impact of these social patterns on members of a stepfamily. ''(SAA)

310. Jorgensen, M., 1983, Stepfamilies: Conflict Tactics and Family Strength, Dissertation Abstracts International, Vol.44/09-A, p. 2899

''This study sought to examine the relationships between: (1) conflict tactics, (2) certain independent variables and perceived family strength in the stepfamily unit. The sample was composed of 85 partners in remarriages from Lincoln, Nebraska. The data were collected during the winter of 1982 by means of a self-administered questionnaire. Percentages, frequencies, Pearson Product-moment correlation coefficient, and one-way analysis of variance were used in the analysis of data. Significant negative relationships were found to exist between family strength and (a) verbal aggression conflict tactics, and (b) violence conflict tactics. Significant positive relationships were found between family strength and (a) marital satisfaction, and (b) satisfaction with handling discipline. No significant relationships were found between family strength and (a)reasoning conflict tactics, (b)length of marriage, (c) family size, (d) age of designated child and (e) type of ex-spouse influence. The stepfamily subjects generally had high family strength and generally handled conflict by employing reasoning tactics and passive verbal aggression tactics. Family strengths identified in an open-ended question coincided with other stepfamily and family strength studies. Issues of conflict identified by the sample also concurred with findings of previous studies. Findings indicate the need for: (1) educational programs focusing on conflict management and parent-child relationships for both children and adults; (2) premarital and marital counseling that addresses the unique issues confronting the remarried family; (3) more research on conflict management, impact of parental status on family strength, children and child-related issues, and a study including a sample representative of various races, socio-economic classes, religions, family sizes, geographical locations, and weak families.'' (DAI)

311. Juroe, D.J. & B.B. Juroe, *Successful Stepparenting,* Fleming H. Renelle, Old Tappan, NJ

Two professional counselors offer a resourceful collection of guidelines based on their personal experiences and training as preparation for the responsibilities and rewards of successful stepparenting. Their sensitive, informative advice provides valuable insights. Biblical emphasis.

312. Kagan, R., 1982, ''Therapy for Children in Placement'', *Child Care Quarterly,* Vol. 11, pp. 280–290

The author postulates that children, though obviously in need of a home, do everything possible to get rejected in a substitute family arrangement. Two ways of helping children with the change from nuclear to substitute family are storytelling and games, which are therapeutic in helping children in coping with their grief, attaching to new families, and returning to their old families. An example is cited in which a child is confronted with the decision of living with a foster family or remaining institutionalized. It is felt that this type of treatment technique can be incorporated into any comprehensive treatment program for children and their families. ''(c) APA''

313. Kagan, R.M., 1982, ''Storytelling and Game Therapy for Children in Placement'', *Child Care Quarterly,* Vol. 11, No. 4, pp. 280–290

''The author postulates that children, though obviously in need of a home, do everything possible to get rejected in a substitute family arrangement. Two ways of helping children with the change from nuclear to substitute family are storytelling and games, which are therapeutic in helping children in coping with their grief, attaching to new families, and returning to their old families. An example is cited in which a child is confronted with the decision of living with a foster family or remaining institutionalized. It is felt that this type of treatment technique can be incorporated into any comprehensive treatment program for children and their families.'' (c)APA

314. Kampman, M., 1981, ''The Impact on Stepchildren When Remarried Parents Divorce'', *National Council on Family Relation annual meeting*

315. Kaplan, M., 1985, Contributors to the Non-Parent's Experience of Becoming a Stepparent: Past Relationships, Current Situational Variables, and Gender (Stepfamilies, Remarried, Stepparenting), Dissertation Abstracts International, Vol. 47/04-B, page 1726

"There are an estimated 34 million stepparents in this country (Visher & Visher, 1979). A large volume of literature—popular and professional—about stepfamilies is available. Most of that literature is about not stepparents but children of divorce and single parents. Most of the literature about stepparents that is available addresses the subject of stepparenting children; it seldom addresses the stepparent's phenomenological experience or the way in which stepparenthood fits into an individual's life. This dissertation describes an exploratory study in which ten stepparents—five women, five men—none of whom have biological children of their own and all of whom have or had full custody of stepchildren, participated in semi-structured interviews of approximately 1 1/4 hours. Subjects were asked about experiences in the family-of-origin as well as about more recent experiences in the stepfamily and in activities outside the stepfamily. In each interview, the subject's genogram (as described by Pendagast and Sherman, 1977) was drawn. In the dissertation, each stepparent's phenomenological experience is described at length. Because this study involves no control group and a sample of only ten (and two samples of only five each, when questions of gender are described), findings are considered not as persuasive findings but as guidelines for future research. These findings include: (1) a stepchild's abandonment by the non-custodial parent was correlated with a negative or partially negative stepparent experience; (2) most of the stepparents reported playing, outside the stepfamily, a "helper" or "mediator" role; (3) most of the stepfathers described distant relationships in the family-of-origin; (4) most of the stepmothers described close relationships in the family-of-origin; and (5) those stepfathers who described a "family feeling" in the stepfamily and who have a stepdaughter, described a romantically tinged dependency on that stepdaughter. Possible explanations of these findings are explored. Research implications are discussed." (DAI)

316. Kaplan, S.I., 1977, "Structural Family Therapy for Children of Divorce: Case Reports", *Family Process,* Vol. 16, pp. 75–83

Describes structural family therapy techniques for treating families of divorce where the child is presented as symptomatic. The author presents five case reports, each case representative of a different stage in the divorce-single parenthood-remarriage continuum. Also: description of work with remarried families.(SAA)

317. Kemp, H.R., 1982, Preparing for a Creative Marriage: Premarital Preparation with Reconstituted Families, Dissertation Abstracts International, Vol. 43/04-A, page 1189

"This project comes as the combination of two concerns: the need for increased skills of pastors doing premarital preparation and the need for an increased awareness on the part of pastors of the unique problems faced by reconstituted families. (A reconstituted family is here defined as a family in which one or both adults is a stepparent.) To address these concerns this project attempts to do four things: first, to delineate some of the unique problems faced by reconstituted families as the parents enter a new marriage and to offer a conceptual framework for understanding the process through which those families move. Second, to struggle with a theology of marriage which takes seriously the need to struggle with a theology of divorce and remarriage. Third, to design a process of four premarital preparation sessions and a fifth session to take place three to six months after the wedding. And fourth, to use and evaluate the premarital preparation design with couples in a local church. This project offers specific suggestions and a detailed design for doing premarital preparation with those who have been previously divorced or widowed and their spouses who will have children or teenagers living in their home and for those noncustodial parents whose children will visit on a regular or occasional basis. Limited attention is given to the problems of those stepparents whose offspring are mature adults. Specific suggestions are made for enhancing sex life, improving communication skills, and understanding role relationships within marriage. This project is undertaken with a growth perspective that recognizes that the immense problems faced by reconstituted families can be met and overcome because stepfamilies are also huge pools of untapped energy and resources to meet those problems. It is out of this growth perspective that the hope comes that given time and proper encouragement stepfamily members can grow to love one another and reconstituted family living can be mutually fulfilling, joyous, and even fun." (DAI)

318. Kendrick, M.L., 1983, The Relationship Between Kindergarten Children's Classroom Behavior and Family Unit Type, Dissertation Abstracts International, Vol. 44/08-A, page 2353

"The purpose of this study was to investigate the relationship between kindergarten children's classroom behavior and family unit type. Three dimensions of classroom behavior were examined: temperament, socialization, and task-orientation. Family unit types were: nuclear, single-parent, and remarried. The sample consisted of ninety-eight subjects divided, according to family unit types, as follows: nuclear-forty, single parent-thirty-one, and remarried-twenty-seven. There were fifty-three males and forty-five females. Subjects were enrolled in kindergarten classrooms of two public school corporations in Indiana. Null hypotheses were formulated to examine kindergarten children's classroom behavior, temperament, socialization, and task-orientation as functions of family unit type. A multivariate and univariate analysis of variance with statistical control for the sex factor was used to test the null hypotheses. The dependent variables, classroom behavior, temperament, socialization, and task-orientation, were measured by the teacher-rated Classroom Behavior Inventory. Data identifying the independent variable, family unit type, and the control variable, sex, were collected on the Personal Data Form. An examination of the statistical analyses yielded the following results: No significant difference in kindergarten children's classroom behavior was found among children of nuclear, single-parent, and remarried families ($p < .4589$). Due to an insignificant F-ratio on the multivariate analysis of variance, univariate analyses of variance could not be performed. Results of this study indicated that there was no significant difference in classroom behavior among kindergarten children of nuclear, single-parent, and remarried families. Results of the sex variance analyses suggested that sex differences existed relative to task-orientation. Although differences in classroom behavior existed they were not caused by family unit type. Concerns of educators that children of non-nuclear families deem special attention were not supported. Children in single-parent and remarried families evidenced classroom behavior similar to that of nuclear family children.'' (DAI)

319. Kent, M., 1980, ''Remarriage: A Family Systems Perspective'', *Social Casework,* Vol. 61, No. 3

A view on remarriage from a family system perspective is presented. Kent addresses the need for the system to re-establish boundaries and integrate new members to achieve a new equilibrium. Specifically, the processes of assimilation and accommodation are two ways in which the system incorporates new members. Knowledge of the functioning of social systems can create new interventions designed to assist family members in the negotiation process.

320. Keshet, J., 1980, ''From Separation to Stepfamily, A Subsystem Analysis'', *Journal of Family Issues,* Vol. 1, No. 4, pp. 517–532

This paper explores the relationships of subsystems within the stepfamily, i.e. the couple, the ex-spouses, the parent-child subsystems, of child to both biological parents (custodial and non-custodial) and child to stepparent(s). An analysis of these relationships can make conflicts explicit, and can thus reduce strain and redefine some of the boundaries.

321. Kirkland, D.C., 1981, *I Have a Stepfamily: But It's Not the End of the World,* Aid-U Publishing Co., Southfield MI 48075

322. Kleinman, J., Rosenberg, E. & M. Whiteside, 1979, ''Common Developmental Tasks in Forming Reconstituted Families'', *Journal of Marital and Family Therapy,* Vol. 5, No. 2, pp. 79–86
The authors give their conceptualization of the developmental tasks with which stepfamilies are faced, e.g., mourning the loss of the nuclear family, formation of a new marital relationship in spite of previous failure and the children's presence to remind at least one partner of this failure; formation of stepparent-stepchild and stepsibling bonds, etc. A case illustration is given to demonstrate how one family achieved these tasks during their family-treatment process.

323. Kompara, D., 1980, ''Difficulties in the Socialization Process of Stepparenting'', *Family Relations,* Vol. 29, pp.69–73
The paper examines the stepfamily literature and highlights the socialization difficulties present in this adjustment process. Three acute problem areas in the stepfamily adjustment are: disciplining the children, adjusting to the habits and personalities of the children, and gaining the acceptance of the children. Clearing up the ambiguity of cultural norms and legal definitions and changing social policy are necessary to provide socialization specifics and to indicate an acceptance of reconstituted families as a legitimate family form. (Gruber)

324. Kosinski, F., 1983, ''Improving Relationships in Stepfamilies'', *Elementary School Guidance and Counseling,* Vol. 17, No. 3, pp. 200–207
In an effort to help school counselors to better understand stepfamilies' so-called typical stepfamily behavior, as well as the roles and expectations of stepfamily members are discussed. The stepmothers' need to create an ''instant love'' climate, and the stepfathers' attempts to join instantly the mother-child dyad which long predated the remarriage dyad, are cited as well as some efforts to deal with these problems.

325. Kupisch, S.J., 1983, ''Stepping In'', *Annual Meeting of the Southeastern Psychological Association, Atlanta*

''A family in which at least one adult has a child prior to the couple's marriage is termed a stepfamily. Although approximately 50 million Americans are members of stepfamilies, there is little research on the nature of stepfamily life. Most authors have projected the stepfamily as a deviant family form, beset with problems and conflict, and less able to provide the appropriate child-rearing environment. Reports from stepparents reflect perceptions of being religiously unsanctioned, legally powerless, and socially denied. However, the stepfamily may be viewed as part of a natural evolution of family life, a reorganization of disrupted family units to accommodate the emotional needs of existing members. While differing in structure from the nuclear family, stepfamilies need not differ along critical dimensions related to healthy family functioning. The necessary tasks in stabilizing the family unit involve establishing appropriate role models, redefining financial and social obligations, establishing consistent leadership for children across households, making custody and visitation arrangements, dispelling myths, and maintaining emotional bonds.'' (ERIC)

326. Lagoni, L. & A. Cook, 1985, ''Stepfamilies: A Content Analysis of the Popular Literature'', *Family Relations,* Vol. 34, No. 4, pp. 521–525

Content analysis of 30 articles in five major parenting magazines, to determine whether in this time of increasing divorce rate and presumed increasing stepfamily formation, significant changes had occurred in the type, number, and content of articles appearing on stepfamilies. The popular literature examined did not seem to reflect the quantity and content of the professional literature on the subject.

327. Lancaster, J.B., Altman, J. & Rossi, A.J. & L.R. Sherrod, 1987, *Parenting Across the Life Span,* Aldine DeGruyter, New York

This book analyzes and discusses the existing human parental behavior and how this behavior differs from or conforms with parental behavior in the past. It analyzes the variety of family forms and the differences in parenting styles in various forms of families, and portrays the various options available today.

328. LaRoche, S.S., 1973, ''The Role of the Stepfather in the Family'', Dissertation Abstracts International, 34: 2792–93-A. (#73–27,800)

"Differences in the roles of stepfathers and natural fathers were examined. Stepfathers were less involved and more passive within several areas of the family structure." (SAA)

329. Lessing, E., Zagorin, S.W. & D. Nelson, 1970, "WISC Subtest and IQ Score Correlates of Father Absence", *Journal of Genetic Psychology,* December 1970, Vol. 117, No. 2, pp. 181–194

"311 boys and 122 girls were given the WISC as part of their diagnostic evaluation at a child guidance clinic. A history of prolonged father absence (found in 138 subjects) was associated with a lower performance IQ and lower scores on Block Design and Object Assembly, regardless of sex and social class, and with lower scores on Arithmetic for boys only. Working-class, father-absent subjects also earned lower mean Verbal and Full Scale IQ scores. Of the two subgroups of subjects with a history of father absence, only those with no father figure in the home at the time of testing differed from father-present subjects in regard to WISC scores. Those with a stepfather did not differ." (SAA)

330. Lightcap, J., Kurland J., & R. Burgess, 1982, "Child Abuse: A Test of Some Predictions from Evolutionary Theory", *Ethology and Sociobiology,* Vol. 3, pp. 61–66

"In a study which included twenty-four families in which there were forty-one parent-child dyads, results showed that stepparents significantly abuse their stepchildren more often than their own children. Males, whether natural fathers or stepfathers, are significantly more likely to be child abusers than females. A handicapped child is much more likely to be abused than a non-handicapped child. Elder children are abused more often than the youngest child, but elder stepchildren aren't abused more often than natural elder children, necessarily. Although this study confirms the studies of other researchers, they still only represent weak confirmation of the evolutionary model." (Gruber)

331. Lippincott, M.A., 1985, Stepfamily Integration: A Study of Stepfamily Issues and Their Impact on Stepfamily Environment (Remarriage, Blended, Alternate Form, Family) , Dissertation Abstracts International, Vol. 46/08-B, page 2788

"The purpose of this study was to investigate how normal stepfamily environment is influenced by the following independent variables: (a) marital adjustment; (b) stepfamily structure (coded: simple = one stepparent spouse; complex = both spouses stepparents); (c) frequency of ex-spouse contacts during previous six months; (d) age of eldest, dependent child at remarriage onset;

(e) percentage of visitation/custody of stepchild(ren); and (f) length of time in the remarriage. The five dependent variables were Moos and Moos' (1981) Family Environment Scale (FES) subscales of: Cohesion, Expressiveness, Conflict, Organization, and Control. The data collected was analyzed by five separate multiple regressions and some follow-up t-tests. The $p < .05$ level of significance was used. Fifty-three volunteer couples, remarried from one month to 27 years, participated in a structured interview in their homes. The interview included Spanier's (1976) Dyadic Adjustment Scale (DAS), the FES, demographic questions, and open-ended attitude questions. The results are summarized as follows: (1) Stepfamilies exhibit greater cohesiveness when only one spouse is a stepparent (i.e. simple structure) and the couple share a strong marital relationship. (2) Family members are more expressive in their communications when the couple's relationship is strong, only one spouse brings a child(ren) from a former marriage to the remarriage, and the stepfamily is still in the process of integrating. (3) There is less intrafamilial conflict when the remarriage is strong. (4) None of the stepfamily variables predict how family organization fluctuates. (5) There is a stronger reliance on rules or control within stepfamilies who have full custody and who are still involved in the integration process. The children's ages at remarriage onset and the frequency of ex-spouse contacts fail to predict family environment. Interpretations of the findings were made using a family systems perspective and the emergent themes from qualitative questions. The results of this study provided numerous implications for the theory, practice and research of normal stepfamily development.'' (DAI)

332. Lowe, P.T., 1970, *The Cruel Stepmother,* Prentice-Hall, Englewood Cliffs, NJ

''Lowe has written the story of her own remarriage, to a man who brought with him his son from his first marriage. The focus throughout is on describing her personal experiences, feelings and reactions, but includes, in the light of hindsight, suggestions and comments about what might have been handled differently. Unique is her inclusion of material from the children—now grown up—who were also asked to look back and reflect on the family experience.'' (SAA)

333. Lutz, E., 1980, ''Stepfamilies: A Descriptive Study from the Adolescent Perspective'', Dissertation Abstracts International, Vol. 41/01-A, p. 992

''The purpose of this study was to ascertain what adolescents believe to be the stressful and non-stressful aspects of stepfamily living and to determine if these aspects coincide or differ with 11 areas suggested by current literature. The subjects used in this study were 103 male and female adolescents between the ages of 12 and 19 who were members of stepfamilies. Thirty-three questionnaire items were used to obtain the data for the study. The Pearson Product-Moment Correlation yielded a reliability coefficient of .90 between the test and retest. The subjects, who were volunteers, were asked to respond to questions which represented 11 areas suggested as stressful by the current literature. These areas included: (a) discipline, (b) divided loyalty, (c) biological parent elsewhere, (d) member of two households, (e) desire for natural parents to reunite, (f) unrealistic expectations, (g) social attitudes, (h) compounded loss, (i) family constellation, (j) sexual issues, and (k) pseudomutuality. Frequency counts were used to determine the areas which the subjects perceived to be stressful and non-stressful. The results of the study indicated that the issues surrounding the areas of divided loyalty and discipline were perceived to be stressful by more adolescents than any of the other categories. The issues surrounding being a member of two households and social attitudes were perceived to be stressful by the least number of adolescents.

In addition, this study attempted to determine if there were significant relationships between the perceived level of stress reported by adolescents in stepfamilies and demographic factors which include: (a) amount of time spent in the stepfamily milieu, (b) residence of the stepfamily, (c) reason for dissolution of the nuclear family, (d) gender of the stepparent, (e) age of the stepfather, (f) age of the stepmother, (g) presence of stepsiblings, (h) presence of half siblings, (i) kinship of stepchild to stepfather, (j) amount of time spent living with one parent prior to remarriage, and (k) age at which the child became a member of a stepfamily. Point biserial correlations revealed significant relationships between the adolescents' perceived level of stress and: (a) number of years spent in the stepfamily milieu, (b) reason for dissolution of the nuclear family, (c) presence of stepsiblings, and (d) kinship of the stepchild to the stepfather.'' (DAI)

334. Magwood, F., 1986, *Blended Families Handbook: Instructor's Resource Kit,* British Columbia Council for the Family, Parliament Buildings, Victoria, B.C., Canada

''This handbook presents the materials used in successful blended family workshops held in British Columbia since 1980. A resource book for group leaders, it gives practical information on how to establish blended family groups or workshops. Designed as a complete package for 6 weekly 2-hour sessions, the goal has been to create an atmosphere where participants can take significant strides toward making their and each other's family lives rewarding. Contents include: separation, discipline, family boundaries, sexuality, clarifying values, in-laws, out-laws, ex-laws, natural parent, and time as a couple.'' (NCFR)

335. Manning, D.T. & M.D. Wooten, 1987, ''What Stepparents Perceive Schools Should Know About Blended Families'', *Clearing House,* Vol. 60, No. 5, pp. 230–235

''Presents the results of a study that examined the effects of stepfamily life on children and adults and what information stepparents would like given to school personnel about their family life.'' (ERIC)

336. Mayleas, D., 1977, *Rewedded Bliss: Love, Alimony, Incest, Ex-spouses, and Other Domestic Blessings,* Basic Books, New York

''Introduces the concept of the ''Synergistic family,'' the family formed after divorce and with remarriage; and develops the thesis that this family is new and different from the ''monogamous family,'' and needs to be so treated. Hypothesizes that failure in the synergistic family comes because of the mistaken identification with the monogamous family, and the refusal of members to recognize the difference, which then results in confusion, frustration, and even divorce. Much of the book highlights these differences, and presents rules and options for creating a new system that is workable for all members, for instance, in the areas of economics, sexuality, ex-spouses.'' (SAA)

337. McClenahan, C., 1979, ''Stepparenting Made Easier'', *Stepping Forward,* Vol. 2, Step Family Association of America, Towson, Md.

Factors influential in lives of stepfamilies: former spouse, lack of courtship and honeymoon, false myths, unrealistic expectations, unclear role definitions, reactions of children and new stepchildren, finances, grandparents, stepparent/stepchild sexuality. (SAA)

338. McCormick, M., 1974, ''Stepfathers: What the Literature Reveals'', *Western Behavioral Sciences Institute,* La Jolla, CA

''Excellent literature review providing an essay in 60 subject areas, including major concepts, issues and trends, as well as an annotated bibliography of approximately 180 articles and books. Conclusions reached are that homes involving step relationships prove more likely to have stress, ambivalence, and low cohesiveness, and organizational disturbance is inevitable. The single most important factor, aside from the general openness to love, appears to be a straightforward recognition that the man is a stepfather, not a father, and the child is a stepchild, not a child, allowing the child emotional room to feel loyal to his own parents and think well of himself. Also surveys the issue of adoption of children by stepfather." (SAA)

339. McCully, R.B., 1978, "The Laugh of Satan: A Study of a Familial Murderer", *Journal of Personality Assessment,* Vol. 42, No. 1, pp. 81–91

"Teenage murderer who killed his mother, his tiny half-brother, and his stepfather studied through Rorschach, Behn/Rorschach, and Ka/Ro plates. Data used to theorize about clues, dynamics, and diagnosis. Family background and developmental history included." (SAA)

340. McGoldrick, M. & E. Carter, 1980, *The Family Life Cycle: A Framework for Family Therapy,* Gardner Press, New York

Chapter on remarriage offers a comprehensive discussion of remarriage, viewing it as a whole additional phase to the family life cycle. The authors think that this process of forming a remarried family is poorly understood. The implications of remarriage at different stages of the family life cycle are discussed. In general, the wider the discrepancy in family life cycle experiences between the new spouses, the greater the difficulty of transition. The authors support a family-therapy approach to intervention, identifying key presenting triangles in remarried families. They advise putting the biological parent in charge of the management of a child's behavior to maintain the new spouse in a neutral position, thereby easing tensions. Case examples are given with specific interventions and their results. The general goal involves establishing an open system with workable boundaries.

341. McKenzie, C.A., 1986, Perceived Satisfaction in Stepfather-Stepchild Relationships, Dissertation Abstracts International, Vol. 47/04-A, page 1486

"The purpose of this study was to investigate those factors associated with the stepfather's and stepchild's perceived satisfaction with their step-relationship. Some factors included: degree expectations for the relationship were met; natural parent contact;

individual interpersonal style of relating; and pre-stepfamily background variables. The population consisted of all stepfather families in an urban school district in Los Angeles County. A random sample of stepfather families (32 white families and 31 black families) participated in this survey. Data was collected from mothers, stepfathers, and children, with questionnaires and interview schedules conducted in the family's home. Instruments used included: an adaption of the Family Satisfaction Scale (Olson, 1982); the FIRO-B Schultz, 1980; the Index of Marital Satisfaction (Hudson, 1982); and an original 13-item scale to assess the degree to which expectations for the relationship were met. Statistical procedures included: Chi Square, t-tests, Analysis of Variance, Spearman's Correlation Coefficient, Pearson's Product Moment Correlation, and multiple regression.

Results provided support for : (1) many of the theoretical notions of a family systems approach; (2) much of the clinical discussions of tasks and issues confronting stepfamilies; and (3) many of the preventative and remedial strategies employed with this population. Several of the study propositions were moderated by the family's race.'' (DAI)

342. Medler, B.W., et al, 1985, ''Identification and Treatment of Stepfamily Issues for Counselors and Teachers'', *Annual Convention of the American Association for Counseling and Development,* New York

''Although the stepfamily has become a significant family system in the United States, the amount of empirical research on stepfamily living is limited. The definitions of a stepfamily as any family in which at least one adult is a stepparent is a simple one, yet the issues and dynamics involved in stepfamilies are complex. The structures, roles, functions, and boundaries of stepfamilies are more ambiguous and complex than are those of nuclear families. Children grieve over the dissolution of their parents' marriage and go through the grieving stages of denial, anger, guilt/depression, and acceptance/resignation.

Children can be at different stages in this cycle when their parents remarry and their stage can determine their ability to adjust to a remarriage. Seven critical issues which children deal with in relation to remarriage are: (1) dealing with loss; (2) divided in two households; (3) deciding where he/she belongs; (4) membership in two households; (5) unreasonable expectations; (6) fantasies of natural parenting; and (7) guilt over causing the divorce. Much of the stepfamily literature suggests that adolescent stepchildren may experience the greatest difficulty in adjusting to a stepfamily system.

Adolescents, in particular, may experience stress related to discipline, having a biological parent living elsewhere, unrealistic expectations, and divided loyalty. The rapid growth in the number of school-age children living in stepfamilies indicates the need for school counselors to initiate programs to assist stepfamilies. There are a number of ways that therapists can help stepfamilies through education and family therapy. A primary consideration for the therapist working with a stepfamily is where the family and the family members are in regard to developmental issues.'' (ERIC)

343. Meier, M., 1961, ''Is There a Stepfather in the House?'', *Parents,* Vol. 42, August, pp. 70–72

A very early article on stepfathering. The author, a social work educator, concludes that although being a stepfather is not an easy role, it can be a very gratifying one. Covers issues such as jealousy, financial responsibility.

344. Messer, A., 1969, ''The Phaedra Complex'', *Archives of General Psychiatry,* Vol. 21, No. 2, pp. 213–218

A case of a stepdaughter-stepfather attraction is presented. It is discussed that the ''family romance'' is repressed in the biological family unit, but may be reawakened in the non-blood relationship in the stepfamily. This is not considered pathological and preventive measures are suggested, such as ways to strengthen the marital bond away from the child, open affection (especially when previous spouse has died), equal responsibility in disciplining, legal adoption.

345. Messinger, L., ''Remarriage Between Divorced People with Children from Previous Marriages: A Proposal for Preparation for Remarriage'', *Aspen Publications,* Gaithersburg, MD

The remarried family after divorce with children from the partners' previous marriages is identified as a high-risk group for which there are no established societal norms. Specific problems, e.g. role stress, finances, children's parenting, and intra-systems as well as inter-systems communications are mentioned. Interviews with 70 couples suggest that pre-remarriage preparation could reduce the stresses considerably, and even prevent them. Specific course content is suggested. ''(c)APA''

346. Messinger, L., 1984, *Remarriage, A Family Affair,* Plenum Press, New York

A family that comes together in remarriage without taking for granted life-style, without common history, customs and traditions gives rise to stress and discomfort. This is unlike the nuclear family which achieves a daily life-style built on common history with shared experiences, customs, and traditions. Implications for practice, e.g. to understand the remarriage household from various perspectives in order to facilitate discussions and a clearer understanding for stepfamily members. Based on the author's extensive work with stepfamilies.

347. Messinger, L. & J. Hanson, eds., 1982, ''Therapy With Remarriage Families'' , *The Family Therapy Collections,* Rockville, MD
The editors collected a series of chapters from different authors, covering both the conceptual issues (e.g. grief and mourning) dealing with remarried families and a variety of interventive approaches. Loss and mourning, changing relationsips after divorce, joint legal and marital counseling, mediation, the formation of stepfamilies and their tasks, and varied treatment approaches, proactive and active, are part of this excellent collection. The editor's emphasis on the continuum from nuclear family (first marriage) to two single-parent households, to remarriage comes through in the selection of authors' papers.

348. Messinger, L., Walker, K., & S. Freeman, ''Preparation for Remarriage After Divorce: The Use of Group Techniques'', *American Journal of Orthopsychiatry,* Vol. 48, No. 2, pp. 263–272
To develop a basis for a program of remarriage preparation, the authors held four series of weekly group meetings with a total of twenty-two couples, in which at least one partner had children from a previous marriage. The leaders' role was informal and non-directive, discouraging members from moving into a psychotherapeutic mode. The findings suggest there are many commonly discussed concerns among participants which they group under five headings. They found the group experience offered reassurance and support that relieved the sense of personal aloneness and inadequacy in coping with problems.

349. Miller, M. & B. Soper, 1982, ''An Emerging Contingency, the Stepfamily: Review Literature'', *Psychology Reports,* Vol. 50, No. 3, pp. 715–722
An annotated bibliography of research on stepfather, stepmother, stepchild, stepfamily, and implications for counseling.

350. Monahan, T., 1958, ''The Changing Nature and Instability of Remarriages'', *Eugenics Quarterly,* Vol. 5, No. 2, pp. 73–85
Demographic data from the population of Iowa, 1953–1955, on marriage, divorce, and remarriage. In Iowa, the widowed who remarry have marriages which last as long as first marriages. In divorce, the opposite holds. Divorce weakens the strength of the marital bond, and a second divorce experience lessens even more the chances of survival for the marriage. However, the fact that the only consideration is the time span makes it difficult to judge remarriage on this fact alone. ''Sequential polygamy'' is the practice of a substantial minority which is entirely within the law. More extensive research on the subject is suggested.

351. Moore, W., 1976, ''The Wish to Steal a Baby in a 15-Year-Old Girl'', *Psychoanalytic Study of the Child,* Vol. 31, pp. 349–388
Case study of a 15-year-old girl referred for psychoanalysis one month after her father's remarriage. Her mother was dead. Episodes of shoplifting were interpreted as symptoms for the girl's wish to have her stepmother's two-year-old child. The baby as a transitional object, as a way of identifying with her mother and an attempt to cope with oedipal anxiety is discussed.

352. Morgan, A., 1980, The Development of Stepfamilies: An Examination of Change Within the First Two Years, Dissertation Abstracts International, Vol. 41/07-A, page 3282
''The purpose of the present study was to examine selected aspects of the initial process of readjustment in reconstituted families. The process was assessed by measuring family interaction as a function of length of time since remarriage. Aspects of family functioning included were the family environment factors of cohesion, expressiveness, control, organization, conflict and problems: the role of the stepfather in the family including participation in discipline of the children and family decision making; and satisfaction with family functioning. Specifically it was hypothesized that cohesion, expressiveness, and more integrated role of the stepfather and satisfaction with family functioning would be positively related to length of time in the remarriage and that conflict, problems, control and organization would be negatively related to length of time in the remarriage. Fifty-three middle-class, white families participated in the personal interview and completed an extensive questionnaire. The families involved were characterized by a marriage between previously divorced persons (one or both spouses) who had at least one child from a previous marriage residing with them. A cross-sectional compari-

son was done and reconstituted 1–6 months, 7–12 months or 13–14 months. One-way multivariate analysis of covariance, done separately for males and females, was used to compare the three stepfamily groups. Results indicated that satisfaction and unity decreased and conflict and problems increased over time. It was found that females were significantly less satisfied as the length of time in the remarriage increased. The trends were consisently in the opposite direction from the stated hypotheses. In addition to the hypotheses tested, correlates of satisfaction were examined for their implications for program development.'' (DAI)

353. Morris, L.J., 1985, A Comparison of Marital Satisfaction and Stepfamily Integration in Stepmother and Stepfather Remarriages, Dissertation Abstracts International, Vol. 46/05-B, page 1695

''*The Problem.* This study was designed to compare the spousal relationship between stepmother families and stepfather families by using certain theories from current literature to address the three variables of perception of personal integration in the stepfamily system, and perception of family functioning. It was hypothesized that differences would be found between stepfathers and stepmothers and between biological parents and stepparents in these perceptions.

Method. The Marital Satisfaction Inventory (Synder, 1981) was used to measure the spousal relationship, and a questionnaire was composed by the writer to address the theories, since no standardized instrument exists at the present time that asks questions about remarried families.

Results. Stepmothers were found to be in significantly more distress in the relationship and in the family system than stepfathers. Where spouses are both biological parents and stepparents, the amount of their distress placed them between the other two groups. That is, stepmothers perceived themselves to have lower personal satisfaction in the remarriage relationship, lower personal integration in the family system, and perception of lower family function, and stepfathers were the least distressed members of the stepfamily groups in the study. Results of the study suggest that the attitude about stepfamilies which each spouse brings to the founding of the stepfamily may be a factor that influences the quality of the family's integration.'' (DAI)

354. Morrison, K., et al, *Stepmothers: Exploring the Myth,* Canadian Council on Social Development, Ottawa, Ontario, Canada

Drawn from more than two decades of personal and professional experience, this book is a practical guide for stepmothers. Exploring the common "pitfalls" of this role and the relationships it creates, it is useful for all members of the stepfamily and those who work with them.

355. Mynatt, E.S., 1984, *Remarriage Reality: What You Can Learn From It,* Elm Publications, P.O. Box 23192, Knoxville, TN 37933
"While mechanics remain the same for any marriage, there are definitely factors and complications which are unique to remarried couples. This book combines the basics that are essential to the strength of any marital or love relationship with the specific areas relevant to blended families, primarily children and ex-spouses. The material and examples in this book were drawn from interviews and questionnaire discussions, written and verbal, on remarried couples throughout the United States, and from interviews with behavioral professionals, including psychologists, psychiatrists, family counselors, and ministers. The opinions are based on the perceptions of people who have "been there." The book is written, not from expertise, but from the experiences of real-life remarrieds. The material in this book is arranged in such a manner that it can be used for reference on a particular topic without loss of continuity. Contents include: before you marry, success in remarriage, problems in remarriage, strengthening your marriage, sex the second time around, merging the families, creating family unity, discipline, affection and sexuality in the home, building a step relationship, visitation, conflict, emotions, financial realities, dealing with the past, social interactions, special considerations, and therapy." (NCFR)

356. Nadler, J.H., 1983, "Effecting Change in Stepfamilies: A Psychodynamic/Behavioral Group Approach", *American Journal of Psychotherapy,* Vol. 37, No. 1, pp. 100–112
"A psychodynamic-behavioral workshop helps stepparents and their partners cope with the intra-psychic stress and interpersonal problems that result from the formation of a new family unit. The program consists of six sessions, each of which runs for an hour and a half. Each session focuses on a separate problem experienced by stepparents. The first session focuses on the commonality of problems in stepfamilies; the second, on roles and conflicting loyalties; the third, on communication skills; the fourth, on problems concerning stepchildren; the fifth, on difficulties in marital interaction; and the sixth, on problems related to visitation and the ex-spouse. Case material is presented that illustrates patterns of interaction in stepfamilies and techniques for intervening effectively in a remarriage." (SWAB)

357. Noble, J. & W. Noble, 1977, *How to Live with Other People's Children,* Hawthorne Books, New York

"The Nobles themselves remarried and in a stepparenting situation, have written a popular book filled with guidance, advice, suggestions, and opinions from experts on 'how to live with other people's children.' Clients have found it extremcly helpful to read in preparation for remarriage, particularly from the parenting perspective and for the understanding they gain about the reactions of the children to their new situation." (SAA)

358. Nolan, J., Coleman, M., & L. Ganong, 1984, "The Presentation of Stepfamilies in Marriage and Family Textbooks", *Family Relations,* Vol. 33, No. 4, pp. 559–566

The authors reviewed 26 textbooks for introductory courses on Marriage and Family. They give detailed descriptions both of the method they used to examine the books and how they were chosen. They also describe the various sub-categories of problems of stepfamilies as they are included or omitted in the books which were reviewed. They are critical of the very cursory treatment which this subject is given and their criticism is well substantiated. The information about stepfamilies could be categorized as to factors relating to successful functioning, sources of stress, and recommendations. These researchers are concerned that most of the material presented in the books are based on clinical observations (in the authors' opinion therefore based on a problem orientation) or on self help models. A subtle application of a deficit model to stepfamilies is pointed out. Though not too much research exists, the authors feel that this does not completely exonerate the editors and writers of the books reviewed. It seems clear that stepfamilies have been a "relatively neglected family style by family researchers and educators."

359. Oakland, T., 1984, *Divorced Fathers. Reconstructing a Quality Life,* Human Sciences Press, Inc., New York

An informative book written for fathers experiencing divorce-related difficulties. The contents covered all aspects of the problems and issues that fathers must face in divorce ranging from basic legal issues to managing a new household. The book provides valuable information to allow fathers to anticipate what lies ahead and to help them establish their goals and objectives for proper planning.

360. Osborne, J., 1983, "Stepfamilies: The Restructuring Process"

"Intended primarily for professionals, this booklet describes a process of psychological restructuring through which, sometimes with help, members of stepfamilies may assimilate the reality of their new situation. Sections of the discussion focus on phases in the restructuring process: fantasy; pretending; panic; and the emergence of a new family reality involving conflict, re-working, and moving on. Characteristics of the fantasy phase are the 'good' and 'bad' fantasies about the new partnership and the new family. In the pretending phase, stepfamily members pretend to be the collection of fantasies they bring to the new family. Essentially, the panic phase arrives when one or more people in the family begin to recognize their unique, individual view of the family and of other family members and, consequently, start to feel like an outsider. The conflict phase is the time in which the couple and/or family as a whole confront highly charged differences in values, traditions, histories, standards, styles, perceptions, and skills. During the re-working phase conflicts are perceived in new and different ways and members begin to create relationships. Now, moving on, stepfamily members are better able to appreciate and explore the differences within their new family, differences which often become assets. Experience suggests that movement through the process takes at least four years.'' (ERIC)

361. Oshman, H.P. & M. Manosevitz, 1976, ''Father Absence: Effects of Stepfathers upon Psychosocial Development in Males'', *Developmental Psychology,* Vol. 12, No. 5, pp. 479–480

Stepfather's importance in mitigating the typically deleterious effects of father absence; effect of early father absence persists into late adolescence.

362. Papernow, P.L., 1984, ''The Stepfamily Cycle: An Experiential Model of Stepfamily Development'', *Family Relations,* Vol. 33, pp. 355–363

The author uses Gestalt and Family Systems theories to develop seven stages of stepfamily development. In-depth interviews with stepfamilies were analyzed in a previous paper by this author (1980). Now the author developed a diagram of the stepfamily cycle (on the basis of the Gestalt Experience Cycle). Due to her observations of stepfamilies through the cycle the author recommends a combination of individual and family therapy interventions, depending on the particular stage of stepfamily development. An easier experiential and cognitive recognition on the part of stepfamily members is expected to aid both the therapeutic and the life process. This stepfamily life-cycle is also perceived as a very good educational tool for work with stepfamilies.

363. Pardeck, J.T. & J.A. Pardeck, 1987, ''Using Bibliotherapy to Help Children Cope With the Changing Family'', *Social Work in Education,* Vol. 9, No. 2, pp. 107–116

''School social workers can use bibliotherapy to help children face such family-life transitions as divorce, single-parent families, and blended, or remarried, family systems. By providing books dealing with such problems, the worker can help children gain greater insight into their problems, focus attention outside themselves, realize that they are not alone in having a particular problem, and share their problems with others. Among the guidelines that social workers should use in determining when to draw on bibliotherapy are these: (1) Bibliotherapy should be used as an adjunct to other forms of counseling; (2) the chronological age and reading level of the child, as well as any handicaps he or she may have, should be considered in selecting books, and (3) bibliotherapy is most effective for children with average or above-average reading abilities. Because bibliotherapy cannot be used with all children, in all settings, or for all purposes, school social workers must use good judgment in its application. Books about problems commonly associated with families in transition are suggested.'' (SWAB)

364. Paris, E., 1984, *Stepfamilies: Making Them Work,* Avon Books, New York

A stepfamily member herself, this well-known Canadian writer concentrates in this very readable book on the pitfalls and rewards of stepfamily living, based on over 100 interviews. She empathizes and makes suggestions. The chapters on the ''Voices of Children'' and ''Accepting Realities: A Portrait of an Integrated Stepfamily'' are noteworthy.

365. Parish, T.S. & T.F. Copeland, 1979, ''Relationship Between Self-Concepts and Evaluations of Parents and Stepfathers'', *Journal of Psychology,* Vol. 101, No. 1, pp. 135–138

''Students from families in which the fathers were absent have self-concepts related to how they evaluated their mothers and stepfathers but not their natural fathers.'' (SAA)

366. Pasley, K & M. Ihinger-Tallman, 1987, *Remarriage and Stepparenting: Current Research and Theory,* Guilford Press, New York

On the cutting edge of the field, this book offers new conceptual frameworks that bridge clinical and theoretical research. The editors address the strengths and weaknesses of existing research;

for example, its tendency to be either theoretical or overcommitted to one particular model. The research of 15 scholars on the effects of remarriage and stepparenting on children and families is collected here. Their major contribution is in their outstanding, innovative efforts to include and encourage a synthesis of clinical, empirical, and research literature, and to identify duplications and gaps, thus pointing the way toward more integrated practice and research. The book is well organized, with sections on social and cultural contexts, conceptual and theoretical issues, the experience of stepfamily living, and prospects for future development. The authors, experts in sophisticated subspecializations, should be familiar to practitioners and theoreticians alike.

367. Perkins, T.F. & J. Kahan, 1979, ''An Empirical Comparison of Natural-Father and Stepfather Family Systems'', *Family Process,* Vol. 18, No. 2, pp. 175–183

''Studied 40 family triads of mother-child-(age 12–15)-father (or stepfather). Stepfather family systems different from natural father systems along several dimensions: psychological adjustment, satisfaction with family, reciprocal understanding, perceived goodness and power, which affect the entire stepparent family system and its ability to function adequately.'' (SAA)

368. Perlmutter, L.H., 1982, Coming of Age in Remarried Families: The Bar Mitzvah , *Journal of Jewish Communal Service,* Vol. 59, No. 1, pp. 58–65

''The Remarried Consultation Service, a division of the Jewish Board of Family and Children's Services, was formed in 1976 to provide counseling, therapy, referral for special services when necessary, and an educational program for remarried couples and their children, for those contemplating remarriage, and for couples living together, one or both of whom are divorced. While treating families for their presenting problems, therapists frequently are called on to deal with particular crises that erupt around times of transition for individual members of the families. Often these transition stages are marked by religious rituals, such as circumcision of a boy at birth, bar or bat mitzvah at the preadolescent stage, the exchange of marital vows of adult couples, or the observance of shiva, the week of mourning after a death. At these times, one may see the emergence of divided loyalties, barely repressed enmities, jealousies, and competition. Some of the dynamics seen in work with families with a boy preparing for his bar mitzvah are explored.'' (SWAB)

369. Perlmutter, L.H., Engel, T., & C.J. Sager, 1982, "The Incest Taboo: Loosened Sexual Boundaries in Remarried Families", *Journal of Sex and Marital Therapy,* Vol. 8, No. 2, pp. 83–96

Sexual abuse is studied in some stepfamilies where the child's presenting problems were depression, suicidal gestures, adolescent rebelliousness, and poor school adjustment. Dynamics of the family as well as each family member's individual dynamics are explored and treatment is discussed. The child's freedom to admit to the act of abuse is perceived as a function of the therapist's comfort in hearing it, his/her ability to deal with anger, and with control issues. Case histories illustrate various forms of sexual abuse and their treatment.

370. Peterson, J.L., 1982, The Relationship of Family Structure to the Psychological Adjustment of Children, Dissertation Abstracts International, Vol.43/07-A, page 2290

"This study investigated children's psychological adjustment as a function of differing family structures. Respondents from the seven year follow-up of the Vermont Child Development Project who indicated remarried, separated, or divorced under 'marital status' were asked to participate, and compared to a group of intact families drawn from the same population. Forty-eight children between the ages of eight and thirteen were asked to complete the Kovacs Child Depression Inventory, the Nowicki-Strickland Locus of Control Scale for Children, and the Piers-Harris Children's Self Concept Scale. All parents were asked to complete the Achenbach Child Behavior Checklist. Remarried and intact parents were also asked to complete the Locke-Wallace Scale of Marital Adjustment. Major findings were that (1) children from separated and divorced families were more depressed and had a lower self-concept than children from remarried and intact families, (2) those children from remarried families appeared to be functioning as well or better than the intact family children on these measures and (3) parents were not found to view their children differently on a symptom checklist across groups. Differences between child self-report and parental reports of child behavior are discussed. The results support a relationship between family structure and psychological functioning in children. Specifically, those children with two parents were better adjusted than those children with one parent irrespective of the biological relationship of the parents to the child. Implications for broader and more longitudinal research are suggested, as well as modifying the model for examining the family to include more systemic indices." (DAI)

371. Pink, J.E. & K.S. Wampler, 1985, ''Problem Areas in Stepfamilies: Cohesion, Adaptability, and the Stepfather-Adolescent Relationship'', *Family Relations,* Vol. 34, No. 3, pp. 327–335

Twenty-eight stepfamilies were compared with twenty-eight nuclear families with reference to family functioning and the (step)father-adolescent relationship. Mother, (step)father, and adolescent ratings were obtained. Quality of the mother-adolescent relationship and marital satisfaction did not differ by family type, but, as anticipated, all ratings revealed lower family cohesion and adaptability, and less quality in the male parent-adolescent relationship in stepfamilies. Length of remarriage, amount and quality of contact with the absent biological father and adolescent gender were not related to stepfamily functioning. However, contrary to expectation, a high amount of contact with the biological father was more positive than either a moderate or low amount, in terms of the regard of the stepfather toward the adolescent. Some of the implications include the authors' suggestions for deliberate nurturing and bonding activities at the beginning of the step-relationship, and any activities aiming at ''unconditionality.'' Attempts to fashion stepfamilies in the mold of nuclear families are felt to be misdirected. Counselors and educators should be helped to recognize and direct their clients in the direction of the issue of greater distancing (perhaps especially between stepfathers and stepdaughters) to provide functionality.

372. Pittman, E., 1983, Remarriage: Expectations, Problems, and Strengths of the Stepfamily, Dissertation Abstracts International, Vol. 44/05-A, page 1595

''This study deals with issues which confront the blended family and identifies expectations, problems, and strengths of these families. The study investigated stepfamilies as to (1) clarification and formulation of expectations, (2) most difficult problems, (3) coping strategies, and (4) strengths or successes. Two research instruments were used, the Remarriage Questionnaire and the Family Life Questionnaire (FLQ). Of the 50 remarried persons who participated in the study, 23 were Black (46%) and 27 were White (54%). Of the sample, 12 (24%) were Black females and 14 (28%) were White females. The group ranged in age from 27–60 years. The mean age for Blacks was 40.4 years and for Whites 34.8 years. The Pearson correlation was used to test questions. T-tests and Chi-square were used to test hypotheses. Significance for all analysis was set at the .05 level.

The results of the test of the hypotheses and the findings related to the research questions are summarized as follows: (1) Do Not

Let Children Divide and Conquer was ranked highest as a strength considered most important for stepparents. Closely ranked were the strengths of Patience and Understanding. (2) The expectations that influenced most repondents to remarry were Love and Companionship. The expectation To Provide a Second Parent was ranked least important. (3) Love was the only one of six expectations significantly related to marital happiness ($r=.344$, $p < .05$). (4) Characteristics of happy remarriages are: higher income ($r=.301$, $p < .05$), knowledge gained from the previous marriage ($r=.301$, $p < .05$), lack of conflict over children from a former marriage ($r=.463$, $p < .01$) and handling of discipline by both partners ($r=.498$, $p < .001$). (5) More Black subjects than White subjects reported regular attendance at church (chi square= 4.43, $p < .05$), and fewer Blacks than Whites reported that they had received marital counseling (chi square=5.24, $p < .05$). More Black stepparents than White stepparents feel as close to their stepchildren as to their biological children (chi square=10.24, $p < .01$), and experience less conflict because of them (chi square=3.88, $p < .05$). More Black stepparents than White stepparents reported that ''one of us'' rather than ''both of us'' handles discipline most of the time (chi square=6.33, $p < .05$). Blacks rated two of six strengths as less important than Whites: Mutual Understanding with Spouse Concerning Discipline and Child Rearing ($t=-2.12$, $p < .05$) and Discuss Problems with Spouse ($t=-2.52$, $p < .05$). . . (Author's abstract exceeds maximum length. Discontinued here with permission of author.)UMI'' (DAI)

373. Podolosky, E., 1955, ''The Emotional Problems of the Stepchild'', *Mental Hygiene,* Vol. 39, January

An early exploration of the position of the stepchild in the stepfamily. The author points out the importance of the age at which a child acquires a stepparent and observes that the older the child, the more difficult the adjustment. Issues of jealousy and the child's feelings of insecurity are also explained.

374. Pouryaghma, M., 1983, A Study of Family Member's Perceptions of Adaptability and Cohesion as Related to Selected Variables in Reconstituted Families, Dissertation Abstracts International, Vol. 44/08-A, page 2363

''The purpose of this study was to determine whether there were relationships between the Family Adaptability and Cohesion Evaluation Scales (FACES) and selected variables for marital partners and acquired children in reconstituted families. Subjects were from white Protestant reconstituted families from the greater

Tuscaloosa, Alabama, area. A 55.5% (61 families) sample of those contacted participated in the study. Demographic data and FACES scores for family adaptability and cohesion were obtained for all subjects. Data were treated by using Pearson product moment r, analysis of variance, and t tests to study relationships between the FACES scales and selected demographic variables. Results indicated that family system balance was perceived as less stable by spouses who were middle-aged and older, who have custody of children from a previous marriage, who are dependent on an ex-spouse for child support, who have themselves been married three or more times or have married a partner who has been married more than twice, and who lived near their ex-spouses. In this study, cohesion or emotional bonding within the reconstituted family was positively related to two variables: (a) spouses being relatively younger and (b) there being no requirement for payment of child support. Children within these reconstituted families viewed their families as being more adaptable if they were younger (preadolescence), but as more cohesive if they were older. The correlation of the two FACES scales was significantly positive, but weak, for both the adult and children groups. Apparently, the two scales share some common loading indicating that families who perceive themselves as being adaptable are likely, also, to be cohesive. However, the correlation was quite small in both groups, allowing the variables of adaptability and cohesion to be treated as essentially independent measures of family adjustment.'' (DAI)

375. Price-Papillo, T.J., 1985, The Visited Stepfamily: A Preliminary Enquiry (Remarriage, Stepchildren, Noncustodial Father, Stepmother), Dissertation Abstracts International, Vol. 46/09-B, page 3229

''In-depth interviews with eleven visited stepfamily couples, noncustodial fathers and their new partners, support the conclusions that the noncustodial father and his new partner can maintain an active, positive place in his child's life and that the difficulties inherent within the visiting structure can be resolved or need not be unmanageable. Exploration of issues identified in the literature as common to all stepfamilies suggest that the structure of the visited stepfamily may have an important impact on the way its members experience these issues. Stepmothers all had positive, although not necessarily problem-free, relationships with their stepchildren. Most discipline issues were handled by the father and daily child care responsibilities were recognized as belonging to the biological mother. Unresolved issues between father and biological mother did not impact on regularity of visiting. Visiting patterns varied widely, from weekly to irregularly, and were described as flexible, depending on work schedules of father, stepmother and biological mother, as well as on the child's school and social needs. Older children tended to visit less frequently than younger children.'' (DAI)

376. Prosen, S. & J. Farmer, 1982, ''Understanding Stepfamilies: Issues and Implications for Counselors'', *Personnel and Guidance Journal,* Vol. 60, No. 7, pp. 393–397

It is postulated that counselors can be helpful in two major dimensions: they can provide direct help to children and their families during difficult transition periods. They can also alert school personnel to the major issues and provide suggestions. Some of the basic differences between nuclear and stepfamilies are reviewed as well as their effects on and manifestations in children's behavior. Suggestions are made for counseling strategies deemed appropriate for this population.

377. Radomisli, M., 1981, ''Stereotypes, Stepmothers, and Splitting'', *American Journal of Psychoanalysis,* Vol. 41, No. 2, pp. 121–127

The author discusses the age-old ''wicked stepmother'' myth, which has influenced children throughout generations, based on the interpretation of the psychoanalytic concept of ''splitting,'' in the examination of fairytales, i.e. the division in the child's feelings about ''good mother'' and ''bad mother.'' While this can serve as a normal outlet for the child's aggressions during the growth process, the author discusses how the concept can lead to continuous negative interaction between stepchild and stepmother, especially since the stereotype is exacerbated by community sentiment.

378. Rallings, E.M., 1976, ''The Special Role of the Stepfather'', Family Coordinator, Vol. 25, No. 4, pp. 445–449

''Extent of Stepfathering in U.S. examined; historical perspective provided. Challenges view of naive male who enters complex web of social relationships with resultant role strain. Children reared in stepfather families not significantly different from those reared by natural fathers. Conceptual model presented for viewing stepfather experience.'' (SAA)

379. Rallings, E.M., 1976, ''The Special Role of the Stepfather'', *Family Coordinator,* Vol. 25, No. 4, pp. 445–449

The author discusses the problems of being a stepfather in the United States, estimates its prevalence, and notes difficulties in defining the role. Contemporary research is reviewed, with the author's stance of a historical perspective. Role analysis is suggested as a model for understanding stepfathering, and directions for future research are offered.

380. Ransom, F., Schlesinger, S. & A. Derdeyn, 1979, ''A Stepfamily in Formation'', *American Journal of Orthopsychiatry,* Vol. 49, No. 1, pp. 36–43

The article advises mental health professionals that they must develop skills for helping two families, the heads of which have remarried, form a new, viable family unit. Stages in the development of the stepfamily are conceptualized. Case material of one family is used to show one child, who is a scapegoat as the focus of conflict in the stepfamily's progression through these stages. ''(c)APA''

381. Reed, B., 1980, *Stepfamilies—Living in Christian Harmony,* Concordia, St. Louis

''Based on interviews with stepfamilies, counselors, pastors, lawyers, educators; includes author's personal experiences, and discussion questions, case histories, enrichment exercises and a 'where to go from here' appendix that lists organizations and addresses.'' (SAA)

382. Reingold, C., 1976, *Remarriage,* Harper & Row, New York

This book, whose author is a happily remarried woman, goes beyond facts and figures directly to people. It is primarily a collection of first-person stories: people talking about spouses and ex-spouses, children and stepchildren, money, lawyers, friends, relatives, and themselves. A psychiatrist and a lawyer, who specialize in matrimonial cases, comment throughout. The book does not attempt to offer advice or answer questions, and clearly shows that no two remarriages are alike. It does, however, recognize and encourage new life-styles, new relationships, and the basic need to seek emotional fulfillment. (DHHS)

383. Reingold, C.B., 1977, *How to Be Happy if You Marry Again: All About Children, Money, Sex, Lawyers, Ex-Husbands, Ex-Wives, and Past Memories,* New York: Harper and Row, Perennial Library

''The author, who married a divorced man with two children after her first husband died, discusses mostly happy second marriages, her own and those of other people she has interviewed. The book encompasses the problems of dealing with stepchildren and natural parents.'' (SAA)

384. Rice, F.P., 1979, *Stepparenting,* Condor Publishing Co., Carol Stream, IL

''Offers a practical guide for those who are stepparents or considering becoming stepparents. The book includes sections on sibling relationships and teen-age stepchildren.'' (SAA)

385. Roberts, T.W. & S. Price, 1986, ''A Systems Analysis of the Remarriage Process: Implications for the Clinician'', *Journal of Divorce,* Vol. 9, No. 2, pp. 1–25

The authors use family systems analysis to examine the transactions described in the literature on the processes of remarriage. Four subsystems are identified: the primary family, the personal, the interpersonal, and the secondary family subsystems. Functional remarried families develop interactional patterns, which confirm family cohesion, appropriate role functioning, and goal consensus, and the clinician is advised to assess each of the subsystems along these dimensions.

386. Roberts, T.W. & S.J. Price, 1987, ''Instant Families: Divorced Mothers Marry Never-Married Men'', *Journal of Divorce,* Vol. 11, No. 1, pp. 71–92

''Interviewed 16 couples involved in marriages between never-married men and divorced women with at least one pre-adolescent child. Findings showed adjustment to remarriage involved the issues of dependence, independence, and interdependence. Findings are presented in 15 propositions which can be utilized as basic hypotheses for future research on these families.'' (ERIC)

387. Roosevelt, R. & J. Lofas, 1976, *Living in Step,* Stein and Day, New York

''Popular style book of 10 chapters, written by Stepfamily Foundation of New York City. Unique in that it explores and uncovers the mythical expectations of all involved in stepfamily relationships, including those parents without custody. It is supported with numerous quotations from experts, whose contributions are acknowledged. The chapter readings are helpful as far as content goes, but have no references and no index. Helpful and reassuring to stepfamilies to read and has been useful and supportive for many in the remarried family situation; has value for the professional.'' (SAA)

388. Rosenbaum, J. & V. Rosenbaum, 1977, *Stepparenting,* Chandler and Sharp Publishers, Inc., Corte Madera, CA

A book by professionals with advice and guidelines for stepparents.

389. Rosenberg, E. & F. Hajal, 1985, ''Stepsibling Relationships in Remarried Families'', *Social Casework,* Vol. 66, No. 5, pp. 287–292

The authors indicate their belief that clinicians nowadays are cognizant of the social tasks for the stepfamily. However, the role definitions still lack clarity and the relationships of stepsiblings heads the list of missing information. Characteristics of these relationships are described, e.g. the common experiences of loss, loyalty issues, changes in family size, personal roles and functions, differential life-cycle needs and tasks. Implications for the children and adults are discussed. The potential for both harmony and disharmony is there and can be affected by clinicians who are better prepared in their understanding of the special differences. Acceptance of and encouragement to live more comfortably with differences and unclear role definitions can go a long way in working toward eventual mastery of the experience.

390. Rosenthal, K.M. & H.F. Keshet, 1978, ''The Not Quite Stepmother'', *Psychology Today,* Vol. 12, No. 2, p. 82

''The nature of the relationship between divorced men with children and the women with whom they are intimate. Tracks the process of ''refamilying.'' 127 divorced fathers had frequent contact with their children and felt torn between spending free time with children and with new partners. Often chose the children. Most did not discuss their sex lives directly with the children. Initially the women did not assume parenting responsibilities or make decisions about children; they were father's helpers. Many fathers kept distance between partner and children, but as emotional closeness developed, they involved women in decisions.'' (SAA)

391. Ross, P.T., 1977, ''The Little Girl, the Family Therapist, and the Fairy Tale, a True Fable'', *Family Therapy,* Vol. 4, No. 2, pp. 143–150

''Case history of successful family therapy in fairy tale form. Prior to intervention, mother was unable to control her children's behavior and stepfather unable to control his temper, frequently beating the two young children violently. Both parents were unfamiliar with the function of therapist prior to first meeting.'' (SAA)

392. Rypma, C.B., 1984, Parent and Teacher Rated Post-Divorce Adjustment of Children Across Four Age Groups From Intact, Single-Parent, and Remarried Families, Dissertation Abstracts International, Vol. 46/06-B, page 2077

"The current study represents an extension of previous research conducted by two research groups (Hetherington, Cox, and Cox, 1976, 1978, 1979; Wallerstain and Kelly, 1975, 1976, 1977) on the impact of divorce on children's adjustment. The study seeks to answer whether remarriage ameliorates or exacerbates post-divorce adjustment of children when compared to groups of children from single-parent or intact families.

Five school districts in the Mid-West were sampled for volunteers by sending permission letters home with school children in grades one through eight. Criteria for inclusion in the study were that single parents be biological mothers divorced at least three years; remarried families were also required to have been remarried at least three years with the biological mother as the custodial parent. The final sample used for analysis consisted of 192 children representing equal number of males and females in one of four age groups (seven and eight year olds, nine and ten year olds, eleven and twelve year olds, and thirteen and fourteen year olds) across the three family types.

Adjustment of children was assessed by parents and teachers using the Louisville Behavior Checklist and the School Behavior Checklist. Teachers also completed the A-M-L Behavior Rating form. A total of fourteen adjustment dimensions were analyzed in a correlational analysis. Overall, children from remarried families were reported to be less adjusted than children from intact families. In addition, differences across sex indicated that males were less adjusted than females, and children who were younger at the time of divorce were better adjusted in remarried families on certain dimensions. Few differences were found between adjustment scores of children from single-parent homes when compared with children from intact or remarried homes and child adjustment did not appear to be affected by reported marital happiness. Furthermore, degree of access by non-custodial family members did not affect child adjustment and access was not affected by the age of the child or reported marital happiness. It is suggested that as a family moves from an intact status to a single-parent status, and finally, to a remarried family status, deterioration in adjustment occurs. (Abstract shortened with permission of author.)" (DAI)

393. Sadler, J.D., 1983, "Stepfamilies, An Annotated Bibliography", *Journal of Applied Family and Child Studies,* Vol. 32, No. 1, pp. 149–152

An annotated bibliography of twenty-one general and three books for juveniles as well as a listing of a variety of sociological studies, research, and guidebooks. Some aspects of step-relations are illustrated, e.g. visitation, shared custody, adoption of stepchildren, stepsibling relationships.

394. Saffady, W., 1973, "The Effects of Childhood Bereavement and Parental Remarriage in Sixteenth-Century England: The Case of Thomas More", *History of Childhood Quarterly,* Vol. 1, No. 2, pp. 310–336

"Fascinating study of the effects on Thomas More of the death of his mother and the subsequent remarriages of his father. More's emotional reactions are analyzed as to (1) pathological reactions to early object loss that persisted in later life; (2) developmental consequences of early object loss; (3) the impact of changes in the family structure produced by his father's remarriages. The effects of parental loss and remarriage on 16th-century children generally are discussed and it is concluded that however prevalent death may have been 16th-century children were no more successful in escaping its effects than children of today." (SAA)

395. Sager, C.J., Brown, H.S., Crohn, H., Engel, T., Rodstein, E. & L. Walker, 1983, *Treating the Remarried Family,* Brunner/Mazel Publishers, New York

Both theory and various treatment modalities of working with remarried families are presented, based on the study of a clinical population of the Remarried Consultation Service of the Jewish Board of Family and Children's Services of New York City. The book's format includes sections on Structure and Theory, on the basic tenets of treatment for remarried families, individuals in remarried families and other significant subsystems. Appendices provide extremely useful guidelines and sample information sheets for schools.

396. Sager, C.J., et al, 1980, "Remarriage Revisited", *Family and Child Mental Health Journal,* Vol. 6, No. 1, pp. 19–33

The strong point is made that the stepfamily, also termed remarried, reconstituted, or blended (abbreviated "Rem") is quite different from the biological or nuclear family unit. The various differences are outlined. Clinical and research studies of remarried families are described and reviewed. The review is divided into children of divorce and the experience of parental loss; the remarried couple; and stepparents and stepchildren, as three distinct target groups.

397. Santrock, J.W., Warshak, R., Lindbergh, C. & L. Meadows, 1982, ''Children's and Parents' Observed Social Behavior in Stepfather Families'', *Child Development,* Vol. 53, No. 2, pp. 472–480

Six- to eleven-year-old children, half boys and half girls, were matched on socioeconomic family status, and family size. Twelve were from father-present nuclear families, twelve from single-parent mothers who were divorced and remarried, and twelve from single-parent divorced mothers who had not remarried. Observations of parent-child interactions revealed that boys in stepfather families showed more competent behavior than those in nuclear families, while girls in those families were more anxious in stepfamilies. Boys showed more warmth toward their stepfather than girls, while girls showed more anger toward their biological mothers. In the comparison of subjects in divorced and remarried families, the boys from stepfather families showed more mature behavior than boys in single-parent families. It is suggested that parenting behaviors, sex of the child, and marital conflict are very important in any family structure to explain children's behaviors.

398. Sardanis-Zimmerman, I., 1977, The Stepmother: Mythology and Self-Perception, California School of Professional Psychology, Dissertation Abstracts International, 77–27618

''Self-perceptions of stepmothers in relation to stepchildren and possible family difficulties; step-mothers' self-concepts compared with those of natural mothers—33 stepmothers and 35 natural mothers. Results: stepmothers more self-confident than natural mothers but do not feel comfortable in stepmother role. Do not feel as close to stepchildren as natural mothers, not as sure of themselves in disciplining stepchildren. Stepmothers appeared affected by mythological views of wicked stepmothers; mothers had similar feelings but had to repress negative feelings because of cultural expectations.'' (SAA)

399. Satterfield, R.K., 1984, The Relationship of Process in Remarried Families to Marital Satisfaction, Family Satisfaction, and Stepparent-Adolescent Communication, Dissertation Abstracts International, Vol. 46/02-A, page 383

''Most previous research on remarried families has focused upon sociodemographic factors and their role in remarital success or failure. Family process has been largely ignored in evaluating remarried families. This investigation examined family process, as indicated by verbal communication behaviors, and its relationship to satisfaction or dissatisfaction for the biological parent, stepparent, and adolescent stepchild.

Twenty-four remarried families were given an interaction task of planning a two-week family vacation together. Their discussion was audiotaped. Using transcripts of these audiotapes, communication behaviors were coded according to twelve categories, which represented the general factors of attachment and separation. Self-report measures were administered to family members to evaluate marital satisfaction, family satisfaction, and parent-adolescent communication. It was hypothesized that families in which the natural parent demonstrated more attachment behaviors toward his or her biological child than toward the spouse would be least satisfactory for all members. Analysis of variance was used to compute the data for the main hypotheses. Analysis of the data did not confirm the hypotheses. Pearson product-moment correlations were performed on the individual communication behaviors to determine their relationships with the three self-report measures. Various individual communication behaviors were shown to be related to family and marital satisfaction for each of the family members.'' (DAI)

400. Schlesinger, B., 1983, ''Remarriage: A Review and Annotated Bibliography'', Chicago: *Council of Planning Librarians*

Many aspects of remarriage and its difficulties are covered in this annotated bibliography. Over 70% of the articles covered from 1961 to 1982, and over 60% of the books covered from 1953 to 1982 were published since 1976.

401. Schlesinger, B. & A. MacRae, 1971, ''The Widow and Widower and Remarriage. Selected Findings'', *Omega,* Vol. 2, pp. 10–18

The authors relate to a previous annotated bibliography by Schlesinger, and to literature on widows and widowers in 1968 and 1970 respectively. This is one of very few writings on remarriage related to widowed persons. 96 couples in Toronto were interviewed in 1968, each by two interviewers. Both males and females had been married an average of five years at the time of the study. The average time lapse was seven years for women, three years for men; ages at remarriage—45 for men, and 37 for women. 57 children were brought into the marriages and 32 mutual children were born after the remarriage. Areas of adjustment considered were the social relationship, personal relationships, sexual adjustment, parent-child relationships, and adjustment problems. The adjustment of children was considered as a separate area. Various responses which were indicative of successful adjustment were described, e.g. compatibility, motivation, a sense of humor. Differences were noted in persons not previously married, both males and females. Advice related to remarriage showed two predominant themes: Don't compare the first spouse with the second, and don't rush into remarriage.

402. Schulman, G.L., 1972, "Myths That Intrude on the Adaption of the Stepfamily", *Social Casework,* Vol. 53, pp. 131–139

This paper is based on clinical experience. It focuses on the unique problems of the stepfamily, particularly the recurring myths and fantasies, of which stepfamilies are often victims. The author thinks that therapists, too, deny the child's special identity by acting as if the child had always lived in this stepfamily. She advocates family therapy both prior to and following remarriage.

403. Schulman, G.L., 1981, "Divorce, Single Parenthood and Stepfamilies: Structural Implications of These Transactions", *International Journal of Family Therapy,* Vol. 3, No. 2, pp. 87–112

The author takes a structural family systems perspective to discuss the family life-cycle stages in the periods of divorce, single-parent family, and stages of the remarried family. Special structural differences of these families are discussed, as well as tasks which make it possible for the new family to function and get through a transitional stage. Three case examples illustrate the conceptual content. The exit of one parent and/or the addition of one parent are perceived as crisis points, at which family therapy is seen as particularly helpful. Awareness of the necessity to include all parts of the family system, both biological and stepfamily members, is emphasized.

404. Schultheis, M., 1981, "Perception of Self Enhanced Through Bibliotherapy", *Journal of the Association for the Study of Perception,* Vol. 13, No. 1, pp. 5–7

"Bibliotherapy is the treatment of childhood emotional problems through the reading and discussion of relevant children's books. A case is presented of a boy who lost interest in school as a result of his mother's divorce and remarriage." (SAA)

405. Sheehy, P.T., 1981, Family Enrichment for Stepfamilies: An Empirical Study, Dissertation Abstracts International, Vol. 42/05-A, page 2317

"The purpose of this study was to develop a home-based, workbook format family enrichment program for stepfamilies, and to compare the effectiveness of this program in an empirical study to the results of a multiple family therapy group for stepfamilies and a no-treatment control group. The following hypotheses were derived for purposes of this research: (1) At post-test, families in both experimental groups will have higher levels of cohesion and lower levels of interpersonal conflict than families in the no-treatment control group. (2) At post-test, families in the home-based group will have higher levels of cohesion and lower interpersonal conflict than families in the multiple family therapy group. (3) At post-test, families in the home-based group will perceive themselves to be closer to one another and to fight less frequently than either the multiple family therapy or the control families. (4) At post-test, parents in the home-based group will perceive themselves to have discussed their views on child discipline and to feel they know their spouses' views to a greater extent than parents in either the multiple family therapy or the control group. Subjects for this study consisted of 64 individuals representing 16 families from two geographic regions of Indiana. To be eligible for participation in the study, there had to be at least one stepparent and one stepchild over the age of four living in the home. The 16 families were then assigned to one of the three groups in this study. All families were pre- and post-tested approximately six weeks apart. All family members over the age of four completed four sociometric questions and two Likert-type questions concerning the amount of interpersonal conflict in the family and their perception of the degree of 'closeness' in the family. In addition to the above instruments, parents were asked to complete the 'Family Environment Scale' (Moos, 1973), and one additional Likert-type question assessing the degree to which they have discussed and have knowledge of one another's views on child discipline. None of the hypotheses was supported by the data analyzed in this study." (DAI)

406. Simon, A.W., 1964, *The Stepchild in the Family: A View of Children in Remarriage,* Odyssey Press, New York

A professional journalist's review and personal experience of the problems of stepchildren. A comprehensive book on the problems of bereavement and divorce, especially as they affect children. It is considered a classic.

407. Sirulnick, C.A., 1980, Primacy of the Couple and Stepfamily Integration: A Case Study Approach, Dissertation Abstracts International, Vol. 41/12-B, page 4690

"This investigation was an exploratory case study examining how four remarried couples reorganized their stepfamilies into integrated units. Past research indicated that confused roles and conflicting kinship systems can impede the development of a sense of cohesion in blended families. The literature suggests that a resilient and strong couple bond can be instrumental in creating a solid foundation for stepfamily's growth, stability, and integration. The present research utilized a case study approach in order to explore the remarried couple's relationship, with special emphasis on reviewing the assimilation of the stepparent into a co-parental role with the biological parent. Structured, open-ended interviews were used to gather information from four sets of Caucasian remarried adults. Children from two of the four stepfamilies were also interviewed. The four stepfamilies varied along certain structural dimensions. The findings revealed that regardless of social class, the number of years married, the number of children and the ages of the children and adults, all family units had similiar concerns in regard to their adjustment and reorganization process. Also although these four families were not currently seeking clinical intervention, they presented problems similar to those clinic families discussed in previous research. Inferences were made that stepfamilies seem to have unique areas of concern that are characteristic to their structure. This research demonstrated that a solid marital relationship contributed to a stepfamily's stability, helped a stepparent enact a parenting role and insured the continuity of a stepfamily's existence. In addition, it was seen that clearly defined roles between parenting adults as well as the development of a strong co-parental alliance enhanced a stepfamily's functioning.

Other aspects emerged as significant. It was found that even when the couple bond was secure and there were clear role definitions, additional elements had a major impact on the development of a sense of integration in a blended family. The primary discriminating finding was that the extent of involvement and degree of flexiblity between the children's two households had a profound effect on stepfamily members. This study emphasizes that if a remarried couple maintain positive ongoing ties with the absent biological parents, the children and ultimately the family benefit. By creating a flexible boundary around their step-family, a couple can contain and preserve their relationship and the stepfamily's sense of cohesion while permitting an easy back and forth flow between the children's separate households. It was found that continued contact between ex-spouses helped family members confront their identity as a stepfamily, thus allowing for a realistic assessment of their situation.

An additional factor that emerged from this study was that children born out of the remarriage seemed to enhance the current marital relationship. On the basis of this research, implications for future research ranged from understanding the role of the absent biological parent, to examining what happens to grandparents when their children divorce and remarry, and to investigating the effects of having chidren in a second marriage. Also further investigations are needed to look at joint custody arrangements and to explore stepfamily situations in non-Caucasian groups. Implications for clinicians were also discussed, and it was suggested that the mental health profession also learn about the unique characteristics in order to better understand the dynamics that stepfamily members are struggling with. This study stressed that stepfamilies need to be considered satisfactory and potentially growth-producing alternative family constellations.'' (DAI)

408. Sitterle, K.A., 1984, The Peer Relations of Children in Stepmother, Stepfather, and Intact Families, Dissertation Abstracts International, Vol. 45/04-B, page 1297

``The effects of remarriage on the child's social competence in peer relations were studied by comparing 26 children whose biological mothers remarried (stepfather families) with 18 children whose biological fathers remarried (stepmother families) and 25 children living with both biological parents (intact families). Approximately half the children were boys and half were girls, aged 7–11 years. Families were matched on SES and the stepparent families had lived together for an average of three years. Only children in which divorce was the reason for dissolution of the parents' marriage were included. A multimethod approach for studying children's social competence with peers was used. The data consisted of videotaped observations of child's interactions with unfamiliar peers in laboratory play groups. Parents and stepparents reported their perceptions; also the children rated their feelings of their social competence with peers. Videotapes were coded using a behavior frequency coding system and also rating scales assessing affect and global social competence categories.

The behavioral observations of the children revealed two patterns of results. First, children in stepmother families, particularly the girls, showed more disruptions in their peer interactions compared to children in stepfather and intact families. Stepmother children of both sexes displayed more aversive, inappropriate, and immature behavior than children in either stepfather or intact families. Additionally, the stepmother girls were viewed as more unhappy, labile, and negative types of emotion were more frequent. In contrast, the stepfather children were found to be as socially competent with peers as children living in intact homes. The second theme indicated that children living with the same-sex remarried parent showed more competent peer relations than children in stepfamilies living with the opposite-sex remarried parent.

No differences between groups were found on the questionnaires completed by parents, stepparents, or the children. Explanation of these findings focused on the consistency of the results with those found in the divorce and stepfather family literature. The importance of the mother as a primary attachment figure and the role of the stepparent as a primary attachment figure and the role of the stepparents as models and identification figures for boys and girls were discussed.'' (DAI)

409. Skeen, P., Covi, R.B. & B.E. Robinson, 1985, ''Stepfamilies: A Review of the Literature with Suggestions for Practitioners'', *Journal of Counseling and Development,* Vol. 64, pp. 121–125

The authors review some of the stepfamily literature around such headings as ''What do we know about stepfamilies?''; ''Primary family versus stepfamily''; ''Special problems associated with stepfamilies.'' In conclusion, they dwell on some of the problems which the differences from nuclear family living may bring and wind up with some specific recommendations aimed at normalizing the situation by open communication.

410. Skyles, A., 1983, Selected Variables Affecting Stepparent Perception of Dyadic Adjustment in Remarriage, Dissertation Abstracts International, Vol. 44/09-A, page 2890

''As divorce and remarriage rates increase, American family life is changing rapidly. It has been predicted that remarriage may come to outnumber first marriages as the predominant form of American family life. Not surprisingly, a concomitant increase in the stepfamily statistics is also occurring. Stepfamily literature suggests that the remarriage dyad is the critical family subsystem reponsible for achievement of stepfamily formation tasks, integration of all family members and family continuance.

The study focused on the relationship between the inclusion of the stepparent in the stepfamily system and the stepparent's perception of dyadic adjustment of the remarriage couple. Data from the second phase of the Binuclear Family Research Project, a five-year longitudinal investigation of divorced family relationships were analyzed in this dissertation. Fifty-four stepmothers and thirty-seven stepfathers, located through their partners, were interviewed in the first to third year of their marriage. Four indicators measured inclusion of the stepparent: (1) shared parenting of the stepchildren with the biological parent partner; (2) discussions between the stepparent and the current partner about the partner's former spouse; (3) acknowledgement of the stepparent by the partner's former spouse; and (4) stepparent participation with the biological parents in family activities. Secondary independent variables used in the study included: (1) residence of the stepchild with the stepparent; (2) adult stepfamily composition; (3) sex of the stepparent; and (4) stepparent feelings toward the current partner's former spouse. The dependent variable, stepparent perception of dyadic adjustment, was measured by Spanier's Dyadic Adjustment Scale. Statistical analysis showed three significant findings. Stepfathers reported higher dyadic adjustment than stepmothers ($p < .05$); high parenting stepmothers reported greater dyadic adjustment than low parenting stepmothers ($p < .05$) , and high frequency of discussion about the partner's former spouse was related to high dyadic adjustment for stepmothers and low dyadic adjustment for stepfathers ($p < .01$)." (DAI)

411. Smith, W.C., 1953, *The Stepchild,* University of Chicago Press, Chicago

"Historical study of the stepchild based on available literature and materials in case records of several agencies. Discusses the background of step-relationship in folklore, drama, fiction, and other centuries; the roles of the stepfather and stepmother; and the stepchild and his adjustment. Historical interest." (E & N)

412. Spann, O. & N. Spann, 1977, *Your Child? I Thought It Was My Child,* Ward Ritchie Press, Pasadena, CA

A humorous account of the experiences of the authors in joining two families.

413. Starks, K.J., 1982, A Descriptive Study of Ten Self-Defined Successful Stepfamilies, Dissertation Abstracts International, Vol. 43/12-A, page 4058

"Little research has been done with stepfamilies and virtually none with successful stepfamilies. The purpose of this study was to explore the successful stepfamily's experiences of remarriage and formation of a new family unit, discovering basic principles and identifying issues for further research. The intent was to focus on the perceptions of the stepfamily members, using a phenomenological approach in which open-ended interviewing is a strategy. The interviews were conducted with ten volunteer families who identified themselves as successful and who have been together for a minimum of two years. These families live in or near a small university community located in mid-Michigan. They are white, in the middle income bracket and all have graduated from high school and the majority have been university educated. All of the volunteer families are "stepfather" families except one in which both parents brought children to the new marriage. Descriptions of each family are given and the interviews are analyzed for common themes in the attempt to uncover structures inherent in the creation of a successful stepfamily. The basic structures that emerged from the sharing of these families are: (1) There is a lack of animosity between the stepfamily and the absent biological parent(s). (2) There are positive relationships between stepparent and stepchild(ren). (3) Most stepparents of adolescents chose to support the system of discipline established before the stepparents entered the family. (4) Conflict was anticipated. When it arose the families indicated that they tried to recognize and deal with it openly. (5) Couples expressed a communication. (6) The couples with adolescent children identified the success of the marital relationship as the measure of the stepfamily's success." (DAI)

414. Stein, P., 1984, Adolescent Drug Abuse as a Function of Family Structure and Family Environment, Dissertation Abstracts International, Vol. 45/03-B, page 1000

"*The Problem.* This study investigated the occurrence of adolescent drug abuse in families according to family structure and family environment. Research indicates that adolescent drug abuse is becoming increasingly prevalent and that single-parent families as well as stepparent families are growing in numbers. The purpose of investigating differences found in families of adolescent drug abusers was to discover factors which influence its occurrence. This study addressed the major dimensions of family environment and family structure that may have contributed to differences in families in which adolescent drug abuse occurred most often and least often.

Method. The research approach utilized was a comparative correlational study analyzed in an ex post facto manner. The sample population consisted of 90 families of adolescent drug abusers. Families were divided into three categories: intact nuclear families, single-parent families, and step-parent families. Each familial category was represented by 30 families. Subjects were given the Moos Family Environment Scale and a self-report questionnaire. Drug usage by family structure hypotheses were subjected to a chi-square analysis. Family environment by family structure hypotheses were subject to an analysis of variance.

Results. Results indicated that adolescent drug abusers used drugs more frequently in stepparent families than in single-parent families and intact nuclear families with significance at the .05 level. Adolescent drug abusers used drugs more often in single-parent families than in intact nuclear families with significance at the .05 level. Differences did not exist at the .05 level in relationship dimensions among family types. Personal growth dimension results indicated that intact nuclear families and single-parent families scored higher than stepparent families at the .05 level, but no significant differences were found between intact nuclear families and single-parent families. System maintenance dimension results indicated that intact nuclear families scored higher than single-parent families and step-parent families at the .05 level, but no significant differences were found between single-parent families and step-parent families.'' (DAI)

415. Steinberg, L., 1987, ''Single Parents, Stepparents, and the Susceptibility of Adolescents to Antisocial Peer Pressure'', *Child Development,* Vol. 58, No. 1, pp. 269–275

''Compared with respect to their susceptibility to peer pressure to engage in deviant activity were fifth-, sixth-, eighth-, and ninth-graders from intact, single-parent, and stepparent families. Youngsters living with both natural parents were less susceptible to pressure than those living in other family environments.'' (ERIC)

416. Stepfamilies/Divorce, *Catalogue of Stepfamilies/Divorce* Published Annually, Stepfamily Assn, of America, Inc. 215 Centennial Mall S. Ste 212, Lincoln, NE 68508

417. Stern, P., 1978, ''Stepfather Families: Integration Around Child Discipline'', *Issues in Mental Health Nursing,* Vol. 1, pp. 49–56

Whether integration into the family occurs smoothly or roughly, there is almost invariably a period of 1.5 to 2 years before things calm down.

418. Stern, P., 1982, ''Conflicting Family Culture: An Impediment to Integration in Stepfather Families'', *Journal of Psychological Nursing,* Vol. 20, pp. 27–33

419. Stern, P.N., 1982, ''Affiliating In Stepfather Families: Teachable Strategies Leading to Stepfather-Child Friendship'', *Western Journal of Nursing Research,* Vol. 4, No. 1, pp. 75–89

This study was done with 30 stepfather families in the San Francisco Bay area in 1975/76. Affiliation was a theoretical construct consisting of 10 steps to determine the process involved in family integration. The author describes the process after a brief review of some stepfamily literature. The findings indicate that the discovery of the affiliating strategies is important, since they confirm that companionable pieces which precede disciplinary activities of stepfathers are much more successful. A 1 1/2 to 2-year time table shows the dimensions of affiliating/non-affiliating activities. It is definitely felt that these strategies are very helpful and it is further felt that these strategies can in the future be taught to other men taking on the surrogate role of resident father figure. Classes and group meetings are suggested, to be led by nurses in primary care and public health settings. A study for stepmother families following the same pattern is suggested.

420. Strother, J. & E. Jacobs, 1984, ''Adolescent Stress As It Relates to Stepfamily Living: Implications for School Counselors'', *School Counselor,* Vol. 32, No. 2, pp. 97–103

This paper reports on a study of 28 male and 35 female high school students, aged 13–18, who completed a 41-item questionnaire designed to perceive stress in 12 areas of stepfamily life. The detailed responses are reported. It seems that the findings disprove at least in some tentative way some of the existing assumptions. Although the stress level in some areas is somewhat higher than in others, the results seem to indicate that the overall stress level of the adolescent participants related to stepfamily issues was not high, but rather seemed to relate to more typical adolescent stresses than to some generated by stepfamily living. Implications for counselors include strong suggestions not to stereotype children living in stepfamilies as problem children per se, but also to offer counseling and advice to families, particularly in the areas of discipline, and informational sessions relating to and promoting family accord as to visiting non-custodial parents and relatives.

421. Thies, J. , 1977, ''Beyond Divorce: The Impact of Remarriage on Children'', *Journal of Clinical Child Psychology,* Vol. 6, pp. 59–61

The author describes some of the difficulties which parental remarriage presents for the children of the resident parent. Her contention is twofold: first, the remarriage usually occurs before the children have had an opportunity to integrate the divorce and resolve the grief over one departing parent; secondly, seemingly even of greater importance, is the institutional lag in our society which permits adults the serial monogamous marriages, but does not extend the privilege of choosing whom to love to the children. Children in our society are groomed to love only their own family of origin, thus the remarriage puts them into a terrible conflict. Institutional reform is recommended.

422. Thomson, H., 1966, *The Successful Stepparent,* Harper & Row, New York

This book is written from a social work perspective and gives case examples. It is a practical guide for stepparents, written in clear popular style. It offers suggestions for handling situations such as: introduction of new parent to child, typical childhood problems to be expected, dealing with visitation of the biological parent, expressing feelings, discipline, jealousy, adoption, and custody. (DHHS)

423. Touliatos, J. & B. Lindholm, 1980, ''Teachers' Perceptions of Behavior Problems in Children from Intact, Single-Parent, and Stepfamilies'', *Psychology in the Schools,* Vol. 17, pp. 264–269

''Teachers gave background information and rated behavior problems of 3644 white children from kindergarten through 8th grade. 2991 children lived with both biological parents, 312 with mother only, 43 with father only, 34 with father and stepmother, 264 with mother and stepfather. Compared with children in nuclear families, those living with mother only had more problems in all of the categories listed, those with father only showed more socialized delinquency; children living with mother and stepfather had more conduct problems and socialized delinquency; those with father and stepmother showed more conduct problems. Sex, social class, and grade in school were found to have some bearing on the findings reported.'' (c) APA

424. Touliatos, J. & B.W. Lindholm, 1977, ''Development of a Scale-Measuring Potential for Foster Parenthood'', *Psychological Reports,* Vol. 40, No. 3, Pt. 2, p. 1190

472 foster families served by 236 caseworkers in 91 agencies were studied during 1975/76 in the U.S. and Canada. A 54-item measure of potential for foster parenthood was developed. This might prove to be of value for custody, adoptive studies, and pre-marriage evaluation of parenting potential. ''(c)APA''

425. Touliatos, J. & B.W. Lindholm, 1981, ''Measurement of Potential for Foster Parenthood,'' *Journal of Psychology* Vol 109(2) pp. 256–263

The same universe is used as in the previous article (1977). This time the authors describe the construction of the scale and summarize evaluations by caseworkers of prospective foster parents. Finally, 54 items are consolidated into 9 factors, e.g. health, employment, opportunities for cultural and intellectual development, flexibility to work with biological parents and/or agency. ''(c) APA''

426. Troon, W., 1980, ''An Examination of Natural Father-Stepfather Responsibility for Parenting'', *Florida Academy of Sciences 44th annual meeting*

427. Tybring, J.B., 1973, ''Remarriage: Parenting Someone Else's Children'', *Forum,* 2: Vol. 27, pp. 19–20

Article examines psychological and interpersonal aspects of remarriage and stepparenthood. Gives summaries of some research findings in Bernard's 1956 study. Discusses the unrealistic expectations of people in a remarriage, ex-spouses, adolescents, and the problems of stepmothers. Recommends that stepparents and parents can help their children by: (1) tolerating not being loved for awhile; (2) acknowledging the place of the biological ex-partner; (3) sharing activities; and (4) being patient.

428. U.S. Bureau of the Census, 1973, ''Remarriages: United States'', Maryland: *National Center for Health Statistics*

''Analysis of national trends in remarriage including data by previous marital status and color variation by state, remarriage rates by age and sex, selection by previous marital status, and selected characteristics of remarrying persons in 1969.'' (SAA)

429. U.S. Bureau of the Census, 1977, ''Marriage, Divorce, Widowhood and Remarriage: 1967'', *Current Population Report,* Series P-20, No. 312. Washington: U.S. Government Printing Office

430. Visher, E. & J. Visher, 1979, *Stepfamilies: A Guide to Working With Stepparents and Stepchildren,* Brunner/Mazel, New York

Although this book is written primarily for clinicians, it is useful to any others involved in advising stepfamilies, and may be helpful to stepparents. Included is an examination of the cultural and structural characteristics of stepfamilies, and the available research literature. Stepparent roles are described as well as the ''recoupling'' process and the role of children in stepfamilies. Therapeutic techniques are described throughout. (DHHS)

431. Visher, E.B. & J.S. Visher, 1978, ''Common Problems of Stepparents and their Spouses'', *American Journal of Orthopsychiatry,* Vol. 48, No. 2, pp. 252–262

The authors address the fact that a half-million adults who annually become stepparents in this country have little guidance available either from mental health professionals or the public. Four common myths that impede family functioning are identified and described. Poorly defined roles, particularly for the stepfather, identified as issues that create conflicts over money, discipline, and guilt feelings. Case examples are used to illustrate. Support groups are recommended. (SAA)

432. Visher, E.B. & J.S. Visher, 1990. *Stepfamilies: Myths and Realities,* Paperback edition of 1979 edition, Citadel Press, Secaucus, NC

A guide primarily for the professional, this book has a non-technical style suitable for self-help reference. Separate chapters are directed to particular family members: mothers/stepmothers, stepchildren, children in stepfamilies, fathers/stepfathers, and others. Includes an overview, a set of guidelines for stepfamilies, references for stepfamilies, and general references for families. (SAA)

433. Visher, E.B. & J.S. Visher, 1978, ''Major Areas of Difficulty for Stepparent Couples'', *American Journal of Family Therapy,* Vol. 6, No. 2, pp. 70–80

Children are one of three major problem areas on which these authors report. Financial difficulties and miscommunication leading to marital misunderstanding are the other two.

434. Visher, E.B. & J.S. Visher, 1982, ''Stepfamilies in the 1980's'', *Conciliation Courts Review,* Vol. 20, No. 1, pp. 15–23

The authors explain that because of complex structural characteristics and normal psychological differences from nuclear families, along with the fact that there is little if any defined legal bond between stepparents and stepchildren, stepfamilies frequently require legal and/or psychological help. It is contended that societal acceptance of the stepfamily as viable and one of many valuable family structures would turn the same characteristics which now create challenges into positives and rewards. Dealing with losses and transitions can lead to lifelong better coping capacity, and the knowledge that family relationships take hard work can lead to better bonding and conscious effort in the future. The adults' deep emotional bonding gives children good role models for their future couple relationships.

435. Visher, E.B. & J.S. Visher, 1988, ''Old Loyalties, New Ties: Therapeutic Strategies With Stepfamilies'', Brunner/Mazel, Inc., New York

''These well-known specialists in working with remarried families show how the therapist's knowledge and skills can help validate stepfamilies as positive and viable units with unique structures that are not imperfect copies of nuclear families but, rather, complex family systems created from the integration of old loyalties and new ties. The volume opens with an overview of American stepfamilies in the 1980's and a review of basic theoretical concepts most helpful to therapists, counselors and stepfamily adults. The authors also outline special therapeutic strategies in working with stepfamilies and factors in assessing whom to see in stepfamily therapy. The rest of the book presents ways in which therapists can help in major areas of difficulty with chapters on change and loss, unrealistic beliefs, insiders/ outsiders, life cycle discrepancies, loyalty conflicts, boundary problems, power issues, and closeness and distance.'' (NCFR)

436. Visher, E.B. & J.S. Visher, 1982, *How to Win As a Stepfamily,* Dembner Books, New York

The authors, who were pioneers in the treatment of stepfamilies and the co-founders of the Stepfamily Association of America, wrote this very useful guide to stepfamily living. They offer advice as to preparation for stepfamily living, on managing and coping with the various pitfalls which arise in the process of two families living together, and they suggest understanding and guidelines particularly for children, grandparents, and legal issues.

437. Visher, E.B. & J.S. Visher, *Workshop Manual,* Stepfamily Association of America, Baltimore, MD

This manual, prepared by the co-founders of SAA, is used at their two-day workshop for professionals.

438. Visher, E.B. & J.S. Visher, 1980, *Stepfamily Workshop Manual,* Palo Alto, CA

The authors, who have been pioneering in the field of stepfamilies, wrote this manual quite early in their efforts at self-help movements and family-life education for stepfamilies. It is a "how to" manual for professionals who offer workshops to stepfamilies. Beginning with information about the stepfamily life cycle and dynamics, they go on to describe common issues, e.g. custody and visitation, consider issues in children's groups, and end with therapeutic strategies and suggestions. References for stepparents, children, and some guidelines are appended.

439. Visher, E.B. & J.S. Visher, 1987/88, "Guidelines for Nurturing Children After Divorce and Remarriage", *Nurturing Today,* p. 9, 14, 17, 20

The authors, who have written much on stepfamilies and whose books and articles on stepfamilies have concerns for children permeating their writings, have focused entirely on children in this article. They stress the importance of continuity for the children and give as examples heart-rending quotes of children where this has not happened. Civil relationships between the biological parents after the divorce and following remarriage of one or both is emphasized. Specific recommendations are included: how former partners could separate marital issues, e.g. support problems and other items which cause ill feelings, and handle visitation and the children's relationships to the non-resident parent separately. The authors' major emphasis is that losses can be turned into gains.

440. Vosler, N.R., 1985, Children in Intact, One-Parent, and Blended Families: Psychological Consequences of Family Structure (Stepparent, Single-Parent Families, Competence), Dissertation Abstracts International, Vol. 46/07-A, page 2077

"Increasing numbers of children in 'non-traditional' one-parent and blended (stepparent) families have resulted in concern over positive, negative, or mixed consequences for children living in such families. A review of the family structure (intact vs. one-parent vs. blended families) literature found that almost two-thirds (nineteen) of thirty studies showed at least some negative differences on a variety of child outcomes for children in one-parent or blended, in comparison with intact, families; the remaining eleven studies found no differences by family structure. Based on findings from nine additional studies that demonstrated that one or more intrafamily contingency variable(s) mediated the relationship between family structure and child outcome, the present study examined both the bivariate relationship between family structure and child outcome, and the same relationship when family competence (measured by the Beavers-Timberlawn Family Evaluation Scale) was controlled. The sample consisted of 136 families who participated in a Department of Corrections family-therapy research project in two urban Virginia locations. Pretest (cross-sectional survey) data were analyzed using regression procedures. Results concerning children's self-esteem showed that children from one-parent families had significantly lower self-esteem than children from two-parent (intact and blended) families, even after family competence, and family income, were controlled. However, the effect was not strong (R('2)= .04); and family competence was a better predictor of self-esteem than family structure. Family structure was not a significant predictor of children's locus of control or communication with parents. Implications of findings for social work practice and for social science knowledge-building are presented and discussed.'' (DAI)

441. Wald, E., 1981, *The Remarried Family: Challenge and Promise,* Family Service Association of America, New York

The book is written from a social work perspective. The author examines the remarried family in relation to the dynamic interactions of person (family)-problem-situation. She provides a framework that serves as a guide for understanding remarried families, their problems and contexts so that a more accurate assessment of this particular family system can be made and thus more individualized interventions can occur. The book offers particularly important chapters on historical and legal contexts.

442. Waldron, J.A. & R. Whittington, 1979, ''The Stepparent/ Stepfamily'', *Journal of Operational Psychiatry,* Vol. 10, No. 1, pp. 47–59

''The factors influencing the stepparent/stepchild relationship and implications for the treatment of the family as a unit are examined. Points: stepparents as a newcomer, social and legal problems of stepparent, existing family's reaction to new parent, feelings of self-doubt, insecurity and inferiority in the stepparent.'' (SAA)

443. Walker, K.W., Rogers, J. & L. Messinger, 1977, "Remarriage After Divorce: A Review", *Social Casework,* Vol. 58, pp. 276–285

This article reviews literature and research on remarriages and identifies the need for research, especially demographic characteristics of remarriages; consequences for children living in stepfamilies; and the rate of remarriages compared to first marriages. Additional questions concern studies to test hypotheses concerning stress in remarriage and case studies of families who successfully adapted to remarriage. Guidelines for therapeutic interventions are also suggested.

444. Walker, L., Brown, H., Crohn, H., Rodstein, E., Zeisel, E. & C.J. Sager , 1979, "An Annotated Bibliography of the Remarried, the Living Together, and Their Children", *Family Process,* Vol. 18, pp. 193–212

An early collection of annotations by the staff of the Jewish Board of Family and Children's Services of New York City, divided into six sections: Demography, Remarried Couples, Stepparents and Stepchildren, Divorce as a Precursor to Remarriage, Children of Divorce in Relation to Remarriage, and Remarriage—Prophylactic and Therapeutic Aspects.

445. Weingarten, H.B., 1987, "Marital Status and Well-Being: A National Study Comparing First-Married, Currently Divorced, and Remarried Adults", *Journal of Marriage and the Family,* Vol. 47, No. 3, pp. 653–662

"A national survey sought to extend knowledge of how particular types of marriages or the loss of the marital role through divorce affect personal well-being. The data set used allowed subsamples of three marital-status groups (first married, remarried, and currently divorced) to be compared across a wide range of indicators of psychological adjustment in order to assess feelings of well-being, self-perceptions, and symptoms of distress. Findings revealed that the enduring impact of divorce on well-being focused on those dimensions of adjustment that involved evaluations of positive affect and strain rather than on evaluations involving assessments of personal adequacy. Regardless of whether people remarry, the divorced respondents differed from the never-divorced first marrieds on adjustment indicators of lifetime experience of stress. In addition, divorced respondents were considerably less exuberant about life than either their first-married or their remarried counterparts. Nevertheless, the current well-being of formerly divorced remarried subjects and the self-esteem and self-confidence of divorced respondents argued against the validity of theories that posit that marital disruption is a product of generalizable and nonreversible pathology among those who divorce.'' (SWAB)

446. Westhoff, L.A., 1975, *The Second Time Around : Remarriage in America,* Viking Press, New York

This book is a journalistic study of remarriage, the material drawn from interviews with a non-clinical population in varying stages of marriage, divorce, and remarriage. There is also a chapter devoted to quotes from children in remarriage families. The author recommends less complicated divorces and more education in preparation for marriage. Most remarriages are better than the first and people find the happiness that first marriages lack. It is also felt that first marriage is a preparation for a better second one.

447. White, L.K. & A. Booth, 1985, ''The Quality and Stability of Remarriages: The Role of Stepchildren'', *American Sociological Review,* Vol. 50, October, pp. 689–698

In an examination of a probability sample of 1673 married individuals interviewed in 1980 and again in 1983, the research attempts to separate the variables affecting a remarriage, such as the fact that one or both partners are remarried, and especially the effects of the presence or absence of stepchildren, in order to determine the compatibility of second marriages. Findings support the perception that the presence of children, while not affecting the quality of the marriage, do affect the quality of family life and the quality of parent-child relationships. Another divorce, especially in the more than once remarried, and a moving out of teenagers are perceived as major strategies to cope with family stress.

448. Whiteside, M.F. , 1983, ''Families of Remarriage: The Weaving of Many Life Cycle Threads'', *Family Therapy Collections,* Vol. 7, pp. 100–119

Sager's and Visher's definitions are used to discuss some of the vicissitudes of remarriage. The process from the resolution of the first marriage through the single-parent households to remarriage, with the wedding itself, are discussed in terms of their special problems, the need for preparation, and the importance of the timing of the remarriage.

449. Williams, M.B., 1984, ''Family Dissolution: An Issue for the Schools'', *Children Today,* Vol. 13, No. 4, pp. 24,25,27–29

The author explicates some of the findings in young children of separation and divorce to emphasize the importance of early intervention in order to deal with the identity confusion in young children. Group programs under the auspices of the school are recommended on the basis of the author's own experience, who with a student as a co-leader, conducted 40-minute group meetings with several small groups (4–6) of kindergarten children who live in single-parent families. Sessions with the children, joint sessions with the separated parents on parent-child issues are described, as is some work with a stepparent. It is felt that mediation efforts in the school can be of considerable help to both children and parents.

450. Wilson, K., Zurcher, L., McAdams, D. & R. Curtis, 1975, "Stepfathers and Stepchildren: An Exploratory Analysis From Two National Surveys", *Journal of Marriage and the Family,* Vol. 37, pp. 526–536

Stereotypes as well as differing opinions in the research studies of social scientists led to this inquiry. The authors did a secondary analysis of two existing research studies. 68 social psychological characteristics were examined. On 58 of them, stepfathers and biological fathers did not differ with statistical significance. 10 of the variables did not emerge as differentiating them with statistical significance. Demographic and religious characteristics, education, and income were some of the characteristics examined. The authors' conclusions, while quite tentative, tend to support their original expectation that their analysis would strongly support the null hypothesis, since only a few of the variables were found to differentiate between stepfathers and biological fathers. Their conclusions are much more tentative, with some indication of questions to be included in future research, but assertive in attempting to dispel popular stereotypes existing in social intervention organizations, that stepfather families a priori are less well functioning families.

451. Wolf, P.A. & E. Mast, 1987, "Counseling Issues in Adoptions by Stepparents", *Social Work,* Vol. 32, No. 1, pp. 69–74

"Although the number of nonrelative adoptions is decreasing, stepparent adoptions are not. These adoptions are viewed as non-problematic family business separate from the general adoption picture. This article examines demographic data in Lancaster County, Pennsylvania, from 55 stepparent adoptions concerning stepparent adopters, birth parents, and adoptees and the stated reasons for adopting." (ERIC)

452. Wolf, P.L. III, 1988, Remarried Families: Adaptability and Cohesion, Dissertation Abstracts International, Vol. 48/12-A, p. 3200

"The purpose of this research was to study the relationship between family structure and family adaptability and family cohesion. Varying with the research hypothesis, the units of attention included 35 biological parent families and 35 stepfather remarried (REM) families. Each family had at least one child between the ages 12 and 16 years participating in the study. An ex post facto comparative/correlation design was utilized. Two standardized data-gathering instruments, an original instrument developed by the researcher and appropriate social characteristics items, were employed as methods of data gathering. Data, thus generated by biological parent families and stepfather REM families, were comparatively analyzed. Descriptive and inferential statistics were used to analyze the study data. The subjects were U.S. Army families. The study also examined three variables which are identified as central to REM family adaptability and cohesion. The three were REM family discipline, cultural myths about the REM family, and how the REM family reacts to the loss of the previous family. The psychological meaning the adolescent attributed to his/her father or stepfather was studied. Chi-square analysis demonstrated that REM families were extreme in family adaptability, whereas intact biological parent families were moderate in family adaptability. Chi-square analysis revealed that REM families were extreme in family cohesion, whereas intact biological parent families were moderate in family cohesion. The study demonstrated that the adolescents in both family types did not rate their father or stepfather differently on evaluation, potency, or activity. REM families that experienced more difficulties around issues related to disciplining of the children were more extreme in family adaptability and cohesion. REM families that were experiencing unresolved issues around loss of the previous family situation were more extreme in their family adaptability and cohesion. The more moderate REM families were in discipline, myths, and loss, the more likely they were to be moderate in adaptability and cohesion. The study contributed: (a) a knowledge base for working with REM families in a clinical and educational model format; (b) support for utilizing role theory when examining situational family problems; (c) information about assessing the REM family in a standardized format." (DAI)

453. Wood, L.E. & S.R. Poole, 1983, "Stepfamilies in Family Practice", *Journal of Family Practice,* Vol. 16, No. 4, pp. 739–744

"The authors suggest that it behooves physicians to become more knowledgeable about recognizing stepfamily problems. They emphasize that these families function differently from nuclear families and thus find themselves without institutional supports. It is stated that the family physician's role includes some direct intervention along the lines outlined in the professional literature on stepfamilies, in order to reduce family stresses and conflicts." (c)APA

454. Woods, L.L. & T.L. Woods, 1974, "Substitute: A Psychological Study", *Elementary School Journal,* Vol. 75, No. 3, pp. 162–167
The authors compare children's reactions to a substitute teacher to those toward a stepparent and advise the substitute along the lines of current thinking about stepparents. The analogy is made that children will react favorably if their relationship to the regular teacher was good and vice versa. The comparison is further related to the feelings the regular teacher has both about this particular class and about the substitute teacher. Training and peer status are recommended for the substitute teacher.

455. Yont, R.H., 1986, A Phenomenological Study of Career-Orented Women in a Stepparenting Relationship: A Qualitative Study, Dissertation Abstracts International, Vol. 47/05-A, page 1671
"Very little data exists on the career woman's experiences as a stepparent. Evidence does exist that maintaining a stepparenting role and meeting the responsibilities of a career creates a stressful situation. The particular area examined in this dissertation is stepmothering as it relates to women in careers. The primary questions to be addressed are how these inherent stresses affect women who value their careers, and how women can adjust to a stepparenting role while maintaining adequate energy to be successful professionally. Based on the author's 1983 pilot study, a questionnaire and an interview protocol, both open-ended in form, were developed to gather data on the subject's stepparenting and career experiences. Nineteen subjects completed the questionnaire, all of them professional women working full-time and actively involved in raising stepchildren. Of this group, 12 were selected for an additional in-depth interview. The data fell into six "themes" or issues with which the women had to deal in their dual roles. Direct quotes from questionnaires and interview tapes were used to support and enlighten each of these themes. A synthesis of the data indicated that the role of stepmother may be more difficult for professional women to accept because of its secondary nature, as compared with their often primary role in the workplace. The

kinds of logical problem-solving techniques which succeed at work often fail at home in the stepfamily. However, the subject's career served as an outlet to family tensions and enhanced the women's self-esteem during the difficult adjustment to stepparenting. While no statistically verifiable conclusions can be drawn, the results provide a framework of information for professionals, helping these women to cope with the combination of career demands and stepparenting stresses.'' (DAI)

456. Zimmerman-Slovack, B., 1985, Stepfamily Experience and Social Environment (Stepchildren, Remarriage, Stepfather, Stepmother), Dissertation Abstracts International, Vol. 46/08-B, page 2792

''The purpose of this study was to come to perceive stepfamily social environment as it is perceived and experienced by stepfamily members themselves, and to identify variables in the stepfamily social environment which relate to stepfamily members' sense of satisfaction with their stepfamilies. Questionnaires were administered to 30 stepfamilies drawn from the nonclinical population. In all stepfamilies this was a second marriage for the wife, her first having been terminated by divorce, and she had custody of at least one child from the previous marriage. The data collected concerned: family background, support network, and perceived and idealized family social environments. Four stepfamilies participated in in-depth follow-up interviews. Statistical (multivariate and univariate) and qualitative analyses were employed. Ten dimensions of family social environment and a typology of six stepfamily types were obtained. An individual's experience of his/her stepfamily social environment was found to be related to the type of social environment s/he lived in, although environment did account for a fairly small portion of the variability in experience. Individual perception of stepfamily social environment was found to be a more powerful predictor of individual experience than was the type of environment itself, thus suggesting the presence of many variables intervening upon the relationship. The results indicate that despite the distinctiveness of each stepfamily type, there are numerous commonalities across types. An overall sense of caring and mutual respect appear to be the essential qualities underlying an environment that fosters a positive experience (i.e. reported satisfaction, small discrepancy between perceived and idealized family social environments, and a perception of family stress that was not high). The data indicate that positive individual experiences are possible in all stepfamily types. A high level of conflict and related aspects of social environment (e.g. competitive tension and lower cohesion) appear to diminish the likelihood of positive individual experience.'' (DAI)

Single-Parent Family

457. Abrams, S., 1983, *Children in the Crossfire. The Tragedy of Parental Kidnapping,* Atheneum, New York

This is an early study of the increasing phenomenon of ''child-snatching.'' Beginning as a journalistic effort, the author interviewed the various participants in the drama of a parent's kidnapping of his or her own child. The terror of the child in this situation and the feelings of the respective parents are observed and developed into a profile of parents motivated by self-serving impulses at the expense of their children.

The problem permeates all classes of people, and a historical perspective on the court's attitude is further developed. Custody struggles in an ever-increasing divorce rate, the role of the courts, and the problems of the ''me generation'' as parents are described. Support groups, the Uniform Child Custody Jurisdiction Act, and the Parental Kidnapping Prevention Act of 1980 are included in the author's chapter on the future.

458. Ahrons, C., 1980, ''Redefining the Divorced Family: A Conceptual Framework for Post-Divorce Family System Reorganization'', *Social Work,* Vol. 25, No. 6, pp. 427–441.

Presents a conceptual framework for the family's reorganization following divorce. Divorce is viewed as a crisis of family transition resulting in structural changes in the family system. Social workers must assist divorced parents in the crucial task of terminating spousal roles while maintaining parental roles.

459. Ahrons, C.R., 1979, ''The Bi-Nuclear Family: Two Households, One Family'', *Alternative Lifestyles,* Vol. 2, No. 4, pp. 499–515.

Based on her study of the dynamics of post-divorce parenting relationships, the author proposes a new term, ''binuclear family,'' to describe a newly emerging family form. The binuclear family is characterized by two nuclear households, maternal and paternal. Both households are important to the children, although not necessarily equally important.

460. Ahrons, C.R., 1981, ''The Continuing Coparental Relationship Between Divorced Spouses.'', *American Journal of Orthopsychiatry,* Vol. 5, No. 3, pp. 415–428

Data from 54 divorced mother custody couples are reported. A range of coparental relationships is documented including many families which fit the author's ''binuclear family'' conceptualization. Differences in the perceptions of men and women are noted and implications of these differences are discussed.

461. Ahrons, C.R., 1980, ''Divorce: A Crisis in Family Transition and Change'', *Family Relations,* Vol. 29, No. 4, pp. 533–540

The author integrates family stress and systems theories in identifying five normative transitions of divorce. With each transition stresses associated with major role changes and common coping strategies are identified. Divorce is presented as culminating in redefinition from a nuclear to binuclear family system. The continuation of meaningful parent-child relationships can reduce the stress associated with this transition. (SAA)

462. Ahrons, C.R., 1980, ''Joint Custody Arrangements in the Post-Divorce Family'', *Journal of Divorce,* Vol. 3, No. 3, pp. 189–205

Describes the post-divorce parental relationships of 41 divorced parents with court awarded joint custody. Reveals a range of shared parenting patterns and concludes that joint custody is a viable option for some divorced parents.

463. Ahrons, C.R. & S. Arnn, 1981, ''When Children From Divorced Families Are Hospitalized: Issues For the Staff'', *Health and Social Work,* Vol. 6, No. 3, pp. 21–28

The article identifies major issues for social workers and other hospital personnel to consider when working with hospitalized children whose parents are divorced.

464. Ambert, A.M., 1984, ''Longitudinal Changes in Children's Behavior Toward Custodial Parents'', *Journal of Marriage and the Family,* Vol. 46, No. 2, pp. 463–467

The authors are examining changes in children's behaviors and in parental satisfaction in a 2 1/2-year interval between interviews with custodial parents and children of divorce. In the first phase of the study, custodial fathers were reported to be the most satisfied of all custodial parents with their children's behavior and elicited more cooperative behavior from them. It was expected that over a two-and-a-half-year period, the behaviors would improve, in all types of single-parent families. The subjects were 27 separated or divorced single parents living in Toronto, interviewed in 1978–1980 and reinterviewed about 20 months after their first interview. Tables present the results of the interviews with three types of custodial parents, and six types of child behaviors.

The exploratory nature of this study and the small sample size, the authors warn us, does not lend itself to generalizations, but rather point the way for future large-scale studies. However, it is quite noteworthy that apart from the gender of the custodial parent, socioeconomic status is the chief variable. This is taken into consideration in the authors' giving two categories of single-mother households such as "children of high SES mothers" and "children of low SES mothers." The improvement in the behaviors and satisfactions of the parent are clearly related to the family's standard of living. A large gain in low SES mothers' families is felt to be more related to the departure of the most difficult children, thus not to be considered a net gain.

465. Anderson, R.E., 1968, " 'Where's Dad?', Paternal Deprivation and Delinquency", *Archives of General Psychiatry,* Vol. 18, No. 6, pp. 641–649.

Effective father is an important "growth factor" in boys 4–7.

466. Angel, R.J. & J.L. Worobey, 1987, "Ethnicity, the Feminization of Poverty, and Children's Health", *American Sociological Association Conference*

"An examination of the impact of single motherhood on several health status indicators for Mexican-American, black, and non-Hispanic white children aged six months to eleven years, based on the recently released Hispanic Health and Nutrition Examination Survey and the earlier National Health and Nutrition Survey II. These two surveys include a physical examination, a medical history, and a household questionnaire. Results show that, for all three racial and ethnic groups, households headed by females suffer serious socioeconomic disadvantages. Also, single mothers who live as sub-families do not appear to greatly improve their economic well-being as a result of this living arrangement. Analysis of the association between health status indicators and a mother's marital status and living arrangement produce inconsistent results. Physical examinations, although they suggest some health disadvantage for black children, indicate no such disadvantage for Mexican-American children. However, mothers' reports of their children's health reveal poorer overall health levels for their children.

These reports were further adjusted for MD's assessments and mother's own depressive affect (using the Center for Epidemiological Studies Depression Scale). Findings reveal that a mother's report of her child's overall health status is largely a reflection of her own distress level. In addition, the poorer health reported by female heads of household is largely a reflection of the socioeconomic disadvantages associated with father absence.'' (Sociological Abstracts)

467. Atkin, E. & E. Rubin, 1977, *Part-Time Father,* Signet Publishers, New York

The authors give advice directed to the divorced father without custody dealing with a variety of emotional and day-to-day problems to which a father and his children must adjust during the stages of children's development. Focus is on the potential opportunities for a fulfilling relationship between father and children. Of particular interest are chapters on remarriage and the extended family with step-relations.

468. Bachrach, C., 1983, ''Children in Families: Characteristics of Biological, Step, and Adopted Children'', *Journal of Marriage and the Family,* Vol. 45, pp. 171–179

58,542 children were compared in terms of different living arrangements: with both biological parents, with one biological parent and one step-parent; with biological mother only, with adoptive parent(s). Results indicate similarity in the lives of children with two parents, biological or step, but differences in several aspects when living in a single-parent family, with poverty being the most outstanding difference, especially when the mother never married. Adopted children were more economically advantaged than others.

469. Baden, C., 1980, *Parenting After Divorce,* Wheelock College Center for Parenting Studies, Boston, MA

''Seven brief presentations discuss social attitudes toward divorce and the experiences and problems families face after divorce. Introductory remarks indicate (1) the extent to which divorced parents are denied consistent and positive support from legal and counseling institutions, schools, and the work-place, and (2) the archaic institutionalized attitudes toward divorced parents which impair adjustment for the families. The first presentation discusses experiences by single parents in coming to terms with their past and managing the present. Subsequently, experiences of mothers without custody of their children are reported and reflected upon. Problems of adjustment of women who have chosen to live separately from their children are also discussed. The following presentation reports on the visiting role experienced by men who wish to remain engaged in the lives of their children. The next topic describes the family forum—a form of therapy for families of divorce. Ways in which the therapist helps to create a setting safe for productive discussion are indicated. Next, several aspects of joint custody are discussed and ways of reducing parental conflict are indicated. The final presentation explores the phenomenon of minifamilies within the stepfamily.'' (NCFR)

470. Baer, J., 1972, *The Second Wife: How to Live Happily with a Man Who Has Been Married Before,* Doubleday, New York
''Baer, herself a second wife, has drawn material from interviews, questionnaires, readings, and her personal experience and observations, to write a popularized journalistic book about 'how to be a second wife.' Her material comes from middle-class families and she covers such issues as courtship, step-parenting, finances, including alimony, dealing with ex-spouses and ex-inlaws and generally how to live with the 'new man,' and his past. Her book is filled with advice and suggestions for handling these issues and she presents many case histories to illustrate her points. Although some of her advice and 'solutions' are highly personalized, this book may be helpful in sensitizing women to the complexity of the issues involved in being a second wife.'' (SAA)

471. Bane, M., 1976, ''Marital Disruption and the Lives of Children'', *Journal of Societal Issues,* Vol. 32
The article surveys data on marital history and divorce statistics to estimate the proportion of children affected by marital disruption (in this century about 25–30%; an estimated 40% over the next few decades). Questions are appropriately raised on how to meet these children's needs. The author's review of literature indicates that opposition to divorce reform ''for the sake of the children'' does not seem to be a solution, but that an examination of the economic problems of single parents (predominantly female) leads rather to a proposal for some income-support policy.

472. Baruth, L.G., 1979, *A Single Parent's Survival Guide: How To Raise the Children,* Kendall/Hunt Pub. Co., Dubuque, Iowa
This helpful book focuses on child-rearing practices and offers sound democratic principles based on Dreikur's ''Children, the Challenge.'' Useful for anyone raising children alone and needing

to win cooperation in sharing household responsibilities and to encourage children to feel good about themselves. (DHHS)

473. Beattie, S. & L.L. Viney, 1980, ''Becoming a Lone Parent, A Cognitive Interactionist Approach to Appraising and Coping During a Crisis'', *British Journal of Social Clinical Psychology,* Vol. 19, pp. 343–351

The Lone Parenthood Scales were administered to 101 members of Parents Without Partners, to test the existence of two separate and systematic relationships between positive and negative appraisals of the event, and possible coping strategies. Positive appraisals were found to be different for men and women, but the perceived instrumentality of the decision to separate proved to be relevant for all negative appraisals. Mutual consent to separate versus spouse decision seemed to be an area which merited further investigation. Handling of the crisis on the basis of a ''cognitive-interactionalist'' framework was found to be expedient.

474. Bettker, D., 1985, ''Fifty Steps You and Your School District Can Do to Help Single-Parent Families'', Paper presented at the Annual Meeting of the American Association of School Administrators

''Fifty strategies developed and used over the past 20 years in school districts throughout New York and California for meeting the needs of single parent families are identified in this brief listing. A single descriptive line is devoted to each of the strategies, which are grouped into seven categories: curriculum/instruction, general, parent group, personnel/staff, public relations, special programs, and support services/attendance guidance.'' (ERIC)

475. Bohannan, P., 1971, *Divorce and After: An Analysis of the Emotional and Social Problems of Divorce,* Anchor Books, New York

Collection of articles dealing with the process of divorce, its aftermath, divorce around the world, and divorce reform. Chapter entitled, ''Divorce Chains, Household of Remarriage, and Multiple Divorces'' outlines eight terminologically recognized relationships based on a first marriage, then outlines and discusses the often large, diverse, and complex chains and kinship links formed by divorce and remarriage. Kinship terms and special-interest groups interested in divorce and remarriage are also discussed. (E & N)

476. Bohannan, P.J., 1970, ''Dynamics of Divorce Interview Schedule'' , Unpublished Instrument, University of California, Santa Barbara

''A nine-page interview guide to be used with a divorced person. Sections include family background, marital history, particulars of the divorce, poor divorce adjustment with ex-spouse and others, financial arrangements, children, remarriage relationships, and attitudes toward divorce and marital counseling.'' (SAA)

477. Bowman, K.L., 1981, The Effects Of Father Absence or Presence, Rapport With Father and the Extended Family on the Academic Performance and Social Adjustment of High School Students, Dissertation Abstracts International, Page 1597, Vol. 42/04-B

''The purpose of the investigation was to examine the effects of father absence or presence in the home on black and white male and female high school students as it pertained to academic and social measures. In addition the rapport with father for father-present subjects and the presence of the extended family for father-absent subjects was studied to see if they also influenced academic and social performance. Approximately 500 students from two urban high schools were given a five-page questionnaire to assess family composition, self-concept and achievement aspirations. After screening procedures 144 subjects were chosen from this total and then divided into sixteen different family groups. In addition school attendance and discipline variables used in this investigation were number of school days absent and tardy, the California Personality Inventory Scales I and V, academic achievement, and discipline. The results indicated that white males were the most negatively affected by father absence or absence of an extended family, while black males appeared to be the least affected. Black and white female subjects also showed some negative effects to father absence, but not to the same degree as white male subjects. The rapport with father for father-present subjects influenced the number of days absent for black female subjects only, but in a manner contrary to the investigator's hypothesis. The results of this study suggested that father absence or presence, the rapport with fathers for father-present subjects, and the presence of an extended family for father-absent subjects were related to the levels of academic and social adjustment for subjects. Societal norms and cultural differences were suggested as possible explanations for differences in results obtained for black and white male and female subjects.'' (DAI)

478. Boyd, D.A., 1984, Children From Divorced and Reconstituted Families: An Examination of Academic Achievement in Light of Familial Configuration, Dissertation Abstracts International, Vol 46/01-B, page 322

"The purpose of this study was to determine whether or not children from divorced homes had significantly poorer academic scores than children from other familial configurations. Subjects were 1451 third through twelfth-grade students from a Kansas school district and may be generally described as urban dwellers of middle-class socio-economic status. Students, once they were identified as either normal or learning disabled, were classified as belonging to one of the following groups: (a) students from intact homes, (b) students from divorced homes, and (c) students from reconstituted homes. The independent variable of the study was family structure. The dependent variable was academic achievement as measured through California Achievement Tests, reading and math subtest scores, and grade point average (GPA). Analysis of variance was used to analyze the data. The following results were noted: (1) Reading and math achievement and GPA were significantly higher ($p < .01$ for reading and math, $p < .01$ for GPA) for normal children from intact families than for normal children from divorced families. (2) While reading and math achievement test scores were significantly higher ($p < .010$) for normal children from intact families than for normal children from reconstituted families, there was no significant difference with regard to GPA. (3) Reading and math achievement test scores were not significantly different for normal children from reconstituted homes and normal children from divorced homes. GPAs were significantly higher ($p < .01$) for normal children from reconstituted homes. (4) There were no significant differences between either the reading or the math achievement test scores for LD children from intact and divorced families. LD children from intact families did score significantly higher ($p < .01$) on the GPA variable than did LD children from divorced homes. (5) Reading and math achievement tests scores and GPAs were not significantly different for LD children from intact homes and LD children from reconstituted homes. (6) Reading and math achievement test scores and GPAs were not significantly different for LD children from reconstituted and divorced families. There was a significant difference ($p < .01$) where GPA was concerned, with GPA being higher for children from reconstituted families." (DAI)

479. Brady, C.P., Bray, J.H. & L. Zeeb, 1986, "Behavior Problems of Clinic Children: Relation to Parental Marital Status, Age, and Sex

of Child'', *American Journal of Orthopsychiatry,* Vol. 56, No. 3, pp. 399–412

''A sample of 703 children with behavioral problems participated in a study that tested for the interactive effects of age and sex of child and family type, for example, divorced families. Data revealed significant differences based on family type, with children of separated, divorced, and remarried parents having more problems. Expected interactions between marital status and age and sex of child were not obtained, although results supported earlier research with regard to the effects of age and sex.'' (SWAB)

480. Brandwein, R., Brown, C. & E. Fox, 1974, ''Women and Children Last: The Social Situation of Divorced Mothers and their Families'', *Journal of Marriage and the Family,* August

Paucity of research on female-headed single-parent households in spite of their numbering 3.5 million families in the U.S. gave rise to this research study. The assumption that this is a deviant or pathological family was considered prejudicial and leading to stigmatization. Two areas of research provided the foci for this study. One area looked at changes in family organization and behavior, taking place when family structure and resources change. Four areas of family functioning are examined (economic, authority, domestic responsibility, social and psychological supports). The second area of research examined societal factors and values that influence the ability of the family to carry out its functions. Literature search revealed the assumption that single-parent state is temporary, which seemed to affect the lack of attention or support to this family unit. It was felt that all areas studied need further exploration and the needs were detailed. It was concluded that there was an urgent need on the part of single-parent women to be more adequately understood in order to discontinue victimization, by prevalent distortions and inadequacy of data, both within their own families and within society. A more realistic and less stigmatized approach to further studies was hoped to be gained, to influence policy makers to create a more equitable milieu for all single parents and their families.

481. Brenes, M.E., Eisenberg, N. & G.C. Helmstadter, 1985, ''Sex Role Development of Pre-Schoolers from Two- Parent and One-Parent Families'', *Merrill-Palmer Quarterly,* Vol. 31, No. 1, pp. 33–46

Pre-schooler's understanding of sex-role identity and stereotypes as well as toy choices were examined by a team of one Costa Rican psychologist and two from Arizona State. Children from single-parent, mother-headed families showed more stereotyped conceptions of sex roles, particularly the masculine ones, and a tendency to be less sex-typed in their use of toys. Behavioral choices were less sex-typed. However, boys from mother-headed families were not "feminized" in their play behaviors. The pattern of developing gender identity was similar for all children.

482. Briggs, B.A. & C.M. Walters, 1985, "Single-Father Families: Implications for Early Childhood Educators", *Young Children,* Vol. 40, No. 3, pp. 23–27

The authors give an overview on the somewhat sparse available literature on single fathers highlighting some of the issues which indicate that this type of family is a viable one. Counselors are admonished to encourage the family, become aware of difficult work schedules, watch for stress, provide parenting information, know about custody arrangements. An important point the authors urge is to change the curriculum for all children to include a more flexible perception of male and female role performance.

483. Bronfenbrenner, U., 1976, "The Family Circle: A Study in Fragmentation", *National Elementary Principal,* Vol. 55, No.5, pp. 11–25.

"Using primary government statistics, author reviews changes in American childrearing. More single-parent families, more unwed mothers, more working mothers, fewer adults at home, greater urbanization, general family fragmentation. Possible solutions: better day care, fairer part-time employment practices, improving position of women, giving youth more responsibilities." (SAA)

484. Broxie, G.J.B., 1987, Parental Participation in Homework Completion As a Predictor of Academic Success of Students in the Single-Parent Family, Dissertation Abstracts International, Vol. 48/11-A, pp. 2806

"Currently over 13 million school-age children are living in single-parent homes. 40 percent of children from single-parent homes earn grades of D and F compared to 24 percent of children from two-parent homes. This descriptive field study was designed to determine if different levels of parental participation in homework completion influence academic success when academic success is defined as grades that average A, B, or C in the single-parent family. Four levels of parental participation were used: (1) supplies materials and resources required for homework completion; (2) directs student to do homework; (3) assures that homework is completed, visually viewed; and (4) assist with homework during time child is working, content teaching or correcting. The sample consisted of 58 fourth, fifth, and sixth grade students and their parents. The parents and students were interviewed in their home setting. Information on academic success was obtained from public school records. The data were analyzed using discriminate analysis statistical techniques to determine group membership and to determine the strength of the four levels or a combination of the four levels of parental participation in homework completion in conjunction with student participation. The results indicate that parental assistance at Levels 3 and 4 are predictors of student grades. However, student time on homework in conjunction with parental assistance at Level 3 was a stronger predictor of student grades.'' (DAI)

485. Burchinal, L., 1964, ''Characteristics of Adolescents from Broken, Unbroken, and Reconstituted Families'', *Journal of Marriage and the Family,* Vol. 26, pp. 44–50

A study which investigates the possible effects of divorce upon the behavior of adolescent children. No significant differences were found within the three groups for the majority of relationships tested, in terms of the detrimental effects of divorce.

486. Burgess, J.K., 1973, ''Children of One-Parent Families.'', *Sexual Behavior,* Vol. 3, No. 1, pp. 9–13

''Society's prejudice against one-parent families plays a crucial role in causing many of the conditions it is complaining about. Discusses sex-role development in one-parent families—depends primarily on how well the single parent functions as self-assured person.'' (SAA)

487. Carlos, P.H., 1981, Family Structure, Locus of Control, Reading Achievement, Manifest Anxiety, and Self-Esteem in Children, Dissertation Abstracts International, Vol 42/02-B, page 741

''The present investigation examined locus of control, reading achievement, manifest anxiety, and self-esteem in four family structures: Class I—residing in a biologically nuclear intact family; Class II—residing with one natual parent, in a single-parent home, as a result of marriage dissolution, for a period of not more than two years: Class III—residing in a single-parent home in the above status for more than two years; Class IV—residing in a reconstituted family in which the custodial parent has remarried. The sample consisted of 237 Anglo children, aged 9 years through 11 years. Subjects were middle class, with no handicapping conditions: not an only child nor with over four siblings, not adopted nor living with guardian or foster parents, and not a member of a racial-ethnic minority. Information was obtained by a self-report, school records, and teacher interview. Subjects were administed the Nowicki-Strickland Locus of Control for Children, Children's Form of the Manifest Anxiety Scale, Coopersmith Self-Esteem Inventory, and the Ginn Reading Achievement Inventory. Using multiple regression statistical procedures, results indicated that a significant difference exists among the relationships between locus of control and each of the independent variables: reading achievement, manifest anxiety, and self-esteem in the four classes of family structure. Further investigation indicated a difference exists in the relationship of manifest anxiety to locus of control between Class I and Class III. Multivariate and univariate analysis of variance statistical procedures indicated that a significant difference exists among the four family structures in the mean vector scores of locus of control, reading achievement, manifest anxiety, and self-esteem. In Class I locus of control internality is significantly higher than in the three other classes of family structure. No differences among the four classes were obtained for reading achievement mean scores. In Class II manifest anxiety is significantly higher than in the three other classes. Self-esteem is significantly higher in family structure Class I and Class III with Class II being the lowest.'' (DAI)

488. Cashmore, E.E., 1985, *Having To,* George Allen and Unwin, London.

The major purpose of this book is the destigmatization of single-parent families. In the effort to contrast the growth-producing and self-enhancing aspects of single parenthood, the author touches on family violence, infidelity, adolescent motherhood, poverty, their meaning to men, women, and children in single-parent families. Much valuable research in the UK and USA is cited as corroborative evidence for the author's perceptions.

489. Chang, C.L. & B.J. Gray, 1983, ''Single Fathers: A Growing Minority in America'', *Health Education,* Vol. 14, No. 7, pp. 37–40

''Health educators can play a vital role in helping provide emotional and social support for single fathers, in helping prepare their children for parent roles, and in educating the community about needs of these parents. Special characteristics and needs of single-father families are discussed.'' (ERIC)

490. Charnas, J., 1983, ''Joint Custody Counseling: Divorce 1980 Style'', *Social Casework,* Vol. 64, pp. 546–554

Joint custody is historically traced, explained, and offered as a viable option in divorced families. A model of custody counseling is presented with case examples. The model is rooted in a problem-solving and educational focus. It builds on the parents' rational and cognitive strengths, and focuses on their stated commitment to their children's welfare. The term "psychological parent" (Goldstein, Freud, Solnit) is explained and adapted to include both biological parents and their importance to the lives of their children on a continuous basis. The model is applicable to practice in many agencies, or in private practice. The counseling process begins with the couple's firm decision to divorce but to continue the relationship to their children. Legal and geographical considerations are mentioned, as are some possible hurdles.

491. Cherlin, A., 1981, *Marriage, Divorce, Remarriage: Changing Patterns in the Postwar U.S.,* Harvard University Press, Cambridge, MA

The author views trends in remarriage, marriage, and divorce through research in these fields since the end of World War II. Data are both presented and analyzed to determine reasons for the changes which have taken place.

492. Clayton, P., 1971, "Meeting the Needs of the Single-Parent Family", *Family Coordinator,* Vol. 20

This article deals with some of the needs of single parents and describes how Parents Without Partners, a self-help organization, attempts to meet these needs. Recent developments such as cooperative services for members, scholarship programs, community service programs, information regarding resources and the therapeutic value leading to personal growth through volunteer work are described in some detail.

493. Cline, B., 1985, "Raising Alan Alone", *Exceptional Parent,* Vol. 15, No. 7, pp. 44–46

"A single parent describes her struggles with her young son whose hyperactive disruptive behavior aggravated an already failing marriage. She notes the help provided by advocacy and support groups." (ERIC)

494. Counts, R. & A. Sacks, 1985, "The Need for Crisis Intervention During Marital Separation", *Social Work,* Vol. 30, pp. 146–150

The authors discuss why marital separation should be considered as a stressor of primary magnitude, since its immediate and long-term results are frequently even more disruptive than separation by death. Vulnerability to mourning, typical stresses during separation, and interventive strategies are discussed, including some emphasis on the impact of these stressful events on children. Family group treatment, i.e. work with the entire nuclear family (without any particular emphasis on any branch of therapeutic endeavor) is recommended.

495. Crossman, S.M. & G.R. Adams, 1980, ''Divorce, Single Parenting, and Child Development'', *Journal of Psychology,* Vol. 106, pp. 205–217

Two recent longitudinal investigations (Heatherington, et al and Wallerstein & Kelly) as well as much current literature indicating that children are likely to experience disorganization, the quality of interaction with the resident parent appears to change, leading to poor patterns of social development. Bloom, Asher, and White use crisis theory to account for the undesirable consequences of divorce for children. Zajonc is cited to provide convincing data re: more limited interaction between child and both resident and absent parent. The authors raise serious questions, since little empirical attention has been given to the investigation of support systems, which could offer additional adult-child interactions. They also emphasize that crisis theory provides conceptualizations for interventions which ''might well mediate the negative consequences of paternal unavailability.''

496. Dager, E.Z. & G.B. Thompson, 1986, ''Family Structure and Family Climate Effects on Black and White Self-Esteem in Single- and Two-Parented Homes.'' ASA conference paper, 22 pp.

''Data from a cross-national representative survey of black and white children aged 7–11 in single- and two-parent homes in 1976 (number of cases = 558 & 1,645, respectively) are used to assess the influence of certain mechanisms of socialization and family structure variables on self-esteem of children. Results of multivariate analyses indicate that perceptions of neglect are critically associated with self-esteem for all cases. The variance in perceptions of neglect is related to problems in family functioning, e.g., lack of helping responsibilities, intermittent mother absence, low levels of family interaction, overpermissiveness in rule enforcement and parent-child argument frequency. While perceptions of neglect are critically associated with self-esteem in all cases, specific family processes that affect those perceptions vary by race and family type. For blacks in single-headed households, not helping and low family activity were significantly related to perceived neglect and low self-esteem. In contrast, for whites, mother-child argument frequency outweighed all other considerations and explained the most variance in self-esteem. In two-parented homes, parental overpermissiveness, parent-child argument frequency and not yelling (i.e., showing concern) were the most critical processes affecting perception of neglect and consequently, self-esteem. Family structure factors that affect family processes, which, in turn, affect self-esteem, include family size and homemaker status. In large families with working mothers, when there are few family activities, and children have few responsibilities, children feel more neglected and tend to have lower self-esteem in single-parent homes. In two-parent homes, children in large families with nonworking mothers who are overly permissive and where the parents argue frequently tend to feel more neglected and have lower self-esteem. Family size and homemaker status affect family processes and consequently the self-esteem of whites more than blacks, irrespective of family type.'' (ASA)

497. Cunningham, N.J. & J.H. Brown, 1984, ''A Parent Group Training Program for Single Parents'', *Journal for Specialists in Group Work,* Vol. 9, No. 3, pp. 145–150

''Describes a group training program in parenting skills for single parents (N=45), emphasizes parent-child communication, child management, and problem-solving skills. Program evaluation indicated improvements in parents' skills and their children's behavior. The group also provided a support system, and positive reinforcement for members' role as parents. (JAC)'' ERIC

498. Despert, L., 1953, *Children of Divorce,* Doubleday, Garden City, NY

The author proposes that it is not divorce, but the emotional situation in the home that is the determining factor in the child's adjustment. Where there is ''emotional divorce,'' and the parents continue in the marriage, it can be more devastating to the child than a legal divorce. She presents case histories to document her thesis and also includes a step-by-step guide for divorcing parents, how to handle this with their children, and where to get help. The child's reactions to divorce are explored and explained and in a chapter on remarriage and the child, expectations and reactions to remarriage are outlined.

499. Doudna, C., 1982, ''The Weekend Mother'', *The New York Times Magazine,* October 3, pp. 72–88

Examines the issue of women without custody of their children—either voluntarily or against their will. The author interviews non-custodial mothers and discusses the conflicts they experience as a result of society's disapproval as well as their internalized value system.

500. Driggs, B.A. & C.M. Walters, 1985, "Single-Father Families: Implications for Early Childhood Educators", *Young Children,* Vol. 40, No. 3, pp. 23–27

The authors give an overview on the somewhat sparse available literature on single fathers highlighting some of the issues which indicate that this type of family is a viable one. Counselors are admonished to encourage the family to become aware of difficult work schedules, watch for stress, provide parenting information, know about custody arrangements. An important point the authors urge is to change the curriculum for all children to include a more flexible perception of male and female role performance.

501. Durst, P., Landes, V., Wedemeyer, N. & L. Zurcher, 1985, "Parenting Partnerships After Divorce: Implications for Practice", *Social Work,* Vol. 30, pp. 423–428

Purpose of the study was to explore the variety of patterns of post-divorce couple interactions to determine how better to evaluate adjustments. Five types of parental partnerships were determined and interpreted from a family systems point of view. The findings are based on semi-structured in-depth interviews with 42 divorced spouses. Two issues were addressed, the variety of parenting arrangements in divorced families, and the viability of each arrangement. The use of the typology to assess the strengths and weaknesses of the family structure is described with examples. Clarity and flexibility of boundaries is identified as a key variable when working with divorcing couples or post-divorce families. The goal of the intervention, while always aiming at maximizing cooperative co-parenting, will have different sub-goals on the basis of the typology-assessment.

502. Eiduson, B.T., 1983, "Conflict and Stress in Nontraditional Families: Impact on Children", *American Journal of Orthopsychiatry,* July, Vol. 53, No. 3

Particular stresses and certain kinds of conflicts seem to be associated with each family's life-style. Aspects of children's intellectual performance and social emotional behavior are negatively affected by stress, but seem to be more related to the kinds of social supports available and thus the handling of stressful events. No family life-style was found to be free of conflict or stress for the developing child.

503. Edmund, J.H., 1986, Long-Term Custody Disputes and Their Effects on Latency Children: A Psychoanalytic and Family Systems Approach , Dissertation Abstracts International, Vol. 47/08-B, page 3503

"The purpose of this study was to develop a synthesis of psychoanalytic, object-relations, and family systems theories as it pertains to families undergoing prolonged divorce and custody disputes. A case study approach was used in selecting families in treatment at the Child and Family Divorce Counseling Service at Children's Hospital, San Francisco. Clinical case materials of three families from the Service's files were analyzed, and synthetic analytic and systemic concepts were formed in light of the material. The custody dispute in each of the selected families focused on a latency-age child. The synthetic concepts were then applied to the sample and in-depth analyses were made. The main themes developed in the analyses included (1) the significance of three generational and family-of-origin materials in relation to the parents' mate selection, marriage and parental; (2) the distinction and relationship between marital and parenting conflicts; (3) and effects of these conflicts on latency-age children in custody-disputing families, particularly in terms of the children's capacity to negotiate the separation and individuation tasks unique to the latency period. Major findings were that marital and parenting conflicts resulted, in part, from each spouses' efforts to repair their own childhoods, and that the effects of the conflicts on their latency children was to revive pre-oedipal and oedipal struggles at a time when, normally, they should be turning their attention to extra-familial matters. It was also demonstrated that long-term divorce and custody-battles are ways for families to stay connected, rather than prolonged ways of separating. The study argued for the saliency of a synthetic theoretical approach in understanding this population of families, through demonstration that neither the psychoanalytic nor the family systems approach, on its own, can adequately comprehend the family dynamics of high-conflict relationships. Finally, the application of this model to other populations, such as intact conflictual marriages and blended families, was suggested." (DAI)

504. Egleson, J. & J.F. Egleson, 1961, *Parents Without Partners: A Guide for Divorced, Widowed, or Separated Parents,* Dutton Publishers, New York

A popular book based on the hypothesis that the "single" parent feels isolated with responsibilities of parenthood. Advice and suggestions for the custodial parent and a chapter on remarriage are included.

505. Ellison, E., 1983, ''Issues Concerning Parental Harmony and Children's Psychosocial Adjustment'', *American Journal of Orthopsychiatry,* January, pp. 73–80

A research project which suggests that parental relationships following divorce directly affect the children's psychosocial adjustment. Early professional intervention to aid successful co-parenting relationships will help the children in their coping process.

506. Epstein, J.L., 1984, ''Single Parents and the Schools: The Effect of Marital Status on Parent and Teacher Evaluations'', Johns Hopkins University, Baltimore, MD, Center for the Study of Social Organizations of Schools

Data from a survey of 1269 parents (of whom 24 percent were single parents) were used to study whether single and married parents differ in their interactions with elementary schools and teachers. Results indicate that initial differences between single and married parents' perceptions of teachers and teachers' evaluations of single and married parents are due to other family and school conditions. Race, parent education, grade level, teacher practices of parent involvement, and overall teacher quality significantly influence parent reports of teacher practices. Single parents also felt more pressure than did married parents to be involved with their children in learning activities at home. Married parents spent more time assisting teachers at school. Study results show the importance of measures of school structures and processes in research on single parents. Single parents had better relations with teachers whose philosophy and practices lead them toward more positive attitudes about parents. Teacher leadership, not parent marital status, influenced parent awareness, appreciation of teachers' efforts, and knowledge about the school program.

507. Espinoza, R., et al, 1983, ''Work and Family Life Among Anglo, Black, and Mexican American Single-Parent Families. Summary of the 1983 Annual Report'', *Southwest Educational Development Lab*

''The focus of the Working Parents Project (WPP) has been on how families adapt and function in relation to workplace policies, with particular attention given to the participation of parents in contexts of child care and socialization, including education-related activities. This report builds on previous data from the WPP by expanding the sample of dual-earner families to include 30 single-working-mother families. Research with this sample focused on processes linking workplace policies and the social supports available to single mothers. Data were collected from Anglo, Black, and Mexican American single-parent (divorced) families through in-depth and structured interviews concerning family demographics, work history, and information about characteristics of the mothers' jobs. Findings are reported under the following headings: (1) involvement in schools; (2) family types, focusing on authoritative, inadequate, no controls, and dependent mothers; (3) family type and school involvement; (4) fathers' involvement; (5) ethnic differences; (6) mother-child relationships; (7) support networks; and (8) dual- earner and single-parent families. The study recommends that employer assistance programs be expanded to include some services related to the mental and financial health of workers and their families, e.g., on-site education and training activities such as stress management, parenting education and financial counseling.'' (ERIC)

508. Ferri, E., 1973, ''Characteristics of Motherless Families.'', *British Journal of Social Work,* Vol. 3, No. 1, pp. 91–100

As part of a longitudinal investigation of the development of all children born in Britain during one week of 1958, the characteristics of motherlessness among 237 11-year olds living with their biological fathers were examined. Interviews with fathers or other adults show that in half of the cases motherlessness was caused by marital breakdown and half by the mother's death. Families in which the mother was missing tended to be smaller than intact families and to contain a higher proportion from lower-class backgrounds. Two-fifths of the children were cared for by their father alone. One in three had a stepmother, remarriage being more common among younger fathers. Comparative data from the larger study indicate that children who had lost their mother before age 11 were less likely to live in a one-parent family than those who had lost their father. (SAA)

509. Francke, L.B., 1983, *Growing Up Divorced,* Linden Press, Simon and Schuster, New York

As a journalist for *Newsweek* the author interviewed a few hundred children and experts on child development. She gives very specific information about the impact of divorce on children in terms of their ability to absorb the facts depending on the stage of their life cycle development.

510. Friedman, H., 1980, ''The Father's Parenting Experience in Divorce'', *American Journal of Psychiatry,* Vol. 137, pp. 1177–1182

The author discusses the possible positive effects of divorce on the (visiting) father-child relationship after divorce. Since the potential for the relationship to develop in a more conflict-free atmosphere exists, greater bonding can take place, if the father can be experiencing his own nurturing qualities, usually with the help of a therapist. The author cautions the professional establishment, especially social workers and psychiatrists, who tend to see post-divorce fathers and children, to examine and lay aside their community-generated prejudices and work on the possibility that post-divorce relationships can be not only non-deleterious, but also positive by generating bonding experiences previously not presented. The sexist attitudes of mothers, fathers, legal professionals, and therapy establishment must be revised.

511. Fuller, M.L., 1986, ''Teachers' Perceptions of Children from Intact and Single-Parent Families'', *School Counselor,* Vol. 33, No. 5, pp. 365–374

''Investigates elementary school teachers' perceptions of the school behaviors of children from intact homes and from single-parent homes. Demonstrates that teachers view the two sets of children differently and that teachers' attitudes affect students' self-perception and behavior. Recommends ways counselors can help single-parent families develop positive coping techniques. (ABB)'' ERIC

512. Furstenberg Jr., F.F., Winquist, C.N., Paterson, J.L. & N. Zill, 1983, ''The Life Course of Children of Divorce: Marital Disruption and Parental Contact'', *American Sociological Review,* Vol. 48, pp. 656–668

Data from a nationally representative sample of U.S. children ages 11–16 in 1981 were examined with reference to the incidence of marital disruption in their lives, the types of living arrangements children experience following such disruptions, and the frequency of contact experienced by the children following marital disruption of their parents. Only 17% experienced frequent contact with the absent parent in both black and white groups. In all other respects, the large racial differences were revealed in both the incidence and aftermath of disruption. Provision of child support, residential proximity of the non-resident parent, and the time period which had elapsed since the separation were critical factors in determining the amount of contact between child and non-resident parent.

A glimpse at more recent data showed little evidence of co-parenting, and came close to predictions found in the professional literature on the subject. The authors conclude that marital disruption typically involves either complete cessation of contact, or what appears to be not very meaningful contact. Some questions are raised about the meaning of a stepparent in the lives of children with cessation of contact with the resident parent, as well as about the meaning of multiple parenting to the lives of children.

513. Galper, M., 1978, *Co-(Sharing Your Child Equally)-Parenting. A Sourcebook for the Separated and Divorced Family,* Running Press, Philadelphia, PA

The author, a social work practitioner with families and children, provides some ideas and very specific guidelines to parents and practitioners. Personal and professional experience are integrated into a careful exploration of new directions both for counseling and living.

514. Gardner, R., 1977, *The Parents Book About Divorce,* Doubleday and Co., New York

This book addresses parents considering divorce, covering counseling, both legal and psychological, the effects of divorce on children, telling the children, dealing with feelings, e.g. anger, depression, abandonment, shame, and guilt. Some sections on parental difficulties that contribute to children's maladjustments, and children's involvements with other significant adults, such as stepparents and therapists. Case situations illustrate the author's concepts.

515. Gardner, R., 1976, *Psychotherapy with Children of Divorce,* Jason Aronson, New York

This book addresses child therapists who specialize in working with children of divorce. Specific techniques for working through feelings such as guilt, anger, abandonment, grief, and depression are covered. Working through feelings engendered by remarriage are included.

516. Gasser, R.D. & C.M. Taylor, 1976, ''Role Adjustment of Single-Parent Fathers With Dependent Children.'', *Family Coordinator,* Vol. 25, No. 4, pp. 397–401

''Fathers faced with role adjustment in home management and child care curtailed former social activities and shifted toward new relationships involving other single parents.''(SAA)

517. Gettleman, S. & J. Markowitz, 1974, *The Courage to Divorce,* Simon and Schuster, New York

The authors attempt to dispel fears that children may be permanently damaged by divorce, that parents would feel guilty, or that children are to be pitied. Divorce is viewed as an opportunity for increased personal growth for both adults and children. (DHHS)

518. Gifford, R.W., 1980, A Content Analysis of Selected Adolescent Novels Dealing with Divorce, Separation, and Desertion Published Between January, 1970 and May, 1979, Dissertation Abstracts International, Vol. 42/01-A, page 117

"As the United States divorce rate constantly rises, more and more children are involved in broken families. One of the important needs of these children is to read about others in a similar situation. Nearly 150 adolescent novels dealing with divorce, separation, and desertion appeared in the 1970's.

The Purpose. The purpose of this study was to determine how selected adolescent novels depict families undergoing a marital breakup and comparing this depiction with psychological and sociological studies to determine the extent of concurrence. As a result, parents, educators, and librarians can be better informed about the kinds of information presented in the novels.

Procedures. The sample for this study consisted of 28 adolescent novels dealing with divorce, separation, or desertion published between January, 1970 and May, 1979. Content analysis was the technique used for analyzing the novels. Seven major categories were employed. Each novel was thoroughly read and all passages referring to he major categories were recorded.

Conclusions. The following results were shown from an analysis of the data: (1) The novels dealt exclusively with Caucasian families and 82 percent of the families were from the middle or upper middle socio-economic classes. This conflicted with actual studies which show that more incidences of divorce occur among blacks than among whites and the majority of divorces occur in the lower socio-economic classes. (2) Twenty-seven of the novels dealt with divorce, where in reality separation and desertion account for nearly forty percent of all single parents. (3) Of the children depicted in the novels, girls outnumbered boys 31 to 17. The average number of children in the fictional families was 1.66 as compared to 1.08 per actual divorce decree. The average age of the fictional children was 13.04 whereas the greatest number of children affected by divorce and separation are in the six to eight-year-old range. (4) The most common reasons for divorce or separation presented in the novels were unfaithfulness, alcoholism, a desire for a new life style or for freedom, constant fighting and arguing and a conflict between marriage and a career. (5) In 85.5 percent of the novels the mother gained custody of the children comparing favorably with the actual figure of approximately ninety percent. (6) A comparison of the fictional children's new life style showed agreement with actual studies in the following areas: many children were forced to relocate after their parents separated and the children usually reacted negatively to the relocation, children viewed their parents dating unfavorably, children's relationships with stepparents and stepsiblings were positive in the majority of the instances, and interpersonal relationships with both parents usually deteriorated after the separation. Disagreement with actual studies occurred where only six fictional children faced a lower standard of living and only six mothers returned to work, where in reality a majority of children experience a lower standard of living and a majority of single-parent mothers begin working. (7) Reactions to their parents' separation which were described in at least three separate instances included the child blaming himself for the separation, the child having a desire to run away, and the child having fits of crying. Several unique individual psychological and physical reactions were noted.'' (DAI)

519. Glenwick, D. & J. Mowrey, 1986, ''When Parent Becomes Peer: Loss of Intergenerational Boundaries in Single-Parent Families'', *Family Relations,* Vol. 35, pp. 57–62

The authors describe the PBP, Parent Becomes Peer, family which occurs not infrequently in single-parent families, in which a late latency-age child resides with his/her mother who does not function in a parental role. In the clinical interventions recommended, the mother is helped to take on parental responsibilities, by re-establishing hierarchical boundaries, teaching regarding age-appropriate behavior and expectations for children, allowing the child expression of feelings, establishing more appropriate communications patterns regarding divorced partner (other parent) etc. Case examples are offered to demonstrate.

520. Glick, P. & A. Norton, 1977, ''Marrying, Divorcing and Living Together Today'', *Population Bulletin,* Vol. 32, No. 50

''This Bulletin presents the most up-to-date figures from the Census Bureau as analyzed by the authors. Documents changing U.S. patterns of marriage, divorce, and living arrangements in the mid-1970's which undoubtedly reflect changed attitudes toward conformity with traditional behavior. 40% of marriages among women now in their late twenties may end in divorce, although the divorce rate has recently stabilized. First marriage and remarriage rates have fallen from previously high levels. Close to two million unmarried men and women currently share living quarters; 15 million adults live alone; and only 67% of children live with their own, once-married parents. About one in three births are premaritally conceived and only half of all pregnancies result in legitimate live births. However, most Americans still experience some variation of the 'typical' family life cycle of the past; two out of three first marriages taking place today are expected to last 'until death do them part'; and young women queried in Census Bureau surveys expect to have an average of two children." (SAA)

521. Golan, N., 1975, "Wife to Widow to Woman", *Social Work,* September 1975

This article discusses the adjustment to the new role of being a widow through the experiences of war widows. The stages of bereavement are explored and a method is described to help others in similar situations better cope with the sudden material responsibilities plus emotional impact of the loss. The final acceptance and new identity of being a different woman is also addressed.

522. Goldman, J. & J. Coane, 1977, "Family Therapy After the Divorce: Developing a Strategy", *Family Process,* Vol. 16, pp. 357–362

Family therapy after a divorce is recommended to facilitate parental relationships. A four-part model of intervention is described. The first task redefines the family as including all members. Next, generational boundaries are worked on in order to reduce parentification which is often intensified by parent's physical absence. Third, the family needs a review of the marriage to correct distortions and offer a chance to mourn the loss of the nuclear family. Finally, the therapist attempts to facilitate the "emotional divorce." A case study is presented to demonstrate.

523. Greif, G., 1986, "Mothers Without Custody and Child Support", *Family Relations,* Vol. 35, pp. 87–93

This is a group of single parents about whom very little is known. A self-selected group from Parents Without Partners answered a questionnaire which was the basis of this study. The authors wanted to develop a profile of the mothers who were paying support as well as the average amounts paid. Fewer women than men pay child support when they do not have custody. The incomes and amounts paid are the same in terms of percentages of their salaries, when they do pay. Some of the differences between paying and non-paying mothers were examined. Some relationship between parental involvement and child support payment is developed, and the authors point to controversial aspects and caution practitioners in their work with this small group of parents.

524. Greif, G., 1985, ''Children and Housework in the Single-Father Family'', *Family Relations,* Vol. 34, pp. 353–357

A self-selected sample of 1136 single fathers (who were members of Parents Without Partners and were asked to complete a questionnaire) raising children alone, after separation and divorce, showed more participation in household chores as the children got older, that girls rendered more help than boys as they became teenagers, and that fathers may expect less from their children in this respect than had been found in a study of two parental families. Though these fathers provided non-traditional role models, their expectations still seemed to be along traditional lines. Age, sex, and financial circumstances were some of the areas more closely studied. Fathers' use of outside help and daughters' use as mother's substitute were further discussed. Implications for practitioners are discussed, and some comparisons are made to life in the single-mother family. The authors caution to ward off the development of a future generation of ''Cinderellas taking care of their brothers and fathers.''

525. Greif, G., 1987, ''A Longitudinal Examination of Single Custodial Fathers: Implications for Treatment'', *American Journal of Family Therapy,* Vol. 15, No. 3, pp. 253–260

''Presents follow-up data gathered 3 years after survey of fathers raising children alone, comparing fathers who remained single custodians and those who remarried. Single fathers' custodial arrangements had not changed significantly. Remarried fathers usually wed mothers with custody, became more involved in housework, and reported that their remarriage had not affected their ex-wives' involvement with children.'' (ERIC)

526. Gurman, A.S., ed., 1981, *Questions and Answers in the Practice of Family Therapy,* Brunner/Mazel, New York

This is a large collection of papers in which experienced family therapists present more than 100 clinical questions and their answers based on a wide variety of theoretical conceptualizations. In Section V, there are 14 papers dealing with Separation, Divorce, and Remarriage. All of these dwell heavily on issues relating to children. Two articles deal specifically with family therapy in child custody cases, one with child management in single-parent families.

527. Hale, L.C., 1983, ''Divorce and Single-Parent Family Counseling. Searchlight Plus: Relevant Resources in High Interest Areas''

''This document, based on a computer search of the ERIC database, presents a review of the literature on divorce and single-parent families. Statistics from the 1980 census are presented which show that 19.7 percent of children under 18 live with a single parent, who in the overwhelming number of cases is the mother. The document presents data on the economic problems, causes, and adjustment issues surrounding divorce. The impact of divorce on children is discussed as well as the particular needs of single-parent families stemming from the dissolution of the marriage and the setting up of a new lifestyle. Areas of strain to the mother and father are identified. Problems inherent in remarriage are reviewed and intervention strategies are suggested. The helping role of society is explored in the areas of legal services, custody laws, conciliation counseling, mediation counseling, personal counseling, and school programs. References and an annotated bibliography from the computer search of the ERIC database complete the document.'' (ERIC)

528. Hanson, S.M.H., 1986, ''Healthy Single-Parent Families'', *Family Relations,* Vol. 35, pp. 125–132

This study attempts to investigate the characteristics of ''healthy'' single-parent families, along a variety of variables including such measures as socio-economic status, social supports, communication, religiousness, problem-solving skills, parents' and childrens' physical and mental health status. Custody arrangements and the sex of the custodial parent were also considered in terms of their effect on the subjects studied. (N-84) Background, method, instrumentation and results are reported in detail. In general, both physical and mental health status of both single parents and their children appeared to be good, with high correlations between the findings on the children and parents. Sex of resident parent and children had significant bearing on the children's health. Custody equally had a bearing on the health and mental health status. Social support and communication were related to health, while socioeconomic status and religiousness did not seem to be related. Problem solving in itself did not seem to be associated with physical or mental health but custody arrangements did appear to wield influence. Implications for practitioners and researchers are outlined.

529. Hanson, S.M.H., 1982, "Variations of Fathering: Implications for Social Policy. Single Fathers with Custody: Implications for Social Policy", *Annual Meeting of the National Council of Family Relations*

"This document summarizes current knowledge about single custodial fathers, and draws implications for social policy. Through a review of the literature, the following characteristics of single fathers are described: socioeconomic status, race, custody status, religion, age, employment, parental history, homemaking skills, motivation for custody, visitation rights and child support, and support systems. Research on the children of single fathers focusing on sex and age, child care arrangements, and father-child relationship is also reviewed. Existing, as well as needed, social policies which affect single-custodial fathers are discussed, i.e., custody laws and issues, child support, income support programs, child care, family counseling, mediation and conciliation services, community program development, business and industry, school systems, health care systems, and cultural messages. A bibliography is included." (ERIC)

530. Hensey, J., 1973, *Help for Single Parents,* Christian Action Commission, Jackson, MS.

Deals with the most pressing questions single parents face from the perspective of family counseling and community pastoral relationships over a period of 25 years. The chapter titled "Should the Single Parent Remarry?" discusses such questions as: What about the other parent? What are we going to tell the children about the stepfather or stepmother? What will be the role of the stepparent? Should the stepparent adopt your child? (E & N)

531. Herzog, E. & C. Sudia, 1971, *Boys in Fatherless Families,* U.S. Government Printing Office, Number (OC) 72–73

A review of studies which examine whether growing up in a fatherless home is likely to affect a child adversely. Generalizations about the adverse consequences of father absence and relevant research are discussed under three headings: 1) overt behavior that is socially condemned (e.g. juvenile delinquency, extramarital pregnancy); 2) intellectual ability and achievement; and 3) psychological and social adjustment. Many of the studies reviewed include stepparents.

532. Hess, P., 1986, ''Promoting Access to Access with Divorcing Parents'', *Social Casework,* Vol. 67, No. 10, pp. 594–604

This article is directed to social workers who are frequently responsible for influencing decisions regarding access of children to divorced parents. The author reviews legal directives and available research on access arrangements. Practice principles are described and suggested, relating to general access, preferred remedies for separation distress, interventions when parents are in conflict. The article concludes with emphasis for some practice principles for which substantial documentation exists, e.g. the majority of children prefer access to both parents; duration and frequency of visits affect both the quality of the interaction and the difficulty in separating at the end of visits; extreme continuing conflict between parents may negatively influence the well-being of the child. The author suggests that the suggested general practice principles be applied in combination with individualized assessments.

533. Hodges, W., Tierney, C. & H. Buchsbaum, 1984, ''The Cumulative Effects of Stress on Preschool Children of Divorced and Intact Families'', *Journal of Marriage and the Family,* August, pp. 611–617

Different types and sources of stress may lead to different methods of coping and adjustment. This article examines how the stresses of divorce affect preschool children.

534. Hofferth, S.L., 1985, ''Updating Children's Life Course'', *Journal of Marriage and the Family,* Vol. 47, No. 1, pp. 93–115

The concern with the statistics indicating that the proportion of children growing up in two-parent nuclear families has declined sharply has given rise to this careful, scholarly research study. The concern was particularly related to the large income differential in single-parent families, and the fact that past studies have focused primarily on children's experiences with divorce and separation. This study attempts to examine the trends and particularly the proportion of children spending some of their growing years in more than one family and with single parents, as well as some of the numerical differences between children in black and in white families, as well as children born between 1950 and 1954, and those born in 1980. Dramatic changes have taken place in the percentages of children living with two biological parents in their first marriage both in white and in black families (in 1950–1954, 19% of white children under 17 had lived with only one parent, while in 1980 almost 70% of the children were projected to have lived with only one parent before they reached age 18. For black children, the figures were 48% and 94% respectively). The authors point out that the missing data of the amount of time the children spend in single versus two-parent families is extremely important. It is also important to consider whether the figures available give the legal status or whether informal arrangements could also be considered. Avenues for further research are outlined.

535. Howard, T. & F. Johnson, 1985, "An Ecological Approach to Practice With Single-Parent Families", *Social Casework,* Vol. 8, pp. 482–489

The authors highlight six components of the ecological model of social work practice for a better understanding of the single-parent family. Strategies are recommended to intervene and prevent post-divorce problems. The orientation of the parent to new roles is emphasized. The assumption of divorce as a crisis state requires intervention in the post-divorce family. Programs emphasizing a variety of formalized support services, early identification of problems, and prevention are described. The immediate environment, e.g. extended family, community, school, etc., as well as the broader environment, including prejudice toward single-parent families (by seeing them all as deviant, and pathological) are described as areas in which social workers can both intervene and influence. A number of factors are cited which can lead to more sophisticated assessments of family needs, and therefore to a much broader range of interventions.

536. Hulbert, J.L., 1987, Social Adjustment and Reading Achievement of Children From Single-Parent and From Two-Parent Military Service Families Enrolled in the DoDDS- Germany, Dissertation Abstracts International, Vol. 48/12-A, pp. 3048

"*Purpose:* It was the purpose of this study to determine the differences between single-parent and two-parent children in their social adjustment and reading achievement in order to develop recommendations to assist DoDDS in providing the best possible academic and social development for single-parent children.

Procedure: The method employed was a nonexperimental design in which matched pairs of 142 second and third grade children from single-parent and from two-parent families, sampled from eleven DoDDS-Germany schools, were compared. Three instruments were used in data collection: the Bristol Social Adjustment Guide (BSAG), the California Achievement Test (CAT), and the scale of reading series equivalence (Houghton Mifflin Reading Series). Demographic data were obtained from school office forms and classroom teachers. The Spearman's Rank Order Correlation, the Pearson Product-Moment Correlation, and the Student t-statistic for both correlated and independent means were employed in the analysis.

Findings and Conclusions: (1) DoDDS-Germany children, in general, are not severely maladjusted. They exhibit mild inconsequence syndrome maladjustment in both syndrome groupings of under-reaction and over-reaction. (2) Single-parent children exhibit twice as much maladjustment as do two-parent children. (3) Over-reaction (inconsequence and hostility) in single-parent children living with mothers is less related to reading achievement than under-reaction (unforthcomingness, withdrawal, and depression). (4) Daughters of single-parent fathers maladjusted in the syndrome grouping of over-reaction are predicted to be good readers. Overreaction is positively related to reading achievement for boys but negatively related for girls.

Recommendations for Practice: (1) DoDDS teachers need to be made aware of single-parent children in their classrooms and to observe their social adjustment development and reading achievement progress so they can request supportive services for single-parent children when needed. (2) DoDDS special service workers, such as counselors and reading specialists, need to assist teachers with home and school communication networking.

Research Recommendation: Further research is needed about the single-parent family structure, especially as it becomes increasingly common.'' (DAI)

537. Humphries, L.S., 1980, A Study of the Relationship Between Family Structure and the Behavior of Students in a Large Surburban Junior High School, Dissertation Abstracts International, Vol. 42/04-A, page 1578

''This investigation was conducted to determine the relationship between behavior in school and the family structure. The family structures that were investigated were: (1) The two-parent family, with one parent working. (2) The two-parent family, with both parents working. (3) The one-parent family; separation, divorce, and death are all included in this category. (4) A stepparent in the home. (5) A student living with someone other than those listed above (grandparent, aunts, uncles, foster parents, etc.). This investigation was conducted in a large surburban junior high school containing grades seven through nine. The school served a predominantly middle-class community. A court-ordered merger with an all-black community resulted in a non-white population of 18% and a white population of 82%. Data were collected from the registration form (superintendent's form) that was completed by each student during registration. The following information was determined from this form: (1) Sex and race of the student. (2) Whether one or both parents worked. (3) Whether two parents were in the home. (4) Whether one parent was in the home. (5) Whether a stepparent was in the home. Data dealing with the behavior of students were collected from the discipline files of the assistant principal. Only those students who had more than two referrals to see an assistant principal for disciplinary action were included in this portion of the investigation. This eliminated those students that were not considered "problems." The various behavior rates of students from the family structure mentioned earlier were compared to the "normal" behavior rate. The normal behavior rate was defined as the ratio of the total number of students referred to the office to the total number of students in the school population. The chi-square statistical test was applied to each hypothesis to determine whether or not there was a statistically significant difference between each group and the normal rate. This study supported the premise that children from broken homes—categories three, four, and five, above—cause a disproportionate share of discipline problems in school. The number of broken homes is continually on the rise—especially among black families. Of all the students, only 18% are responsible for 45% of the problems." (DAI)

538. Kalter, N., 1977, "Children of Divorce in an Outpatient Psychiatric Population", *American Journal of Orthopsychiatry,* Vol. 47, pp. 40–51.

"Reviews the records of 400 children who were referred for outpatient psychiatric evaluation to the youth services of the Department of Psychiatry at the University of Michigan, October 1974 through July 1975. The population was low socioeconomic class to lower middle-class and included 14.5% of children living with a stepparent. Kalter found that children of divorce appeared in the clinic sample at nearly twice the rate of their occurrence in the general population and that in all subsamples (analyzed by age and sex) there was a greater tendency for children of divorce living in both single-parent and remarriage families to manifest aggression toward their parents, compared with children in intact familes. More specific to remarriage families, he found that a significantly greater proportion of adolescent boys with stepparents manifested aggression toward parents and conflict with the law and that for girls age 12 and over, there were also higher incidences of aggression toward parents and peers, sexual behavior, drug involvement, and school-related difficulties than for children in intact families. He suggests that such children are particularly vulnerable and at risk. Kalter cautions that this is a clinic population and proposes that the child's age at the time of divorce needs further study and understanding.'' (SAA)

539. Kalter, N., Pickar, J. & M. Lesowitz, 1984, ''School-Based Developmental Facilitation Groups for Children of Divorce: A Preventative Intervention'', *American Journal of Orthopsychiatry,* Vol. 54, No. 4, pp. 613–623

''A model of time-limited, school-based groups for children of divorce is presented. Common themes that emerged in groups conducted in three schools suggest that youngsters continue to wrestle with divorce-related conflicts years after the marital disruption. Developmental tasks created by specific post-divorce stresses are described, and the multiple brief interventions tied to nodal points in child development are proposed. Although early intervention may be helpful to youngsters amidst the upset of parental divorce, the combination of post-divorce stresses and developmental changes in children suggest both the need and opportunity to intervene beyond the point of the immediate familial disruption.'' (SWAB)

540. Kammerman, S.B., 1980, *Parenting in an Unresponsive Society,* Free Press, New York

Describes the concrete problems facing a single parent and takes a look at the various support systems available. In general, the author feels that society is unresponsive to single parents' greatest need—satisfactory child care arrangements.

541. Kaplan, S.I., 1977, ''Structural Family Therapy for Children of Divorce: Case Reports.'', *Family Process,* Vol. 16, pp. 75–83.

Describes structural family therapy techniques for treating families of divorce where the child is presented as symptomatic. The author presents five case reports, each case representative of a different stage in the divorce-single parenthood-remarriage continuum. Also: description of work with remarried families. (SAA)

542. Kaslow, F.W., 1984, ''Divorce Mediation and its Emotional Impact on the Couple and Their Children'', *American Journal of Family Therapy,* Vol. 12, No. 3, pp. 58–66

The author discusses the recency of the application of the concept of developmental stages to the process of divorce. She stresses the necessity to base the point of therapeutic entry and the selection of treatment strategy, i.e. the approach to divorce mediation, on a clear and accurate assessment. What needs to be assessed is the individual and couple identity of the divorcees, their intrapsychic and interpersonal resources, as well as the life-cycle stages of the individual family members.

543. Keith, P.M. & R.S. Schafer, 1982, "A Comparison of Depression Among Employed Single-Parent and Married Women", *Journal of Psychology,* March, Vol. 110, pp. 239–247

Study of 139 structured interviews with single-parent (n=52) and married (n=87) employed women; examined employment characteristics, psychological resources, and management of domestic activities in relation to depression. Stress and overload were said to be contributory to depression, and especially stressfully to single parents, in economic and domestic areas. This study compared work and home factors associated with depression and examined the extent to which deficits attributed to the single-parent family were linked with depression. Data were analyzed and measured in relation to depression. Non-traditional sex-role attitudes, more time at work, higher income with less work and family strain were associated with less depression among single-parent employees. High self-esteem, positive work orientation, less time spent at work, and satisfaction with domestic tasks were associated with lower depression among married women.

544. Kelly, J. & J. Wallerstein, 1976, "The Effects of Parental Divorce: Experiences of the Child in Early Latency", *American Journal of Orthopsychiatry,* Vol. 46, pp. 20–42

After a description of age-appropriate developmental tasks for children in this age range, the authors show differences in the 7–8 year olds in their study. The children of divorce seemed to be immobilized by intense suffering and longing for their absent fathers with few avenues of finding relief for their suffering and with weaker ego structures, less able to tolerate grief. The authors commonly found thoughts about the instability of the family and fears of the future. Fantasies of reconciliation and possessiveness seemed to mask deep sense of loss and deprivation, and loyalty conflicts were pervasive. Follow-up a year later depended on the post-divorce family structure. There was generally a resigned, sad attitude about divorce, with strong expression of wishes for more time with the absent father. Twenty-three percent of the children were in worse condition than when seen originally.

545. Kelly, J. & J. Wallerstein, 1977, ''Part-Time Parent, Part-Time Child: Visiting After Divorce'', *Journal of Clinical Child Psychology,* Vol. 6, pp. 51–54

This paper is an early report of the authors' study of divorced families focusing on the visiting and relationship between non-resident parent and child. Visiting patterns were very closely studied in relation to the pre-divorce relationship, the frequency and content structure of the visits, and the dynamics of the visiting parent. When age and sex were studied as independent variables, strong differences emerged in the visiting contacts. However, continuity in the parent-child relationship and increased bonding (perhaps because of the short-term counseling interventions connected with the research project) were observed as beneficial. Anger and instability of the family discontinuance can be overcome, and it appeared that the highly complex variables related to the divorce process strongly influence the continued contact of child with absent parent, rather than the pre-divorce relationship or the frequency factors. Continued study of the post-divorce relationship patterns and their effects on the child's emotional development is recommended.

546. Kelly, J. & J.S. Wallerstein, 1977, ''Brief Interventions with Children in Divorcing Families'', *American Journal of Orthopsychiatry,* Vol. 47, pp. 23–29.

This paper is a partial report of the authors' five-year clinical research project studying the impact of divorce on children. Preventive clinical interventions developed for children of various ages are described. Formulations regarding assessment, strategies, and the limitations of brief interventions with children at the time of divorce are presented.

547. Keshet, H. & K. Rosenthal, 1978, ''Fathering After Marital Separation'', *Social Work,* Vol. 23, No. 1, pp. 11–18

Describes a study dealing with the experiences of a group of separated or divorced fathers, who chose to remain fully involved in the upbringing of their children. Deplores the processes they went through from the initial adjustment following separation through to ''single fatherhood.'' Found that the men learned that meeting the demands of child care facilitated and contributed to their own stability and personal growth.

548. Kitson, G.C., Lopita, H.Z., Holmes, W.M. & S.M. Meyering, 1980, ''Divorcees and Widows: Similarities and Differences'', *American Journal of Orthopsychiatry,* Vol. 50, No. 2, pp. 291–301

The authors report on a substantial study of widows and divorced women in the Chicago and Cleveland areas. Based on findings from age-standardized survey data, divorced women reported that they felt more restricted in their relationships with others and had less favorable attitudes toward their former spouses. Remarriage was also viewed very differently. Though influences by or on children are not considered in this study, the findings would seem to have considerable impact since the two categories of single women are not usually separated in other ongoing research.

549. Klaas, T.A., 1985, The Effects of Divorce and Single-Parenting on the School Adjustment of Fourth and Fifth Grade Students, Dissertation Abstracts International, Vol. 46/09-A, page 2630

"This research examined the effects of two-parent, single-parent (through divorce), and remarried households on student adjustment to the educational milieu. In addition, it explored specific variables related to maternal post-divorce adjustment and how these variables influenced children. The subjects for this study included 183 mother/child pairs selected from a midwestern school district, representative of a white, middle-class community. Those students in the divorced categories were from families of long-term (greater than 15 months) divorce. The Family Environment Scale (Moos, 1981) was selected to evaluate the role of family interactions in the school adjustment of children. School adjustment was measured by the Walker Problem Behavior Identification Checklist (Walker,1976) which consists of five categories designed to measure behaviors which interfere with successful classroom adjustment. The Separated/Divorced Parent Questionnaire was designed and used to assess separated/divorced mothers' perceptions of circumstances relating to separation and divorce. The study included fourth and fifth-grade students not identified or suspected of a handicapping condition. The teacher of each participating student rated their respective students as to school adjustment on the Walker Problem Behavior Identification Checklist (WPBIC). Next, the Family Environment Scale (FES) was administered in a group format to all participating students in their individual schools. The mother of each student was then asked to fill out the FES, and single-parent and remarried mothers were asked to fill out the FES plus the Separated/Divorced Parent Questionnaire (S/DPQ). In addition, each mother was asked to complete a general information sheet which requested background information about themselves and their families. The results of the data analysis indicated that children residing in single-parent families of divorce were not distinguishable from their intact classmates on the Walker Problem Behavior Identification Checklist. The results also suggested that children from remarried families, especially males, demonstrated a higher level of classroom distractibility than did their classmates. Additional analysis, regarding mothers' perceptions of circumstances surrounding separation/divorce, revealed that children's school adjustment did not appear to be influenced by their mothers' reaction to the divorce process. (Abstract shortened with permission of author.)'' (DAI)

550. Kohn, J.B. & W.K. Kohn, 1978, ''My Children's Grief'', In *The Widower,* Beacon Press, Boston

Actual case reports of family members' reactions to death help us understand where communications break down and the grieving process becomes stunted. Sensitive guidelines for helping children cope with grief are offered. Underlying feelings children often experience in reaction to death and how to help children through this period are also outlined in a practical way.

551. Krantzler, M., 1974, *Creative Divorce,* M. Evans & Co., New York

Realistic assessment of children's reactions to divorce. Children, too, must mourn the ''death of parents' relationship.'' The author describes what to expect, how long negative reactions might last, and cites some tested ideas about how to improve relationships with children. The author feels that divorce may be a positive event and an opportunity for growth for all concerned. (DHHS)

552. Krell, R., 1972, ''Problems of the Single-Parent Family Unit'', *Canadian Medical Association Journal,* Vol. 107, No. 9, pp. 867–872

Six case histories of single-parent families are presented to demonstrate some unique problems. Single mothers frequently present children with specific complaints. The symptoms may reflect special problems of the single-parent family or unresolved issues from the marriage, such as the circumstances of death or divorce with the attendant separation anxiety, grief, anger, and/or depression as well as difficulties with the visitation rights and the effects of visits. Additional parental concerns relate to the child's developing sexual curiosity and sexual identity, loneliness due to the restricted social life of working mothers, and thoughts about remarriage and its implications.

553. Kurdeck, L.A., Blisk, D. & A.E. Siesky, 1981, "Correlates of Children's Long-term Adjustment to Their Parents' Divorce", *Developmental Psychology,* Vol. 17, pp. 565–579.

554. Kurdek, L., 1981, "An Integrative Perspective on Children's Divorce Adjustment", *American Psychologist,* August 1981, pp. 856–865

A description of four components thought to be related to children's adjustment to their parents' divorce. Describes the difficulty of professional assessment of the impact of divorce on children.

555. Kushner, S., 1965, "The Divorced, Non-Custodial Parent and Family Treatment", *Social Work,* July 1965, pp. 52–58

Discusses the neglect of professional services and counseling for the non-custodial, absent parent, usually the father. Urges the treatment person to reach out to the non-custodial parent when only the child or the custodial parent are involved in treatment.

556. Lamb, M.E., ed., 1982, *Nontraditional Families: Parenting and Development,* Lawrence Erlbaum Associates, Hillsdale, NY

Well-known authors in their respective fields discuss a variety of non-traditional family types. All chapters relate to the crucial question of the effect of these family types on the children. Among the families discussed are those with increased or decreased father involvement, single-parent families, divorce and its consequences, extra familial child care. Sex role development and appraisal of the necessity of male models are given some attention. Statements re: normative practices are evaluated against emerging evidence of alternate styles.

557. Landis, J., 1962, "A Comparison of Children From Divorced and Non-Divorced Unhappy Marriages", *Family Life Coordinator,* Vol. 3, pp. 61–65

Report on a research study comparing children from divorced and non-divorced unhappy marriages. Found that the unhappy marriage is more disturbing to children than the fact of divorce. Also considered parent/child relationships, sex education, dating, competence in college, and self-evaluation.

558. Leader, A.L., 1973, "Family Therapy for Divorced Fathers and Others Out of the Home", *Social Casework,* January, 1973, pp. 13–19.

"Treatment article advocating the inclusion of the separated member of the family in family therapy. Case studies used to demonstrate that work on the affective ties which remain, despite divorce, is essential in order for the family members to move beyond the symbol of finality, trauma and old wounds, to an exploration of present ties." (SAA)

559. Leahy, M., 1984, "Findings From Research on Divorce", *American Journal of Orthopsychiatry,* Vol. 54, No. 2, pp. 298–317

The author analyzes results of research on divorce, and develops implications that are useful for the development of skills on the part of professionals in education, law, mental health, health care, etc. Lawyers and judges are called to task for their cultural biases in favor of stereotypical sex roles; mental health clinicians who have the opportunity to see and work with these families are also cautioned to be aware of their own theoretical biases which influence their work with single-parent families. The author explicates conceptual skills and changes necessary for each of the target groups and finally recommends professional collaboration to maximize professional know-how and resources.

560. Lessing, E., Zagroin, S.W. & D. Nelson, (1970) "WISC Subtest and IQ Score Correlates of Father Absence", *Journal of Genetic Psychology,* December 1970, Vol. 117, No. 2, pp. 181–194

"311 boys and 122 girls were given the WISC as part of their diagnostic evaluation at a child guidance clinic. A history of prolonged father absence (found in 138 subjects) was associated with a lower performance IQ and lower scores on Block Design and Object Assembly, regardless of sex and social class, and with lower scores on Arithmetic for boys only. Working-class, father-absent subjects also earned lower mean Verbal and Full Scale IQ scores. Of the two subgroups of subjects with a history of father absence, only those with no father figure in the home at the time of testing differed from father-present subjects in regard to WISC scores. Those with a stepfather did not differ." (SAA)

561. Levitin, T.E., 1979, "Children of Divorce: An Introduction", *The Journal of Social Issues,* Vol. 35, No. 4, pp. 1–182

This whole issue is devoted to children of divorce. Both positive and negative effects of divorce on children are addressed by professionals of a variety of theoretical persuasions. The children's perspective, the parents' point of view, custody issues, and children of divorced parents in demographic perspectives are considered. In an introduction, Teresa E. Levitin of the National

Institute of Mental Health presents an overview of the major research and approaches on children of divorce and some questions for future research. She reviews each paper in this special issue.

562. Lewis, W., 1986, ''Strategic Interventions with Children of Single-Parent Families'', *School Counselor,* Vol. 33, No. 5, pp. 375–378

The author describes in detail the helping process to a single parent whose child has shown behavior problems or academic malfunctioning, on the basis of family systems theory, particularly C. Madanes' family therapy model. Counselors are referred to other readings on family systems models. Some familiarity with this form of treatment would be quite helpful, although the author is explicit in his description of the process.

563. Liston, W., 1984, ''Professional Attitudes Toward Single-Parent Families'', *Counseling and Values,* Vol. 29, No. 1, pp. 74–78

The purpose of this study was to ascertain whether counselors perceive single-parent families differently from other educators. Approximately 343 questionnaires were distributed randomly at a counseling workshop in Louisiana in 1983. 114 counselors and 44 teachers and administrators broadly represented 22 school systems. Analysis revealed some differences in the perceptions of counselors and other educators. A chart explains these in detail as does the discussion. The authors conclude that the study offers reassuring evidence that educators are knowledgeable and quite in agreement with research findings on the subject. Counselors are not as compatible with the findings of recent research. A problem orientation and lack of up-to-date information on research are postulated as possible reasons. More extensive research is suggested.

564. Long, T.J. & L. Long, 1988, ''Hotlines for Children: What Makes Them Effective?'', *Children Today,* March/April, pp. 22–25

The authors report on the existence and effectiveness of telephone hotlines for children and support the notion that a national help line would bring comfort and support to thousands of children who are at home alone. The denominators underlying the philosophy of successful hotlines are described as pro-family philosophy, highly trained volunteers, regular consultation, support, and supervision of the volunteers, sensitivity to cultural and language differences. Interagency contact, record keeping and evaluation are also recommended.

565. Manley Jr., D.B. Jr., 1987, Selected Determinants of Parenting Behaviors in Single and Dual-Parent Families, Dissertation Abstracts International, Vol. 48/11-A, p. 2989

"This study compared mothers of adolescent children from single-parent and dual-parent families in terms of their parenting styles and also on factors which may influence parenting (parents' personal resources, social support, and adolescent behaviors). The data came from questionnaires completed by a sample of mothers recruited primarily through contacts with church groups in the West Texas area. Based upon several models of parenting, parenting style was conceptualized as involving two key dimensions: (a) separating (encouraging adolescent independence), and (b) connecting (maintaining positive affective relationships with the adolescent). Each of these dimensions was measured by three scales derived from factor analyses of items from existing measures of parenting and family environment. There were no significant differences between the single and dual parent groups of mothers on the measures of social support, parental competency, and adolescent behaviors, nor on five of the six parenting scales. As expected, single-parent mothers did have significantly lower incomes than did dual-parent mothers. In addition, single-parent mothers reported a higher level of expressiveness among family members than did dual-parent mothers. Comparisons of the relationships between these variables for each group revealed that the patterns were quite similar for mothers from single and dual-parent families. For both groups, perceived parental competency, parental enthusiasm, coping style, and adolescent behaviors were significantly related to parenting behaviors which emphasized verbal praise and connecting positively with adolescents, and with parenting behaviors which allowed adolescent separateness (low emotional and verbal parental control). Contrary to some previous research, the results of this study indicate that single-parent mothers are equivalent to mothers in dual-parent families with respect to their feelings of parental competency, enthusiasm for parenting coping style, social support, and most parenting behaviors. Further, patterns of relationships between these variables are comparable for the two groups. Implications for the development of children with single-parent families and for future research are discussed." (DAI)

566. Marotz-Baden, R., Adams, G.R., Bueche, R., Munro, B. & G. Munro, 1979, "Family Form or Family Process? Reconsidering the Deficit Family Model Approach", *The Family Coordinator,* Vol. 28, No. 1, pp. 5–14

The authors question the popular notion that a different from norm, i.e. nuclear family, is considered a deficit family, which a priori produces deviance, frequently equated with pathology. They reconsider the assumption that the nuclear family is the ideal way to rear and socialize children. A literature review on recent works on alternate family forms and their effects on children's personality, behaviors, and school achievements suggests the more productive avenue of focusing on family and social interactional dynamics that may lead to a particular outcome, than to consider the family form or structure the critical independent variable. The suggestion is made that future research be more heavily based on family actions and interactions along demographic, social, and historical dimensions.

567. McKay, R. & G. Blades, 1984, *The Divorce Book,* New Harbinger Publications, Oakland, CA

The effects of divorce on children and adults are presented along with issues that develop from divorce, e.g. legal, financial, and social. How and why children react to divorce is discussed. The process of grieving and how parent(s) can help children cope as well as guidelines for telling children about the divorce are discussed.

567a. Mengerink, R.A., 1987, The Relationship of School Achievement and Disciplinary Problems to Single-Parent Families Among Selected Tenth and Twelfth Grade Students in the United States, Dissertations Abstracts International, Vol. 47/11-A, p. 4048

"The purpose of this study was to examine the relationship of school achievement and discipline problems to students from single-parent families. The investigation used a National data base collected in 1980 by the National Opinion Research Center entitled 'High School and Beyond' (HSB). Over 55,000 high school sophomores and seniors in the working file of this investigation each completed a questionnaire and a battery of tests as part of the data collection for HSB. Portions of these instruments were used to create the 8 general and 32 specific hypotheses for this investigation. Single, non-single, maternal single and paternal single-parent families were analyzed to predict teacher assigned grades and discipline problems in school while taking into account the effects of sex, socioeconomic status, race and ability score. This study used an ex post facto research design and multiple linear regression to analyze the variance accounted for in each hypothesis. An F-Test to determine statistical significance and a .05 alpha level was established. Due to the extremely large sample size, practical significance was also examined. The results of this study found statistical significance for all hypotheses. Family configuration accounts for a significant amount of unique variance in predicting achievement and discipline problems. The results also indicate that students from single parent families tend to have lower grades and more discipline problems in comparison to their peers from non-single parent families and students from maternal single parent families tend to have lower grades and more discipline problems in comparison to students from paternal single-parent families. Practical significance, however, was not established for any hypotheses in this study.'' (DAI)

568. Mitchell, A., 1985, *Children in the Middle. Living Through Divorce,* Tavistock Publications Ltd., London

As a researcher at the University of Edinburgh the author interviewed adolescents who have experienced separation and/or divorce of their parents about their recollections of the event or process. It became clear that children do not share the popular belief that divorce is preferable to living with feuding parents. The living circumstances also received less attention of the children than the feeling that they had not received sufficient explanations, and insufficient regard of their feelings and problems in coping. The book is intended for all professionals dealing with children as well as being a guide to parents who are considering separation or divorce. The recommendations are made that non-custodial parents should be more fully included in planning, and friends and relatives were also considered to profit from this type of information, and could thus help at periods of time when the (custodial) parent cannot carry the tasks fully.

569. Moore, R.T., 1986, ''The Androgynous Black Parent: One Answer to the Single-Parent Dilemma'', *Annual Convention of the American Association for Counseling and Development,* Los Angeles

''A crisis exists in the black family today due to the high unemployment of black men, the high separation rates of parents, the dramatic increase in the number of unwed mothers, and the subsequent heading of nearly one-half of black families by women. There is nothing necessarily wrong with being raised in a home with a single mother. Biographies of 25 successful educators, physicians, lawyers, ministers, and politicians who are black showed common experiences which include: (1) a working mother outside the home; (2) black elementary school teachers; (3) extended family and friendly neighbors; (4) belief in education as a way out of poverty; (5) intervention by an important person during adolescence; (6) firm discipline from the mother; (7) nurturing from the grandmother; (8) expectations from mother and teachers that the children would be successful; and (9) job responsibilities in the home from age 8 and part-time job as a teenager. Strategies are needed to help black single-parent families. An androgynous black single parent who is a female head of household and who uses masculine (instrumental) and feminine (expressive) behavior routinely may provide a useful parenting model for black single mothers. Blending these behavior skills increases the chances of heading a functional family. An androgynous mother still needs male allies to intervene when her male children need them.'' (ERIC)

570. Morrison, J.R., 1974, ''Parental Divorce as a Factor in Childhood Psychiatric Illness'', *Comprehensive Psychiatry,* Vol. 15, No. 2, pp. 95–102

The author starts on the principle that too much research emphasis has been on the consequences of divorce to the child, and not enough on examining the antecedents of the divorce and the possibility that divorce and childhood psychiatric illness may be related secondarily to a common background factor. In 1972, 127 children at the Iowa College of Medicine were evaluated by interviews with a parent or relative as to extensive familial history. The children's diagnosis was not revealed to the relatives; the diagnoses of family members were made on the basis of information obtained along DSM II criteria. Several tables are offered to show comparative figures in the symptom picture of parents and children, in both divorced and non-divorced families. From the data available, the author finds no clear-cut relationship between marital status and symptomatology of the children. However, the role of parental pathology prior to the divorce is also found to be a matter of conjecture at this point. The author raised many questions and suggests further studies, and care in evaluating all facts available before concluding ''what is cause and what is effect.''

571. Mueller, D.P. & P.W. Cooper, 1986, ''Children of Single-Parent Families: How They Fare as Young Adults'', *Family Relations,* Vol. 35, No. 1, pp. 169–176

1448 persons, aged 19–34, representing 1% of the residents in a midwestern metropolitan county, were surveyed. The differences between being raised in two-parent or one-parent families at young adulthood were the subject of this inquiry. Persons raised by single parents, primarily mothers, tended to show lower educational, occupational, and economic attainment in young adulthood. Differences in family formation and marital stability were also observed, and it appeared that the economic disadvantages of the single-parent family were clearly responsible for the former, but the latter remained after controlling for this factor. Policy implications for Welfare and school programs as well as the importance of preventive programming are discussed.

572. Newman, G., *101 Ways to Be a Long Distance Superdad,* Blossom Valley Press, Mountain View, CA
The purpose of this book is to aid mothers and fathers who are separated from their children. Offers ideas for "together type" activities that can be enjoyed despite distance.

573. Norton, A.J., 1987, "Families and Children in the Year 2000", *Children Today,* Vol. 16, No. 4, pp. 6–9
"Describes social, economic, and demographic trends affecting children and families. Discusses how patterns of marriage, childbearing, divorce, remarriage, and mothers' employment in the paid labor force influence the lives of children." (ERIC)

574. Nunn, G., Parish, T. & R. Worthing, 1983, "Perceptions of Personal and Familial Adjustment by Children from Intact, Single-Parent, and Reconstituted Families", *Psychology In The Schools,* Vol. 20, pp. 166–174
"Personal and family adjustment of 566 children in grades 5–10 were examined by a variety of tests. The results revealed less positive adjustment in children of divorce, regardless of their living in single-parent or remarried households. Mixed results were observed when comparing children in single-parent and remarried families, in terms of their psychological adjustment. Finally, in examining significant family interactions and family type, it was found that males were favorably affected in the single-parent family, while females were more favorably affected within stepfamilies." (c) APA

575. Nye, E., 1957, "Child Adjustment in Broken and in Unhappy Unbroken Homes", *Marriage and Family Living,* Vol. 19, pp. 356–361
A study comparing adjustment of adolescents in "broken" homes with those in unhappy, "unbroken" homes. Those in broken homes showed less psychosomatic illness, less delinquent behavior and better adjustment to their parents, did not differ

significantly with respect to school adjustment, church or delinquent companions.

576. Oakland, T., 1984, *Divorced Fathers: Reconstructing a Quality Life,* Human Sciences Press, Inc., New York

An informative book written for fathers experiencing divorce-related difficulties. The contents covered all aspects of the problems and issues that fathers must face in divorce, ranging from basic legal issues to managing a new household. The book provides valuable information to allow fathers to anticipate what lies ahead and to help them establish their goals and objectives for proper planning.

577. Osborne, J., 1983, "Stepfamilies: The Restructuring Process," Unpublished booklet.

"Intended primarily for professionals, this booklet describes a process of psychological restructuring through which, sometimes with help, members of stepfamilies may assimilate the reality of their new situation. Sections of the discussion focus on phases in the restructuring process: fantasy; pretending; panic; and the emergence of a new family reality involving conflict, re-working, and moving on. Characteristics of the fantasy phase are the 'good' and 'bad' fantasies about the new partnership and the new family. In the pretending phase, stepfamily members pretend to be the collection of fantasies they bring to the new family. Essentially, the panic phase arrives when one or more people in the family begin to recognize their unique, individual view of the family and of other family members and, consequently, start to feel like an outsider. The conflict phase is the time in which the couple and/or family as a whole confront highly charged differences in values, traditions, histories, standards, styles, perceptions, and skills. During the re-working phase conflicts are perceived in new and different ways and members begin to create relationships. Now, moving on, stepfamily members are better able to appreciate and explore the differences within their new family, differences which often become assets. Experience suggests that movement through the process takes at least four years." (ERIC)

578. Perkins, W.H., 1981, Adolescent Children of Divorce in an Outpatient Psychiatric Population, Dissertation Abstracts International, Vol. 42/04-B, page 1616

"The purpose of this study was to investigate the kinds and degree of risk associated with the impact of divorce on the family and the children involved. The variables included were :(a) family status at the time of referral, i.e., intact, divorced, separated, stepparent, widowed, and "other"; (b) sex of the child; (c) race; (d) age of the child at the time of referral; (e) age of the child at the time of the family break; (f) referral source; and (g) type of problem for which the child was referred for psychiatric evaluation and treatment. The subjects of the study were 510 children between the ages of 12 and 17, taken as a consecutive series, who were referred to a publicly financed mental health center for psychiatric evaluation and treatment. The study covered the three-year period of time between January 1977 and December 1979. The information describing the problem behaviors for which the children were referred was coded onto a 22-item checklist of problem categories. For the statistical analysis, these 22 categories were sorted into two major clusters, on the basis of a conceptual model available from the literature, corresponding to the two major dimensions of behavior disorders: (a) anxious/neurotic symptoms and (b) conduct disorder symptoms. The data were then analyzed on the basis of the analysis of variance technique, using the General Linear Models procedure of the Statistica Analysis System of computer data analysis. For the anxious/neurotic dimension, these adolescent children did not differ significantly among themselves, within the overall statistical model. However, it was found that there were significant differences among the children on the basis of sex and the interaction effect of sex and race. Females showed significantly more anxious/neurotic symptoms than did males. Black females showed the highest number of these problems, followed by white females, white males, and black males, respectively. Children from widowed families showed significantly more of these symptoms than did those from stepparent families. On the conduct disorder dimension, the overall statistical model was highly significant. Children from the stepparent family situation showed significantly more of these problems than did children from the other family status categories. Males showed significantly more conduct disorder symptoms than did females. There was also a significant interaction of family status, sex, and race on the conduct disorder variable, with black male children in stepparent families appearing to be particularly at risk for this type of problem. Age of the child at the time of referral was found to be unrelated to the expected number of either anxious/neurotic or conduct disorder symptoms. Neither was the age of the child at the time of the family break found to be statistically significant. Children who were younger when the break occurred were no different from those who had been older, in terms of the number of symptoms on either dimension at the time of referral." (DAI)

579. Peters, J. & V. Haldeman, 1987, ''Time Used for Household Work: A Study of School-Age Children from Single-Parent, Two-Parent, One-Earner, and Two-Earner Families'', *Journal of Family Issues,* Vol. 8, No. 2, pp. 212–225

''Time-use charts and survey questionaires were used to compare the actual and relative amounts of time spent on household work by school-age children in single-parent/one-earner, two-parent/one-earner, and two-parent/two-earner families (SIGMA number of cases = 170). Findings reveal that employment of the homemaker did not appear to contribute to differences in children's actual time spent on individual household tasks, but it did seem to contribute to differences in the children's share of the workload. When total time for all tasks was compared, children in two-parent families were found to spend less actual and relative amounts of time on household work than children in single-parent families. It was concluded that while children from single-parent families spent only a little more actual time than children from two-parent families on individual tasks, the apparent effect was cumulative for time spent on all tasks.'' (Sociological Abstracts)

580. Peterson, J.L., 1982, The Relationship of Family Structure to the Psychological Adjustment of Children, Dissertation Abstracts International, Vol. 43/07-A, page 2290

''This study investigated children's psychological adjustment as a function of differing family structures. Respondents from the seven year follow-up of the Vermont Child Development Project who indicated remarried, separated, or divorced under 'marital status' were asked to participate, and compared to a group of intact families drawn from the same population. Forty-eight children between the ages of eight and thirteen were asked to complete the Kovacs Child Depression Inventory, the Nowicki-Strickland Locus of Control Scale for Children, and the Piers-Harris Children's Self-Concept Scale. All parents were asked to complete the Achenbach Child Behavior Checklist. Remarried and intact parents were also asked to complete the Locke-Wallace Scale of Marital Adjustment. Major findings were that (1) children from separated and divorced families were more depressed and had a lower self-concept than children from remarried and intact families, (2) those children from remarried families appeared to be functioning as well or better than the intact family children on these measures and (3) parents were not found to view their children differently on a symptom checklist across groups. Differences between child self-report and parental reports of child behavior are discussed. The results support a relationship between family structure and psychological functioning in children. Specifically, those children with two parents were better adjusted than those children with one parent irrespective of the biological relationship of the parents to the child. Implications for broader and more longitudinal research are suggested, as well as modifying the model for examining the family to include more systemic indices.'' (DAI)

581. Phelps, R.E. & D.K. Huntley, 1985, ''Social Networks and Child Adjustment in Single-Parent Families'', *Annual Convention of the American Psychological Association,* Los Angeles

''While research with divorced adults has revealed a positive correlation between their social support networks and their adjustment after divorce, there has been little direct examination of the influence of the child's support network on the child's adjustment to parental divorce. The relationship of social network variables to child adjustment in one-parent families was examined in 119 6- to 10-year-old eldest children who were living with their separated or divorced custodial mothers. Mothers rated their children on the Revised Behavior Problem Checklist, and provided information about the child's quality and frequency of contact with various members of his or her social network. Children (N=94) rated themselves on the Child Depression Inventory. Multiple regression analyses were conducted using one criterion variable (a measure of psychopathology of the child) and ten predictor variables (time since parents' separation; child's age; and both the quality and quantity of the child's contact with peers, other adults, the custodial mother, and the non-custodial father) for each analysis. The results revealed that only the network quality measures were significant predictors of child adjustment. Sex differences were also found, with boys' interactions with peers and the custodial mother more salient, while interactions with the non-custodial father and other adults were more salient for girls.'' (ERIC)

582. Platt, K.S., 1987, Successful Single-Parent Families, Masters Abstracts

''This is a study of the healthy post-divorce family using a group of case studies. The literature review examines the family systems work on healthy family function and the literature on divorce and single-parent families. The families in the study were interviewed in depth, given an interactional family task and observed informally. The researcher explored the social support system, household management and child rearing as well as analyzing the families' interactional functioning using family systems concepts.'' (DAI)

583. Pollack, G.K., 1970, ''Sexual Dynamics of Parents without Partners'', *Social Work,* Vol. 2, pp. 79–85
''Discusses some adjustments that PWP must make in their social, dating and love relationships as revealed in seminar groups conducted by a metropolitan area family service. Problems encountered included unrealistic expectations or other stereotypes of the opposite sex, and confusion about and fear of promiscuity as opposed to sexual relations in love relationships. Ways of regaining one's emotional freedom, planning for remarriage, and living a full life if one remains single.'' (SAA)

584. Ramos, S., 1975, *Teaching Your Child to Cope with Crisis: How to Help Your Child Deal with Death, Divorce, Surgery, Being Adopted, Moving, Alcoholic Parents, Sick Parents, Leaving Home, and Other Major Worries,* David McKay, New York
This book is intended to assist parents in dealing effectively with child-rearing problems to anticipate and avert crises, and to utilize life stresses and even tragedies to strengthen the child's emotional growth.

585. Rice, P.L. & S. Bernstein, 1983, Androgyny in the Single-Parent Family, *Annual Meeting of the Midwestern Psychological Association,* Chicago
''The single parent who has to assume the role and the responsibilities of both mother and father provides a different sex-role model for the child than that provided in the two-parent family. Research has indicated that single parents are more androgynous than parents in intact families. To investigate the sex roles of 332 college students (213 females; 119 males) who were raised in single-parent (N=48) and intact nuclear families (N=284), the BEM Sex-Role Inventory, the Spence-Helmreich Personal Attributes Questionnaire, the Family Environment Scale-Short Form, and the Marital History Survey were administered. An analysis of the results showed that children reared in a single-parent environment did not differ substantially from those reared in a nuclear parent home on scales measuring androgyny. However, single-parent family environments did produce a significant change in the distribution of sex-role types, i.e., androgynous males appeared more frequently in single-parent families, while androgynous females appeared less frequently; undifferentiated males appeared less frequently and undifferentiated females

appeared more frequently. Neither age nor maternal employment were found to be significant factors determining androgyny.'' (ERIC)

586. Rios, J.D. & J.M. Gutierrez, 1985–86, ''Parent Training with Non-traditional Families: An Unresolved Issue'', *Child and Family Behavior Therapy,* Vol 7, No. 4, Winter, pp. 33–45

''Although behavioral parent training has been shown to be effective with a variety of child behavior problems, the adaptation and generalization of this treatment across family populations has not met with consistent success. Therapists have only recently recognized the needs of families with diverse backgrounds and those facing interpersonal and intrafamilial conflicts. To promote effective and generalized treatment success across this population, some therapists recommend adjunctive or alternate treatment strategies that encompass the specific needs and characteristic makeup of a family. Despite the therapeutic merit of many recommended adaptations, little empirical information exists on the implementation of the various treatment adaptations. Other clinical issues related to the needs of nontraditional and other non-Mc families are suggested.'' (ASA)

587. Risman, B.J., 1986, ''Can Men 'Mother'? Life As a Single Father'', *Family Relations,* Vol. 35, No. 1, pp. 95–102

With divorced fathers who raise children increasing in numbers, this study sets out to show that social service providers and policy specialists must pay attention to the fact that ''mothering'' is not an exclusively female skill. They surveyed 141 single fathers about their overall role satisfaction. All of those were influenced by economic status and the reason for custody. The author discusses a careful methodological approach to the study. The results indicate that more than 80% of the father respondents took care of the children themselves, showed concern for making their homes child centered, spent considerable time with the children in both functional household and recreational activities. Health care was very adequately provided for. The emotional tasks of child rearing suggested a great amount of ''dyadic intimacy.'' Instrumental and expressive functions seem to be well carried out. Findings bear out past research in that respect. However, they also differ in some respects with other research efforts. The author concludes with the need for professionals to re-examine traditional community and theoretical concepts with reference to child rearing by fathers alone.

588. Robson, B., 1982, ''A Developmental Approach to the Treatment of Children of Divorcing Parents'', In Hanson, Messinger, eds., *Therapy with Remarriage Families,* Aspen Systems Corporation, Rockville, MD, pp. 59–78

The author traces the children's reaction along their life-cycle development with particular emphasis on her conviction that counselors, lawyers, mental health professionals, teachers must be attuned to these developmentally related symptoms in order to prevent development of later pathology. Educational programs for parents within the school system are recommended.

589. Roddy, P.P., 1984, ''A Closer Look at Children in Single-Parent Families'', ERIC Clearinghouse on Urban Education, New York

''Schools are more and more called upon to accommodate students' differences in background and experiences; this picture of diversity includes the growing number of one-parent families. However, educators need to be cautioned against expecting ''trouble'' from the child from a one-parent family. The diversity among research findings suggests that while, as a group, single-parent children tend to have more behavioral problems in school and are at greater risk in terms of truancy and dropout rate, the likelihood of any particular child having cognitive or behavioral problems depends upon the interaction of many factors. Among those factors are the adequacy of child care arrangements; the number of siblings; the structure of the child's environment in both the home and the school; the amount of nurturing the child receives; the age, sex, and race of the child; the socioeconomic level of the family; and the circumstances surrounding the separation of the parents. Therefore, the only accurate answer to the question of whether single-parentness is harmful to a child's academic or behavioral development may well be, it depends.'' (ERIC)

590. Roman, M. & W. Haddad, 1979, *The Disposable Parent: The Case for Joint Custody,* Penguin Books, New York

The authors advocate joint custody; their point of view is sympathetic to the father's rights and they present evidence against the court's assumption that one parent, the mother, is the sole legal and custodial caretaker.

591. Rosenthal, D., Leigh, G.K. & E. Richard, 1986, ''Home Environment of Three- to Six-Year Old Children from Father-Absent and Two-Parent Families'', *Journal of Divorce,* Vol. 9, No. 2, pp. 41–48

Thirty single-parent (mother) families and two-parent families were studied by a home visit and the administration of a home scale. Examination of the data seemed to dispute previous findings, and it is argued that the quality of the mother-child relationship one year after a divorce is similar to that in two-parent families. It is suggested that other areas may need to be looked at to explain developmental differences found in children of divorce in previous studies. Income, relationship to father and other variables may well be of influence. However, the authors point out that their study dispels assumptions which have been held on the basis of other studies, with reference to the quality of the mother-child relationship.

592. Rudolph, M., 1978, *Should the Children Know? Encounters with Death in the Lives of Children,* Schocken Books, New York

Alternatives, such as writing about feelings, for children unable to cry provided within a real-life context. Short chapters, well written in story-like themes convey how to relate death concepts to children. Author uses different levels of loss, e.g., moving, death of a pet, to help adults incorporate ideas of loss into child's cognitive framework.

593. Ryan, P., 1981, *Single-Parent Families,* Administration for Children, Youth, and Families (DHHS), Washington, DC

"This booklet attempts to reassure single parents that they can raise healthy, happy children and provides some suggestions for parents' specific questions and concerns. The first section discusses the emotional stages children pass through when they lose a parent, ways to explain to children the loss of a parent, and ways to handle children's questions and feelings when they do not remember the absent parent. The second section deals with problems of daily living (child care, home chores, and budget management) and the special concerns of single mothers and fathers. The third section gives suggestions for handling problems within the nuclear family, such as disciplining children and adolescents, listening effectively to children, showing children affection, providing sleeping arrangements and privacy, and deciding whether the child has serious emotional problems. The fourth section gives suggestions for managing relationships with relatives, friends, dates, and community agencies. Particular types of single parents (unmarried mothers and fathers; divorced parents; widowed parents; single adoptive parents; and parents who have been separated from their spouses because of a job, illness, etc.) are given suggestions in the fifth section. The final two sections list community agencies and books that may be useful to single parents and their children." (ERIC)

594. Ryberg, R.A., 1985, Noncustodial Father's Involvement with Their Children After Divorce, Dissertation Abstracts International, Vol. 46/10-A, page 3159

"This panel study investigated the effects of role strain perceived by noncustodial fathers on their involvement with their children over the first five years after divorce. The population for this study was identified from public divorce records of 1977–1979 in Dance County, Wisconsin. Noncustodial fathers with at least one minor child were interviewed at one, three, and five years postdivorce. Key variables measured were father-child involvement, the quality of the father-stepfather relationship, fathers' recoupling, father-stepchildren involvement, and fathers' regard for their former spouses as parents. The sex and age of the noncustodial father's youngest child, the target child, were statistically controlled by analysis of covariance (ANCOVA). Repeated measures ANCOVA was used to test the differences in noncustodial fathers' involvement across the three time periods. Results indicate that noncustodial fathers' involvement increased over time for fathers with high regard for their former spouse's parenting ability. Significant post hoc findings demonstrated that fathers with adolescent children had less involvement with their children than noncustodial fathers with young children, mother-custody fathers had less involvement with their children than fathers with other types of custody, and noncustodial fathers with high involvement with their stepchildren were less involved with their own children than noncustodial fathers without stepchildren." (DAI)

595. Sack, W.H., Mason, R. & J.E. Higgins, 1985, "The Single-Parent Family and Abusive Child Punishment", *American Journal of Orthopsychiatry,* Vol. 55, No. 2, pp. 252–259

This retrospective study attempted to compare over 800 adults through in-person interviews, as to the frequency of child abuse in single-parent versus nuclear families and attempted to distinguish the impact of single parent sex, reason for breakup, and the role of parental compatibility on the incidence of child abuse. Sex of the single parent had no bearing on the incident of abuse, nor did the reason for breakup. The major distinguishing factor seemed to be the child's compatibility with the father, suggesting that the parent-child relationship continued after family breakup. However, abuse frequencies were nearly twice as high for single-parent families, and in families separated by divorce rather than by death.

596. Santrock, J.W. & K. Sitterle, 1985, "The Developmental World of Children in Divorced Families: Research Findings and Treatment Implications", In Goldberg, D.C., ed, *Contemporary Marriage: Special Issues in Couples Therapy,* The Dorsey Press, Belmont, CA

The chapter identifies three traditions of research in this area, then goes on to chart them. Intervening problems in the adult world which heavily influence the development of children are given attention. Clinical implications and recommendations for interventions conclude the chapter. The interventions include both educational and clinical considerations.

597. Schamgar-Handelman, L., 1982, "The Concept of Remarriage Among Israeli War-Widows", *Journal of Comparative Family Studies,* Vol. 13, No. 3, pp. 359–372

Most writings on remarriage focus on divorced people; this study attempts to differentiate the remarriage of widowed women who lost their husbands in one Israeli war, a relatively homogenous group. There are differences from other single parents, in that these women have considerable status in terms of their husbands' status as war heroes, and also because they and their children are economically provided for. Provisions for the children continue after remarriage. Therefore, the outer circumstances, which shape much of the feelings about remarriage, are different from those in which most other research on remarriage was done. Three types of expectations were outlined: (1) Second "First Marriage," where romantic love and the formation of a new unit with additional children are seen as the objective; (2) "Remedial" marriage to repair the damage done to the family, with the expectation of the second husband to be very different from the first one; (3) "Postponed" Marriage, until such time as "the children had left the home." While seemingly compatible with certain life-cycle stages, this actually did not seem to be so in terms of the women's ages. The considerations seem quite child-focused as well as taking into consideration the feelings of the widow's family of origin, perhaps features more typical for Israeli society. The children's feelings were not researched, though they seemed to be very much in the foreground of their mothers' perceptions—positive or negative—about remarriage.

598. Scherman, A. & S.L. Tedder, 1987, Training Counselors in Divorce Intervention: A Course Approach, Paper presented at the

Annual Convention of the American Association for Counseling and Development

"This paper recognizes an increasing demand for counseling services for children and adults affected by divorce and notes that counselors traditionally have not been trained to provide such services. It presents a six-unit training outline which can be used as a course or as an inservice workshop for training mental health workers in offering services to persons affected by divorce. The first unit, "Review and Trends in the Literature," examines pre-1970 and post-1970 literature as two distinct periods in reported research concerning divorce impact on children. Unit 2, "Models of Intervention," presents the model developed by Wallerstein and Kelly, the Grief Model, the Rebuilding Model, and a Multimodal Therapy Model. Unit 3, "Working with Children," lists instruments useful for informational or research purposes and describes activities in school-related problems. Unit 4, "Working with Parents," identifies five areas of intervention for working with single parents. Unit 5, "Working with Step-Families," addresses problems associated with remarriage. The final unit, "Child Custody Law and Mediation," examines the legal problems of divorce. Content materials and references for each of the six units are described. (NB)" ERIC

599. Schlesinger, B., 1986, "Single-Parent Families: A Bookshelf, 1978–1985", *Family Relations,* Vol. 35, No. 1, pp. 199–204

The author, who has written on single parents in journal articles and who has published books on the subject since 1969, gives in this paper 80 annotations relating to books and special issues of journals published between 1978 and 1985 in Canada and the U.S. The bibliography was divided into various categories of single parents, e.g. Separated Single Parents, Non-Married Mothers and Fathers, Children and Single Parent Families. The author has also written 490 annotated entries in his 1985 book published in Toronto.

600. Schulman, G., 1975, "The Single-Parent Family", *Jewish Communal Service*

In the single-parent family, as a result of external events, one parent must assume daily roles and responsibilities toward the children. The economic and social status of the family, the ages of the children, and the basic emotional and physical health of the family as well as important social networking affect how the family will deal with the change. Many of the problems could be avoided if the feelings of anger, helplessness, jealousy, etc., were expressed jointly and in the presence of the children.

601. Schulman, G.L., 1981, "Divorce, Single Parenthood and Stepfamilies: Structural Implications of These Transactions", *International Journal of Family Therapy,* Vol. 3, No. 2, pp. 87–112

The author takes a structural family systems perspective to discuss the family life-cycle stages in the periods of divorce, single-parent family, and stages of the remarried family. Special structural differences of these families are discussed, as well as tasks which make it possible for the new family to function and get through a transitional stage. Three case examples illustrate the conceptual content. The exit of one parent and/or the addition of one parent are perceived as crisis points, at which family therapy is seen as particularly helpful. Awareness of the necessity to include all parts of the family system, both biological and stepfamily members, is emphasized.

602. Schwartzberg, A.Z., 1981, "Divorce and Children and Adolescents", *Adolescent Psychiatry,* pp. 119–132

The prominent effects of divorce on the older child are sadness and a sense of loss and betrayal by the parents. There is evidence of a recurrent theme of anxiety about future marriage, intense loyalty conflicts, abrupt de-idealization of parents and awareness of parents as sexual objects. Divorce affects the superego development and resolution of oedipal conflicts primarily with boys and the custodial mother. Early and effective intervention during the separation period would prevent severe development issues with children. Adolescents need help to deal with losses, express anger and sadness and anxiety to enhance their growth and development.

603. Skolnick, A. & J. Skolnick, 1980, *Family in Transition,* Little, Brown and Co., Boston

This book reviews changes in the family over the last decade as well as controversies about how to interpret these changes.

604. Stein, P., 1984, Adolescent Drug Abuse as a Function of Family Structure and Family Environment, Dissertation Abstracts International, Vol. 45/03-B, page 1000

"*The Problem.* This study investigated the occurrence of adolescent drug abuse in families according to family structure and family environment. Research indicates that adolescent drug abuse is becoming increasingly prevalent and that single-parent families as well as stepparent families are growing in numbers. The purpose of investigating differences found in families of adolescent drug abusers was to discover factors which influence its occurrence. This study addressed the major dimensions of family environment and family structure that may have contributed to differences in families in which adolescent drug abuse occurred most often and least often.

Method. The research approach utilized was a comparative correlational study analyzed in an ex post facto manner. The sample population consisted of 90 families with adolescent drug abusers. Families were divided into three categories: intact nuclear families, single-parent families, and stepparent families. Each familial category was represented by 30 families. Subjects were given the Moos Family Environment Scale and a self-report questionnaire. Drug usage by family structure hypotheses were subjected to a chi-square analysis. Family environment by family structure hypotheses were subject to an analysis of variance.

Results. Results indicated that adolescent drug abusers used drugs more frequently in stepparent families than in single-parent families and intact nuclear families with significance at the .05 level. Adolescent drug abusers used drugs more often in single-parent families than in intact nuclear families with significance at the .05 level. Differences did not exist at the .05 level in relationship dimensions among family types. Personal growth dimension results indicated that intact nuclear families and single-parent families scored higher than stepparent families at the .05 level. System maintenance dimension results indicated that intact nuclear families scored higher than single-parent families and stepparent families at the .05 level, but no significant differences were found between single-parent families and stepparent families.'' (DAI)

605. Steinzor, B., 1969, *When Parents Divorce: A New Approach to New Relationships,* Pantheon Books, New York

The author, a practicing psychotherapist, presents his personal philosophy on divorce and marriage. He takes exception to the child-centered and friendly divorce approach, preferring direct dialog and confrontation. Believes that divorce based on an artificial friendship with the ex-partner is no solution. The book is meant for both parent and child. Discusses choosing a lawyer, separation agreements, child support, living independently, visitation relations, custodial relations, and remarriage. (E & N)

606. Stolberg, A. & A.J. Ullman, 1984, ''Assessing Dimensions of Single Parenting: The Single Parenting Questionnaire'', *Journal of Divorce,* Vol. 8, No. 2, pp. 31–45

This study developed and attempted to validate a research instrument which assesses five dimensions of single parenting. The dimensions are described, as is the methodology of the researchers. 239 divorced, custodial parents and their children were administered the test, 179 single mothers, 31 single fathers. (6 children were pre-schoolers, 102 elementary school children, 86 adolescents, and 11 young adults, 121 boys, 84 girls.) A great deal of care was taken in explaining the instrument, its development, and how it was validated. It is felt that the strength of the single-parent questionnaire both statistical and predictive makes it a good measure to be used in both research studies and clinical interventions of the divorced.

607. Stuart, I.R. & Abt, L.E., eds., 1981, *Children of Separation and Divorce,* Van Nostrand Reinhold Company Inc., New York

The authors have presented a very good and increasingly popular collection of papers dealing with the impact of divorce on children, and the development of new therapeutic approaches to the resulting consequences. The first edition of this book in 1970 viewed problems from the point of view of parting parents and the effects on children from the children's point of view. This edition includes a much heavier emphasis on interventions by a variety of professional helpers. The four parts in which management and treatment are examined deal 1)with legal issues and problems, 2) with psychodynamic problems, e.g. developmental issues, custody, and loss, 3) with ''management problems,'' resulting from separation and divorce, e.g. placement in foster care, joint custody, or special issues such as gay parents, or adolescent pregnancy, 4) treatment of problems within the family unit focusing on a systems approach to stepfamilies, on preventive treatment among others. A chapter on visiting relationships concludes the selection, with contributions by a large array of professionals.

608. Terre, L., 1987, Contribution of Proximal Versus Distal Stressors to Children's Divorce Adjustment: Methodological and Theoretical Considerations, Dissertation Abstracts International, Vol. 48/11-B, p. 3427

''The present study examined the relationship between family constellation, family interaction patterns, parent-child relationships, and child adjustment in divorced, intact, and remarried households, using a biracial sample of rural school children from predominately lower and lower-middle class families. Among the most striking features of the results was that, across a variety of child adjustment domains, the proximal conditions associated with daily family life better predicted child adjustment than family type itself. Moreover, in the divorced and remarried families, parent-child relationships quality was more strongly associated with child adaptation than parent-child contact per se. Finally, some differential adjustment patterns emerged as a function of child gender, age, and race. The implications of these results are discussed in terms of methodological, conceptual, and intervention efforts in the area of divorce.'' (DAI)

609. Tessman, L.H., 1978, ''Children of Parting Parents'' in *The Human Relations Network: Its Supports and Lacunae,* Jason Aronson, New York

Children of parting parents must deal with the loss or drastic alteration of relationship to at least one parent. The components of the human interaction network change and grow in importance as the child experiences this loss and new status. An understanding of the current social structure in relation to the more immediate environent of the single-parent family can aid families and professionals in the development of needed supports for individual families in the divorce crisis and after. Tessman, an experienced clinician, provides guidelines for therapy, an extensive bibliography and more than 50 case examples of work with children and parents.

610. Trevisano, M.A.A., 1982, The Effects of Sole and Joint Custodial Arrangements on the Emotional Functioning and Behavioral Adaption of Children of Divorce, Dissertation Abstracts International, Vol. 43/02-B, page 537

''The high divorce rate in the United States has produced a need to consider the custody needs of children involved in these family changes. Are the emotional needs of children of divorce best served through joint custody by both parents or through sole custody by one or the other parent? This study addresses the relative merits of joint and sole custody arrangements through an examination of the empirical data related to these two custodial styles. The researcher investigated the behavioral adaptation and emotional functioning of three groups of children between the ages of seven and eleven: eight joint custody children, fourteen sole custody children, and a control group of ten children from intact families. Three objective measures were used in the survey: The Adaptive Behavior Inventory for Children, the California Test of

Personality, and the Children's Attitude to Parental Separation Inventory. A subjective measure was also conducted to determine parents' and children's reactions at the time of marital separation. No statistical significance at the .05 level was found between the behavioral adaptation and emotional functioning of the three groups of children. However, children who had been identified as gifted and children with stepparents functioned at a statistically more significant level than other children in the study on several scales of the California Test of Personality. Results on the subjective measure (Kidd & Kidd: Experimental Method) indicated that both parents and children underwent emotional pain at the time of the marital separation irrespective of custodial arrangement. A correlation matrix between the scales of two objective measures—the Adaptive Behavior Inventory for Children and the California Test of Personality—evidenced no significant correlations. Given that children in this study raised in joint custody families evidenced neither significantly higher behavioral adaptation nor higher emotional functioning than sole custody children, serious questions and challenges emerge regarding the suitability of the joint custody law now existent in the State of California. Thoughtful assessment of the results of this survey suggests that further research is needed on families from different ethnic groups and socioeconomic levels. It becomes more evident also that each case of child custody needs to be individually assessed by mental health counselors without court intervention. Research is further recommended on children of unfit parents.'' (DAI)

611. Troyer, W., 1979, *Divorced Kids,* Harcourt Brace Jovanovich, New York

Interviews with children of divorce revealing their feelings, insights, and adjustments. Helps the professional understand how children feel in terms of their family situation.

612. Turner, N.W. & S. Strine, 1985, ''Separation and Divorce: Clinical Implications for Parents and Children'', in Goldberg, D.C., ed., *Contemporary Marriage: Special Issues in Couples Therapy,* The Dorsey Press, Belmont, CA

The process of separation and its implications for treatment are considered. The conflicting needs of children and adults in these situations are described, in terms of the phases of divorce. A chart is developed to consider the parent's need, the child's need, and the therapist's role.

613. Wagaw, T. & M. Achatz, 1985, "The Effects of Absence of a Parent on the Cognitive and Social Performance of Adolescents: Research Results from Africa", *Annual Meeting of the American Educational Research Association,* Chicago

"The importance of family life on the development of the child has been undertaken to assess the influence that family life and marital status of parents have on child development. It was hypothesized that African adolescents from broken homes would experience: (1) less involvement in informal social relations and organized group activities; (2) less popularity with peers; (3) more personal, social, and disciplinary problems; and (4) more fluctuation in academic performance when compared to peers from homes where two parents were present. To test these hypotheses, 8th and 11th grade students in Addis Ababa, Ethiopia were interviewed. The experimental group consisted of 173 students from broken homes. Students (N=150) from intact families, matched with the experimental group in age, sex, and socioeconomic background, comprised the control group. Data were collected from a questionnaire and sociometric rating scale administered to all students; interviews with instructional staff; and academic records. Overall, the findings indicated that one out of three adolescents attending secondary schools in Addis Ababa came from broken homes. The social and academic profile of these students differed from that of students from intact homes, with the students from broken homes generally at a disadvantage. However, the incidence of broken homes and the magnitude of their effects on aspects of emotional, social, and academic performance varied according to the age, sex, and socioeconomic background of students." (ERIC)

614. Wallerstein, J.S., 1984, "Children of Divorce: Preliminary Report of a Ten-Year Follow-Up of Young Children", *American Journal of Orthopsychiatry,* Vol. 54, No. 3, pp. 444–458

This describes the results of a ten-year follow-up study of children now in their teens who were between two and one-half and six at the time of their parents' divorce. Few conscious memories of the nuclear family's separation were retained, although at the time these children had shown distress and anxieties. The children had spent two-thirds of their lives in single-parent or stepfamilies, showed normal school adjustment, nevertheless expressed feelings of loss and deprivation along with reconciliation fantasies. Relationships with the non-custodial father had retained centrality, and a heightened need to re-establish such ties during adolescence. However, these children fared better than their older siblings, had less troubled memories, and presented a more optimistic outlook for the future.

615. Wallerstein, J.S., 1985, "The Overburdened Child: Some Long-Term Consequences of Divorce", *Social Work,* March/April, pp. 116–123

An article which suggests that divorce is not a time-limited crisis but an ongoing series of adjustments. The author also describes how the professional can shift focus from interventions that treat a time-limited crisis to helping the family deal with some of the persisting problems of divorce.

616. Wallerstein, J.S. & J.B. Kelly, 1974, "The Effects of Parental Divorce: Experiences of the Preschool Child", *Journal of the American Academy of Child Psychiatry,* Vol. 14, No. 2, pp. 600–616

Research data on the response of 34 preschool children to their parents' separation through divorce was obtained by four to six interviews with individual family members over a period of six weeks, with a follow-up one year later. The school system was also used to obtain information about the children. The findings indicated that separation triggered regression, bewilderment, aggression, and need in the two-and-a-half and three-and-a-quarter year old group, guilt, diminished self-esteem, and depression in the three and three-quarter to four and three-quarter year olds, while five to six year olds were able to go through the separation experience without noticeable developmental interruption or regression. However, 55% of all children had regressed psychologically one year later, and the mother (resident parent)-child relationship had deteriorated, and father-child relationship had improved. At follow-up, 63% of the girls and 27% of the boys had deteriorated.

617. Wallerstein, J.S. & J.B. Kelly, 1986, "The Effects of Parental Divorce: Experiences of the Child in Early Latency", *American Journal of Orthopsychiatry,* Vol. 46, No. 1, pp. 20–42

This is a partial report on the authors' research on the impact of divorce on children. Criteria of age-appropriate developmental tasks are used as a base. The children showed deep suffering and longing for their absent fathers, with little help for their hurt, since their ego structures could not tolerate such intense pain and grief. Feelings of loss and deprivation, fears about the very existence of the family and its future were expressed by loyalty conflicts, reconciliation fantasies, and possessiveness. At follow-up, one year later, the nature of the post-divorce family structure had strong bearing on the outcome. Twenty-three percent of the children were worse, manifested by sadness, resignation toward the divorce, and strong reconciliation wishes.

618. Wallerstein, J.S. & J.B. Kelly, 1976, ''The Effects of Parental Divorce: Experiences of the Child in Later Latency'', *American Journal of Orthopsychiatry,* Vol.46, No. 2, pp. 256–269

Report on part of a larger study, this one concentrating on 9–10-year-olds (later latency), at the time of parental divorce and one year later. These children seemed to function more on age-appropriate levels. They seemed to struggle actively to master their experience by denial and avoidance activities, thus appearing courageous, and containing their grief, while functioning well. Anger continued to exist, but was quite consciously expressed by temper tantrums and/or demanding, dictatorial attitudes and identification with the non-resident fathers. There were not infrequently cases of poor school performance, somatic symptoms, fears, and loneliness. At one year follow-up, fifty percent of the children were significantly worse and one-third remained enraged with either one of the parents. Low self-esteem, depression, peer and school difficulties were observed.

619. Wallerstein, J.S., Kelly, J.B., 1974, ''The Effects of Parental Divorce: The Adolescent Experience'', in *The Child In His Family,* John Wiley & Sons Pub., New York

Report on part of the larger research study, in which 21 youngsters over 13 years of age were studied as to the effects of family disruption on the developmental tasks of adolescence. Findings indicated that all adolescents experienced a great deal of pain, and anger at their parents. Sadness and a feeling of betrayal, as well as embarrassment vis-à-vis their peers and community adults, as well as anxiety about their own future roles as marital partners were expressed. Concern over family finances were expressed, but no responsibility for the divorce was expressed, unlike by younger children. In vulnerable children there was a greater number of deeper pathological problems, e.g. substance abuse, or developmental regression. The functioning of the adolescents was particularly strongly affected by the blurring of generational boundaries, which seriously affected their family tasks. Those who were able to distance themselves from their parents' crises, with the parents' approval or tolerance of this, fared best.

620. Walters, J. & L.H. Walters, 1980, ''Parent-Child Relationships: A Review 1970–1979'', *Journal of Marriage and the Family,* Vol. 42, pp. 807–822

This article includes a summary of the state of research at the beginning of the seventies and identifies 10 primary issues in this decade, and examines some major contributions in the literature on parent-child interactions, including a review of some of the changes in professional conceptualizations. They point out that the research reflects a departure from the unidirectional model to the reciprocal model of causality of child behavior. Fathers are increasingly included in considering adult-child interaction. This article also included some of the issues which are not given too much attention elsewhere, such as physiological influences on child behavior, and last but not least, the effects of the law on parent-child interaction, relationships and interpretations of sexuality.

621. Waters, F.H., 1983, The Effect of Family Structure on Behavior and Attendance of Central Bucks High School Students, Dissertation Abstracts International, Vol.44/04-A, page 952

''A study of 2,813 high school students from a suburban Philadelphia school district was conducted to determine if family structure—two natural parents, single-parent, one-natural and one-stepparent, or neither natural or adoptive parents—had an effect on the student's behavior or attendance patterns. A review of cumulative record cards, attendance records, principals' reports, and special education records plus a series of interviews with disciplinarians, attendance officers, and counselors provided the information on each student. The data was analyzed to determine if differences existed in behavior based on family structure, as well as by sex, grade level, and school. The study showed significant differences in attendance patterns between students from two-parent families and those from the other three family structures. (1) Students from two-parent families had a significantly lower proportion of days tardy than did students from single-parent families. (2) Students from two-parent families had a significantly lower proportion of legal absences than did students from either single-parent families or stepparent families. (3) Students living with neither parent had significantly higher proportion of illegal absences than did students from each of the other three family structures. The following differences were found regarding behavior: (1) Students from two-parent families had a significantly lower proportion of suspensions and of less duration than students from each of the other family types. (2) Students from two-parent families had a significantly lower proportion of class cuts and disciplinary problems than did students from one-parent families. (3) Students from stepparent families had significantly more disciplinary contacts than students from the other two non-two-parent families. (4) Students placed in special programs for socially-emotionally disturbed children more frequently came from homes where there were not two natural parents. (5) There were no significant differences in placement in the Alternative School. (6) The numbers of students who committed alcohol or drug violations, withdrew from school, or were expelled were so small that individual comparisons of family type could not be made. (7) Some two-way and three-way interactions of family type, sex, grade level, and school were significant.'' (DAI)

622. Weinraub, M. & B.M. Wolf, 1983, ''Effects of Stress and Social Supports on Mother-Child Interactions in Single- and Two-Parent Families'', *Child Development,* Vol. 54, No. 5, pp. 1297–1311

14 single mothers and 14 matched married mothers and their respective children were studied as to their interactions along the parameters outlined. Single parents tended to be more isolated, receiving fewer parental and social supports, and to experience more potentially stressful life changes. But only in the household area did they report more difficulty in coping. No significant differences were found in any of the 5 mother-child interactions. Implications for intervention are discussed.

623. Weisfeld, D. & M.S. Laser, 1977, ''Divorced Parents in Family Therapy in a Residential Treatment Setting'', *Family Process,* Vol. 16, pp. 229–236

''Treatment article highlighting the importance of including the divorced or separated parents in the treatment of their child. Divorced parents are required to participate together in the family therapy of their child placed in the residential treatment center. Different sources of resistance and treatment techniques are identified and discussed through theoretical analysis and case study presentations. The therapy of these fractured families contributed to an elimination of recidivism and according to follow-up reports, to significant and sustained improvements in the children's functioning in school, home and community activities.'' (SAA)

624. Weiss, R.S., 1979, *Going It Alone,* Basic Books, New York

This book is based on reports of widowed and never-married parents as well as those of divorce. The problems of child-rearing with only one adult in the home and the different stresses as well as positives for the children and their relationships to the resident parent are fully described. Women and men, as heads of single-parent households tell their stories, including considerations of remarriage. This book also develops an understanding of parenting in our society.

625. Weiss, R.S., 1975, *Marital Separation,* Basic Books, New York
This book offers discussion and verbatim reports of the social and psychological realities of ending a marriage and single-parenting. Positive as well as less successful ways of coping are illustrated. Extreme sensitivity of the custodial parent to signs of behavior problems, and the overload of roles, tasks, and responsibilities are highlighted. Suggestions for easing single-parent burdens are included. (DHHS)

626. Weitzman, L.J., 1985, *The Divorce Revolution,* Free Press, New York
This book is based on a ten-year scientific study (1970–1980) of the divorce reform by way of the ''no fault'' divorce law. Starting with a very positive attitude, the author found surprising data, indicating that the so-called ''enlightened'' legal reform and the court's interpretation of ''equality'' tend seriously to disadvantage women and children, too, since in most cases children still live with their mothers. Divorced women and the children with them suffer an immediate 73% drop in their standard of living while their male counterparts show a 42% rise in theirs. A systematic analysis of court records, interviews with hundreds of attorneys, judges, and recently divorced men and women are reported on. The book is a valuable resource both for divorcees, especially women, and for professionals who are dealing with them. The impact of child custody and child support decisions which very seriously disadvantage children, and may have very far-reaching consequences in every aspect of their lives, are particularly noteworthy.

627. No entry.

628. Weltner, J.S., 1982, ''A Structural Approach to the Single-Parent Family'', *Family Process,* June 21, Vol. 21, No. 2, pp. 203–210

This paper lists some core problems encountered by all single-parent families, and presents a sequence of therapeutic approaches for dealing with these problems on the basis of structural family theory with the emphasis on sub-systems, generational boundaries, and organizational patterns a la Minuchin, Haley and Aponte. The single parent, predominantly the mother, is beset by emotional and physical demands, needs validation from other adults, to achieve generational boundaries from offspring and family of origin, and mother and children need avenues of emotional expression. Suggestions for treatment are: 1. Support the Executive System Function; 2. Define and delineate the children's functions, especially the ''parental child's''; 3. Establish a ''family cabinet''; 4. Use the extended family constructively; use friends, groups, home health resources; 5. Help parent and children have lives of their own; 6. Therapy in its formal sense is the last helping resource to be considered.

629. Williams, M.B., 1984, ''Family Dissolution: An Issue for the Schools'', *Children Today,* Vol. 13, No. 4, pp. 24,25,27–29

The author explicates some of the findings in young children of separation and divorce to emphasize the importance of early intervention in order to deal with the identity confusion in young children. Group programs under the auspices of the school are recommended on the basis of the author's own experience, who with a student as a co-leader, conducted 40-minute group meetings with several small groups (4–6) of kindergarten children who live in single-parent families. Sessions with the children, joint sessions with the separated parents on parent-child issues are described as is some work with a stepparent. It is felt that mediation efforts in the school can be of considerable help to both children and parents.

630. Wodarski, J.S., 1982, ''Single Parents and Children: A Review for Social Workers'', *Family Therapy,* Vol. 9, No. 3, pp. 311–320

''A literature review discusses the significance for families and schools of the rapidly increasing divorce rate. The characteristics of families and children who are at risk are explored, and the effects of the divorce process on children's academic and social behavior are examined. Implications for school personnel are highlighted, and suggestions for future research are presented.'' (SWAB)

631. Wolf, B.M., 1987, Stress and Social Supports: Impact on Parenting and Child Development in Single-Parent and Two-Parent Families, Dissertation Abstracts International, Vol. 48/04-B, p. 1171

"This study explored the nature of parental behaviors and child development in one- and two-parent households. The differing social situations of these mothers were examined. Attention was focused on life events and social supports as these hinder or promote optimal parenting and successful child development. The sample consisted of 19 pairs of single mothers and their pre-school children, and a comparison group of 19 married mothers and children. There were no differences between the groups in income, maternal education and age, and child's age. However, single mothers worked more hours. Several dimensions of maternal behavior associated with optimal child outcomes were examined: maternal control, maturity demands, parent-child communication, nurturance and a summary parenting measure. Child outcome measures included intellectual functioning, compliance with maternal requests, readiness to learn, moodiness, aggressiveness and an overall risk factor for social and learning problems. In many aspects, single and married mothers and their children functioned equally well. No differences between the mothers in the handling of their daughters were found. Nor were there any differences in the quality of maternal communications and nurturance. No differences in intellectual functioning, readiness to learn, or moodiness were apparent between children in these families. Difficulties among single mothers in exercising control and setting appropriate maturity demands with their sons were noted. Concurrently, boys in single-parent homes were less compliant with their mothers' requests and commands than boys from two-parent homes. The life situations of single and married mothers differed. Besides working more hours, single mothers tended to experience more life events. Simultaneously, single mothers reported receiving fewer social supports both for themselves emotionally and as parents. Social supports and maternal satisfaction with supports were reflected in more optimal parenting behaviors for both single and married mothers. Life events were associated with reduced parental effectiveness and increased child behavior problems in single-parent families. Differences in mother-child interactions in single-parent and two-parent households were discussed as these related to the differing social situations of the two groups and to father-absence." (DAI)

632. Woody, J.D., Colley, P.E., Schlegemilch, J., Maginn, Paul & J. Balsanek, 1984, "Child Adjustment to Parental Stress Following Divorce", *Social Casework,* Vol. 65, No. 9, pp. 405–412

This article reports on a study which analyzed the relationship between parental stress and the children's adjustment following the divorce process. A number of studies enhanced the knowledge base and understanding of divorcing and divorce families, leading to the hypothesis that the amount of parental stress (or life change) which is experienced during the divorce process will have a bearing on the degree of active symptoms and/or other indicators of problems on the part of parents and children alike. The findings showed that high levels of parent stress predict a greater number of child symptoms which do not decrease with the passing of time. Therefore, the need for prevention programs is emphasized, as well as for outreach both to create programs and to make a wide variety of programs available to divorcing couples. The responsibility of the clinician beyond treatment and referral is highlighted as well as the creation of new roles for the clinician.

633. Worell, J., 1986, ''Single Mothers: Issues of Stigma'', *Annual Convention of the American Psychological Association,* Washington, DC

''This paper examines psychological and social issues for single mothers in the context of therapeutic strategies for effective intervention. Never married, previously married, and Lesbian mothers are considered in terms of sociocultural myths and sources of stigma; research findings related to these myths; and interventions targeting the single-mother family, the community, and governmental policies that influence legislation affecting these familes. Sources of societal stigma are discussed which are related to morality, sex-role violation, and victimization. Dispelling myths related to these areas requires careful consideration of the major sources of stress impinging on these families: economic stress, social isolation, and role-strain. It is suggested that mental health interventions treat these families in the context of the massive effects of poverty, societal oppression, and victimization. Therapeutic strategies that include only psychological processes of the single mother will fail to address the larger context of her social situation and will further contribute to her victimization and despair. Interventions must be preventive, remediative, educative, and aimed at involving community resources. Therapists are encouraged to become knowledgeable about single mothers and the economic and legal issues facing them, and to take an active role as mediators and advocates. Research requirements discussed include increased attention to models of prevention and intervention into the factors that facilitate the strength and well-being of single-mother families. Forty references are included.'' (ERIC)

634. Zaslow, M., 1988, ''Sex Differences in Children's Response to Parental Divorce'', *American Journal of Orthopsychiatry,* Vol. 58, No. 3, pp. 355–378

The author gives a comprehensive review of the research literature on the differential reactions of boys and girls to parental divorce. She contests the notion that boys are more negatively affected. She suggests a more sophisticated and differential hypothesis on the basis of evaluating the strengths and weaknesses of the research to date.

635. Zaslow, M., 1989, ''Sex Differences in Children's Response to Parental Divorce: Samples, Variables, Ages and Sources'', *American Journal of Orthopsychiatry,* Vol. 59, No. 1, pp. 118–141

This second of a two-part review concentrates on finding and possibly explaining the differences in the research findings on sex differences in children's response to parental divorce. The research literature is again examined from different vantage points and tables are presented for clarity. A number of sub-hypotheses are presented, e.g. ''the prediction that boys do indeed respond more negatively to parental divorce both immediately and over a period of years if they are living with an unmarried mother; whereas in post-divorce families involving a stepfather or father custody, girls fare worse.'' The author examines the data carefully along various dimensions and makes specific, valuable suggestions for further research.

636. Zill, N., 1978, ''Divorce, Marital Happiness, and the Mental Health of Children: Findings from the Foundation of Child Development National Survey of Children'', *NIMH workshop on Divorce and Children,* Bethesda, MD

637. Zimmerman, I.L. and M. Bernstein, 1983, ''Parental Work Patterns in Alternative Families: Influence on Child Development'', *American Journal of Orthopsychiatry,* Vol. 53, No. 3, July

The increasing return to work by mothers of young children was documented for matching samples of mothers in families representing traditional marriages, single-mother units, social contract relationships, and communal living groups. Mothers appear to be returning to work in increasing numbers, with 13% working full time by the end of the first year. In-depth comparisons of children's functioning revealed few differences attributable to life-styles, no matter at what age the child was assessed. Overall no evidence was found of negative effects on children's social, emotional, and cognitive development attributable to maternal absence due to employment.

Extended Family

638. Bronfenbrenner, U., 1970, *Two Worlds of Childhood, U.S. and U.S.S.R.,* Russell Sage Foundation, New York

Description of life in the U.S. and U.S.S.R. Discussion of cultural differences and the use in other countries of extended family and community persons as role models and enforcers of discipline.

639. Dornbusch, S., Carlsmith, J., Bushwall, S., Ritter, P., Leiderman, H., Hastorf, A. & R. Gross, 1985, "Single Parents, Extended Households, and the Control of Adolescents", *Child Development,* Vol. 56, pp. 326–341

The authors study decision-making patterns and their relationship to adolescent deviance in a representative national sample done in 1970. They regret the unavailability of similarly comprehensive data of more recent origin. Findings in the data of that time indicate a definite association between "mothers only" households and adolescent deviance, as well as adolescent decision making without parental input, especially for males. The presence of an additional adult in the household brings the single-parent resident youngster closer to the patterns seen in two-parent households. Some implications for the suggestion that nontraditional group parenting may provide a functional task distribution which cannot as easily be carried by one mother (person) alone are outlined.

640. Fisher, E.O., 1981, "Impact of Divorce on the Extended Family", *Journal of Divorce,* Vol. 5, No. 1/2, pp. 3–171

"We speak about divorce as having reached epidemic proportions but have largely ignored that an epidemic is not confined to those who are initially distressed. Much of professional writing is devoted to the marital couple and their children in relation to the onset and impact of divorce and little to the study of what was concomitantly happening to other family members. This special double issue of the journal focuses on the impact of divorce on the extended family. It is divided into four sections: psychology, sociology, law/economics, and clinical practice. The articles are: "Divorce and the Dynamics of the Family Kinship System" by M. Duffy; "Divorce, the Family Life Cycle, and Its Empirical

Deficiencies'' by W. Bytheway; ''The Role of Extended Kin in the Adjustment to Marital Separation'' by G.B. Spanier and S. Hanson; ''Changes in Family Relationships Following Divorce of Adult Child: Grandmother's Perceptions'' by C.R. Ahrons and M.E. Bowman; ''Support of the Parent When an Adult Son or Daughter Divorces'' by E.S. Johnson and B.H. Vinick; ''Grand-parent Visitation: Vagaries and Vicissitudes'' by H.H. Foster and D.J. Freed; ''The Economic Choice in Divorce: Extended or Blended Family?'' by W.D. Johnson and M.H. Minton.'' (SWAB)

641. Gladow, N.W. & M.P. Ray, 1986, ''The Impact of Informal Support Systems on the Well-Being of Low-Income Single Parents'', *Family Relations,* Vol. 35, No. 1, pp. 113–123

The authors examined 63 families in a rural county in Eastern Washington who were living below 125% of the nationally established poverty level. The study cites previous research, its own measures, tentative conclusions and suggestions for future studies. A discussion section details the pros and cons of the findings. The overall result of the study attests to the hypothesis that informal support systems do have a positive impact on the well-being of single parents in low-income strata. Friendship support, relative support, and romantic involvement are examined separately. Comparisons are made of some of the findings about the lonely elderly. The implications seem to refute the popularly held notions of the self-suffiency of the nuclear family and point in the direction of advising agencies dealing with poor single-parent families (or perhaps even with others) to encourage family and friend networks, and to help create new ones by a variety of support groups, and by direct encouragement to expand the clients' life space.

642. Hartman, A.L., 1979, ''The Extended Family as a Resource for Change'', In *Social Work Practice,* Columbia University Press, New York

This article discusses innovative approaches for utilizing the extended family as a resource for change. Emphasis is on the use of the genogram as a vehicle for contracting, assessment, and intervention. System and individual changes are addressed.

643. Johnson, C.L. & B.M. Barer, 1987, ''Marital Instability and the Changing Kinship Networks of Grandparents'', *Gerontologist,* Vol. 27, No. 3, pp. 330–335

''Focuses on the effects divorces of children have on the kinship networks of the older generation. Found a common source of expansion among paternal grandmothers who retained relationships with their former daughters-in-law and her relatives at the same time that they added new relatives with sons' remarriages.'' (ERIC)

644. Johnson, W.D. & M.H. Minton, 1981, ''The Economic Choice in Divorce: Extended or Blended Family?'', *Journal of Divorce,* Vol. 5, No. 1–2, pp. 101–113

This study examines the economic situation of the divorced family. It is hypothesized that the nuclear family is reshaped into an extended family in the post-divorce period. The dissolution-fragmentation process is felt to result in changing the environment in which the family functions. The extended family is described as stepping in as a surrogate protector.

645. Kalish, R. & E. Visher, 1981, ''Grandparents of Divorce and Remarriage'', *Journal of Divorce,* Vol. 5, pp. 127–140

At least three perspectives are suggested for viewing the grandparents in divorce situations: the older individuals themselves and their changed interactions with their children and grandchildren, the perspectives of the adult child and child-in-law and new in-laws upon remarriage, and last but not least the perspectives of the grandchildren and potential stepgrandchildren. Grandparents may be grand- or greatgrandparents who get divorced; parents of adult divorcing children; grandparents of adults who get divorced. The focus of this paper is on the middle group, but the others are also considered. While pre-divorce relationships are important, there are extraneous and societal factors which play an important part, e.g., who has custody and for how much of the time, has another adult become involved, are other stepgrandchildren added? Several scenarios are described by the authors to sensitize people to the role complexities, and six stress-producing patterns of grandparenting are outlined, with case examples. Growth potential is also suggested.

646. Kammerman, S.B., 1980, ''Family Support Systems: Natural Helping Networks and Community Resources'', in *Parenting in an Unresponsive Society,* Macmillan, New York

This chapter discusses a study done in a population of working mothers from different family types and socioeconomic backgrounds. The focus of the study involved to what extent these mothers utilized the extended family, friends, and relatives as a support system.

647. Kaslow, F. & R. Hyatt, 1981, ''Divorce: A Potential Growth Experience for the Extended Family'', *Journal of Divorce,* Vol. 5, pp. 115–126

Contrary to the usual perception of divorce as a painful and primary experience, it can become positive and a growth experience for the extended family. After predictable suffering through crisis, the developing coping mechanisms of the divorcing relative may ultimately model self-esteem and survival skills to other extended family members. New and more mature relationships may develop with the family of origin and potential for family support may be utilized. A secondary beneficial effect on the children of the divorcing couple is also noted.

648. Kornhaber, A., 1983, ''The Vital Connection—The 1983 Grandparents Are Coming of Age in America'', *Children Today,* July-August 1983

The author discusses the unique contribution which grandparents can and do make to the lives of their grandchildren. The Foundation for Grandparenting, a nonprofit organization, is mentioned with varied tasks, such as research, creating programs, educating the public, etc. A legal attempt has been made to propose grandparents' visitation rights. A proposition called a Uniform Grandparents Visitation Law was proposed and unanimously approved by the U.S. House of Representatives in 1983. The author speaks for the enhancement of family relationships and depth in family bonding with positive help from grandparents.

649. Littner, N., 1978, ''The Art of Being a Foster Parent'', *Child Welfare,* Vol. 57, No. 1, January

Dr. Littner, an early consultant psychiatrist to Child Welfare Agencies who has written elsewhere about child rearing, discusses the inherent difficulties of foster parenting versus biological parenting. The pressures on foster parents are much greater than on biological parents, both in terms of community expectations, those of family, neighbors and friends, and in terms of extraordinarily high self-expectations. Nevertheless the reality is that many foster parents do a tremendous job. Negative responses from foster children, lack of responsiveness, the child's ''protective wall,'' manipulation, pressures of the biological parents, agency ''supervision,'' the threat of losing a child, and the shift in balance in the foster parents' own family are some of the hurdles cited. Those who managed to cope well were found to be aware of the problems as a first step. Recognition of the importance of contact with the biological parents on the part of the child also leads to parent-to-parent contact. Trust of the agency (worker), sharing of information and feeling, courage to view one's own upset and come to see it not as a personal failure but as inherent in the special situation help with effective coping. Get-togethers and talking to other foster parents was perceived as helpful. All of the above combines to increase the coping ability of foster parents and make their task interesting and fulfilling.

650. McGoldrick, M., et al, 1982, *Ethnicity and Family Therapy,* Guilford Press, New York

Discussion of the use of ethnicity in therapy. Description of aspects of culture to be considered within the intervention. Articles of these cultures and orientations to be considered during treatment.

651. Norman, M., 1980, "The New Extended Family: Divorce Reshapes the American Household", *The New York Times Magazine,* Nov. 23, 1980

Presents information on divorce and remarriage and the increased role of the extended family as a helping network.

652. Phelps, R.E. & D.K. Huntley, 1985, "Social Networks and Child Adjustment in Single-Parent Families", *Annual Convention of the American Psychological Association,* Los Angeles

"While research with divorced adults has revealed a positive correlation between their social support networks and their adjustment after divorce, there has been little direct examination of the influence of the child's support network on the child's adjustment to parental divorce. The relationship of social network variables to child adjustment in one- parent families was examined in 119 6- to 10-year-old eldest children who were living with their separated or divorced custodial mothers. Mothers rated their children on the Revised Behavior Problem Checklist, and provided information about the child's quality and frequency of contact with various members of his or her social network. Children (N=94) rated themselves on the Child Depression Inventory. Multiple regression analyses were conducted using one criterion variable (a measure of psychopathology of the child) and ten predictor variables (time since parents' separation; child's age; and both the quality and quantity of the child's contact with peers, other adults, the custodial mother, and the non-custodial father) for each analysis. The results revealed that only the network quality measures were significant predictors of child adjustment. Sex differences were also found, with boys' interactions with peers and the custodial mother more salient, while interactions with the non-custodial father and other adults were more salient for girls.'' (ERIC)

653. Saulnier, K.McC. & C. Rowland, 1985, ''Missing Links: An Empirical Investigation of Network Variables in High-Risk Families'', *Family Relations,* Vol. 34, No. 4, pp. 557–560

Since social network support has been found to influence personal health and well-being positively, the authors undertook an examination of 32 families where a child was at risk of placement away from home. Descriptive data regarding function and size of social networks for this group are studied and their relationship to the clients being rated as particularly difficult and perhaps demanding on the agency workers who interacted with them. The results indicate that clients rated by clinicians as high in case difficulties engaged in lower numbers of community interactions than those who were perceived as low in case difficulties. Some reasons for the lower interactions by difficult families are postulated. The authors emphasize the importance of assessing network parameters when working with troubled families and of designing network interventions.

654. Tessman, L., 1978, *Children of Parting Parents,* Ch. 1, The Human Relations Network: Its Supports and Lacunae, Jason Aronsen, New York

Children of parting parents must deal with the loss or drastic alteration of relationship to at least one parent. The components of the human interaction network change and grow in importance as the child experiences this loss and new status. An understanding of the current social structure in relation to the more immediate environment of the single-parent family can aid families and professionals in the development of needed supports for individual families in the divorce crisis and after. Tessman, an experienced clinician, provides guidelines for therapy, an extensive bibliography and more than 50 case samples of work with children and parents.

654a. Van Cleve, L., 1985, ''Achievement Dynamics in a Single-Parent Anglo- American Family: A Case Study'', *Annual Meeting of the American Educational Research Association,* Chicago

''The purpose of this case study was to look closely at one single-parent Anglo-American family, members' daily patterns of living, and psychosocial patterns that may set them apart as an achieving family. The major assumption guiding the research effort was the thesis that home environments of interpersonally competent American youngsters show some rather consistent psychological patterns—regardless of race or socioeconomic background. The mother of the family observed was drawn from a volunteer sample of 32 Los Angeles mothers and interviewed in depth regarding her perceptions of present and past family dynamics related to her fourth grade son's school situation, as well as about her family and community network perceptions. The emphasis was on identifying key elements or components of the patterns of social interaction in this family that contributed to this fourth grader's achievement. The study of the emotional family tone, role behavior of the parents and child in a typical day, and socialization processes during leisure and labor events all revealed evidence of a supportive functional environment with these patterns well established.'' (ERIC)

655. Wallerstein, J.S., 1984, ''Children of Divorce: Preliminary Report of a Ten-Year Follow-Up of Young Children'', *American Journal of Orthopsychiatry,* Vol. 54, No. 3, pp. 444–458

This study describes the results of a ten-year follow-up study of children, now in their teens, who were between two and one-half and six at the time of their parents' divorce. Few conscious memories of the nuclear family's separation were retained, although at the time these children had shown distress and anxieties. The children had spent two-thirds of their lives in single-parent or stepfamilies, showed normal school adjustment, but nevertheless expressed feelings of loss and deprivation along with reconciliation fantasies. Relationships with the non-custodial father had retained centrality, as had a heightened need to re-establish such ties during adolescence. However, these children fared better than their older siblings, had less troubled memories, and presented a more optimistic outlook for the future.

656. Wolf, A.M., 1983, ''A Personal View of Black Inner-City Foster Families'', *American Journal of Orthopsychiatry,* Vol. 53, No. 1, pp. 144–151

A 21-year-old medical student lived in a black inner-city area and reported on her experiences and observations. She compares the special form of extended family which she observed to the parts of current literature which deal with black families and family ties. The ''informal'' adoptions which are quite prevalent in this community are discussed and the author stresses the need for mental health professionals to understand that these families have special strengths in their extended family system which serves the children well and must be appreciated better by the professionals who serve the community.

Foster Family

657. Aldredge, M.J. & P.W. Cautley, 1976, ''Placing Siblings in the Same Foster Home'', *Child Welfare,* Vol. LV, February, pp. 85–92
This study addresses the issue of placing siblings together. One hundred and fifteen placements were researched. Each placement involved a 6 to 12-year-old foster child and sibling. Foster parents and social workers involved in cases were interviewed periodically to discuss attitudes, problems, and changes in children. No conclusive results were found.

658. Aust, P. , 1981, ''Using the Life Story Book in Treatment of Children in Placement'', *Child Welfare,* Vol. 60, pp. 536–560
Various uses for this technique are described in this article, especially its utility for a practitioner skilled in a variety of treatment modalities to use this method to help children in foster care placement to connect their past and present lives. It can also be used therapeutically to enhance the children's self-image.

659. Bloomfield, S.I., 1982, Foster Care: An Interactional Perspective, Dissertation Abstracts International, Vol. 43/04-A, page 1044
''This study investigated the structure and interactional patterns of systems formed by the initiation of foster care. These systems were composed of a child in foster care, a natural family, a foster family and a Department of Social Services case worker. Four such systems were studied through a case study methodology, and were conjointly interviewed; all of the interviewers were videotaped and analyzed by the researcher and two raters, using a modification of the family structural assessment format developed by Minuchin. In each case an adolescent child had been removed from his or her home and placed in foster care through the Massachusetts Department of Social Services; in each case a Child in Need of Services petition had been filed by the child's natural parents. Exploring and describing foster care from an interactional perspective, this study applied the psychological theory of structural and strategic family therapy to the area of child welfare and foster care; while focusing on the work of Minuchin and Haley, the study expanded both an understanding of family therapy and of child welfare. In addition the study applied structural and strategic family therapy to a social system, inclusive of, yet more complex

than a family. The analysis of the data revealed trends in patterns and structure concerning triadic interactions, hierarchical relationships, developmental transitions, systems myths and homeostatic tendencies of systems. In particular it was found that the child was in an inappropriate hierarchical status, and that these systems maintained a rigid homeostasis. Suggestions were made for future research and for a model of family therapy applicable to such systems. It was suggested that the system formed be framed as a decisional subsystem. Suggestions were also made concerning the applicability of five hierarchical principles developed by the researcher: of inclusion, complexity, dominance, situation, and generativity. Suggestions were also made regarding the application of structural and strategic family therapy to the assessment, diagnosis and treatment of complex social systems.'' (DAI)

660. Canning, R., 1974, ''School Experiences of Foster Children'', *Child Welfare,* Vol. LIII, November, pp. 582–587
This study explored the educational experiences of 25 foster children. Separate interviews were conducted with children and teachers. Three common characteristics cited in children included: withdrawal, aggression, seeking to comply with teacher and peers. Foster children's perceptions of school also are mentioned. Useful guidelines included how to reduce transition problems and enhance more positive educational experiences.

661. Chestang, L.W. & I. Heymann, 1976, ''Preparing Older Children for Adoption'', *Public Welfare,* pp. 35–40
Focus on preparing children, ages five through twelve, for adoption. A framework is included which provides a dialogue of points to clarify to children and responses that they may have. Approaches with foster and adoptive parents are also detailed.

662. Clifton, P.M., 1975, ''An Approach to Working with the Placed Child'', *Child Psychiatry and Human Development,* Vol. 6, Winter, pp. 107–117
This paper presents a therapeutic approach to working with the placed child (foster care, adoption or separation and divorce). Emphasis is placed on professionals to become aware of the placed child's emotional needs, based on the separation crisis (crisis-oriented approach). Three case reports are described in detail.

663. Cutler, J.P., 1984, A Study of Children in Foster Care: Problems Related to the Separation of Siblings, Dissertation Abstracts International, Vol.45/05-A, page 1526

''Social support systems have been found to moderate the effects of stressful events on individuals. This ex post facto natural support group can help a child cope with placement in foster care. Thirty-one children placed in foster care with siblings, and thirty-one children placed away from siblings were selected from four public child welfare agencies. Children were between the ages 6–12, and were living in family foster care. The two groups were compared on four dependent variables: self concept, familial relationships, behavior, and school performance.

Data collection was conducted from October 1982 to February 1983. The children completed the Children's Self Concept Scale, the Family Relations Test, a life space diagram, and an interview. Social workers, foster mothers, and foster fathers of each child completed the Child Behavior Characteristics form. Social workers also completed an interview about the child's background and school record. Overall, there were no statistically significant differences between groups on the four dependent variables. Children in both groups were more emotionally involved with their birth families than with their foster families. The entire sample had numerous academic and social problems in school. There were, however, indications that siblings are a source of social support. The children themselves expressed strong feelings that siblings should be placed together. They reported being happier and less anxious when placed with a sibling. Other findings suggest that children separated from their siblings were at a greater risk of emotional detachment, and were more disruptive and demanded excessive adult attention in school. These findings give rise more to speculation than to definitive conclusions. The indications are that siblings are very important to the child in foster care. In the absence of findings that contraindicate joint placements, it is recommended that siblings be placed together, and that visitation be mandated when separate placements exist. Further research on sibling relationships is encouraged.''(DAI)

664. Dando, I. & B. Minty, 1987, ''What Makes Good Foster Parents?'', *The British Journal of Social Work,* Vol. 17, No. 4, pp. 383–399

''A study attempted to describe the characteristics, personal background and motivation of all the foster mothers used by two inner-city teams who had had at least one child placed with them for a year or more. A total of 80 foster mothers were interviewed. The chief motivations and childhood experiences of the foster mothers were compared with ratings made by the fostering officers of their excellence as foster parents. The study confirmed that two motivations for fostering that have often been held to be reasonably good predictors of success in caring for deprived children were, in fact, associated with an acknowledgement on the part of experienced fostering officers that the parents who claimed to act from such motives had a good capacity to fulfill the demanding role of a foster parent: firstly, a desire to parent a child, when it was impossible to conceive a child of one's own; and secondly, an identification with deprived children as a result of unhappy experiences in childhood—experiences that the foster mothers had had the resilience to cope with and use creatively. In addition, it emerged that foster parents who claimed to act from motives of social concern and altruism were also seen by fostering officers to have demonstrated a real ability to foster children. Nearly three-quarters of the foster mothers were emphatic that the experience of fostering had enhanced the quality of family life. For childless couples, the satisfaction seemed to come from caring for children; but for couples who had children of their own, the satisfaction seemed particularly to lie in helping children who had been deprived of a normal home life and in bringing up children whom they could not see as extensions of themselves.'' (SWAB)

665. David, J., 1982, The Effects of Placement in Foster Family Homes on Selected Aspects of School Adjustment and Academic Achievement, Dissertation Abstracts International, Vol 43/05-A, page 1474

``The present study investigated the effects of foster families' levels of democratic permissiveness and intellectual climate, the age at which the child was separated from his biological parents, and the length of time in care with the current foster family on latency-age, male, foster children's school adjustment and mathematics and reading achievement. Subjects were 66 male foster children, age 6 1/2 to 14 years, who were under the auspices of seven agencies. They resided with foster families within the five boroughs of New York City and Westchester County. School adjustment was measured by six subscales of the Child Behavior Characteristics Form (CBC), an adjective checklist constructed specifically for use in evaluating foster children's adjustment. Caseworkers rated subjects' behavior in the school setting and a mean adjustment score was obtained for each subject. Foster family characteristics were measured by two indices of the Foster Parent Appraisal Form (FPAF): Intellectual Climate and Democratic Permissiveness. Caseworkers rated foster families with mean scores obtained on each index for each family. Children's reading and methematics grade levels, as well as IQ scores and number of previous placements were recorded. Data were subjected to three multiple regression analyses in order to test the hypotheses. The three null hypotheses were accepted, in part, indicating minimal relationships among the independent and dependent variables. IQ and number of previous placements, two variables included for control, accounted for more of the variance in school adjustment and academic achievement than the originally hypothesized independent variables. Results strongly suggest that characteristics of children prior to entering care and stability of placement affect school adjustment and academic achievement more than other child-related or systemic variables. The implications for preventive enrichment programs for preschool children at risk of placement and for policies regarding stability of placement were discussed.'' (DAI)

666. Davids, L., 1973, ''Foster Fatherhood: The Untapped Resource'', *Child Welfare,* Vol. LII, February, pp. 100–107

An enlightening study focusing on foster fatherhood. Interviews were conducted with foster fathers, mothers and boys (ages 8–11) in 40 foster homes. Ordinary versus foster father roles are compared as are the foster fathers' relationship with caseworkers. Implications for social work practice are included, emphasizing that contributions of foster fathers be included in criteria of homefinding process.

667. Davidson, H.A., 1980, ''Periodic Judicial Review of Children in Foster Care: Issues Related to Effective Implementation'', *American Bar Association, National Legal Resource Center for Child Advocacy and Protection*

''In 1974, the National Council of Juvenile and Family Court Judges initiated a special project to promote, in courts throughout the country, periodic review of the status of all children in foster care. This paper explains the development of these judicial review systems, describes several alternative review mechanisms, and discusses key issues related to the successful implementation of court monitoring of the status of all children in foster care. In addition, the expected impact of a new Federal law germane to this subject, the Adoption Assistance and Child Welfare Act of 1980 (P.L. 96–272), is briefly analyzed. Concluding remarks suggest that periodic court review is an excellent mechanism to assure that public agencies legally responsible for children in foster care plan effectively to meet those children's long-term, permanent needs. With the help of a properly functioning judicial review process, harms perpetrated by child welfare systems on children and parents can be corrected.'' (ERIC)

668. Davis, R.T., 1983, Foster Family Environments in Relation to Social Competence of Adolescent Foster Children: Perceptions of Foster Mothers, Dissertation Abstracts International, Vol.45/02-A, page 644

''The purpose of this study was to assess the relationship between factors of foster family environments and differential levels of social competence of adolescent foster children. Developed within a framework of normalcy, health, and competence, this investigation used measures that had been standardized on the normal population and resulted in a comparative profile of foster families and foster children. The independent variables were four factors of the foster family environment—cohesion, conflict, control, and organization—as measured by the Moos Family Environment Scale, and the age of foster mothers. The dependent measure—social competence—was measured by the Achenback Child Behavior Checklist. Hypotheses 1 through 5 addressed the bivariate relationships between the independent variables and social competence. Hypothesis 6 examined how much of the dependent measure could be explained by a combination of the independent variables. The bivariate relationships were analyzed using Kendell Rank-Order Correlation, and the combined effects were analyzed using a multiple regression analysis. The significance level was set at $< .05$. The sample consisted of 50 foster families in Piedmont, North Carolina, who had had a foster child between the ages of 12 and 16 in their homes for at least one year. The data were collected in a personal interview with the foster mothers. The findings showed that perceived cohesiveness, by itself, was significantly related to social competence. That relationship was positive and not curvilinear as hypothesized. None of the hypotheses was supported as stated. A number of the variables were restricted in range and may have contributed to the low correlations. The four factors of family environment hypothesized as discriminators of social competence were in fact those factors that differed the most from the norm. Because of the selection criteria, it may be that this was a sample of good foster parents, and these factors may be discriminators of competence among foster parents. Nationwide, about 50 percent of all foster children are adolescents. Their needs differ vastly from those of infants and young children for whom the foster care system was developed. Direct application of this study could be used in the recruitment, screening, and selection of foster parents who serve this adolescent population.''(DAI)

669. Dennis, D., 1987, Foster Care Experience in Relation to Locus-of-Control, Learned Helplessness, and Effectance Motivation, Dissertation Abstracts International, Vol. 48/03, pp. 908

''Relatively few studies have addressed the impact of foster care experience on children. A recent study by McIntyre, Lounsbury, Berntson, and Steel (in press) identified a pattern of responses to the Tasks of Emotional Development (TED) Test which was unique to foster children. This pattern of responses was interpreted as reflecting a 'reliance upon and exploitation of externally determined events.' The similarity of this pattern of TED responses to the personality constructs of locus of control (Rotter, 1966), learned helplessness (Seligman, 1976), and effectance motivation (White, 1959) was noted by the authors of the TED study. The present study investigated the relationship between two foster care experience variables (total time in care and number of placements) and the three personality constructs discussed above. The Children's Nowicki-Strickland Locus of Control Scale was used to assess locus of control orientation. An instrumental response task previously used in a number of studies of learned helplessness was used as a measure of that construct. A game choice situation was used as a measure of effectance motivation. All three measures were administered to 62 foster children, ages 9–18. A significant correlation was found between external locus of control and increasing number of foster placements. Tendencies toward significance were found between increasing number of placements and some of the learned helplessness submeasures. The unusual response of 21 of the children to the learned helplessness task compromised the use of statistics conventionally employed for measures of performance on this task, and this behavior was interpreted as reflecting extreme passivity. No other significant correlations were found. The results of the study were interpreted as consonant with those of McIntyre and her associates (in press). Implications for social service policy were discussed in terms of promoting the development of an internal locus of control orientation.'' (DAI)

670. Derr, D.R.F., 1983, The Crisis of Fostering for the Foster Family, Dissertation Abstracts International, Vol. 44/12-A, page 3814

''The impact of a foster child's entrance into a family system was explored in a six-month longitudinal study. Three aspects of family life were conceptualized: family functioning, role expectations and flexibility, and the developmental life cycle stage. The St. Paul Scale of Family Functioning was the major instrument; in addition the Child Functioning Scale was used to measure the foster child's functioning level. An Expectation Scale was developed to measure the family's expectations of the placement and a Role Flexibility-Rigidity Scale was devised to indicate the parents' ability to be flexible in their role allocations. The sample of 120 foster families, experienced and inexperienced, was evaluated at four time periods: before placement, two weeks after placement, at three months, and at six months. At preplacement all of the foster families were functioning at levels that could be considered highly adequate. During the course of the study the majority of families experienced some decline in their level of functioning; in only three situations did the level of functioning fall below what was considered to be an adequate range. Families that entered foster care with lower levels of functioning experienced greater declines than those with higher scores. Each of these findings were at statistically significant levels. Decreased functioning adequacy was also correlated with lower family income. The foster family with no previous experience had a greater tendency to suffer a decline in functioning level, as did the family with a more malfunctioning foster child. Family functioning also tended to vary directly with role performance and flexibility. Role flexibility data suggested that the more flexible families experienced fewer declines in some areas than the rigid-role ones. Families with optimistic yet realistic expectations sustained fewer declines in functioning level than those whose expectations were not as realistic. No consistent pattern emerged relating foster family function to its developmental stage. Finally, despite the apparent stress of foster care, and a concomitant decrease in family functioning following the addition of a foster child, the level of functioning for most foster families remained fairly high.''(DAI)

671. Eastman, K., 1979, ''The Foster Family In a Systems Theory Perspective'', *Child Welfare,* Vol. 58

Viewing the foster family as a social system sheds some light on understanding and adding credibility to known problems. Boundary problems, the need for more permeability of boundaries and opening up the foster family system to entry of both members of the nuclear family and agency staff members is explicated. The uncertain length of time children are placed adds to the strains of determining separation-connectedness issues. Lack of role clarity and lack of clearly defined norms, and uncertain family identity detract from the stability of the family system. Coming and going of members stresses the system, and agencies sometimes demand so much that the foster family withdraws rather than live with all the stresses. Flexibility seems to be the most desirable feature to make the system work.

672. Edelstein, S., 1981, "When Foster Children Leave: Helping Foster Parents to Grieve", *Child Welfare,* Vol. LX, July-August, pp. 467–473

Article relates the theories of grief and its resolution of separation and loss. A brief discussion on grieving and four obstacles to a healthy resolution are mentioned, with particular emphasis on foster parents being at high risk. Obstacles include: difficulty of grieving in an ambivalent relationship, the demands of the foster parenting role, social expectations, and personality. Possible supports to foster parents in the grieving process are discussed, e.g. communication with parents, relationship with social worker, educational programs, and self-help groups.

673. Ellison, C.E., 1982, A Study to Determine the Credibility of Foster Home Situations Portrayed in Contemporary Realistic Fiction for Purposes of Reading Guidance, Dissertation Abstracts International, Vol 43/05-A, page 1454

"The purpose of this descriptive study was to determine the credibility of foster home situations as depicted in realistic fiction written for adolescents, for use in reading guidance situations. The realistic fiction used for this study were twenty-three novels which depicted children who were living with a foster family. To accomplish this, ten volunteer adults who lived in foster homes during childhood read three of the sample novels and responded to a questionnaire. Three social workers who placed and supervised foster children also read the three novels and responded to the questionnaire. An interview was conducted with five of the adults who experienced foster care and the three social workers to obtain information regarding their opinions of the three novels. Each of the ten adults who experienced foster care completed a personal history questionnaire to obtain additional information regarding their experiences. The data gathered from the two questionnaires and the interviews were used to help determine the credibility of the sample novels which depicted foster home situations. A content analysis of the twenty-three adolescent fiction novels was conducted. The conclusions of this study were that there were aspects of real life which were portrayed by the authors of the three sample novels, according to the responses made to the books by adults who had experienced foster care and the social workers.

However, authors of adolescent literature need to become more informed about the life experiences of the foster child in order to portray foster home situations as credibly as possible. Only a small percentage of the twenty-three novels exhibited "excellent" overall literary quality, though many of the novels were considered "good." Because this is a sensitive area for many children involved in foster care placement, an implication of this study was that caution should be used when introducing novels of this genre to children, particularly young adolescents who may be experiencing difficult situations within their home life." (DAI)

674. Euster, S.D., Ward, V.P., Varner, J.G. & G.L. Euster, 1984, "Life-Skills Groups for Adolescent Foster Children" , *Child Welfare,* Vol. 63, No. 1, pp. 27–36

A curriculum designed by child development specialists in collaboration with child welfare workers and other experts provides workers with concrete tools for conducting life-skills groups with foster adolescents. Developed by the University of South Carolina, the curriculum focuses on six general topics: foster care, self-concept and friendship, sex education, human sexuality, problem solving in relationships, and drug and alcohol abuse. In a time of reduced resources, the program equips practitioners with an additional tool for extending effective services to foster adolescents.

675. Fanshel, D., 1978, "Children Discharged from Foster Care in New York City: Where to—When—At What Age?", *Child Welfare,* Vol. LVII, September-October, pp. 467–483

Article examines data available about the discharges of children from foster care, with emphasis on destinations. Data was collected by a computerized information system for 1974 to 1977. Length of foster care, age at entry, and discharge destinations were studied. Results support premise that biological parents are major source of permanency for foster children.

676. Fanshel, D., 1975, "Parental Visiting of Children in Foster Care: Key to Discharge?", *Social Service Review,* December, pp. 493–514

This study explores the visiting patterns of parents with regard to discharge of foster children over a five-year investigation. A sample of 624 children, ranging in age from infancy to twelve years, was studied. Sequential telephone interviews were carried out, and a visiting scale was created. Author discusses ethnicity as a factor in visiting, a reduction of visiting over time, and association of frequent parental visiting with discharge of children from care.

677. Fanshel, D., 1976, ''Status Changes of Children in Foster Care: Final Results of the Columbia University Longitudinal Study'', *Child Welfare,* Vol. LV, March, pp. 143–171

The Columbia University 5-year longitudinal study of foster children was near completion when this article described the final results of an analysis of status changes experienced by 624 children. The article gives details with regard to the issue of impermanence.

678. Fox, M. & K. Accuri, 1980, ''Cognitive and Academic Functioning in Foster Children'', *Child Welfare,* Vol. LIX, September-October, pp. 491–496

A study of the cognitive and academic skills of foster children from the Children's Aid Society of Penn. The sample included 163 children ranging in age from 4 years to 18 years, with mean age of 9.6. The average length of time in placement was 5.2 years. Wechsler intelligence tests and Wide Range Achievement Test (WRAT) were administered. The results support the hypothesis that foster care does not necessarily affect cognitive functions and learning ability of children and in fact these are comparable to functional levels of children from low-income groups.

679. Frank, G., 1980, ''Treatment Needs of Children in Foster Care'', *American Journal of Orthopsychiatry,* Vol. 50, No. 2, pp. 256–263

The author did a substudy of a sample of 50 children in long-term foster care, from a large Child Welfare Research program done at Columbia University School of Social Work (624 children who entered foster care in 1966 were followed for a five-year period). While the authors themselves modestly indicate that this is not definitive research but rather an exploration, it is made clear, the assumption that substitute family care (or residential institutional care to a lesser degree) will serve the needs of children who cannot live with their own families of origin is an enormous one. The vulnerability of these children whose families had problems in caring for them plus the separation experiences make it imperative that additional efforts other than mere family placement are mandatory. In addition there is emphasis in the article on the need for much greater professional efforts with the biological parents to provide continuity and eventual rehabilitation.

680. Gambrell, E.D. & K.T. Wiltse, 1974, ''Foster Care: Prescriptions for Change'', *Public Welfare,* Vol. 32, Summer, pp. 39–47

The purpose of this article is to describe guidelines which address the negative aspects of foster care. The negative aspects include: long-term care, easy access into foster care and little support as to emotional stability of foster children.

681. Glickman, L.L., 1981, Foster Parenting: An Investigation of Role Ambiguity, Dissertation Abstracts International, Vol 42/01-A, page 385

''Statement of the Problem. The foster parent role has undergone major transitions since the development of foster family care policy during the last half of the nineteenth century. A review of the professional literature reveals consistent references to the lack of clarity in role definition and the problems arising from role ambiguity. The foster parent is alternately seen as a client, a staff member, a natural parent, a volunteer, a 'professional parent,' or unclassifiable. The purpose of this study is to examine foster parent role ambiguity from a role theory perspective and to analyze its implications for policy. The research explores the relationships among foster parents' role perceptions, demographics, foster parenting experience, and difficulties in role performance.

Methodology: The research is based on Massachusetts Department of Public Welfare data derived from: (1) a survey questionnaire of 427 foster parents including 313 participants in spring 1979 Title XX training sessions and 114 non-participants; and (2) interviews with a sample of 10 foster parent volunteers chosen from training participants and with their respective social workers. Cross-tabulation tables were generated with Chi Square and Spearman correlation coefficients computed where appropriate. Interview responses for each foster parent-social worker set were scored and ranked to measure the level of policy agreement and the degree of effectiveness of their working relationships. In addition, interview data formed the basis for individual case vignettes and analyses of each foster parent-social worker set.

Major Findings. (1) Foster parents evidenced pervasive ambiguity in their role perceptions. Although role perception differences did not fall into predictable 'parent' and 'worker' typologies, there was, when compared with earlier studies, an increase in foster parents who perceived themselves as workers in terms of desiring remuneration. (2) Demographic variables contributed little to understanding differences in role perception or role performance. (3) Experimental variables contributed to explaining one measure of role perception—the desire for remuneration.

Foster parents with more experience were more likely to want extra payment for their work than were foster parents with less experience. (4) Almost half of the foster parents surveyed reported inconsistent role perceptions over time in that the role was more difficult than originally anticipated. (5) Both foster parents and social workers exhibited a low level of knowledge regarding foster care policies with workers having even less knowledge than foster parents. (6) A strong direct relationship was found between foster parents' and social workers' level of policy agreement and the degree of effectiveness of their working relationships.

Conclusions and Policy Implications. Foster care policy is not clearly communicated to either social workers or to foster parents. The data revealed a need for foster parents to have a greater understanding of the demands of their role prior to role assumption. Suggested methods for achieving this goal include more comprehensive training through education and peer support. Data further indicated that the relationships between role-set members, particularly between foster parents and social workers, are often sporadic and need to be more structured to reduce ambiguity through methods such as contracting. Finally, given foster parents' increased desire for remuneration in addition to their widespread sense of frustration, the study suggests the need for a 'paraprofessionalization' of the foster parent role involving payment for foster parents' work and certification based on specialized training.'' (DAI)

682. Goldstein, J., Freud, A. & A. Solnit, 1973, *Beyond the Best Interest of the Child,* Free Press, New York

The authors address the issues of child placement within the framework of protecting the physical and emotional development of the child. They focus on the development of legal guidelines for contested child placements in cases of adoption, divorce, abuse, or neglect. Using psychoanalytic theory as a framework, the authors evaluate the psychological and biological needs of the child. (The term psychological parent is created here.) They propose changes in existing custody laws enhancing continuity in the lives of children. They propose that non-custodial parents have no legal right to visit, and that custodial parents have the right to decide whether visits are desirable for the child.

683. Gross, G., 1975, ''Fosterhome Placements: Conjoint Family Therapy for the Foster Family's Role Dilemma'', *Family Therapy,* Vol. 2, pp. 57–61

More serious problems in foster family living are compared

with those of biological families. Potential role conflicts between foster and biological family, child and biological family, and all of these with the community are examined. Joint therapy of foster family and child is suggested, with inclusion of biological family, especially in the termination stage of placement. ''(c) APA''

684. Gross, M., 1984, ''Custody Conflicts Between Foster and Birth Parents in Pennsylvania'', *Social Work,* Vol. 29, pp. 510–515

The author reviews the development of legal decisions related to foster care and traces recent history of custody conflicts between foster parents and birth parents in Pennsylvania as significant in portraying the relationship of the courts to social agencies. The seemingly neutral position of agency staffs as representing both foster and biological family is in sharp contrast to the adversary position of the courts. Legal position and changes in the standards, e.g. a more flexible interpretation of the ''best interest of the child,'' as well as the significant cessation of the ''tender year doctrine'' which automatically made the mother the most logical custodian are discussed. Visitation as a right or as the child's need for continuity is debated. The question of the child's bonding to a psychological parent seems to be rejected by the court. The author sees the court's ''either or'' position of foster parents versus birth parents as unfortunate.

685. Hardin, M. , 1983, ''Court Review: Making It Work'', *Child Welfare,* Vol. 62, No. 4, pp. 367–371

''A good court review system should help accomplish permanence for foster children by (1) setting firm goals and timetables, (2) being useful in later court proceedings, and (3) helping parents become more involved in the case plan. The review process, however, can make it difficult to develop and adapt the plan as the case progresses when the court freezes the planning process by adhering to a particular case plan. Court review can be time-consuming for workers. Judges may make snap decisions or rulings that are impractical to implement. In addition, review proceedings may stimulate antagonism between the court and the child welfare agency and may be demoralizing to the social worker. Six methods by which the court-review process might be improved are detailed.'' (SWAB)

686. Hegar, R., 1988, ''Legal and Social Work Approaches to Sibling Separation in Foster Care'', *Child Welfare,* Vol. 67, No. 2, pp. 113–121

''Urges greater attention of siblings as a critical sub-system in families of child welfare clients. Identifies gaps in knowledge about siblings. Points out social trends that call for increased responsiveness to siblings' needs. Examines both social work and legal opinions regarding sibling separation in foster care. Considers child welfare implications.'' (ERIC)

687. Hegar, R.L., 1983, ''Foster Children's and Parents' Right to a Family'', *Social Service Review,* Vol. 57, No. 3, pp. 429–447

''A discussion presents evidence from court decisions, state laws, and model statutes that demonstrates the emerging legal interest of foster children in stable parental relationships. The children's need for stable figures is discussed, and a historical overview of the legal status of children and the family is provided. The issue of balancing the child's emerging interest in stable and permanent relationships against established interests of the natural family is explored as an outgrowth of society's heightened recognition of children's interests in custody and other child-placement cases.'' (SWAB)

688. Jenkins, S., 1969, ''Separation Experiences of Parents Whose Children are in Foster Care'', *Child Welfare,* Vol. XLVIII, June, pp. 334–341

This study focuses on separation feelings of biological parents at the time of placement. Data were derived from field interviews with 297 biological mothers and 137 biological fathers conducted under the Child Research Program at Columbia University School of Social Work. Expressions of feelings were related to ethnic groups, religion, jurisdiction of case, and socioeconomic status. Feelings with regard to reason for placement also observed. Commentary afterward implies that providing supportive services might prevent need for placement.

689. Jones, M., 1978, ''Stopping Foster Care Drift: A Review of Legislation and Special Programs'', *Child Welfare,* Vol. LVII, November, pp. 571–579

Reviews legislation addressing the lengthy foster care stays. Legislation from New York, Virginia, Ohio, and New Jersey, and in addition, special projects addressing this issue are cited. (SWAB)

690. Jurich, A.P., 1979, ''Coping with Moral Problems of Adolescents in Foster Care'', *Child Welfare,* Vol. LVIII, March, pp. 187–195

Examines in a concise manner the moral development of an adolescent in foster care. The social influences of parents and peers and the impact that is made on the adolescent is discussed. Basic guidance techniques encouraging positive moral development are described which include: open discussion accepting the adolescent's perspective, sharing news and alternative choices, compromising and dealing with parent's own feelings.

691. Kagan, R.M., 1982, ''Storytelling and Game Therapy for Children in Placement'', *Child Care Quarterly,* Vol. 11, No. 4, pp. 280–290
The author postulates that children, though obviously in need of a home, do everything possible to get rejected in a substitute family arrangement. Two ways of helping children with the change from nuclear to substitute family are storytelling and games, which are therapeutic in helping children in coping with their grief, attaching to new families, and returning to their old families. An example is cited in which a child is confronted with the decision of living with a foster family or remaining institutionalized. It is felt that this type of treatment technique can be incorporated into any comprehensive treatment program for children and their families. ''(c)APA''

692. Katz, L.L., 1987, ''An Overview of Current Clinical Issues in Separation and Placement. Special Issue: The Foster Care Dilemma'', *Child and Adolescent Social Work Journal,* Vol. 4, No. 3–4, pp. 209–225
This is a very informative article which elucidates treatment issues for children of separation, their parents, other caretakers, and therapists, although the author focuses specifically on children in foster care and adoption. A historical and contemporary review of pertinent literature provides the reader with information to develop a sound knowledge base to work with children in foster care and adoption and with their caretakers, be they foster or adoptive parents. Age-old pitfalls in the work with these children are identified. Of special importance is the presentation of treatment approaches both in the clinical and research literature which include work with the whole family rather than an overfocus on the child as the primary client.

693. Kirgan, D.A., 1983, ''Meeting Children's Needs through Placement: The Placement Evaluation Program'', *Child Welfare,* Vol. LXII, March/April, pp. 157–166
The author describes a time-limited family model group home used for the purpose of evaluating the most suitable placement plan for foster children. The rationale and evaluation criteria of the home are discussed. Also, results of 65 children evaluated between

January 1977 and September 1980 are cited. The author believes that effectiveness of this program supports the idea that similar programs be included in the placement process.

694. Klee, L. & N. Halfon, 1987, ''Mental Health Care for Foster Children in California'', *Child Abuse and Neglect: The International Journal,* Vol. 11, No. 1, pp. 63–74

''Interviews with 154 program administrators, social workers, foster parents, and health care providers in California found that only one county performed routine mental health evaluations of all foster children. Mental health problems were identified by informants as more severe than medical problems among foster children.'' (ERIC)

695. Kufeldt, K., 1984, ''Listening to Children—Who Cares?'', *British Journal of Social Work,* Vol. 14, No. 3, pp. 257–2648

''Child welfare workers should listen to children in foster care. When given the opportunity to be heard, children can provide observations that are both relevant and important. To illustrate this, verbatim comments of children obtained as part of a larger research endeavor are presented, as are observations extracted from children's evaluations of a Canadian 'Who Cares?' conference held in 1979, the Year of the Child.'' (SWAB)

696. Lemieux, D.J., 1984, The Effects of Foster Placement on the Biological Children of Foster Parents: An Exploratory Investigation, Dissertation Abstracts International, Vol 45/06-B, page 1917

''This study investigated the initial effects on biological children of a foster child's placement in the family, in the general context of the foster families' adjustment to care. Six new foster families, recommended by the Tennessee Department of Human Services, participated in the project for a period of five to six months. Families were interviewed before placement and four months after placement to collect general information and to compare the families' expectations for fostering with their actual experiences. Foster parents were also interviewed weekly by phone to collect behavioral data on each child. Analysis of behavior data suggests that although biological children exerted constant effort to accommodate the foster child and to help their parents at home throughout the study, mothers reported feeling more dissatisfied with their children's behavior four months after placement than they had before placement. However, changes in the number of positive and negative behaviors reported by mothers were not significant. Mothers also reported having less contact and feeling less intimate with their own children four months after placement. Mothers and their children evaluated the reduction in contact and intimacy negatively when a situational stress was high. Although interview data suggested that family members decided to foster to balance their own personal needs, the findings of this study suggested that initially, fostering actually disrupted family functioning. When a caseworker was able to help a family cope with situational stress, the family reported a positive foster care experience and began to integrate the foster child into their home. If the stress level became too high, however, families reported feeling "burned-out," family functioning was disrupted and the placement was threatened. Biological children in this study influenced their parents' decisions whether to continue to foster." (DAI)

697. Levant, R. & M. Geer, 1981, "A Systematic Skills Approach to the Selection and Training of Foster Parents As Mental Health Paraprofessionals: Project Overview and Selection Component", *Journal of Community Psychology,* Vol. 19, No. 3, pp. 224–230

Describes a project for education of foster parents as paraprofessionals in Mental Health. Selection was based on a definition of the role of foster parents, of their helping skills, and the quality of the family's emotional climate. Assessments were made along these two dimensions. The results of a pilot study of 30 first-time foster parents are reported on, suggesting the efficacy of the Family Concept Test as a selection instrument.

698. Littner, N., 1978, "The Art of Being a Foster Parent", *Child Welfare,* Vol. LVII, No. 1, January 1978

Dr. Littner, an early consultant psychiatrist to Child Welfare Agencies who has written elsewhere about child rearing, discusses the inherent difficulties of foster parenting versus biological parenting. The pressures on foster parents are much greater than on biological parents, both in terms of community expectations, those of family, neighbors, and friends, and in terms of extraordinarily high self-expectations. Nevertheless the reality is that many foster parents do a tremendous job. Negative responses from foster children, lack of responsiveness, the child's "protective wall," manipulation, pressures of the natural parents, agency "supervision," the threat of losing a child, and the shift in balance in the foster parents' own family are some of the hundreds cited. Those who managed to cope well were found to be aware of the problems as a first step. Recognition of the importance of contact with the biological parents on the part of the child also leads to parent-to-parent contact. Trust of the agency (worker), sharing of information and feeling, courage to view one's own upset and come to see it not as a personal failure but as inherent in the special situation help with effective coping. Get-togethers and talking to other foster parents was perceived as helpful. All of the above combines to increase the coping ability of foster parents and make their task interesting and fulfilling.

699. Maas, H.S., 1979, ''Assessing Family and Child Welfare Practice'', *Social Work,* Vol. 24, No. 5, pp. 365–372

A learned article in which the author discusses the fact that Child Welfare Agencies have been more likely to assess their practice than other social agencies. In reviewing some basic tenets in the child welfare field he reminds us that particularly some of the research efforts in Child Welfare Agencies have highlighted the need for early assessment. He points out the consequences of heeding good research results available toward studying our practice and moving toward earlier implementation on the basis of what we have learned.

700. Maluccio, A., Fein, E. & K. Olmstead, 1986, *Permanency Planning for Children: Concepts and Methods,* Tavistock, UK; Routledge Chapman & Hall

The authors dispel the misconceptions that these concepts deal (only) with moving children into adoptive placements. The key question suggested is, ''Will the child have a family when he/she grows up?'' To ensure that the answer is ''yes,'' planning must be a central component of all child-care work and must focus on prevention and rehabilitation, not only on adoption. The ecological approach to child placement is the central focus, away from the traditional ''Medical Model'' toward identifying family strengths, and providing services. The child is always the central focus of planning but parents must be involved as full partners in decision making and the implementation of the plan.

701. Maluccio, A., Sinanoglu, P.A., eds., 1981, *The Challenge of Partnership: Working With Parents of Children in Foster Care,* Child Welfare League of America

This is a collection of papers presented under a grant of the Children's Bureau at the University of Connecticut School of Social Work. The focus is on the untapped resources of biological parents. Preface, foreword, and the first paper, which identify issues and trends in the literature, quickly identify the fact that parents are rarely, if ever, offered the kinds of continuous help that would enable them to function as true physical or emotional resources to their children, and more efforts—though also not enough—are invested in substitute arrangements. The papers offered give both a theoretical, research, and hands-on view of the child-placement process, both foster home and institutional care, and discuss means of continuity between biological parents and their children through the process to avoid the proverbial ''drift'' and insure maximum bonding despite separation experiences.

702. Mayfield, J. & J.N. Branch, 1983, ''Group Treatment for Children in Substitute Care'', *Social Casework,* No. 10, December

The authors describe the expected effects of a support group of children in substitute care by promoting self-awareness and by teaching communication and coping skills. Specifically, basic survival roles used by children of alcoholics are identified, and a comparable treatment approach is developed for children who have seemingly coped with the separation from their families but have much underlying turmoil and lack of understanding of what has happened to them and why. An eight-session program is described in some detail along with some of the expected goals for each session.

703. Mech, E., 1985, ''Parental Visiting and Foster Placement'', *Child Welfare,* Vol. 64, pp. 67–72

''Analyzed the association between parental visiting and time spent in foster care using data on 1559 children included in the National Study of Social Services to Children and Their Families by A.W. Shyne and A.A. Schroeder (1978). Controlling for race/ethnicity and geographical region, analysis underscored the importance of parental visiting for achieving permanency in foster care.'' (c) APA

704. Meegan, W. & J.F. Shireman, 1982, ''Foster Parent Adoption: A Literature Review'', *Child Welfare,* Nov-Dec, pp. 525–535

Not until the 1970's did information about the use of foster homes for adoption receive somewhat more regular attention in the literature. Agency policies and legal constraints had been liberalized. The philosophy on adoption now incorporated an inclusion of the child's continuing ties to biological parents (no more legally mandated total severance). An open acknowledgment and working through of the relationship, an opportunity for bonding to the foster family, assistance with possible financial burden to the adoptive family, etc., were all relatively new concepts which turn up in the literature. The conclusion of the review points to the fact that foster homes are an even more reasonable resource for children now that they may become permanent adoptive homes. There is also a discussion of reasons for the foster parents' decision to become or not to become adoptive parents.

705. Meyer, C., 1984, ''Can Foster Care Be Saved?'', *Social Work,* Vol. 29, No. 6, Editorial Page

The author, as editor-in-chief, addresses the gap in social workers' armamentarium of contemporary ideas, theories, and skills, and the lack of change and adaptation in the field of child welfare, which is among the oldest social work efforts. She points to the fact that adversarial legal practices seem to define the foster care system, untrained staff represents the profession, and the public erroneously believes that the field is still the domain of (trained) social workers. Poor and minority children and their parents continue to need many services other than child placement as attempted solutions to their multiple problems. A family-focused social service could begin to avoid the vast problems brought on by separating children from their parents and might stimulate clinical social workers to return to the child welfare field.

706. Meyer, C. , 1985, ''A Feminist Perspective on Foster Family Care: A Redefinition of the Categories'', *Child Welfare,* Vol. 64, No. 3, pp. 249–258

The author uses the feminist perspective to demystify mothering. It helps to differentiate the notions of parenting functions in many areas of caring for children not to be automatically characterized as mother love. A separate analysis of mothering and parenting opens new possibilities to redefine foster parenthood as a social service, instead of a ''pretend'' biological family. This would clarify the role relationship of foster mother to agency worker, increase accountability of service, and free up clinical workers' skills where and when needed.

707. Miller, K., Fein, E., Bishop, G., Stillwell, N. & C. Murray, 1984, ''Overcoming Barriers to Permanency Planning'', *Child Welfare,* Vol. LXIII, No. 1, January/February

After defining the parameters of permanency planning and giving background history, the authors describe a project in Connecticut in which the state agency contracted with voluntary agencies to provide permanency planning services for children who were or were likely to become victims of foster care drift. 55

children were selected for study, and joint planning monitored by a project co-ordinator included treatment, assessment of an optimum plan, recruitment and home study, placement planning and preparation, post-placement supervision, and services after legal adoption. As part of the project a training program was conducted for all workers on a local and state level, and continuing evaluation of the project was carried out by the research department of a voluntary agency.

708. Murray, L., 1984, ''A Review of Selected Foster Care-Adoption Research from 1978 to mid-1982'', *Child Welfare,* Vol. 63, No. 2, pp. 113–124

Continuing Kadushin's ''scholarly analysis of foster care and adoption literature up to mid-1977,'' the author summarizes recent research studies which contributed to the knowledge base with regard to permanancy planning, adoption outcomes, foster parents, and recidivism in foster care. Findings seem to point in the direction of recent know-how to find permanence for more children, some interesting adoption outcomes with regard to single-parent and transracial adoptions, the importance of education for foster parents, and first steps toward recognizing and therefore developing strategies to cope with recidivism in foster care.

709. Kadushin, Alfred, ''Children in Foster Families and Institutions'' in Henry Maas (ed), Service Research: Review of Studies, Washington, DC, NASW 1978

710. Norton, F., 1981, ''Foster Care and the Helping Professions'', *Personnel & Guidance Journal,* Vol. 60, pp. 156–159

Counseling children placed in foster homes is recommended, with the focus on knowledge of and sensitivity to issues of separation and age-appropriate coping behaviors. Only if the stages of separation are dealt with can the placement be of positive value. ''(c) APA''

711. Orlin, M., 1977, ''Conflict Resolution in Foster Family Care'', *Child Welfare,* Vol. LVI, January, pp. 769–775

Describes a method of helping workers understand conflict in foster family care and ways of constructively resolving it. Conflictual aspects of foster care are listed and propositions for constructive conflict resolution are applied with dialogue between worker and foster mother.

712. Pardeck, J.T., 1984, "Multiple Placement of Children in Foster Family Care: An Empirical Analysis", *Social Work,* Vol. 29, No. 6, pp. 506–509

The author examines the relationship between factors related to the foster child him/herself, the biological family, and the placement agency's caseworker to the number of placements by examining data from a large national study. Older children after three years of placement are more likely to move, and initially identified problems of the child may continue to be the cause of multiple placements. Parents' problems seem to have less of an impact than expected, but turnover of the caseworker was found to have a statistically significant relationship with multiple placements. The author indicates in his conclusions the importance of his findings of the presence of good continuous relationships with foster families and advocates a middle road between the two extremes of surrender for adoption and return to the biological parents, i.e. the viability of permanent long-term foster care, since the foster parents do become the psychological parents of the child, thus providing him/her with more of a sense of identity.

713. Paulson, M.J., Grossman, S. & G. Shapiro, 1974, "Child-Rearing Attitudes of Foster Home Mothers", *Journal of Community Psychology,* Vol. 2, January, pp. 11–14

This study explores child-rearing attitudes of foster mothers with attitudes of biological mothers. Two hundred thirty-three foster mothers and several biological mothers were assessed by the Parent Attitude Research Instrument. The findings showed a greater trend to dependency, strictness and conformity in parenting by foster mothers.

714. Proch, K. & J. Howard, 1984, "Parental Visiting in Foster Care: Law and Practice", *Child Welfare,* Vol. 63, No. 2, pp. 139–147

The authors examine and critique the legal basis for using visitation or lack of visitation as a major criterion in the reunification with parents or the termination of parental rights. They review some of the existing provisions at state and federal levels and contrast them with some model acts. Recommendations for statutory reform and changes in child welfare practice are made.

715. Proch, K.O., 1980, Adoption by Foster Parents, Dissertation Abstracts International, Vol 41/02-A, page 808

"Adoption by foster parents was studied by personally interviewing a randomly selected sample of adoptive foster parents and children residing in the Chicago area. The children were between the ages of seven and 13 at the time of the interview. The typical adoptive foster child who was studied was black, without severe physical or psychological problems, and placed in infancy with older, low-income black parents who had a high school education or less. The child had lived with the adoptive foster family an average of five years prior to the adoption. The majority of the parents became foster parents because they wanted to add children to their family, not to provide temporary care to a child. They adopted primarily for one of three reasons: they wanted to adopt a child when they applied to be foster parents; they became attached to a child in their care and wanted to make the child legally theirs; or they thought that the only way they could keep a child in their care was to adopt him or her. The last group of parents did not want to adopt the child; they would have remained foster parents if they were not threatened with the child's possible removal.

Foster parents and children received little preparation for adoption. The topic most often discussed with the parents was subsidy, and least often discussed was how the family would meet the child's needs in the future. A caseworker did not discuss adoption with the child in the majority of cases. Many parents stated they had not received sufficient information about their child. In addition, some parents were unwilling to discuss adoption with their child, and a few parents stated that their child did not know that he or she was adopted. Despite the lack of preparation, parents were satisfied with their experience with adoption and with the service they had received from the agency.

The foster parents tended to see foster care as permanent. They felt that adoption did not change their relationship with their child but that it eliminated the fear that the child might be removed from their care. Children who could not remember living in another home could not distinguish foster care from adoption. Children who remembered living with another family defined foster care as temporary and adoption as permanent. Based on the interviews, specific recommendations were made for care planning and for adoptive assessment and preparation of foster parents and children." (DAI)

716. Rzepnicki, T.L., 1987, "Recidivism of Foster Children Returned to Their Own Homes: A Review and New Directions for Research", *The Social Service Review,* Vol. 61, No. 1, pp. 56–70

"Problems leading to recent changes in foster care services are outlined, stressing the current emphasis on returning children in foster care to their biological families. Research addressing the problem of reentry is summarized, and it is suggested that children may be returning home too soon and that families may not be receiving appropriate services while their child is in foster care, leading to recidivism. Little data on how service characteristics, case decision-making processes, and the quality of aftercare services relate to placement stability are found. Suggestions for future investigation of these issues are offered.'' (Sociological Abstracts)

717. Thomas, C.B., 1967, ''The Resolution of Object Loss Following Foster Home Placement'', *Smith College Studies in Social Work,* Vol. XXXVII, June, pp. 163–234

Investigated the process through which children respond to object loss initiated by placement as it relates to efforts in establishing new relationships within a foster family. Thirty-five foster children were selected based on no previous placement and continuation in placement for no more than eighteen months (between ages of seven and twelve). Case records and interviews with foster parents provided data. Questions asked of foster parents to provide evidence of presence or absence of grief process were described in detail. One finding concluded that children studied showed some kind of reaction to placement, and they were observed to be in different phases of the grief process. Author suggests specific information concerning the grief process should be shared with foster parents to promote understanding and acceptance of children's reaction to placement.

718. Titus, K., 1984, Attitudes and Values Held by Adolescents in Foster Care That Help Them Successfully Adapt to Their Foster Care Experience (Child Welfare), Dissertation Abstracts International, Vol 45/10-A, page 3213

''The purpose of this study was to survey adolescents (age 12–18 years) who had been in foster family care six months or more to determine what attitudes or values within a foster home and what attitudes or perceptions held by the adolescents in care had assisted the adolescents to adapt successfully to foster care. A successful foster care experience was defined as one that did not disrupt the adolescent's developmental process. Four criteria were used in determining success: regular school attendance, maintenance of peer relationships, no arrests, no habitual substance abuse. The research design was an exploratory survey. There were ninety adolescents in foster family care. Of this group, 42 consented to be interviewed. Three data-gathering questionnaires were used. A chart/record review was done to provide a demographic profile of the successful and unsuccessful group. A foster parent questionnaire asked how the foster parents felt the adolescents were adjusting. The major questionnaire was used in interviewing the adolescents. This questionnaire was based on previous works done by Malcolm Bush, who assessed foster children's satisfaction of their care, and Rudolf Moos' attitude scales which have been used to survey human adaptation in other treatment environments. The three attitude scales that showed the greatest difference between the successful and unsuccessful adolescents were Recreation, Independence/Autonomy, and Support. Essentially, this meant that successful adolescents responded to structured environments where family activities were planned and occurred with regularity. They trusted and consulted with their foster parents about decisions and felt that foster parents went out of their way to help them. Another interesting finding indicates that unsuccessful adolescents tended to blame themselves for being placed in foster care, while successful adolescents tended to blame others (parents, agency or situation). A final pattern that requires further research revealed that successful adolescents had their primary attachment to their foster families while unsuccessful adolescents maintained their primary attachment to their biological families.'' (DAI)

719. Touliatos, J. & B. Lindholm, 1981, ''Measurement of Potential for Foster Parenthood'', *Journal of Psychology,* Vol. 109, pp. 256–263

In this article the same universe is used as below. This time the authors describe the construction of the scale and summarize evaluations by caseworkers of prospective foster parents. In the final form, 54 items are consolidated into nine factors: health, employment and income, time, opportunity for cultural and intellectual development, opportunity for religious and spiritual development, marriage, ability and motivation for foster parenthood, flexibility, working with the agency and the child's biological parents. ''(c) APA''

720. Touliatos, J. & B.W. Lindholm, 1977, ''Development of a Scale-Measuring Potential for Foster Parenthood'', *Psychological Reports,* Vol. 40, No. 3, Pt. 2, p. 1190

472 foster families served by 236 caseworkers in 91 agencies were studied during 1975/76 in the U.S. and Canada. A 54-item measure of potential for foster parenthood was developed. This might prove to be of value for custody, adoptive studies, and pre-marriage evaluation of parenting potential. ''(c)APA''

721. Turner, J., 1984, ''Reuniting Children in Foster Care With Their Biological Parents'', *Social Work,* Vol. 29, No. 6, pp. 501–505

The author reports on a study which contrasted 50 children who returned and remained at home after foster care, with 50 children who were returned to the foster care system. The study found a relationship between recidivism and the absence of services following a child's return to his/her home. It postulates the need for a continuum of services from placement through return to the home in order to insure a level of family functioning which will permit children to return home under more auspicious conditions or to provide alternate services. The quality of services in the non-recidivist cases is also commented upon.

722. Walker, C.W., 1974, ''Separation and Object Loss: The Plight of the Foster Child'', *Childhood Deprivation,* Thomas, Springfield, Ill.

The author explores the stages, feelings, experiences and defenses used in coping with the trauma of separation. It is imperative that the worker and foster parents know the facts about prior relationships in order to help resolve the effects of this trauma. It is further imperative that both the child's biological family and foster family be included in treatment.

723. Wallinga, J.V., 1966, ''Foster Placement and Separation Trauma'', *Public Welfare,* American Public Welfare Association

Dr. Wallinga discusses the psychological trauma experienced by children in separation, elaborating on the feelings and fears of the child, as well as the coping patterns and long-term effects. He stresses the importance of establishing a positive casework relationship prior to, during, and after the separation with emphasis on the child's expression of his or her own feelings.

724. Watson, K., 1982, ''A Bold New Model for Foster Family Care'', *American Public Welfare Journal,* Spring

This article discusses the changes affecting foster home placement. In the past, foster home placement was viewed only as substitute care, social workers working only with the child, the foster family taking the place of the biological parent(s). This new model views the foster family as an extended family, the biological family continuing involvement in decision making concerning the child. This involvement helps the family in crisis, forcing positive change or termination of parental roles.

725. Wenger, C., 1982, "The Suitcase Story: A Therapeutic Technique for Children in Out-of-Home Placement", *American Journal of Orthopsychiatry,* Vol. 52, No. 2, pp. 353–355

"A story developed as a vehicle for the expression of many of the feelings experienced by children in out-of-home placement is presented. The story has helped children in therapy to express their anger, acknowledge their fears of abandonment, and talk about their longing for performance. It has also enabled foster parents to better understand the child's situation and viewpoint." (SWAB)

726. Wilkes, J.R., 1974, "The Impact of Fostering on the Foster Family", *Child Welfare,* Vol. LIII, June, pp. 373–379

This paper selected four stresses that foster families react to which include: (1) coping with child in transition, (2) dealing with strange agency, (3) great expectation, (4) coping with disruption of family equilibrium. Successful ways of coping with stress included.

Adoptive Family

727. Allen, E., 1983, *Mother, Can You Hear Me?,* Dodd, Mead and Company, New York

A true story of self-discovery, tenderness, and devotion. Elizabeth finds her mother and shares her brief intense relationship due to her mother's death in the little time left after her discovery.

728. Arms, S., 1983, *To Love and Let Go,* Alfred A. Knopf, New York

Sensitive and moving accounts by mothers giving up their children for adoption, an adoptee searching for biological parents, a lawyer involved in adoptions, and parents working to adopt.

729. Aumend, S.A. & M.C. Barrett, 1984, "Self-Concept and Attitudes Toward Adoption: A Comparison of Searching and Nonsearching Adult Adoptees", *Child Welfare,* Vol. LXIII, May/June, pp. 251–259

Author's study attempts to compare adoptees searching for biological parents with those not searching. One hundred thirty-one adoptees were drawn from search groups and adoption agencies. Findings include differences between the two groups and do not support the idea that adoptees generally have low self-concepts and identity conflicts.

730. Auth, P.J. & S. Zaret, 1986, ''The Search in Adoption: A Service and a Process'', *Social Casework,* Vol. 67, No. 9, pp. 560–568

The authors give a brief history of the search, a consequence of the sealed record, which originated in the laws of many states in the 1930s and 40s. They believe the quest for identity to be at the root of the search, which has its peak during adolescence. They treat the search as a professional service during a developmental task, which may become a growth experience. The process is described and case examples are given.

731. Baran, A., Pannor, R. & A.D. Sorosky, 1974, ''Adoptive Parents and the Sealed Record Controversy'', *Social Casework,* Vol. 55, No. 9, pp. 531–536

The authors examine the background of the relatively recent trend of adoptees to search for their birthmothers, and the historic background of the adoption practice which was to conceal the information as a safeguard to all involved in the adoption triangle. The writers suggest that adoption agencies would do well to examine their position with regard to sealed records, since the past standards seem to have been the cause of big problems in the lives of adoptive families. The secrecy seemed to be more of a burden than a protection. It is suggested that the adult adoptee be accepted as a full client with the right for complete information.

732. Bass, C., 1975, ''Matchmaker-Matchmaker: Older Child Adoption Failures'', *Child Welfare,* Vol. LIV (July), pp. 505–512

Discussion is focused on exploration of adoptive placements of older children, with emphasis on innovative approaches and preparation of child and adopting family. Two cases are included.

733. Bellucci, M.T., 1975, ''Treatment of Latency-Age Adopted Children and Parents'', *Social Casework,* May, pp. 297–301

Discusses a group therapy program for newly placed adopted children, nine to thirteen years old, who experienced at least five foster homes. The children's themes in therapy are discussed in detail. Author stresses value of the group modality.

734. Benet, M.K., 1976, *The Politics of Adoption,* The Free Press, New York

This book takes a look at adoption in different cultures and societies as well as in the United States, from the viewpoints of the adoptees, biological parents, and the adoptive parents. It also gives insight into the experiences and the difficulties encountered by adoption agency workers in dealing with both birth parents and adoptive parents.

735. Berman, L.C. & R.K. Bufferd, 1986, ''Family Treatment to Address Loss in Adoptive Families'', *Social Casework,* Vol. 67, No. 1, pp. 3–11

All partners in the adoptive triangle experience serious losses, usually without an opportunity to mourn them adequately. This article explores the major issues for the various participants and develops a treatment approach based on family systems theory in which adopted children and their adoptive families are seen together to deal with these issues. The article also points out the pitfalls about seeing only the child or only the parent(s). Case examples are given.

736. Borgman, R., 1985, ''The Consequences of Open and Closed Adoption for Older Children'', *Child Welfare,* Vol. LXI (April), pp. 217–225

An interesting discussion of open vs. closed adoption for older children. Both types of procedures are discussed. The needs of the children, the biological parents, and the adoptive parents are also examined. The author emphasizes the importance for school-age children to be permitted to have a flexible approach to adoption which acknowledges the need to continue past relationships with the biological family and significant others.

737. Boyne, J., 1978, ''A Mental Health Note in Adoption of School-Age and Teen-Age Children'', *Child Welfare,* Vol. LVII (March), pp. 196–199

This concise article cites some mental health findings emerging from experience with 275 placements of the Spaulding for Children Agency. Suggests that maladaptive behaviors may be triggered by adoption. Recommendations in dealing with this behavior include: pre-adoption education, value clarification techniques, sensitizing workers and parents with symptoms, encouraging parental decision making, and fighting for subsidized psychiatric counseling for adoptees if needed.

738. Brockhaus, P.D. & R.H. Brockhaus, 1982, ''Adopting an Older Child—The Emotional Process'', *American Journal of Nursing,* February, pp. 288–291

Discusses phases in the emotional process of adopting and being adopted and how these can be timed to establish family equilibrium.

739. Brodzinsky, D.M., Schecter, D.E., Braff, A.H. & L.M. Singer, 1984, ''Psychological and Academic Adjustment in Adopted Children'', *Journal of Consulting and Clinical Psychology,* Vol. 52, pp. 582–590

This study attempted to answer two questions relating to psychological adjustment of adopted children: (1) whether or not adoptees are more vulnerable to emotional and academic problems, and (2) whether adjustment problems are related to age and sex. The sample consisted of 260 adopted and nonadopted children ranging in age from 6–11 years. Two measures were used. Results support position that adopted children are more vulnerable than other children to emotional, behavioral, and educational problems.

740. Brodzinsky, D.M., Singer, L.M. & A.M. Braff, 1984, ''Children's Understanding of Adoption'', *Child Development,* Vol. 55, pp. 969–978

Two hundred adopted and non-adopted children, ranging in age from 4 to 13 years, were interviewed concerning their understanding of adoption. During interviews, open-ended questions and Q-sort tasks were used. Results show developmental trends in the children's understanding of adoption with little difference between adopted and non-adopted children.

741. Churchill, S.R., Carlson, B. & L. Nybell, 1979, ''No Child is Unadoptable'', *Sage Human Services Guide,* Vol. 8

A series of papers dealing with some updated notions on adoption, e.g. even ''hard to place'' children are adoptable; single-parent adoptions are acceptable, may even be chosen for particular children; adolescents or children with medical problems can be placed in adoptive homes; black children are adoptable and black homes can be found. The authors then select papers in which special treatment techniques are described. Finally, a series of papers describe innovative programs.

742. Clifton, P.M., 1975, ''An Approach to Working With the Placed Child'', *Child Psychiatry and Human Development,* Vol. 6, Winter, pp. 107–117

This paper presents a therapeutic approach to working with the placed child (foster care, adoption or separation and divorce). Emphasis is placed on professionals to become aware of the placed child's emotional needs, based on the separation crisis (crisis-oriented approach). Three case reports are described in detail.

743. Cordell, A., Cicely, N. & V. Krymow, 1985, ''Group Counseling for Children Adopted at Older Ages'', *Child Welfare,* Vol. 64, pp. 113–124

The high-risk nature of later adoptions and the vulnerability of adolescents to stresses, as well as the experience from other studies showing that adoptees feel they do not get sufficient information from adoptive parents, led to an agency experiment. The format consisted of counseling group sessions for teens and pre-teens, culminating in an overnight retreat for these children as well as for a group of children whe were being prepared for adoption, so that the adoptees were in the role of consultant to the newcomers. The program is described in detail. It was started by a group of adoptive mothers who became the coordinators of the program and worked with two professionals in the agency. Concurrent meetings were held with the parents of the participating adoptees. It can be inferred that the meetings enhanced the children's self-concept and opened up future channels of communication, especially with peers who have had similar experiences.

744. Depp, C.H., 1982, ''After Reunion: Perceptions of Adult Adoptees, Adoptive Parents, and Birth Parents'', *Child Welfare,* Vol. LXI (February), pp. 115–119

A concise, informative study, tapping the feelings of adoptees, adoptive parents, and birth parents regarding reunion. The information was obtained through letters and questionnaires which were sent to 12 adult adoptees and their parents, both adoptive and birth. Results support the idea that the reunion experience enhanced the relationship between adoptee and adoptive parents.

745. DiGiulio, J., 1979, ''The 'Search': Providing Continued Service for Adoptive Parents'', *Child Welfare League of America*

This article deals with an agency's new ideas for a program that will lessen the fears raised in adoptive parents by the current controversy over sealed records. The author deals with issues concerning the adoptees, whose search for biological parents proved to be generally effective.

746. Dukette, R., 1979, ''Adoption 1979: Sleeping Beauty Awakes'', *Social Thought,* Fall, pp. 5–13

The author explores briefly the history of adoption and then raises questions concerning the present adoption practices. With regard to opening records, some questions included are, ''How will the role of adoption-practitioner change? Can we find enough comfort with the freedom an adoptee might have at some time to help him and both sets of parents with their relationship?''

747. Elbow, M., 1986, ''From Caregiving to Parenting: Family Formation with Adopted Older Children'', *Social Work,* Vol. 31, No. 5, pp. 366–370

''Families adopting older children are faced with three unique transitional tasks: boundary establishment, resolution of losses, and affirmation of roles. Describes these tasks, as well as the challenges to family development, and reframes stresses of adoptive families as normative to the transition process. Presents implications for practice.'' (ERIC)

748. Eldred, C.A., Rosenthal, D., Wender, P.H., Kety, S.S., Schulsinger, F., Welner, J. & B. Jacobsen, 1975, ''Some Aspects of Adoption in Selected Samples of Adult Adoptees'', *American Journal of Orthopsychiatry,* Vol. 46, February, pp. 279–290

Three groups of adoptees were studied with respect to biological parent with psychiatric disturbance, adoptive parent with psychiatric disturbance, and biological parent without psychiatric history. The data was collected from psychiatric interview and from placements. This information was used as part of a study of environmental and hereditary factors in etiology of schizophrenia. Various findings are discussed.

749. Feigelman, W. & A. Silverman, 1986, ''Adoptive Parents, Adoptees, and the Sealed Record Controversy'', *Social Casework,* Vol. 67, No. 4, pp. 219–226

372 adoptive families received questionnaires in the mail, of which 2/3 had at least one teenage adoptee. The authors review the history leading to the open-record controversy, then describe the study and the results of the questionnaire. Their description of trends reveals that today's adoptive parents seem to be more receptive to the idea of contact between their adopted children and the children's birth parents than earlier studies revealed. There is greater acceptance of a variety of adoptees, e.g. older or handicapped children, interracial or foreign adoptees. All parties in the adoption triangle have expressed frustration at the lack of information they received. The findings suggest that agency policies be changed to include routine medical and background information, and that contact between adoptees and birth parents be facilitated if both so desire. Opposition to such ideas is also reported.

750. Festinger, T., 1986, *Necessary Risk, A Study of Adoptions and Disrupted Adoptive Placements,* Child Welfare League of America, New York

A scholarly study beginning with a literary review, then describing the nature of the study, data collection, and design. The child population and parent population are studied along various criteria, as are the agencies and service characteristics. Several very interesting tables are included. The study ends on a note of hope that disruption is not the end but that over 75% of the children were replaced directly into another family of which over 25% went directly into another adoptive home. However, some suggestions are made which could strengthen the adoption services in order to minimize disruptions.

751. Fisher, F., 1973, *The Search for Anna Fisher,* Arthur Fields Books, Inc., Fawcett Crest, New York

Florence Fisher, founder of ALMA (Adoptees' Liberty Movement Association), tells her exhausting and dramatic story of a 20-year search for her biological parents to discover her identity.

752. Gill, M.M., 1978, ''Adoption of Older Children: The Problems Faced'', *Social Casework,* Vol. 59, No. 5, pp. 272–278

Presents many of the common post-placement concerns of parents and children gathered from the author's review of 22 hours of taped sessions of one such group.

753. Gilman, L., 1984, *The Adoption Resource Book, A Comprehensive Guide To All the Things You Need to Know and Ought to Know About Creating an Adoptive Family,* Harper & Row, New York

As indicated in the title and subtitle, this book truly describes what is going on in the adoption field, both formal and informal, today. It informs prospective adoptive parents about the available resources and options, details of the process of pre-adoption and adoption procedures, e.g. paperwork and legal issues, as well as agency procedures. Adoption agencies, parent groups, and legal resources are listed. Wisely the book does not end with the adoptive placement, but the author continues to discuss parenting issues and a number of questions which arise at later points in adoptive families. A must reading for adoptive families, better sooner than later.

754. Hartman, A., 1979, *Finding Families,* Sage Human Services Guide, Vol. 7

The author uses a family systems framework to develop a novel, more realistic approach to assess adoptive families. Making it a mutual assessment leads to a mutual decision-making process, which is considered an educational process as well, hopefully resulting in a better decision about the kind of plan and the kind of child who would best meet the family's life-style and expectations. As applicants learn more about themselves, some may withdraw, having found other ways to fulfill family needs, thus avoiding failure in adoptive placements. Others may be helped to work through certain problems which would then make them enter the adoptive process more realistically and become better adoptive families. Preparation for adoption and post-adoptive work are stressed. An appendix gives a training program for staffs to use the ecological approach described earlier.

755. Hartman, A., 1984, *Working With Adoptive Families Beyond Placement,* Child Welfare League of America, New York

The author provides the reader with the first post-placement model intended for professionals working in the adoption field. On the basis of the known complexities of the adoption process over the years of raising a child, the author reconceptualizes the kinds of help an adoptive family needs. The "probationary period" is not perceived as constructive. A sharing relationship between pre-adoption homestudy worker and family will set the tone for continued agency-family relationship on an as-needed basis. For instance, the resurging questions related to the adoptee's identity which surface during adolescence may well require professional help. This monograph provides a model for such services, based on family systems theory. Group help and self-help approaches are also considered.

756. Jaffee, B., 1974, "Adoption Outcome: A Two-Generation View", *Child Welfare,* Vol. LIII, April, pp. 211–223

This research attempted to determine how adoptees felt about their adjustment, related to adoption. More than 50 adoptive parent couples were interviewed, and 33 adult adoptees participated. One of the findings suggested that adoptees and their adoptive parents agreed on the quality of the adoptee adjustment. Additional information regarding adoptees' perceptions of their placement is included.

757. Jones, M., 1970, "Preparing the School-Age Child for Adoption", *Child Welfare,* Vol. LVIII (January), pp. 27–34

A useful reference that provides stages or guidelines for the emotional preparation of the school-age child for adoption. These stages include: (1) termination with biological family, (2) differentiation between foster and adoptive placement, (3) clarification of self-concept, (4) development of adoptive relationship. Each area is explored in detail.

758. Kadushin, A., 1971, ''Adoption Failures: A Social Work Post-Mortem'', *Social Work Journal,* Vol. 16, No. 3, pp. 32–38
This article looks at adoptions which have failed and discusses implications for practice in the field of adoption.

759. Katz, L., 1977, ''Older Child Adoptive Placement: A Time of Family Crisis'', *Child Welfare,* Vol. 56, March
Suggests that the family crisis that inevitably follows the adoptive placement of an older child can be surmounted if the social worker applies techniques based on crisis theory and family systems theory.

760. Kirk, H.D., 1981, *Adoptive Kinship, A Modern Institution in Need of Reform,* Butterworth, Toronto
This book is the result of the author's thirty years' involvement with the subject. He rejects what he calls the trivialization of adoption in the current literature and places it conceptually into the realm of kinship studies and family arrangements, rather than a peripheral social service activity. The central theme is sharply critical of the tendency in the adoption literature to eradicate or deny the difference between consanguinal and adoptive kinship. A detailed examination of the differences between birth parenthood and adoptive parenthood form the basic thesis and the author proceeds to amass considerable empirical evidence for this. He makes a good case for his thesis that, contrary to the traditional view, the acceptance rather than the rejection of the differences would be appropriate as the basis for public policy and would benefit the functioning of adoptive families. A chapter on a theory of bonding, one on legal contradictions, and several chapters dealing with institutional problems, legal contradictions, and barriers to institutional reform make this a very comprehensive and informative book.

761. Knight, M., 1985, ''Termination Visits in Closed Adoptions'', *Child Welfare,* Vol. 64, No. 1, pp. 37–45
A final contact is recommended by the author, to allow both child and parent some reaction to the separation, to decrease the

child's sense of guilt and responsibility for the separation, to diminish the realm of fantasy, and to leave the road open for new bonding. It is emphasized that this must be "a process rather than an event" and that the worker's influence on both parent and child is crucial. Some of the more negative factors are cited but seem outweighed by the positives, according to the author's experience.

762. Kowal, K. & K. Schilling, 1985, "Adoption Through the Eyes of Adult Adoptees", *American Journal of Orthopsychiatry,* Vol. 55, No. 3, pp. 354–362

This research study presents the results of a survey of 100 adopted adults who went to the adoption agency to search for information and/or biological relative. The perspectives of the search were compared with data from the clinical literature and with recommendations in adoption practice which were prevalent a generation ago. Other research findings are reported on as a background. The results show that adoptees who come to adoption agencies are a priori a self-selected group. However, the findings do have practice implications: Fantasies about biological parents are present in a non-clinical sample of the population, and cannot be assumed to be uncommon without further study. There seems to be different salience to male and female adoptees to search. Adults who enter a search in the majority are not looking for a surrogate family or for contact, but find the search important in an existential sense to enhance their knowledge and sense of identity. As a result of the study, the authors suggest adolescence and pregnancy/childbirth as appropriate life-cycle stages to offer post-adoption services.

763. Lifton, B.J., 1975, *Twice Born: Memoirs of an Adopted Daughter,* McGraw-Hill, New York

As a journalist and a playwright, the author uses her considerable writing skills and her intense emotional experiences, both while growing up as an adopted child and later in her search for her biological parents, to lead the reader through the identity conflicts of the adopted child, especially fostered by the taboo of secrecy about adoption which is both legally required and societally more acceptable.

764. Lifton, B.J., 1981, *Lost and Found,* Bantam Books, New York

The author delves into the emotional and psychological impact of being adopted by describing the "adoptive life-cycle" as being different from that of biological children. She looks at the fact as differently perceived by all participants, the adoptive parents and biological parents as well as the adoptees. The search and the reunion are elaborated upon. The adoptee's spouse and children are separately considered in terms of their perception of the consequences of being married to and/or born to an adopted person.

765. Littner, N., 1974, ''The Challenge to Make Fuller Use of Our Knowledge About Children'', *Child Welfare,* Vol. LIII, No. 5
   Discusses some common consequences of the separation and placement conflicts for children.

766. Miall, C.E., 1987, ''The Stigma of Adoptive Parent Status: Perceptions of Community Attitudes Toward Adoption and the Experience of Informal Social Sanctioning'', *Family Relations,* Vol. 36, No. 1, pp. 34–39
   ''Examined role of informal social response by having involuntarily childless women (N=71) detail their perceptions of societal beliefs about adoption concerning the importance of the biological tie for bonding and love, the unknown genetic past of adopted children and the view that adoptive parents are not 'real' parents. Discusses how family practitioners can alleviate the stigma potential of adoption.'' (ERIC)

767. Mikawa, J.K. & J.A. Boston, 1968, ''Psychological Characteristics of Adopted Children'', *Psychiatric Quarterly,* Vol. 42, July, pp. 274–281
   The purpose of the present study was to determine if normal non-adopted children differ from normal adopted children with regard to personality dimensions. (''Normal'' refers to the absence of emotional disturbances.) Twenty adopted children were compared to twenty non-adopted children as to ratings of behavior at school, interviews with mothers. The Rosenzweig Picture Frustration test, Sarasen's Test Anxiety Scale for Children, and General Anxiety Scale for Children were used. Results indicated similarity in personality structure in both groups studied and that implications of emotional stress in adoptees might be related to parent-child relationship difficulties.

768. Munisinger, H., 1975, ''The Adopted Child's IQ: A Critical Review'', *Psychological Bulletin,* Vol. 82, September, pp. 623–659
   This article summarizes and critiques adoption studies pertaining to IQ. The importance of the nature-nurture controversy is taken into account.

769. Murray, L., 1984, "A Review of Selected Foster Care Adoption Research from 1978 to Mid-1982", *Child Welfare,* Vol. LXIII, March/April, pp. 113–124

Explores research findings regarding (1) permanency planning, (2) adoption outcomes, (3) foster parents, and (4) recidivism in foster care from 1978 to 1982.

770. Offord, D.R., Aponte, J.F. & L.A. Cross, 1969, "Presenting Symptomatology of Adopted Children", *Archives of General Psychiatry,* Vol. 20, January, pp. 110–116

Study addresses the question of whether clinical symptoms differ between emotionally disturbed adopted and non-adopted children. 25 adopted children (experimental group) and 25 children living with biological parents seen clinically over a 5-year period. Findings show adopted children were not more seriously disturbed than non-adoptees.

771. Pannor, R. & E.A. Nerlove, 1977, "Fostering Understanding Between Adolescents and Adoptive Parents Through Group Experience", *Child Welfare,* Vol. LVI, October, pp. 537–545

An enlightening article describing in detail the experiences of two groups, an adopted adolescent group and an adoptive parent group. Parent group consisted of 5 couples and 3 single parents while adolescent group consisted of 13 children. Focus of groups is on vulnerability of adoptive families during adolescence of the child.

772. Pardeck, J.T. & J.A. Pardeck, 1987, "Bibliography for Children in Foster Care and Adoption", *Child Welfare,* Vol. 66, No. 3, pp. 269–278

"The bibliotherapeutic technique can help children adjust to the foster care and adoption experience. Appropriate children's books for grades 1 to 6 are described. The application and limitations of bibliotherapy are discussed." (ERIC)

773. Prentice, C.S., 1940, *An Adopted Child Looks at Adoption,* D. Appleton-Century Company, New York

An early study of problems and processes of adoption by a woman who was herself an adopted child and who added an adopted daughter to her two biological sons. With a knowledgeable view of contemporary Child Welfare Practices the author looks at adoption as a process, considers many of the popular notions on adoption, the assets and pitfalls, the people who adopt, the children who tend to be adopted. A courageous and lucid, reality-oriented picture emerges, at a time at which not many people tended to challenge existing practices. A manual for adopting parents which is appended, goes into motives, finding a child, legal procedures, probation period, special problems. A forerunner of many studies to come.

774. Proch, K., 1982, "Difference Between Foster Care and Adoption: Perceptions of Adopted Foster Children and Adoptive Foster Parents", *Child Welfare,* Vol. LXI, May, pp. 259–268
Author explored how foster care and adoption are viewed by adoptive foster parents. Between January and June, 1979, interviews were conducted with adoptive foster parents of 56 children and with 29 adopted foster children. The children were between the ages of 7 and 13 and had "special needs" or were considered "hard to place." It is concluded that foster parents did not define their roles as temporary and indicated a psychological parent/child relationship can develop without adoption; children viewed adoption as significant if they were the result of multiple placements.

775. Ramos, S., 1975, *Teaching Your Child to Cope with Crisis: How to Help Your Child Deal with Death, Divorce, Surgery, Being Adopted, Moving, Alcoholic Parents, Sick Parents, Leaving Home, and Other Major Worries,* David McKay, New York
This book is intended to assist parents in dealing effectively with child-rearing problems to anticipate and avert crises, and to utilize life stresses and even tragedies to strengthen the child's emotional growth.

776. Raymond, L., 1955, *Adoption and After,* Harper and Row, New York
This book is a general text that deals with all aspects of adoption to give the reader an understanding about the different phases of adoption and what problems are likely to arise in the interpersonal, emotional, legal, and community aspects.

777. Reece, S. & B. Levin, 1968, "Psychiatric Disturbances in Adopted Children: A Descriptive Study", *Social Work,* January, pp. 101–109
This study was intended to explore the degree to which psychiatric disturbance is prevalent in adopted children under the age of 18. Authors determined the number of adopted children under age 18 in population of 1,017 cases which were opened consecutively at a children's service psychiatric unit. Goal was to

form impressions about factors related to psychiatric disturbance in these children.

778. Rickarby, G. & T. Single, 1981, "Making New Bonds Between Adults and Children", *Australia Family Physician,* Vol. 10, No. 10, pp, 780–781

Discusses relationships of fathers and grandparents to children and of parents to adopted, fostered, or stepchildren, who may need special attention.

779. Rohr, F., 1971, "How Parents Tell Their Children They Are Adopted", *Child Welfare,* Vol. L, May

A brief excerpt from booklet for adoptive parents regarding suggestions when discussing adoption with their adopted children. Author stresses sensitivity of parents to the needs and concerns of the children when exploring this issue with them.

780. Schwartz, E.M., 1970, "The Family Romance Fantasy in Children Adopted in Infancy", *Child Welfare,* Vol. XLIX, July

Explores the fantasy that parents with whom children live are not their true parents, and there is another set of "all loving, all-permissive parents." Twenty-five boys adopted before age 6 were compared to non-adopted boys. Boys were between 8 and 11 years at time of study. Results support idea that children adopted in infancy in stable family situations do not show greater significance of family romance fantasy.

781. Shireman, J.F. & P.R. Johnson, 1986, "A Longitudinal Study of Black Adoptions: Single Parent, Transracial, and Traditional", *Social Work,* Vol. 31, No. 3, pp. 172–176

"A longitudinal study of 76 black children who were adopted as infants and who were reared in single-parent, transracial, and traditional adopted homes revealed that most children did well in their adoptive families. Interview data collected from parents and their children were supplemented with standardized test material. In regard to overall adjustment, the three groups of children were similar to one another, as well as to adopted children who participated in earlier studies. Interest at this reporting, when the children were 8 years old, focused on transracially adopted children because their pattern of racial-identity development differed from that of children reared in black homes. The stress associated with low income and the close nature of the parent-child relationship was noted in the single-parent adoptions. Different patterns of handling issues of adoption also emerged among the three groups.'' (SWAB)

782. Silverman, P.R., Campbell, L., Patti, P. & C. Style, 1988, ''Reunions Between Adoptees and Birthparents: The Birthparents' Experiences'', *Social Work,* Nov/Dec, Vol. 33, No. 6, pp. 523–528

Reunions of 170 birth parents and their children are described. 79% of the birth parents, and 21% of the children (placed at birth) initiated the reunion. The authors themselves describe the limitations of the study before coming to tentative conclusions. However, this initial exploration is very valuable as a data base, which explored mainly the experiences of the birth parents. Contrary to expectations, the reunion did not seem to disturb the lives of the participants. Even birth mothers who did not search or did not wish to do so were pleased to be found. The findings generally support the need to re-examine the notion that the legal surrender must sever all relationships between birth parents and their children.

783. Sorich, C. & R. Siebert, 1979, *Toward Humanizing Adoption,* Child Welfare League of America, New York

This article discusses the benefits of exploring alternatives to the traditional closed adoption placement. It explores open adoption, and the sharing of a meaningful relationship between adoptive parents and biological parents, in order to provide adopted children with continuity and a sense of identity.

784. Sorosky, A., 1979, *The Adoption Triangle,* Anchor Press, New York

This book discusses the adoption triangle as it relates to the biological parents, adoptive parents and adoptee, both in depth and with critical, analytical perspective.

785. Sorosky, A., Baran, A. & R. Pannor, 1976, ''The Effects of the Sealed Record in Adoption'', *American Journal of Psychiatry,* Vol. 133, August, pp. 900–903

Authors recommend opening records for adult adoptees, with assistance of the helping professionals. Their suggestions are supported by research with 50 adult adoptees who experienced reunions with their birth parents.

786. Sorosky, A., Baran, A. & R. Pannor, 1975, ''Identity Conflicts in Adoptees'', *American Journal of Orthopsychiatry,* Vol. 45, No. 1, pp. 18–27

Explores adoption dynamics and more specifically psychological issues pertaining to them. Four categories of psychological difficulties with regard to adoptees are given in conjunction with a detailed review of the literature. Authors interviewed a large number of adoptees searching for biological parents and support the view along with literature findings, that adoptees are more vulnerable than population in development of identity problems.

787. Sorosky, A., Baran, A. & R. Pannor, 1974, "The Reunion of Adoptees and Birth Relatives", *Journal of Youth and Adolescence,* Vol. 3, pp. 195–206

Eleven adoptees were interviewed regarding the outcome of reunion with their mothers. A statistical breakdown of the group given and brief summaries of reunion included.

788. Starr, P., Taylor, D.A. & R. Taft, 1970, "Early Life Experiences and Adoptive Parenting", *Social Casework,* October, pp. 491–500

This study empirically tests the relationship between early life experiences of couples and their ability to perform as adoptive parents. Three hundred ninety-five couples who had adopted children participated. Self-reporting inventories of childhood experiences and the Roe-Siegelman Parent-Child Relations Questionnaire used. Findings indicate minimal association between childhood experiences and performance as adoptive parents.

789. Triseliotis, J., 1985, "Adoption With Contact," *Adoption and Fostering,* Vol. 9, No. 4, 19–24

Discusses adoption with the condition of access by original family members within the changing legal and demographic environment of the childcare system. Tested evidence about the outcome of adoption with contact is limited, but related research is encouraging. The main issue about access and contact in present-day adoption practice refers mostly to those adolescents who, even though they may be looking for a new family, do not wish to give up existing attachments to members of their original family. It is contended that professionals in the childcare system should focus on the quality of these existing attachments among family members when dealing with each case. "(c)APA"

790. Turkeimer, E.N., 1986, Cognitive Development of Adopted and Fostered Children (Genetics, Environment, IQ), Dissertation Abstracts International, Vol. 47/09-B, page 3987

"Adopted and fostered children provide a unique opportunity for the study of genetic and environmental influences on cognitive development, but fifty years of adoption studies have not succeeded in resolving the debate between environmentalists and hereditarians. This study attempts to subsume two classic adoption designs that have often led to opposite conclusions. One design compared the mean IQ's of adoptees and a control group of similar but nonadopted children. These studies have usually found an IQ advantage for the adopted children, suggestive of an environmental effect. The second involves regressing IQ's of adoptees on characteristics of their biological parents and adoptive rearing environments. These studies have shown adoptees' IQ's to be more strongly related to their biological than adoptive parents, indicative of a predominant genetic influence. In the present study, 338 adopted or fostered children were selected from the Natural Collaborative Perinatal Project, a large-scale longitudinal study. These children were compared to two groups of matched controls, one matched to characteristics of the biological families on the index cases, and the other matched to characteristics of their adoptive or foster families. All children were administered infant development scales at eight months of age, and intelligence scales at four and seven years. Structural equation modelling techniques were used to perform simultaneous regressions of cognitive measures on family variables in the three groups, while constraining regression coefficients to be equal across groups. IQ differences predicted by the regressions were then compared to actual differences among the groups. Adopted children scored significantly higher than controls on most IQ measures. Foster children scored substantially lower than either control group on all tests. Some of the adopted childrens' IQ advantage could be attributed to their adoptive environment, especially for white children. Biological mother's education predicted biological children's IQ's for adopted children of both races. The low IQ's of the foster children appeared largely to be caused by biological deficits predating their fostering, although those raised in poor foster environments showed especially large IQ deficits. Genetic relationships between maternal education and child IQ appeared to have been attenuated by neurological impairment in this group.'' (DAI)

791. Vida, A., 1979, *Adoption Agency: Who Needs It!,* Dorrance and Company, Philadelphia, PA

This book contains the observations and experiences of a journalist who visited an adoption agency to do an article for a newspaper. He becomes more involved and learns how the agency operates and functions, how it works with its clients, and the way the workers handle the stress and joys of working in the area of adoption. This book provides an inside view of the adoption world which is very complete and describes conflicts that workers experience. It enables one to have a better understanding of adoption agencies.

792. Wilder, H., 1977, "The Family Romance Fantasies of Adopted Children", *Psychoanalytic Quarterly,* Vol. 46, April, pp. 185–200
Focuses on being told of adoption and the effect it has on romance fantasies. The author defines family romance fantasies and discusses research with regard to this. Analyses of three adoptees are given. It was found that adoptee's fantasy is to deny adoption and establish a blood tie to adoptive parents, erasing the humiliation adoption implies.

793. Wilder, H., 1977, "On Being Told of Adoption", *Psychoanalytic Quarterly,* Vol. 46, pp. 1–22
Focuses on the consequences of disclosure about adoption to children under three years of age. Three case studies are included: a nine-year-old, an adolescent, and a twenty-seven-year-old adult. The author stresses the possible traumatic effects of early communication to the child of adoption.

794. Wolf, A.M., 1983, "A Personal View of Black Inner-City Foster Families", *American Journal of Orthopsychiatry,* Vol. 53, No. 1, pp. 144–151
A 21-year-old medical student lived in a black inner-city area and reported her experiences and observations. She compares the special form of extended family which she observed to the parts of current literature which deal with black families and family ties. The "informal" adoptions which are quite prevalent in this community are discussed and the author stresses the need for mental health professionals to understand that these families have special strengths in their extended family system which serves the children well and must be appreciated better by the professionals who serve the community.

795. Wolf, P.A. & E. Mast, 1987, "Counseling Issues in Adoptions by Stepparents", *Social Work,* Vol. 32, No. 1, pp. 69–74
"Although the number of nonrelative adoptions is decreasing, stepparent adoptions are not. These adoptions are viewed as non-problematic family business separate from the general adoption picture. This article examines demographic data in Lancaster County, Pennsylvania, from 55 stepparent adoptions concerning

stepparent adopters, birth parents, and adoptees and the stated reasons for adopting.'' (ERIC)

796. Work, H.H. & H. Anderson, 1971, ''Studies in Adoption: Requests for Psychiatric Treatment'', *American Journal of Psychiatry,* Vol. 127, January, pp. 948–950

Reports a survey of all children seen at the Neuropsychiatric Institute of U.C.L.A. School of Medicine from 1964 to 1969. Authors found that parents of adopted children frequently seek psychiatric treatment for them. Authors believe that there is some possible relationship between child-rearing practices and adopted children's difficulties.

III. INTERVENTIONS

Prevention

797. Bray, J.H., et al, 1985, Behavior Problems with Children: Relationship to Parental Marital Status, Paper presented at the *Annual Convention of the Southwestern Psychological Association*

"As the divorce rate continues to rise, increasing attention is being paid to the impact of parental divorce and remarriage on the children from these families. A study was undertaken to investigate the impact of family process and organization, in intact, divorced, and stepfather families. Subjects were 36 families (12 families from each group) with a 6- to 12-year-old boy, who were clients at a child guidance center. Subjects were assessed using self-reports, structured interviews, and behavior ratings of family interactions. The results indicated that there were no significant differences in family process and organization between the intact, divorced, and stepfather families. In addition, no differences in boys' behavior problems were observed based on family type. Significant correlations were found between more pathological family process variables and boys' behavior problems, suggesting that problems and conflict in marital and family relationships are related to behavior problems with children. (NRB)" ERIC

798. Coleman, M., Ganong, H. & J. Henry, 1984, "What Teachers Should Know about Stepfamilies", *Childhood Education,* Vol. 60, pp. 306–309

Popular stereotypes about stepfamilies are warned against and specific suggestions are made for helping teachers become more aware of common differences (not necessarily problems) of stepfamilies such as difference in names, legal complications. Sensitivity to the children's feelings and awareness of the positive aspects of stepfamily living are emphasized.

799. Engebretson, J., 1982, "Stepmothers as First-Time Parents, Their Needs and Problems", *Pediatric Nursing,* Nov/Dec

The author defines mothers having their first parenting experience with stepchildren as a group with special needs and recommends that they be considered as much in crisis as new mothers. Nurses must get involved and expose the ''bad stepmother'' myth, and other problems such as the expectation of instant love. The nurse, it is felt, can help the stepmother deal realistically with her expectations, frustrations, and anger as well as advise her about disciplining techniques and child development. Interventions are quite detailed and some literature is recommended. The article takes in the major problems of stepparenthood and is prevention oriented. It is not specified where and how nurses meet these stepfamilies, nor how first-time stepmothers differ from stepmothers who have had biological children before.

800. Feiner, R.D. & S.S. Farber, 1980, ''Social Policy for Child Custody: A Multidisciplinary Framework'', *American Journal of Orthopsychiatry,* Vol. 50, No. 2, pp. 341–347

The authors identify divorce as a prime target for preventive efforts on behalf of children due to its high incidence and its potentially negative impact. The authors view continuity of relationships, minimal interference of the court, and according the child party status, as recommended by Goldstein, Freud, and Solnit with some question, and cite other research studies, e.g. Zill, Heatherington, et al, to highlight the importance of continuity not only with the resident parent, but also with the non-custodial parent, mostly the father. Other proponents of single custody as well as those of joint custody have produced some research efforts which show considerable problematic areas in each. The authors attempt to make a case for the development of a preventively oriented social policy for child placement which attempts to combine the best efforts of both legal and mental health knowledge. Future research is recommended along with efforts at true interdisciplinary collaboration.

801. Fuller, M.L., 1986, ''Perceptions of Children from Intact and Single-Parent Families'', *School Counselor,* Vol. 33, No. 5, pp. 365–374

The author attempts to dispel the ''self-fulfilling prophecy'' inherent in the popular perception of school personnel that children from non-nuclear families will behave differently, i.e. worse than children from intact homes. She therefore investigates school teachers' perceptions of the school behaviors of children from intact homes versus those from single-parent homes and arrives at some suggestions of changing their views. She makes a strong point that the teachers' (negative) perceptions have a strong influence on the self-perceptions of the children they teach. The author gives a literature review, states her hypothesis clearly and describes her pilot study, then discusses the results. The study corroborated the assumptions made initially. Specific suggestions are made in which school counselors can help: individual and group counseling of children, support groups for children and single parents, in-service training for teachers, counselors, multicultural awareness, and reviews of school policies.

802. Funk, J., 1983, "Special Problems in Divorce Management", *Journal of Development and Behavioral Pediatrics,* Vol. 4, pp. 108–112

"It is assumed that pediatricians are involved in helping families solve divorce-related problems, as well as problems with remarriage. Parents are to be advised to let the school system know as soon as possible, since the child's school behavior and performance may be adversely affected. Research is cited indicating that the child's continued access to both parents is desirable, and when conflict is minimal such access enhances the child's adjustment. Counseling measures for stressful visitations are presented. Pediatricians are said to have the opportunity to provide guidance with reference to unrealistic expectations and lack of clarity in family roles." (c) APA

803. Furstenberg, F.F., Nord, C.W., Peterson, J.L. & N. Zill, 1983, "The Life Course of Children of Divorce: Marital Disruption and Parental Contact", *American Sociological Review,* Vol. 48, No. 5, pp. 656–668

The authors offer a preliminary analysis of data from a nationally representative sample of U.S. children 11–16 in 1981. The incidence of marital disruption in children's lives, the type of alternate living arrangements, and the amount of contact children have with the non-resident parent are the subjects of analysis. Large differences in incidence and consequences of disruption were found based on racial factors. Black children were much more likely to have undergone a family disruption by early adolescence, and were much less likely to wind up in a stepfamily within 5 years of family of origin disruption. Frequent contact with the non-resident parent occurred rarely, irrespective of race (17% showed once-a-week visits within the year preceding the study). The length of time since separation was a crucial factor in the visiting or contact pattern. Children whose non-custodial parent was not living were not included, nor the number of children whose parents had not been married. If these were included, close to 40% of all children experience some time in single-parent families. It was felt that the predominant pattern, at least for whites, involves the replacement of the biological parent with the sociological or stepparent. Much needs to be studied about this transition and the consequences to the well-being of the children, the authors feel.

804. Galaway, B.R., 1980, Role Consensus and Satisfactions in Foster Family Care Systems, Dissertation Abstracts International, Vol. 41/03-A, page 1215

"In foster family care services parenting responsibilities are typically divided among natural parents, social workers and foster parents which may result in problems of role ambiguity and conflict. Role theorists suggest that role conflict may lead to a reduction in gratification and increased strain. This exploratory study examined the extent to which participants in foster family care systems were in consensus or agreement regarding authority to make a series of child care decisions in five areas—management of foster youth in the foster home, foster youth's use of community resources, involvement of natural parents with the youth in placement, the foster youth's assumption of adult privileges, and appropriate communication patterns within the foster family care systems. A foster family care system consists of the foster mother, natural mother, adolescent girl, and the youth's social worker. Data was also secured regarding the satisfactions of participants in these foster family care systems with the role behavior of reciprocals. A cross-sectional design was used involving 18 foster care systems serving Caucasian girls ages 12 through 18 who were non-state wards but were in foster family placements under auspices of a single public welfare agency. A structured interview schedule was used to collect data. Data was secured from 16 foster youth, 18 foster mothers, 12 natural mothers, and 16 social workers; complete data was available for nine systems. Consensus was analyzed across groups as well as within each of the systems. The groups of foster youth, foster parents, natural parents, and social workers were generally in consensus as to who should make decisions concerning management of the foster youth within the foster home, the foster youth's assumption of adult privileges, and appropriate communication patterns within foster family care systems. Consensus was not present in regard to the decisions concerning the foster youth's use of community resources and involvement of the natural parents with the youth in placement. The participants disagreed as to whether the foster parent or social worker did and should have authority to make decisions regarding the foster youth's use of community resources; there was no pattern in regard to decisions concerning the natural parents involvement with the foster youth in placement with wide differences of view as to who does and should make these decisions. The level of consensus within each of the individual systems paralleled the cross group consensus. Satisfaction with the role behaviors of reciprocals was generally high although the natural parents consistently expressed lower levels of satisfaction than did any of the other participants. Likewise, all participants, including natural parents, expressed lower levels of satisfaction with the role behavior of natural parents than with the role behavior of other participants. Because the measures of satisfaction did not discriminate, the exploration of associations between consensus on decision-making authority and satisfactions was not useful. Additional study is necessary to further clarify the nature of dissensus in foster family care systems and to determine if the patterns found in this study are present in other populations. This study was unable to test for possible effects from a lack of role consensus; role theory postulates, however, that these effects might be strain, lack of stability and reduced sense of gratification. Given this theoretical orientation, social work interventions could be directed towards increasing consensus within foster family care systems; the development of teamwork among all participants in these systems and the use of contracting foster family care services are approaches which may increase the level of consensus.'' (DAI)

805. Gray, B.J. & G.D. Pippin, 1984, ''Stepfamilies: A Concern Health Education Should Address'', *Journal of School Health,* Vol. 54, No. 8, pp. 292–294

''Health educators need to recognize that many children are in a stepfamily situation, where they may have trouble coping with changes. Through subunits included in the family life curriculum, young people can be taught how to deal with the issues involved.'' (ERIC)

806. Guisinger, S., 1984, The First Years of the Second Marriage: Changing Parental and Couple Relations in the Remarriage Family (Stepmothers, Divorced Fathers, Stepfamilies), Dissertation Abstracts International, Vol. 45/09-B, page 3071

''This study investigates factors related to parental and couple relations in the first five years of the remarriage of divorced fathers and their new wives. Sixty-three couples, recruited primarily from marriage license records, were assessed by interviews and questionnaires; 22 couples were in their second year of marriage, 24 had been married three to five years, and 17 were assessed as newlyweds and again in their third year of marriage. For women, several variables examined in this study changed systematically over time. Satisfaction declined in the areas of child care division of household tasks and stepparenting over the first three years of the remarriage. Wives' marital satisfaction also declined. Stepchildren were perceived as being increasingly difficult, while the evaluation of former wives by the present wives was extremely negative at both assessment times. Women who were more satisfied with their marriages at both times tended to have self-esteem, to be more satisfied with division of household tasks and child-care, to report a good relationship with their stepchild, to see the child as not too difficult, to describe the former wife in more favorable terms, and to be nurturing, accepting, and well-adjusted individuals. Men's marital satisfaction also decreased over the course of the study. Men who were more satisfied with their marriages at both times tended to be more satisfied with couple decision-making, to report a good relationship with their child, and to be less negative in their evaluation of their former wives. The more satisfied men had wives who tended to see stepparenting of the child as less difficult, reported a good relationship with the stepchild, and were more positive in their evaluation of the former wife. More satisfied husbands also tended to be better adjusted, more insightful and to have higher self-esteem. These findings suggest that marital satisfaction emerges from an interaction of variables including the couple's role arrangement, relations with the children from the previous marriage, relations with the former wife, and personality factors. Information from the present study may be helpful in designing preventive interventions to make the early years of remarriage less stressful and more satisfying.'' (DAI)

807. Herndon, A. & L.G. Combs, 1982, ''Stepfamilies as Patients'', *Journal of Family Practice,* Vol. 15, No. 5, pp. 917–922

In view of the increase in the stepfamily population the authors think it is important for family physicians to be aware of the special stepfamily characteristics which are not present in nuclear families: formation out of loss, previous history of only some family members, and also previous child bonds; a biological parent elsewhere, legal limitations, children as part of more than one household. Recommendations for the training of residents and continued education for physicians are made. The article's special contribution is on the normalization of other-than-nuclear family patterns.

808. Huntington, D., 1982, ''Attachment, Loss, and Divorce'', *Therapy With Remarried Families,* Aspen Systems Corporation, Rockville, MD, pp. 19–29
The author gives an update of recent theories of attachment and then applies a reconsideration of attachment to the bonding processes of all children, and details the importance of this understanding to children of divorce. The crucial importance of extended family, even early peer group attachments, different functioning of parental role models, and the total context of familial and societal support systems needs to be considered. The strong point is made that parents (adults) are allowed to love many people while children are reared to love and trust only two people, their biological parents. This must change in order to adjust to the reality in the lives of children of divorce.

809. Johnson, H., 1980, ''Working With Stepfamilies: Principles of Practice'', *Social Work,* Vol. 25, pp. 304–308
Johnson discusses common characteristics of stepfamilies: their complexity, variability, unclear expectations, losses and gains, questions of turf, and suggests there are some positive, beneficial elements of stepfamilies. Principles for practice are drawn, in particular, the need to understand the sociological and economic basis for the breakup of nuclear families to reduce the tendency to later development of pathology. It is emphasized that groups can be very helpful, especially in prevention.

810. Jones, F., 1977, ''The Impact of Divorce on Children'', *Conciliation Courts Review,* Vol. 15, pp. 25–29
Three studies initiated since 1970 are reviewed in this paper in terms of the impact of divorce on children (Hetherington, Wallerstein & Kelly, Oregon Study). The author concedes the importance of understanding crisis theory and suggests that the difficulties notwithstanding, the negative impact on children may have been overestimated. More research comparing those children who are doing well with those who are not is suggested. The professional bias of focusing on problem situations is mentioned. Specific recommendations for practitioners include working with both parents, encouraging their coming to counseling, opportunity for children (especially older ones) to express feelings in counseling, and last but not least, a view of counseling as a support structure during a transition phase for (non-pathological) families.

811. Kalter, N., Pickar, J. & M. Lesowitz, 1984, ''School-Based Developmental Facilitation Groups for Children of Divorce: A

Preventive Intervention'', *American Journal of Orthopsychiatry,* Vol. 54, pp. 613–623

This is a model for time-limited school-based support groups for children of divorce. The sparse history of work with groups of children of divorce is reviewed and a rationale for this work is developed. ''Nodal points'' such as moving into school, adolescence, pre-high school graduation are suggested as good entry points. This report is on several groups in three public schools but the authors feel that the system could be used in many sites, e.g. child guidance centers, courts. The plan, content and format are described, as is the need to share with parents the general purpose and aims of the group. Specific foci, such as fighting parents, changed custody, mother's dating, stepparents, or live-in partners were discussed. Evaluations were done and were favorable in almost all instances. Earlier interventions are recommended wherever possible.

812. Kantor, D. & W. Lehr, 1965, *Inside the Family: Toward a Theory of Family Process,* Jossey-Bass, San Francisco

The authors develop a systems model for examining components of family process and show how it is employed in regulating family members' behaviors. They describe and analyze behaviors family members use in specific situations, identify clear-cut family types and member roles, and discuss marital, sibling, and parent-child relationships. The model is based on reports of trained observers who lived with families of various religious, ethnic, educational, and class backgrounds.

813. Kinney, J.M., Madsen, B., Fleming, T. & D.A. Haapala, 1979, ''Homebuilders: Keeping Families Together'', *Journal of Consulting and Clinical Psychology,* Vol. 45, pp. 667–673

This study examined the use of therapists in the homes of 80 families in crisis to avoid family members' being placed elsewhere (foster home, institutional care). Therapists used techniques which included crisis intervention, behavior modification and assertion training. Results indicated 121 out of 134 family members did not seek outside placement after therapists worked with families. Example of a case study is included.

814. Lindsay, D., Nov. 1982, *Achievements for Children in Foster Care,* NASW, Inc.

Through research, evidence has been cited of inefficient and inadequate delivery of child welfare services to neglected and abused children. Lindsay examines three projects: CES, Alameda,

Oregon. All three seek to reduce the number of children in foster care by limiting the length of time in care, and, for those whose situations indicate extended long-term care, to provide permanency. All projects seek to attempt return to biological parents by helping to remedy the initial problems which caused placement.

815. Lowery, C.R., 1985, "Child Custody in Divorce: Parents' Decisions and Perceptions", *Family Relations,* Vol. 34, No. 2, pp. 241–249

55 divorcing couples were given questionnaires and interviews about factors involved in decisions about child custody. Both mothers and fathers agreed on the importance of such issues as continuity in the child's environment and quality of parent-child relationship but their interpretation of these issues in relation to the decision of who should have custody were at variance. Fathers were generally less satisfied with the custody arrangements (75% had agreed on mother custody, 13% on joint custody and 10% had not yet decided). The study is described in terms of its origin and findings, with provision of specific subdata. In the light of the difference in satisfaction between men and women, and the fact that over one-third reported somewhat less than a consensual decision, along with known facts of judicial decision which favor mothers as primary custodians, plus surprising subdata, the authors suggest some follow-up research. Early intervention to insure continued concern and participation of fathers, new techniques such as divorce mediation, joint custody, attention to mothers' economic plight are included in the author's suggestions to practitioners.

816. Lutz, P., 1983, "The Stepfamily: An Adolescent Perspective", *Family Relations,* Vol. 32, pp. 367–375

A study involving 103 adolescents aged 12 to 18 living in stepfamilies. Found divided loyalties and discipline to be the most stressful areas in stepfamily living. Experiencing one biological parent talking negatively about the other received the highest stress rate with all respondents. Discipline is very stressful for all adolescents because they are seeking autonomy. Other perceived areas of stress were cited, such as divided loyalty. Prevention of developmental problems by knowledgeable professionals is emphasized to maintain a sense of roots and identity.

817. Mace, D., 1983, *Prevention of Family Services: Approaches to Family Wellness,* Sage Publications Inc., Beverly Hills, CA

Preventive approaches in family therapy are viewed, with

emphasis placed on working with families in the pre-crisis state. The main focus of the book is on the need for educating the family and insuring awareness by family members to prevent potential dysfunctioning. The development of appropriate coping mechanisms prior to crisis is stressed.

818. Maluccio, A., Fein, E. & K. Olmstead, 1986, *Permanency Planning for Children: Concepts and Methods,* Routledge, Chapman & Hall, Tavistock, UK

The authors dispel the misconceptions that these concepts deal (only) with moving children into adoptive placements. The key question suggested is, "Will the child have a family when he/she grows up?" To ensure that the answer is "yes," planning must be a central component of all child care work and must focus on prevention and rehabilitation, not only on adoption. The ecological approach to child placement is the central focus, away from the traditional "Medical Model" toward identifying family strengths, and providing services. The child is always the central focus of planning but parents must be involved as full partners in decision making and the implementation of the plan.

819. McKinnon, R. & J.S. Wallerstein, 1988, "A Preventive Intervention Program for Parents and Young Children in Joint Custody Arrangements", *American Journal of Orthopsychiatry,* Vol. 58, No. 2, pp. 168–178

The authors describe a pilot program aimed at being a preventive intervention model for voluntary joint custody counseling of parents of very young children. The first group of parents (25) who had come to the "Center for Family Transition," all of whom had chosen joint custody voluntarily, were followed in this project for periods ranging from 1 to 4 years. A comprehensive assessment of both parents and children was followed by a planning conference and continued periodic monitoring. Counselors were very available on request. As the program continues, its "efficacy," the authors state, "remains to be evaluated more formally."

820. Messinger, L., Walker, K. & S. Freeman, "Preparation for Remarriage After Divorce: The Use of Group Techniques", *American Journal of Orthopsychiatry,* Vol. 48, No. 2, pp. 263–272

To develop a basis for a program of remarriage preparation, the authors held four series of weekly group meetings with a total of twenty-two couples, in which at least one partner had children from a previous marriage. The leaders' role was informal and non-directive, discouraging members from moving into a psychotherapeutic mode. The findings suggest there are many commonly discussed concerns among participants which they group under five headings. They found the group experience offered reassurance and support that relieved the sense of personal aloneness and inadequacy in coping with problems.

821. Meyer, C., 1984, ''Can Foster Care Be Saved?'', *Social Work,* Vol. 29, No. 6, Editorial Page

The author, as editor-in-chief, addresses the gap in social workers' armamentarium of contemporary ideas, theories, and skills, and the lack of change and adaptation in the field of child welfare, which is among the oldest social work efforts. She points to the fact that adversarial legal practices seem to define the foster care system, untrained staff represent the profession, and the public erroneously believes that the field is still the domain of (trained) social workers. Poor and minority children and their parents continue to need many services other than child placement as attempted solutions to their multiple problems. A family-focused social service could begin to avoid the vast problems brought on by separating children from their parents and might stimulate clinical social workers to return to the child welfare field.

822. Miller, C.C., 1981, ''Primary Prevention of Child Mistreatment: Meeting a National Need'', *Child Welfare,* Vol. 60, No. 1, pp. 11–23

Abuse and neglect were reported to be the primary reason for public services given to children, but with reporting difficulties, it is uncertain how many children in the U.S. never come to the attention of the authorities and therefore never receive services. Obstacles to an increase in the provision of preventive services are seen not only in the shortage of resources but also in such factors as 1) the historical perspective in which values of self-sufficiency have led to non-use of services, and parents' rights have superseded children's rights; 2) prevention has not been adequately defined; therefore services have been rendered at a secondary level of prevention instead of the primary level, never reaching families at early stages of prevention; 3) information gaps, narrow policy focus, and a fragmented constituence are seen as further obstacles. Recommended actions include an institutionalized approach to primary prevention by a broad-based national family policy, a continuum of developmental services to coincide with the growth of the child, coordination of preventive efforts across human service agencies, rehabilitation as a major objective of family-focused legislation, and publicity and citizen involvement in developing a constituency for primary prevention.

823. Mueller, D.P. and P.W. Cooper, 1986, "Children of Single-Parent Families: How they Fare as Young Adults", *Family Relations,* Vol. 35, No. 1, pp. 169–176

1448 persons aged 19–34 representing 1% of the residents in a midwestern metropolitan county, were surveyed. The differences between being raised in two-parent or one-parent families at young adulthood were the subject of this inquiry. Persons raised by single parents, primarily mothers, tended to show lower educational, occupational, and economic attainment in young adulthood. Differences in family formation and marital stability were also observed, and it appeared that the economic disadvantages of the single-parent family were clearly responsible for the former, but the latter remained after controlling for this factor. Policy implications for Welfare and school programs as well as the importance of preventive programming are discussed.

824. Papp, P., Silverstein, O. & E. Carter, 1973, "Family Sculpting in Preventive Work with 'Well Families' ", *Family Process,* June 1973

Use of sculpting in families before a crisis has arisen, with a goal being motivation for change not based on a desperate situation. Uses a model of concepts including labeling, triangles, and family ghosts.

825. Sager, C.J., Brown, H.S., Crohn, H., Engel, T., Rodstein, E. & L. Walker, 1983, *Treating the Remarried Family,* Brunner/Mazel Publishers, New York

Both theory and various treatment modalities of working with remarried families are presented, based on the study of a clinical population of the Remarried Consultation Service of the Jewish Board of Family and Children's Services of New York City. The book's format includes sections on Structure and Theory, on the basic tenets of treatment for remarried families, individuals in remarried families and other significant subsystems. Appendices provide extremely useful guidelines and sample information sheets for schools.

826. Schaeffer, M., Gilbert, W., Friedman, M. & B. Pasquariella , 1981, "Children in Foster Care: A Preventive Service and Research Program for a High-Risk Population", *Journal of Preventive Psychiatry,* Vol. 1, pp. 47–56

"The authors are engaged in long-term preventive research related to meeting (through social service structures) the needs of children in foster care with an emphasis on intervention, both short term, and permanency planning. It is hypothesized that the disruptive and frequently provocative behavior of foster children which foster parents have a difficult time accepting and often reject, is frequently a pathogenic reaction to the crisis of removal from unknown circumstances. It is further shown that short-term clinical intervention involving foster children, foster parents, biological parents, and placement agency workers with clinicians can make a difference. Varying lengths of treatment are examined and some predictions and hypotheses are discussed." (c) APA

827. Schwartz-Borden, G., 1986, "Grief Work: Prevention and Intervention", *Social Casework,* Vol. 67, No. 8, pp. 499–505

This is a paper describing the clinical application of theoretical knowledge about the need for grief work in bereavement. Though specifically tailored to work with bereaved people in groups, especially with widows and widowers, and parents who lost a child, there is a good deal of generic content which is applicable to working through losses in "normal" groups of adults or children. The methods used in such groups are described, and the description of disabling symptoms which are either helped to disappear, or are normalized, inferentially indicate that further problems or deterioration can be prevented by such groups.

828. Schwartzberg, A.Z., 1981, "Divorce and Children and Adolescents", *Adolescent Psychiatry,* pp. 119–132

The prominent effects of divorce on the older child are sadness and a sense of loss and betrayal by the parents. There is evidence of a recurrent theme of anxiety about future marriage, intense loyalty conflicts, abrupt deidealization of parents and awareness of parents as sexual objects. Divorce affects the superego development and resolution of oedipal conflicts primarily with boys and the custodial mother. Early and effective intervention during the separation period would prevent severe development issues with children. Adolescents need help to deal with losses, express anger and sadness and anxiety to enhance their growth and development.

829. Simon, D., 1976, "Systematic Approach to Family Life Education", *Social Casework,* October 1976

The scope and rationale for family life education is discussed. Methods for developing family life education programs described and an example of such a program given. Detailed explanation in considering the primary areas to be considered in planning a Family Life program. Identifying community needs, establishing a focus, developing thematic content, establishing the group structure, recruiting participants, establishing fees, evaluation of effectiveness.

830. Stanton, G.W., 1986, ''Preventive Intervention With Stepfamilies'', *Social Work,* Vol. 31, No. 3, May/June, pp. 201–206

The author discusses the child's need to grieve losses and to clarify both biological and psychological continuity, before bonding can take place. Professionals and educators are reminded of the impact which absent biological parents have on the child, even in successful stepfamily systems. The importance of clear understanding, and continuity of biological ties to the establishment of a positive sense of self is stressed. Analogy is drawn to children in foster care, adoption, and those living with extended family members. A reversal of traditional treatment is recommended, beginning with consultation to self-help groups, concentrating on family life education and short-term family group intervention, with individual and group treatment.

831. Strayhorn, J.M., Jr., 1983, ''A Diagnosis Axis Relevant to Psychotherapy and Preventive Mental Health'', *American Journal of Orthopsychiatry,* Vol. 53, No. 4, pp. 677–696

The author attempts to integrate a number of commonly known and used theoretical concepts into a diagnostic axis using the language of performance skills. The skills axis is expected to have more therapeutic relevance than a symptom cluster scheme, to be less pejorative than personally disordered designations. It is further argued that this scheme would promote clarity in outcome research, and last but not least, could be translated into mental health and preventive principles which could be looked for and taught to the natural caregivers who have always instilled good mental health such as parents, teachers, and other character-forming role models.

832. Sundel, M. & C.C. Homan, 1979, ''Prevention in Child Welfare: A Framework for Management and Practice'', *Child Welfare,* Vol. 58, No. 8, pp. 510–521

The authors concentrate on much needed research during a 3-year program to strengthen social agencies' growing interest in prevention. They attempt to build a bridge between academic research and theory, practitioners, and administrators. A framework is developed and different levels of activity are described.

Good examples and charts support the study. In summary, the authors conclude that the competition of preventive efforts with ongoing badly needed services disadvantages preventive efforts, and limits remedial efforts.

833. Weber, J.A. & D.G. Fournier, 1985, ''Family Support and a Child's Adjustment to Death'', *Family Relations,* Vol. 34, No. 1, pp. 43–49

Ninety-one children from fifty families who had an experience with death were interviewed, along with their parents. Variables studied to determine family influence on a child's understanding and adjustment to death included family cohesion, adaptability, decisions about the child's participation in mourning, etc., as well as the child's ability to conceptualize death. The role of the family as an educator and socializer of the child's understanding of death as well as a support factor are addressed. The child's understanding of death appeared to be strongly mediated by family characteristics and adaptation. In general, children were found to be willing to talk about their feelings and to understand more about death than their parents were willing to accept. Great varieties were found in children's cognitive understanding. Participation in the rituals, open communication, opportunity for the child to decide on participation, family support seemed important implications highlighted by the authors.

834. Woody, J.D., 1978, ''Preventive Intervention for Children of Divorce'', *Social Casework,* Vol. 59, No. 9, pp. 537–544

An early concern for children of divorce as a high-risk population is expressed. Contemporary studies are reviewed and important questions are raised. Children's rights are emphasized. Collaboration with the legal community, outreach activities, counseling, educational strategies, and liaison with community caregivers and resources are described. This is a seminal article drawing the attention of the therapeutic community to the existence of some available data on children of divorce pointing away from the traditional ''pathological lens'' of viewing family disruption, allowing for environmental factors as a strong influence. Remedial approaches are not sufficient, unless prevention is addressed on a policy level to socioeconomic and other long-range factors which tend to lead to family disruption and/or deterioration affecting children's mental health and behaviors.

835. Worell, J., 1986, "Single Mothers: Issues of Stigma", *Annual Convention of the American Psychological Association,* Washington, DC

"This paper examines psychological and social issues for single mothers in the context of therapeutic strategies for effective intervention. Never married, previously married, and Lesbian mothers are considered in terms of sociocultural myths and sources of stigma; research findings related to these myths; and interventions targeting the single-mother family, the community, and governmental policies that influence legislation affecting these families. Sources of societal stigma are discussed which are related to morality, sex-role violation, and victimization. Dispelling myths related to these areas requires careful consideration of the major sources of stress impinging on these families: economic stress, social isolation, and role-strain. It is suggested that mental health interventions treat these families in the context of the massive effects of poverty, societal oppression, and victimization. Therapeutic strategies that include only psychological processes of the single mother will fail to address the larger context of her social situation and will further contribute to her victimization and despair. Interventions must be preventive, remediative, educative, and aimed at involving community resources. Therapists are encouraged to become knowledgeable about single mothers and the economic and legal issues facing them, and to take an active role as mediators and advocates. Research requirements discussed include increased attention to models of prevention and intervention into the factors that facilitate the strength and well-being of single-mother families. Forty references are included." (ERIC)

Family Life Education and Self-Help

836. Ahrons, C. & M. Perlmutter, 1982, "Therapy With Remarriage Families: The Relationship Between Former Spouses: A Fundamental Subsystem in the Remarriage Family", *Family Therapy Collections,* Vol. 2, pp. 31–46

The importance of the relationship of former spouses to the formation of the remarriage relationships is emphasized. The authors work on the assumption that a continuing relationship of the former spouses will enhance the success of co-parenting their mutual children. They find that education is necessary to help remarried families with their new tasks of restructuring the stepfamily.

837. Ambrosino, S., 1979, "Integrating Counseling, Family Life Education, and Family Advocacy", *Social Casework,* Vol. 60, No. 10, pp. 579–587

The author, who is executive director in a family service agency on Long Island, defines and uses descriptive examples for the three essential components of service in family agencies. Counseling, family life education, and family advocacy are seen as three distinct services, both in purpose and goals, although in effect both the skills used and the results often overlap. The author believes all three components should be practiced in an agency and the agency focus should be quite flexible, ready to shift its emphasis on the basis of agency data which would provide documented need for change.

838. Apgar, K. & J. Coplon, 1985, "New Perspectives on Structured Life Education Groups", *Social Work,* Vol. 30, pp. 138–143

Contrary to traditional practices and popular misconceptions, the authors find that the content of these groups is informational as well as affective, and when carried out by experienced professionals didactic and experiential methods are used, based on the theoretical base of adult education and learning theory. Shared responsibility of teaching-learning engages the total person of the learner. A definitive structure and pre-planned topics tend to help participants to universalize and normalize their experiences, without promoting insight or highlighting personal experiences as one would in therapy. The therapeutic component of this educational venture seems to be the group process aided by the manner in which problems are handled. Among other groups, the authors indicate that children too respond to adult education principles and methods, which aim at growth-producing results relevant to their current life experiences. These educational groups then serve through their anticipatory guidance on both preventive and interventive levels.

839. Armstrong, D.P., 1980, "Developing Services for Single Parents and Their Children in the School", *Social Work in Education,* Vol. 3, No. 1, pp. 44–57

"As a result of the rising divorce rate and other factors, there has been a dramatic increase in the number of one-parent households. Problems related to this trend are discussed. A comprehensive approach to providing supportive services to children and their parents may include the following: (1) counseling on an individual basis, (2) working with groups of single parents, (3) leading children's groups, (4) founding programs of professional development for teachers, and (5) developing innovative alternative ways of serving children and parents affected by divorce.'' (SWAB)

840. Arnold, E.L., 1978, *Helping Parents Help Their Children,* Brunner/Mazel, New York
A collection of articles by experts in the field of child guidance, focusing on guidance for parents, representing an early effort of professionals to concentrate on parents. A wide variety of theoretical approaches are represented. The topics include general principles, help with specific problems of children, specific problems of parents, and guidance by other than mental health professionals. A chapter on stepparents and their spouses, one on adoptive and foster parents, guidance for separated and divorced parents, and a chapter on parents and the divorce court worker are noted especially.

841. Barsh, E., Moore, J. & L. Hamerlynck, 1983, ''The Foster Extended Family: A Support Network for Handicapped Foster Children'', *Child Welfare,* Vol. 62, pp. 349–359
The Foster Extended Family (FEF), was established to alleviate isolation among foster families caring for handicapped children. The FEF model provides the foster parent with education and a certificate in child care and management. Extra payments for specialized services and crisis intervention are also provided. The family's resources are augmented through the use of friends, neighbors, relatives, and the community people. A child's foster parents, together with these other adults, constitute a ''foster extended family'' system. This model seems transferable to other stressful family situations.

842. Becker, W.C., 1971, *Parents Are Teachers, A Child Management Program,* Research Press, Champaign, IL
A ''How To'' book for parents using descriptive behavioral objectives, to help reinforce parents' belief in themselves as primary educators of their children. Aimed at disadvantaged parents and teachers' aides, as well as parents of children with special problems originally. The program has been tested in many different settings before this book was published. It was now expanded to reach ordinary parents who are seeking to improve their parenting skills.

843. Benson, L., 1969, *Fatherhood: A Sociological Perspective,* Random House, New York
At that time the book addressed the fact that there was a

surprising absence of studies about fathers and fatherhood in the modern industrial United States. While mothers or prospective mothers were deluged with information, instruction, advice, etc., and were the subjects of intensive study, fathers or prospective fathers were virtually ignored, and their roles, problems, behavior, etc., absent from most scientific literature. To the end of correcting this oversight, the author reviews and integrates available material on fathers, and has a very short section concerning stepfathers. A comprehensive bibliography is included.

844. Bonkowski, S., Bequette, S. & S. Boomhower, 1984, ''A Group Design to Help Children Adjust to Parental Divorce'', *Social Casework,* Vol. 65, pp. 131–137

Children are perceived as a very vulnerable and largely unreached population. This is an attempt to reach children who usually do not receive help through a semi-structured group intervention. Crisis intervention and current literature on loss are used as guiding principles, with the objective of allowing the children freedom to express their feelings, increase their peer relationships, and give professionals the opportunity to learn both about the content and process of involvement. The sessions are described and evaluated. Questions of group membership, confidentiality, and setting are examined. The conclusions confirm the feeling that this could be the treatment of choice for latency-age children not confined to traditional therapy agencies and persons.

845. Brooks, J., 1981, *The Process of Parenting,* Mayfield Publishers, Mountainview, CA.

''This book presents information on physical, intellectual, social and emotional growth from birth to adolescence. Parents need a variety of techniques for handling situations with children, depending on the specific characteristics of the child and the problem. To provide a range of techniques, the book describes five strategies of parenting and shows how they are applied to particular problems. Three strategies emphasize communicating feelings and establishing relationships with children. Two strategies emphasize ways of changing behavior. Parents can find solutions in these different approaches if they adopt a problem-solving method that consists of defining the problem, thinking about alternative actions, taking action, evaluating the results and sometimes starting over.'' (Gruber)

846. Burdick, A.R., 1988, ''A Model for Group Intervention With Pre-School Children Experiencing Separation and Divorce'', *American Journal of Orthopsychiatry,* Vol. 58, No. 3

A short-term model of six sessions with preschoolers is described. The program aims at easing the adjustment of the children to parental separation. Session plans, goals, and some thought about outcome are shared with the readers. Group cohesion, dealing with the feeling of abandonment and alienation, and providing an atmosphere for openness are identified as not only serving this particular group, but as a generic factor with which to deal in similar crisis situations.

847. Cantoni, L., 1975, ''Family Life Education—A Treatment Modality'', *Child Welfare,* November 1975

Families need new coping skills to adapt to the period of rapid change because transitions becoming more difficult. Family Life usually developed around transitional crises.

848. Cantoni, L., 1975, ''Family Life Education: A Treatment Modality'', *Child Welfare,* Vol. LIV, No. 9, pp. 658–665

The author who is the district director of a family agency in Wayne County describes a program of 6 sessions in the agency. She also gives a good indication both of the history of family life education and of its utility. The process of one particular program is described. The paper directs the attention of practitioners to a valuable tool in working with families.

849. Cantor, D., 1977, ''School Based Groups for Children of Divorce'', *Journal of Divorce,* Vol. I

Dr. Cantor, a school psychologist describes an existing program, and from this experience makes some programmatic suggestions. Beginning with some statistical and literature research and concluding that divorce has reached ''epidemic proportions,'' the author is appropriately concerned with the fact that most children in divorce situations do not receive help, though changed behavior is often observed particularly in schools. The paper proposes the establishment of situation/transition groups led by school mental health personnel, school social workers, school psychologists, guidance counselors, to provide immediate crisis intervention and on-going support as a means of preventing the development of psychopathology. School is thought to be the logical place for such interventions and school mental health personnel are encouraged to see the expansion of their services to include preventive programs available to large numbers of children as their obligation.

850. Clayton, P., 1971, "Meeting the Needs of the Single-Parent Family", *Family Coordinator,* Vol. 20

This article deals with some of the needs of single parents and describes how Parents Without Partners, a self-help organization, attempts to meet these needs. Recent developments such as cooperative services for members, scholarship programs, community service programs, information regarding resources and the therapeutic value leading to personal growth through volunteer work are described in some detail.

851. Cline, B., 1985, "Raising Alan Alone", *Exceptional Parent,* Vol. 15, No. 7, pp. 44–46

"A single parent describes her struggles with her young son whose hyperactive disruptive behavior aggravated an already failing marriage. She notes the help provided by advocacy and support groups." (ERIC)

852. Cohen, R.S., Cohler, B.J. & S.H. Weissman, eds., 1984, *Parenthood: A Psychodynamic Perspective,* New York, Gifford Press.

A team of social worker, psychologist, and psychiatrist selected a large number of very pertinent papers dealing with parenthood from a psychoanalytic and psychodynamic point of view. Parenthood, just as childhood, is identified as a dynamic developmental process throughout the life cycle. The influence of early childhood experiences with parents on adult parent functioning, as well as the parenting by middle-aged adults of their aged parents, are considered. The chapters on the "effect of parental loss on future parenthood," parenting responses in divorce and bereavement of a spouse, judges and other people's children as well as "the parental couple in successful divorce" are particularly relevant to professionals dealing with the target population.

853. Coleman, M., Ganong, L. & R. Gingrich, 1985, "Stepfamily Strengths: A Review of Popular Literature", *Family Relations,* Vol. 34, No. 4, pp. 583–589

The authors, who have been involved in stepfamily work and research, wrote this paper to review the popular literature, which had been proliferating within the last ten years; they identified self-help books, magazines, and adolescent fiction as to content which identified family strength. 243 pieces of literature in all were reviewed. Though potential strengths were identified in all three types of literature examined, the major emphasis was found to be on the problems of stepfamilies. The details of the review reveal interesting sub-data. Perhaps the most specific contribution found was the notion that the literature emphasized problem-solving skills. Adolescent fiction, written from the child's point of view, was found to be more geared to situations where a parent had died, thus perhaps being atypical, since most of the stepfamily literature written deals with children of divorce. However, it was found to be more contructive to problem solving than the general notions seen in the adult self-help literature. The authors point the review in the direction of less problematic aspects of stepfamily life which they recommend for greater attention.

854. Coplon, J. & J. Strull, 1983, ''Roles of the Professional in Mutual Aid Groups'', *Social Casework,* Vol. 64, pp. 259–266

Authors address the fact that professionals and self-help groups tend to view each other with suspicion, while they could be helpful and learn from each other. The article is based on the authors' personal experience and on data collected in 1979 from 55 questionnaires completed by mutual aid groups in the Boston area. The concept of the professional as a leader in the self-help group as well as in an array of roles dependent on the nature and function of the group is further developed. Their concept develops a type of teacher-leader role different from the more traditional therapeutic stance and one in which mutual collaborative efforts are emphasized. The five stages of group development according to Garland et al are utilized to describe the group process. The fifth or termination stage is especially mentioned in which the consultant can help the group to separate and move on to a more autonomously functioning stage. The benefits for both professional and self-help group are emphasized with the increased mutual understanding enhancing the roles of each in future encounters.

855. Dinkmeyer, D. & Dinkmeyer Jr., D., 1979, ''A Comprehensive and Systematic Approach to Parent Education'', *American Journal of Family Therapy,* Vol. 7, pp. 46–50

The authors give a review of the history of parent education and emphasize the importance of such educational and preventive work. A new program, called ''Step''—Systematic Training for Effective Parenting (no relation to stepfamilies)—is discussed in detail, based on the theories of Alfred Adler.

856. Dreikers, R., 1964, *Children: The Challenge,* Meredith Press, Des Moines, IA

This is a widely read book useful to both professional and lay persons. The approach presented, rooted in Adlerian theory, offers both conceptual and concrete ideas for parenting. Specific techniques for coping with problems between children and parents are recommended. (DHHS)

857. Dreikers, R., 1974, *Family Council,* Henry Regnery, Chicago

Based on Adlerian principles, Dreikers outlines a conceptual and operation strategy for family decision-making and problem-solving in this guidebook. The notion of a family council is rooted in the value of a democratic and cooperative family system. During the family council, which involves regularly scheduled meetings, family rules are negotiated and agreed upon by all family members. This book details both the techniques and procedures for conducting a family council and offers concrete guidelines for its continued functioning. (DHHS)

858. Einstein, E., 1982, *The Stepfamily,* Macmillan Publishers, New York

The myth of instant love in a remarriage is destructive. Children may be angry at the missing parent and direct this toward the stepparent. There needs to be a time for mourning and the child worries about where he will fit into the new family. Not only does the ex-spouse use the child/children as a scapegoat, but so does the extended family. Establish a workable system with boundaries, noting where the child is in his/her life cycle and also educate the ex-spouses and their extended families as to the problems children go through in dealing with remarriage.

859. Ellis, A., 1984, ''Second Time Around: A Preventive Intervention for Remarried Couples'', *Australian Journal of Sex, Marriage & Family,* Vol. 5, pp. 139–146

''Reviews role theory and second marriages, problems experienced in second marriages, effects of remarriage on children and systems theory and the remarried family. A preventive intervention program for remarried couples with children from previous marriages is described. The Second Time Around program is aimed at strengthening the family relationship by presenting an alternative family model that is realistic and attainable. Issues addressed by the program include becoming a couple, unfinished mourning, rejection themes, power issues, and guilt over loving another's children. One group of four couples and one group of five couples (men aged 30+ years, women aged 30–45 years) completed and evaluated the twenty-hour program and discussed the program's long-term effects at 6–8 week follow-up. Findings show that most Ss were satisfied with the group. All Ss stated that their relationships had improved since joining the program, and 75% reported that the group helped them to cope better with parenting and to feel more positive toward their stepchildren. All Ss viewed the program as an integral part of divorce-remarriage counseling and said they would recommend the program to others.'' (c) APA

860. Euster, S. & L. Noble, 1981, ''A Unique Approach to Foster Training: Preparing Caseworkers as Instructors'', *Journal of Continuing Social Work Education,* Vol. 1

This article describes research which indicated the need to educate caseworkers for their roles as educators of foster parents. Knowledge base, skills, and experience to design and conduct training programs are detailed. A ten-session descriptive course sample is prepared and included in this article, developed as part of the Foster Parent Training Curriculum at the University of South Carolina. Outcome data reported attest to the success of the program.

861. Euster, S., Ward, V., Varner, J. & G. Euster, 1984, ''Life Skill Groups for Adolescent Foster Children'', *Child Welfare,* Vol. 63, pp. 27–36

A University Department and a Social Agency combined resources to design a curriculum for adolescents to conduct life skill groups. Child Development specialists and Child Care Workers developed the program together. Geographic separation not only from family but from other support systems makes it necessary for the teenagers in foster care to be exposed to experiences which will enhance their self-confidence, minimize their feeling of difference from their peers, develop relationship skills and a sense of control over their lives. Developing a clearer sense of identity and clarity in sexual and emotional confusion were some of the areas of the youngsters' known vulnerabilities. A structured curriculum and some simple ground rules allowing them to set their own pace in participating were offered along with some age-appropriate activities and pre-structured exercises. The initial response to the program was an enthusiastic one by the participating practitioners.

862. Fisher, B., 1978, *When Your Relationship Ends,* Family Relations Learning Center, Boulder, CO

This manual, developed by the author for use in his educationally oriented seminars for divorced adults, is a useful book for both the professionals and lay persons. It clearly identifies the emotional process of divorce and offers constructive approaches for adjustment. The chapter devoted to children of divorce is particularly useful for parents. Each chapter identifies the important concepts embodied in that chapter and also provides homework assignments related to these concepts. (DHHS)

863. Fooner, A., 1981, ''Split Families, Stepfamilies: Helping Students Through a Difficult Time'', *Forecast for Home Economics,* Vol. 27, pp. 23, 24, 26

The author quotes extensively from Robert Allers, a school psychologist in Grand Rapids, Michigan. The message is clearly that children see teachers as allies; 80% when asked in an informal survey indicated that they would choose a teacher as someone who could understand their feelings when they needed to talk to someone. Some specific steps are recommended for teachers, e.g. evaluate your own attitudes, be alert for symptoms, be available, do not wait for parents, find other resources, initiate a lesson or discussion, be sensitive, you can make a difference, use other professionals.

864. Ganong, L. & M. Coleman, 1983, *Journal of Children and Youth,* Fall 28–37.

''(Step) Parent education: a proposal''(SAA)

865. Ginott, H.G., 1965, *Between Parent and Child,* Avon Books, New York

The author, an expert in child psychology who contributed significantly to child rearing literature in his all too short lifetime, published this book which quickly became a best seller. He talks to parents, and he knows how to talk to children. His expertise attempts to bring adults and children closer together. Teachers and other adults who work with children will profit greatly from his suggestions. He was considered an enlightened professional whose direct dialogue can both inspire and teach and invite imitation. An early consideration of the influence of problem parents on child behavior is noteworthy.

866. Ginott, H.G., 1969, *Between Parent and Teacher,* Avon Books, New York

The author suggests a variety of ways for parents and teenagers to reach a better understanding of each other. As always, the author is lucid, easy to understand, and able to convey profound concepts in an easily comprehensible manner. His vignettes are illustrative both of specific issues and of general principles. He is helpful and empathic to both youngsters and adults.

867. Gitterman, A. & L. Shulman, eds., 1986, *Mutual Aid Groups and the Life Cycle,* Peacock Publishers, Inc., Los Angeles, CA

The editors introduce the theoretical model which underlies the practice described in this book: the life model, a mutual aid approach with groups, and mediation as a role for the group leader. The various stages of the life cycle and some of the possible problem areas encountered guide the selection of authors of the various chapters. Group work with bereaved children, with single parents, dealing with the death of a group member, and the concept of mutual aid are some of the content areas of relevance to this collection.

868. Gordon, T. , 1970, *Parent Effectiveness Training,* Peter H. Wyden, New York

This book is the text used in the well-established, educationally oriented Parent Effectiveness Training (PET). It identifies and elaborates upon specific skills such as active listening, constructive responding, conflict management, authority and power, discipline and the "no lose" method of problem solving. Specific techniques for handling parent-child problems are presented throughout. In addition, very good exercises related to parenting skills are included in the appendix. These exercises could be very useful for an educationally based parenting program. (DHHS)

869. Hartman, A., 1984, *Working With Adoptive Families Beyond Placement,* Child Welfare League of America, Inc., New York

This book provides a post-placement plan designed for practitioners to aid the adoptive family in dealing more effectively with feelings surrounding placement. Hartman discusses a model for providing services to all members of the adoptive family throughout the development phases of the adopted child's life cycle for the child's and family's better understanding.

870. Helfer, R.E., 1978, *Childhood Comes First: A Crash Course in Childhood for Adults,* Ray E. Helfer, East Lansing, MI

This book is written for and dedicated to those adults who were unable to learn interactional skills when they were children. It is written in the form of a manual which can be used and rehearsed with friends on a regular basis. It is based on the conviction that learning and improving relationship skills is possible at any age, even when it was missed in childhood. It is particularly important to develop relationship skills in parents who have never had a chance to experience positive parenting themselves. A separate section is written for the ''coaches'' who will help with this crash course.

871. Isaacs, S., 1986, *Who's In Control? A Parent's Guide to Discipline,* Putnam Publishing Group, New York

Disciplining children can be hard work and is often frustrating. The author provides instruction for parents on how to assess their needs, attitudes, and skills concerning discipline and then shows them how to apply their new knowledge.

872. Jacobsen, D., 1979, ''Stepfamilies: Myths and Realities'', *Social Work,* Vol. 24, pp. 202–207

The author focuses on ''the three D's: denial, denigration, and disorientation. These confront the stepfamily, especially in our society, where remarriage—usually following divorce—is an unpleasant subject, and differences from the nuclear family tend to be denied. Absence of clear role models for parenting, and societal guidelines for behavior tend to disorient members of stepfamilies. A program was developed and is recommended, the better to help stepfamilies deal with societal expectations and prejudices. After six well-focused discussion group meetings, findings showed a diminution of initial anger and fruitful movement in the direction of better reality perception and improvement of daily functioning. The author concludes that professionals, too, may frequently operate on the basis of societal myths (e.g. instant love, or recreated nuclear family), and need to retool to consider other than the traditional forms of intervention.

873. Jacobson, D., 1980, ''Stepfamilies'', *Children Today,* Vol. 9

The author discusses outcome of research on stepfamilies especially with regard to the adjustment of children. There is a description of the author's own preventive and therapeutic work, especially in leading and coordinating groups of stepfamilies. Pre-marriage consideration of the issues is strongly suggested.

874. Jenkins, S., 1978, ''Children of Divorce'', *Children Today,* Vol. 7, pp. 16–20

In view of the very high divorce rate, the high remarriage rate and the rising percentages of divorce involving young children, in the U.S., the author selects four areas for special attention: economic problems and child support; custody issues and court involvement; emotional problems and intervention, including peer group support; and kinship patterns in step-relationships and the stepfamily. Solutions for economic problems need to be worked out in general policy areas for the population at large, such as income maintenance, jobs, day care, etc. This could avoid stigmatizing a large segment of the population. Custody decisions are continuing to be based on state laws, though the 1968 Uniform Child Custody Jurisdiction Act which was instituted to curb child snatchings is gaining in some states. Empirical research is missing as a base for decision making.

875. Jertson, J.M., 1975, ''Self-Help Groups'', *Social Work,* Vol. 20, No. 3
The author offers a brief discussion of the heightened professional interest in self-help groups, which opens up new exciting opportunities for practice. He describes some of the possibilities for professionals to help organize and facilitate self-help groups or to act in consultant roles. The possibilities for professionals to provide training to leaders is considered, as are the possible conceptual difficulties and inconsistencies which juxtapose self-help and its natural structural processes with the traditional values of therapists to assume full responsibility for leadership. The questions raised are challenging and point the way for many novel professional approaches.

876. Johnson, H., 1981, ''A Family Life Education Group for Working with Stepparents'', *Social Casework,* March
It is the author's contention that a primary goal when working with stepfamilies is to prevent repetition of family dissolution. A family life program is described. Membership was limited to five or six couples to maximize group participation. Goals were geared to attentiveness to the couple's relationship, helping to reassess expectations, identify and cope with pressures, and help cut through the stepfamily's isolation. Evaluation of the program was done through questionnaires. A significant rate of satisfaction with the group experience was reported by participants.

877. Kalish, R.A. & E. Visher, 1981, ''Grandparents of Divorce and Remarriage'', *Journal of Divorce,* Vol. 5, No. 1/2, pp. 127–140
At least three perspectives are suggested for viewing the grandparents in divorce situations: the older individuals themselves and their changed interactions with their children and grandchildren, the perspectives of the adult 'child-in-law,' and new in-laws upon remarriage, and last but not least, the perspec-

tives of the grandchildren and potential stepgrandchildren. Grandparents may be grand or greatgrandparents who get divorced. The focus of this paper is on the middle group, but the other age groups are also considered. While pre-divorce relationships are important, there are extraneous and societal factors which play an important part, e.g. who has custody and for how much of the time, has another adult become involved, are other stepgrandchildren added? Several scenarios are described by the authors to sensitize people to the role complexities, and six stress-producing patterns of grandparenting are outlined, with case examples. Growth potential is also suggested.

878. Kessler, S. & S. Botwick, 1977, "Beyond Divorce: Coping Skills for Minors", *Journal of Clinical Child Psychology,* Vol. 6, No. 2, pp. 38–41

This paper describes a workshop model for children aged 10 to 17 whose parents are involved in a divorce process. It is perceived as a group which provides both support and coping skills. The workshop is six hours long and its rationale, dynamics and format are described. Needs and problems of the participants as well as treatment efforts and skills are detailed. Conclusions indicate that the model would best serve 11- to 17-year-olds, but could be adapted for younger groups (6 to 10). Participants' evaluations revealed positive enthusiasm.

879. Koller, M., 1974, *Families: A Multigenerational Approach,* McGraw-Hill Book Company, New York

This book attempts a unique multigenerational approach to organize marriage and family data. Two distinct themes are utilized. One is family life education; the second theme is family theory and research.

880. Levant, R.F., 1987, "The Use of Marketing Techniques to Facilitate Acceptance of Parent Education Programs: A Case Example", *Family Relations,* Vol. 36, No. 3, pp. 246–251

"Presents case example to illustrate use of market assessment to inform the marketing of preventive parenting programs for fathers, working parents, single parents, and stepparents. Discusses results from survey of 300 parents in terms of how findings can be used in marketing areas of product, price, place, and promotion." (ERIC)

881. Littner, N., 1978, "The Art of Being a Foster Parent", *Child Welfare,* Vol. 57, No. 1, January

Dr. Littner, an early consultant psychiatrist to Child Welfare Agencies who has written elsewhere about child rearing, discusses the inherent difficulties of foster parenting versus biological parenting. The pressures on foster parents are much greater than on biological parents, both in terms of community expectations, those of family, neighbors, and friends, and in terms of extraordinarily high self-expectations. Nevertheless the reality is that many foster parents do a tremendous job. Negative responses from foster children, lack of responsiveness, the child's ''protective wall,'' manipulation, pressures of the biological parents, agency ''supervision,'' the threat of losing a child, and the shift in balance in the foster parents' own family are some of the hurdles cited. Those who managed to cope well were found to be aware of the problems as a first step.

Recognition of the importance of contact with the biological parents on the part of the child also leads to parent-to-parent contact. Trust of the agency (worker), sharing of information and feeling, courage to view one's own upset and come to see it not as a personal failure but as inherent in the special situation help with effective coping. Get-togethers and talking to other foster parents was perceived as helpful. All of the above combine to increase the coping ability of foster parents and make their task interesting and fulfilling.

882. Lyon, E., Silverman, M., Howe, G. & Bishop, 1985, ''Stages of Divorce: Implications for Service Delivery'', *Social Casework,* Vol. 66, No. 5, pp. 259–267

A three-stage model (pre-separation decision making; litigation-reconstructuring; recovery post-dissolution stages) is studied in terms of the adults' and children's perceptions, and their use of legal and other support systems. All respondents in the study (adults) had attended divorce education groups in a family service agency over a thirty-two month period. Questionnaires and interviews were used. The different reactions in the three stages were addressed, and the perceptions and feelings of the participants were described. Their perceptions of their children's feelings were also described. In spite of the respondents' participation in various forms of help processes plus the divorce education group, conflicts, especially over visitation, continued for nearly half the group. The data suggest differential needs during the various phases and recommend professional sensitivity, with different forms of intervention. Early mediation and counseling programs are suggested, as well as organized support groups. Lawyers seemed to concur, since much of their time with clients seemed to be spent on non-legal issues.

883. Marks, N.P., 1980, Fostering Growth, Dissertation Abstracts International, Vol, 42/02-B, page 777

''Fostering Growth has two parts: the first section contains a report of a five-session training program for foster parents and caseworkers; the second part consists of a training manual which was devised for the program and revised as a result of it. The workshops were two hours long and ran for five consecutive weeks. Each workshop was a complete unit to enable participants to come to any one or all workshops in the series. Workshops were geared for a maximum of twenty people. The five topic areas, identified through a needs assessment, were the foster child's natural family, the foster child's relationship to the foster family, dealing with typical foster child behavior and foster parenting an adolescent. Advocating an adult education model, the co-leaders employed various techniques to enable participants to take responsibility for their own learning. Encouraging activity rather than passivity, leaders utilized methods such as goal setting and self-evaluation, role play, one-to-one dialoguing, and other structured exercises. Material for evaluation was gathered from three sources: the caseworkers, the foster parents, and the co-leaders. Evaluation showed that the participants gained in knowledge, skill, and understanding as a result of the workshops. Suggestions are made for future use and extension of the program and the training manual.'' (DAI)

884. Messinger, L., ''Remarriage Between Divorced People with Children from Previous Marriages: A Proposal for Preparation for Remarriage'', Aspen Publications, Gaithersburg, MD

The remarried family after divorce with children from the partners' previous marriages is identified as a high-risk group for which there are no established societal norms. Specific problems e.g. role stress, finances, children's parenting, and intra-systems as well as inter-systems communications are mentioned. Interviews with 70 couples suggest that pre-remarriage preparation could reduce the stresses considerably, and even prevent them. Specific course content is suggested.

885. Messinger, L., Walker, K. & S. Freeman, ''Preparation for Remarriage After Divorce: The Use of Group Techniques'', *American Journal of Orthopsychiatry,* Vol. 48, No. 2, pp. 263–272

To develop a basis for a program of remarriage preparation, the authors held four series of weekly group meetings with a total of twenty-two couples, in which at least one partner had children from a previous marriage. The leaders' role was informal and non-directive, discouraging members from moving into a psychotherapeutic mode. The findings suggest there are many commonly discussed concerns among participants which they group under five headings. They found the group experience offered reassurance and support that relieved the sense of personal aloneness and inadequacy in coping with problems.

886. Miller, S., Nunnally, E.W. & D.B. Wackman, 1975, *Alive and Aware,* Interpersonal Communication Programs, Minneapolis, MN

This book provides extensive guidelines for effective communication skills. Although it is oriented toward a wide audience, the principles and examples are often related to the family. Specific communication techniques are identified and discussed in detail. Each section of the book concludes with a summary of the key ideas and concepts. A workbook with experiential exercises useful for educational programs is also available. In addition, a classroom instructor manual which offers suggested activities related to the concepts and skills is available from the authors. (DHHS)

887. Nelson, P.T., 1986, ''Newsletters: An Effective Delivery Mode for Providing Educational Information and Emotional Support to Single-Parent Families?'', *Family Relations,* Vol. 35, No. 1, pp. 183–188

A research-based newsletter for single parents (*) was evaluated in terms of its utility as an educational experience. Twenty-seven percent of the readers of the publication were reached by telephone interview and questionnaire, after one year of subscription. Attitude and behavior changes without face-to-face contact were reported. The author feels that this mode of education offers promise of reaching people on this level and of cutting program costs without diminution of quality service. The characteristics of those who found the newsletter most beneficial and those who found it at least useful are described. Suggestions for a suitable target audience and ways of reaching such an audience are made. (*) (''Solo-Parenting: A Newsletter for Mothers and Fathers on their own,'' Ed. Janet Cranston)

888. Nichols, W.C., 1977, ''Divorce and Remarriage Education.'', *Journal of Divorce,* Vol. 1, pp. 153–161.

''Nichols addresses the need for helping the many people

involved in marital and family disruption and describes using an educational approach, first for those adjustments to divorce and then to those both contemplating and already in a remarriage. The content of the latter seminar—'Problems of a Second Marriage'—are described by the author in detail. The advantages of using a trained professional as leader are underscored.'' (SAA)

889. Papernow, P.L., 1984, ''The Stepfamily Cycle: An Experimental Model of Stepfamily Development'', *Family Relations,* Vol. 33, pp. 355–363

The author develops a road map through seven stages of development in a stepfamily. It helps the various members of a stepfamily to recognize, cope with, and/or avoid the pitfalls on the road to the formation of a stepfamily. Both therapists of any ilk, and stepfamilies themselves, can benefit from this step-by-step approach.

890. Pasley, K. & M. Ihinger-Tallman, eds., 1985, ''Portraits of Stepfamily Life in Popular Literature'', *Family Relations,* Vol. 34, No. 4, pp. 527–534

This paper discusses the results of a content analysis of popular articles on stepfamily life from 1940 to 1980. The articles were evaluated in terms of the audience to which they were directed as to source, citations of authorities, problems identified. The analysis revealed an increased interest in this family form over the time span evaluated. The appeal is mostly to an audience of women, included more factual information over time, and showed a more diversified view of this family life style. The number of references to authoritative resources has increased. Since these magazines reach millions of people, the authors' recommendation is very important, that authors continue to have ready access to professional literature and to the views of respected authorities, as the professionals' empirical knowledge expands. As in other writings, it is noted that the clinicians' as a sole resource may tend to influence a more problem-oriented view than is warranted in looking at the totality of this population.

891. Penna, R.G., 1987, Design and Implementation of a Support Group for Stepparents in a Local Church (United Methodist, Texas), Dissertation Abstracts International, Vol. 48/05-A, p. 1327

''The purpose of this project was to design and implement a support group for stepparents in a local church. This included six monthly meetings which investigated the unique issues confronting stepparents and brought the Church into a direct dialogue with a group of twenty stepparents willing to allow their faith and particular social status to inform each other. This support group considered resources from Scripture that provided a theological base and identity as it engaged research that brought focus and understanding to stepparent life. The group participants were helped to appreciate and reflect upon the stepparent experience and to receive support, information, and faith stimulus as they developed their own ways to achieve fulfillment. The group process helped the participants receive necessary data in order to intelligibly make choices as stepparents appropriate to their own particular situation. This project illustrates the need for the Church to be aware and sensitive to its stepfamily membership and the stepfamily community at large if it is to remain faithful to being representative of God's love and support.'' (DAI)

892. Pereira, A.M., 1988, Foster Parents Support Group: Its Impact on the Attitudes of Foster Parents and Department of Children and Youth Service Social Workers, Masters Abstracts, Vol. 26/01, n.p.

``Department of Children and Youth Service Social Workers and foster parents must work cooperatively in a partnership in which commitment and investment are shared. Over the last several years, there has been a breakdown in communication between workers and foster parents resulting in the development of negative attitudes and lack of trust. Due to this, foster children do not receive the benefit of coordinated services. Pre/Post attitudinal tests were administered to social workers and foster parents. Statistical results showed no significant change in attitude after five foster parent group interventions. Clinical changes were significant for the foster parents. Limitations of research indicate the need for further research after more time has elapsed and social workers/foster parents are given more opportunity to involve themselves in the foster parent group.'' (DAI)

893. Pill, C.J., 1981, ``A Family Life Education Group for Working with Stepparents'', *Social Casework,* Vol. 62, No. 3, pp. 159–166

The author describes some of the most common problems occurring in stepfamilies and the intent of the program to prevent repetition of family dissolution. A group program offered as part of the FLE—family life education program—in a family counseling agency in Massachusetts is described. It starts with the recognition that stepfamilies tend to be isolated; therefore efforts at recruitment are described. A description of the group goals and of the group sessions follows. The stepfamily issues which form the topics for discussion are considered. Evaluations of the program, considerations of other types of programs, and some thoughts about the utility of family life education programs with such families conclude the article.

894. Prochaska, J. & B.F. Creager, 1975, "Preparing a Community for Family Life Education", *Child Welfare,* Vol. 8, No. 10, pp. 665–672
As social agencies discontinue their total adherence to the medical model of therapeutic interventions, the number of family agencies which offer family life education programs has more than doubled from the mid-fifties to the mid-seventies. This article describes what family life education (FLE) does, i.e., to give families (normal or pathological) the opportunity to learn about sound family relationships under the guidance of a professional. This article describes how to initiate such programs, and what kinds of issues are involved in starting programs, implementing them, and evaluating them. Among the programs listed under family transitions are Divorce, Single Parenthood, Remarriage, and Death of a Spouse.

895. Reingold, C., 1976, *Remarriage,* Harper & Row, New York
Problems that remarried couples and their children need to confront affect the success of the marriage. The rates of divorce, remarriages, and divorces of the remarried all affect the remarried couple, as does the comparison of ex-spouses to new-spouses, the comparisons of spouses by their children and the use of children as pawns in the new marriage. The author suggests educating both children and parents as to what to expect in a remarriage and especially focusing on the confusion and fear of the children involved.

896. Rothenberg, B.A., 1987, "Parent Educators Train Pediatric Residents", *Children Today,* Nov/Dec, pp. 11–14
The author, a child/parent psychologist, describes a training program for pediatric residents at Stanford University Medical School, which aims at helping MD's who go into pediatric medicine to deal with the questions about child rearing which invariably come up in pediatric practice. Training in normal child development was felt to encourage and interest more MD's to go into pediatric medicine, and to this end a four-week special program of 15 hours per week was developed. Tutorial sessions, reading, parenting classes, structured home visits and "play care" with children were part of the curriculum. Though admittedly a short program, it was felt to be suc-

cessful in developing competence and compassion in the residents.

897. Salk, L., 1978, *What Every Child Would Like Parents to Know About Divorce,* Harper & Row, New York
The book is written from what Dr. Salk terms "your child's point of view" and helps parents to understand clinical concepts by translating them into conversational language, concluding chapters with his response to questions he was asked. He emphasizes the essentials of honesty, to help preserve or strengthen the child's sense of security and self-esteem, reminding parents that divorce can be a stage of growth for both children and parents. He also addresses the professional's responsibility to deal with the parent, not only with the child.

898. Stanton, G.W., 1981, "Child in Stepfamily: Extended Family Bliss or Nuclear Family Nightmare?", APHA Social Work Section, Los Angeles, CA, unpublished paper
The author discusses the child's need to grieve losses and to clarify both biological and psychological continuity, before new bonding can take place. Professionals and educators are reminded of the impact which absent biological parents have on the child, even in successful stepfamily systems. The importance of clear understanding, and continuity of biological ties to the establishment of a positive sense of self are stressed. Analogy is drawn to children in foster care, adoption, and those living with extended family members.

899. Toseland, R.W. & L. Hacker, 1985, "Social Workers' Use of Self-Help Groups as a Resource for Clients", *Social Work,* Vol. 30, No. 3, pp. 232–237
This paper reports on the results of a survey which attempts to identify some factors influencing the use or non-use of self-help groups by professionals. Knowledge of, attitudes toward these groups, agency practices, policies and procedures, and need for educating and informing agency personnel, as well as better communication to address the discrepancy in the view in which the two groups—professionals and members of self-help groups—regard each other are recommended, as well as further research on specific findings.

900. True, J. & D. Googins, 1984, "Extended Learning Opportunities for the Single-Parent Family", *National Reading and Language Arts Educator's Conference,* Kansas City, MO

"Changes in family lifestyles, particularly the increase in single-parent families, can affect children's behavior in school. Apparently, teenagers are able to cope more successfully with the conflict of loyalties and demands of their parents' divorce than are younger children. Educators designing support systems to provide families with opportunities to have positive interactions with their children's school need to consider the limitations encountered by single parents in terms of time, earnings, and energy. Two programs in Minneapolis, Minnesota at St. Anthony Village, New Brighton School District 282 have been designed to meet the needs of the single-parent home as well as the needs of more traditional family lifestyles in promoting the reading needs of children at school and at home. The first, Extended Learning-A Family Affair, attempts to partially modify elementary schoolhouses and to provide appropriate facilities, time, and direction for parents to help their children become more efficient readers. The Saturday Morning School operates with the cooperation of the education departments of local colleges and universities. In this second program, college students needing beginning practicum experiences with children are enlisted to provide adult models for young readers in local public libraries and elementary schools." (ERIC)

901. Varner, J.G., 1984, Effects of Group Work on Foster Children's Adjustment to Foster Care, Dissertation Abstracts International, Vol. 45/09-A, page 2767

"The usual developmental adjustments of childhood and adolescence are made more difficult for the foster child by the separation from an unstable or untenable family situation and adjustment to a new, but temporary, family. Group work can be an effective way to help foster children develop the confidence they need to improve their relationships with others in their families and with peers. This study measured the effects of group work with a population of foster adolescents who took part in a structured group experience. Seven groups met during the summer. Each group had two co-leaders and followed the same eight-week mini-curriculum taken from the manual for Life Skills Training for Foster Adolescents. Each pair of co-leaders determined their potential group members. Eight to ten of the children were randomly assigned to participate in the groups, and the remaining children served as a control group. Behavior rating scales were filled out for each child within two weeks of the first group meeting, two weeks after the last group meeting, and four to six weeks after the last group meeting. The rating scale was filled out by the child's caseworker and foster parent. A self-report adaptation of the scale was filled out by the child. Four composite scores of the scale were analyzed to determine if changes in behavior were perceived after children had participated in these groups. Differences between means for the controls and treatment groups were compared for the immediate and delayed posttests. Means for the treatment group at the pretest, immediate, and delayed posttests were compared to determine if there is a pattern of perceived change over the time being measured.'' (DAI)

902. Visher, E.B. & J.S. Visher, 1979, *Stepfamilies: A Guide to Working with Stepparents and Stepchildren,* Brunner/Mazel, New York

To varying degrees adults, especially women, in stepfamilies expect themselves to (1) make up to the children for the upset caused by the divorce or death in the original family; (2) create a close-knit, happy family in an attempt to return to the nuclear family; (3) keep all members of the family happy and contented; (4) be living examples that the wicked stepmother myth is untrue; (5) love their step-children instantly and equally with their biological children, and receive love from their stepchildren instantly. Implications for practice are spelled out, both for therapy and for self-help movements.

903. Warren, N. & I. Amara, 1984, ''Educational Groups for Single Parents: The Parenting After Divorce Program'', *Journal of Divorce,* Vol. 8, No. 2, pp. 79–96

Parent groups were offered as part of a research study, the Parenting After Divorce (PAD) Project, designed to assess the usefulness of educational programs for divorcing parents. The data collected was from 10 groups given to a total of 35 parents (4–6 single custodial parents per group). The group impact on child, adult, and family was measured, and was found to be helpful. Parent ratings were uniformly high and emphasized the importance of learning new skills in understanding and communicating with their children more effectively. It was felt that the parent group model—though in this case designed to fit the research and the particular legal structure based on the state in which it was carried out—would be quite useful and could be adapted to many populations and clinical settings. It was found that parents with greater post-divorce stress, e.g. parental disagreement, less visitation, drop in quality of life, tended to benefit the most. A session-by-session discussion and data from surveys, as well as suggestions for adaptation of the model are included.

904. Nadler, J.H., 1983, "Effecting Change in Stepfamilies: A Psychodynamic/Behavioral Group Approach", *American Journal of Psychotherapy,* Vol. 37, No. 1, pp. 100–112

"A psychodynamic-behavioral workshop helps stepparents and their partners cope with the intra-psychic stress and interpersonal problems that result from the formation of a new family unit. The program consists of six sessions, each of which runs for an hour and a half. Each session focuses on a separate problem experienced by stepparents. The first session focuses on the commonality of problems in stepfamilies; the second, on roles and conflicting loyalties; the third, on communication skills; the fourth, on problems concerning stepchildren; the fifth, on difficulties in marital interaction; and the sixth, on problems related to visitation and the ex-spouse. Case material is presented that illustrates patterns of interaction in stepfamilies and techniques for intervening effectively in a remarriage." (SWAB)

IV. CHILDREN'S BOOKS

905. Adams, F., 1973, *Mushy Eggs,* Putnam, New York
Two boys and their life with their single-parent mother. For school-age children.

906. Alexander, A., 1975, *To Live a Lie,* Atheneum, New York
A 12-year-old girl imagines she is unloved and unwanted by divorcing parents. She tells people that her mother is dead, instead of being able to acknowledge that she lives with her father and that her non-custodial mother is going to college. (DHHS)

907. Anker, C., 1975, *Last Night I Saw Andromeda,* H.Z. Walck, New York
Eleven-year-old Jenny discovers she really needn't try so hard to earn her divorced father's love and appreciation. (DHHS)

908. Arundel, M., 1972, *A Family Failing,* Thomas Nelson, New York
A girl matures after her parents' separation by learning to view them as people separate from herself. This story is set in Scotland. (DHHS)

909. Bach, A., 1977, *A Father Every Few Years,* Harper, New York
Schemes and searches are used to try to find Tim's stepfather. Finally, Tim and his mother realize that they have been deserted and must learn to go on living without him. (DHHS)

910. Barman, A., 1976, *Helping Children Face Crises,* Public Affairs Committee, National Institute of Mental Health, U.S. Dept of Health, Education, and Welfare, Rockville, MD
This pamphlet describes what a crisis might be for a child and how it can best be handled by a parent. Issues covered include children's reactions to crises, the need for the parent to share truth, discuss family problems, and include children in grieving. Crises discussed include death in the family (of a parent, sibling or other

relative), separation and divorce, the child's own illness, starting school, and going away from home. (DHHS)

911. Bates, B., 1977, *Bugs in Your Ears,* Archway Paperback, New York
"Fiction. Parent and stepparent assume that adoption will bring them closer. It does not, but this unlikely combination of stepfamily members develop caring relationships in time, after some struggles."(SAA)

912. Berger, T., 1974, *A Friend Can Help,* Children's Press, Chicago, IL
Illustrated with color photographs, showing how friends can be helpful in mastering an experience.

913. Berger, T., 1977, *How Does It Feel When Your Parents Get Divorced?,* Messner, New York
In this narrative a little girl discusses her feelings about her parents' divorce. Although she experiences anger, fear, and frustration, she finds that it is still possible to be happy. The text is accompanied by photographs. (DHHS)

914. Bernstein, J.E., 1977, *Books to Help Children Cope With Separation,* Bowker Books, New York
The author developed a list of books which are designed to help children between the ages of 3 and 16 cope with issues of separation and loss. Other sections deal with selected readings for adults and some guidelines on how to use books to help children with these problems.

915. Blue, R., 1972, *A Month of Sundays,* Franklin Watts, New York
This is the story of a 10-year-old's adjustment to living with his mother and visiting his father. In the process of illustrating how painful conventional custody and visitation can be, the book presents some stereotyped ideas regarding the role of women. (DHHS)

916. Blume, J., 1972, *It's Not the End of the World,* Bradbury Press, New York
Karen and her sister cope with their feelings after their parents' divorce. This book is helpful for those experiencing similar situations. (DHHS)

917. Butterworth, W.E., 1970, *Steve Bellamy,* Little, Brown and Co., Boston

After his mother and stepfather are killed in an auto accident, Steve goes to live with his father, whom he had never met. (DHHS)

918. Byars, B., 1982, *The Animal, the Vegetable, and John D. Jones,* Delacorte, New York
The story of three children and their stepmother.

919. Carlson, D., 1977, *Triple Boy,* Atheneum, New York
Paul retreats to the safety of a split personality after his parents divorce and his little brother dies. Understanding friends, professional help, and his strong will help to get him back together. (DHHS)

920. Cleaver, V. & B. Cleaver, 1967, *Ellen Grae,* Lippincott, New York
A girl survives the aftermath of her parents' divorce, even though she does not live with either of them. (DHHS)

921. Clifton, L., 1976, *Everett Anderson's Friend,* Holt, Rinehart and Winston, New York
Everett's mother is angry because he lost his house key. He thinks about what his father might have said if he had been there. Single-parent problems are reviewed from the young child's point of view. (DHHS)

922. Clifton, L., 1978, *Everett Anderson's Nine Months Long,* Holt, Rinehart and Winston, New York
For children 4–7, dealing with stepfather relationships.

923. Clymer, E., 1973, *Luke Was There,* Holt, Rinehart and Winston, New York
It seemed that whenever Julius began to rely on an adult, something would go wrong. His father left, his mother was in the hospital, and he had to stay in a children's home. He develops a trusting relationship with one adult, Luke, a social worker. (DHHS)

924. Cottle, T., 1980, *Children's Secrets,* Anchor Press, New York
This book is a collection of a psychologist's interviews with children. Children tell their perceptions on parental abandonment, infidelity, physical battering, divorce, remarriage, and other family problems. This is an excellent book for counselors who deal with children. (Gruber)

925. Eichler, M., 1971, *Martin's Father,* Lollipop Power, Chapel Hill, N.C.

The daily life of a young boy who lives with his father. Encourages open communication between children and resident fathers. (DHHS)

926. Emery, A., 1980, *Stepfamily,* The Westminster Press, Philadelphia, PA

Written from the perspective of a child whose mother had died and whose father remarried, the book describes the feelings of this young teenage girl in moving into a new big home with her father, stepmother, and her three children. The book is descriptive of some of the thinking, feeling, and actions of this young group which is thrown together in a new community.

927. Evans, M.D., 1988, *This is Me and My Two Families,* Marla Evans, Omaha, NE

This self-awareness ''scrapbook'' for young children offers the opportunity to explore, share, and develop issues relevant to both children and adults in divorce and remarriage.

928. Ewing, K., 1975, *A Private Matter,* Harcourt Brace Jovanovich, New York

Marcy must give up her dream father, an elderly man next door, for the reality of her mother's second husband. (DHHS)

929. Gardner, R., 1971, *The Boys and Girls Book About Divorce: With an Introduction for Parents,* Bantam Edition, New York

A review of problem areas children face in divorce, e.g. anger, abandonment, blame, etc. The author talks in children's language of how they react to divorce, stepparents, and how to adjust to these situations. He thinks that children should know the truth even if it is painful, but also includes coping methods.

930. Getzoff, A. & C. McClenahan, *Stepkids: A Survival Guide for Teenagers in Stepfamilies,* Walker and Co., New York

Packed with solid, realistic advice. Unusually aware of the teenager's own point of view, this book will be helpful even to the most well-adjusted stepkids.

931. Glick, P., 1976, ''Living Arrangements of Children and Young Adults'', *Journal of Comparative Family Studies,* Vol. 7, pp. 321–333

This study documents some of the substantial changes in the

living arrangements of children and young adults in the United States during the short span since 1960. In addition, it relates the living arrangements of children under 18 years old in the marital history and socioeconomic level of the parents.

932. Goff, B. , 1969, *Where Is Daddy? The Story of a Divorce,* Beacon Press, Boston
A little girl learns not to blame herself for her parents' divorce. The story has been criticized as too sad by some, but it does stimulate open discussion of a young child's fears. (DHHS)

933. Green, C., 1969, *A Girl Called Al,* Viking, New York
Alexandra is unhappy and finds that her father's money for support is no substitute for his love. This story is useful if other books are read to give a more positive perspective. (DHHS)

934. Green, C., 1975, *I Know You, Al,* Viking, New York
The sequel to *A Girl Called Al* in which Al attends her father's wedding. (DHHS)

935. Green, P., 1978, *A New Mother for Martha.,* Human Sciences Press, New York
''Deals sensitively with the feelings of a young girl whose mother has died, and whose father remarries.''(SAA)

936. Gripe, M., 1971, *The Night Daddy,* Delacorte Press
The young heroine, whose mother works at night, becomes friends with the baby-sitter. (DHHS)

937. Hazen, B.S., 1978, *Two Homes to Live In: A Child's Eye View of Divorce,* Human Sciences Press, New York
Especially appropriate for the preschool and early school-age child, this book deals with guilt about ''causing the divorce'' and getting it all together again afterwards.

938. Holland, I., 1972, *The Man Without a Face,* Lippincott, New York
A somewhat controversial story about a much-divorced mother and her family. Charlie has quite a time adjusting but is helped by his friendship with an older man. (DHHS)

939. Holland, I., 1975, *Of Love and Death and Other Journeys,* Lippincott, New York
After a nomadic existence with her mother, Meg learns that her mother is dying and that she must live with her father, whom she

does not remember. After a bad start, her relationship with him improves as both talk honestly about their feelings. (DHHS)

940. Hoopes, J.L. & L.M. Stein., 1986, *Identity Formation in the Adopted Adolescent: The Delaware Family Study,* Child Welfare League of America
Following the same 50 child adoptees first reported on in ''Prediction in Child Development,'' this study examines their development during their high school years. The results of this study challenge the myth that adoption in itself has a negative impact on adoptees.

941. Hunter, E., 1976, *Me and Brenner,* Lippincott, New York
This is the story of an 11-year-old girl coping with her mother's divorce and remarriage. She learns to accept the new man whom her mother will marry, and finds that she can have her stepfather and her biological father. (DHHS)

942. Hunter, E., 1976, *Me and Mr. Stenner,* Lippincott, New York
Tells story of an eleven-year-old girl who has a stepbrother.

943. Kindred, W., 1973, *Lucky Wilma,* Dial Press, New York
A story about a girl who enjoys both parents after a divorce. Her loving father visits every Saturday. Demonstrates how important visitation is. (DHHS)

944. Klein, N., 1972, *Mom, The Wolfman, and Me,* Pantheon, New York
Real people cope with separation after remarriage. The father is portrayed as a nurturing person. (DHHS)

945. LeShan, E., 1979, *What's Going to Happen to Me? When Parents Separate or Divorce,* Four Winds, New York
This book offers a positive approach to divorce. The inclusion of numerous anecdotes serves to assuage children's loneliness and fears. The author stresses that divorce is never the fault of the child, and that parents should not try to keep a bad marriage together. Anecdotes on remarriage are included as well. The book may help children to discuss feelings about divorce with parents. (DHHS)

946. Lewis, H.C. , 1980, *All About Families—The Second Time Around,* Peachtree Publishers, Atlanta, GA
Explores children's feelings and leads to discussion around

important basic stepfamily issues.

947. Lexau, J., 1972, *Emily and the Klunky Baby and the Next Door Dog,* Dial Press, New York
Little Emily's feelings of being neglected after her parents' divorce are cited and finally resolved. (DHHS)

948. Lisker, S., 1976, *Two Special Cards,* Harcourt Brace Jovanovich, New York
A young girl feels angry and afraid when her parents fight and talk about divorce. She later finds ways to make the best of having separated parents, both of whom love her. (DHHS)

949. Madison, W., 1975, *Marinka, Katinka, and me (Susie),* Bradbury Press, New York
This story portrays friendship among three fourth-grade girls whose non-traditional families are accepted. Susie's father is dead, Marinka's parents are divorced, and Katinka's father is in prison. Realistic problems, including divorce, are put into perspective. (DHHS)

950. Magid, K. & W. Schreibman, 1980, *Divorce is . . . A Kid's Coloring Book,* Pelican Publishing Co., Gretna, LA
"A coloring book for young children illustrated with scenes and captions regarding the common dilemmas of children of divorce. Preface for parents."(SAA)

951. Mann, P., 1973, *My Dad Lives in a Downtown Motel,* Doubleday, Garden City, NY
This book deals with a child's feelings immediately following separation and during the early single-parent phase.

952. Mazer, N., 1971, *I, Trissy,* Delacorte, New York
Trissy uses her typewriter to vent frustrations about her parents' divorce and the problems brought on by her unwillingness to understand her parents. Finally she begins to question her own identity and eventually becomes better able to face her problems. (DHHS)

953. McHargue, G., 1975, *Stoneflight,* Viking Press, New York
Janie suspects a divorce but no one tells her. She wishes she were like the invulnerable stone Griffon. Through her uncle, she becomes included in family discussions of the problem. (DHHS)

954. Neville, E.C., 1975, *Garden on Broken Glass,* Delacorte, New York
Brian, age 13, grows into a sensitive youngster despite an absent father and an alcoholic mother. This book was considered outstanding by the Child Study Association of America. (DHHS)

955. Newfield, M. , 1975, *A Book For Jordan,* Atheneum, New York
Jordan, age nine, doesn't believe her parent's reassurances of their love for her after their separation. Both parents work to promote her constructive adjustment, even though her father lives far away. The book details a creative project for fathers. (DHHS)

956. Noble, J., 1979, *Two Homes for Lynn,* Holt, New York
"Lynn's makebelieve friends help her adjust to her two homes after her parents divorce."(SAA)

957. Okshaker, B., 1971, *What Shall We Tell the Kids?,* Dell Publishing Co., New York

958. Perl, L., 1975, *The Telltale Summer of Tina C.,* Seabury Press, New York
Trying to untangle the confusing relationships of divorce and remarriage, Tina begins to understand her loved ones. The story portrays positive, open relationships with both parents. (DHHS)

959. Pevsner, S., 1975, *A Smart Kid Like You,* Seabury Press, New York
A realistic view of some of the aftereffects of divorce. Nina finds her new math teacher is her father's second wife. (DHHS)

960. Pfeffer, S.B., 1975, *Marly the Kid,* Doubleday & Co., New York
During her sophomore year, Marly decides to live with her father instead of her mother. She also refuses to tolerate insulting remarks of her history teacher. The stepmother in this story is a positive figure. (DHHS)

961. Phillips, C.E., 1981, *Our Family Got a Stepparent,* Regal Books, Ventura, CA
Two young children adjust to a new stepfather.

962. Pursell, M.S., 1976, *A Look At Divorce,* Lerner, New York
Text and photographs describe the changes children and parents may make following a divorce. The pictures make it a good book to read and discuss with small children. (DHHS)

963. Rand, D., 1977, *I'm Going to Visit My Daddy,* Academic Therapy, San Rafael, CA.

Illustrated book for young children who go on an airplane trip to visit their father. (DHHS)

964. Ricci, I., 1980, *Mom's House, Dad's House,* Macmillan, New York

A practical guide to post-divorce parenting. How to make shared custody work and build two homes for children after divorce. Goes beyond the concept of legal custody to a new way of reorganizing family life after divorce. For all types of living arrangements.

965. Richards, A. & I. Willis, 1976, *How to Get It Together When Your Parents Are Coming Apart,* David McKay, New York

The book deals with family troubles before, during, and after divorce. It is addressed to adolescents to help them deal with the effects of their parents' marital troubles on their own lives. The chapter titled "The Family Circle" discusses the problems and feelings related to remarriage.

966. Robson, B., 1979, *My Parents Are Divorced, Too,* Dorset Publishing, Inc., Toronto

"What teenagers experience and how they cope, with comments by the author, a child psychiatrist."(SAA)

967. Rofes, E. (Editor), 1981, *The Kid's Book of Divorce,* Lewis Publishing Co., Lexington, KY

"Written by 20 kids, 11–14 ,14 of whom have divorced parents. Gives practical ways of getting along that would never be accepted or heard if it came from adults. Deals well with important stepfamily issues."(SAA)

968. Sachs, M., 1971, *The Bear's House,* Doubleday Press, New York

Difficult emotional situations confront a young girl and her older brother who take responsibility for the younger sibling and their mentally ill mother after their father leaves. Painful to read, but value may lie in readers' realizing that others have terrible problems too. (DHHS)

969. Sheffield, J.N., 1975, *Not Just Sugar and Spice,* William Morrow and Co., New York

Lani is jealous, self-centered, and losing friends rapidly. Only to get rid of a domineering housekeeper does she decide to pull herself together, cooperate with her future stepfather, and help out while her mother is in the hospital. (DHHS)

970. Shyer, M., *Stepdog,* Charles Scribner's Sons, New York
A delightful story for children from the perspective of the new family's dog, who deals with becoming the ''stepdog''.

971. Sinberg, J., 1978, *Divorce Is a Grown Up Problem,* Avon Books, New York
A story for young children about their emotional reactions in a divorce situation, with a preface for adults.

972. Sinberg, J., 1978, *Now I Have a Stepparent and It's Kind of Confusing,* Avon Books, New York
This book, dealing with the confusion children may experience when a parent remarries, was written to help children, parents and stepparents better understand the issues they all face.

973. Smith, D., 1974, *Kick a Stone Home,* Crowell, New York
After three years, Sara Jane still hopes her father will come back. She hates visiting him and his new wife and has no one with whom to share her feelings. Gradually, her negativism and resentment toward the remarriage soften. A positive portrayal of real people is presented. (DHHS)

974. Snyder, Z.K., 1971, *Headless Cupid,* Atheneum, New York
Fun and intrigue result when stepbrothers and sisters begin adjusting to each other and to their new parents. (DHHS)

975. Sobol, H.H. & P. Agre, 1979, *My Other Mother, My Other Father,* Macmillan, New York
''Photo illustrations and story appropriate to younger children. Twelve-year-old Andrea, whose parents have divorced and remarried, discusses the complexities of her new, larger family.'' (SAA)

976. Spilke, F., 1979, *What About Children?,* Crown Publishers, Inc., New York
A handbook for parents that gives practical information on how to tell children about an impending divorce through to helping children deal with a remarriage. It includes important practical knowledge that a professional will find useful in practice.

977. Stenson, J.S., 1980, *Now I Have a Stepparent and It's Kind of Confusing,* Avon Books, New York

"To be read to younger children, with a preface for adults. Older children also respond well to the book, which deals with conflicts that may arise in children—frustration of the child who secretly hopes the parents will get back together, jealousy of sharing the parent, fear of betraying lost parent by loving stepparent. The child can begin to respect and trust the stepparent and understand that he is safe, secure, and loved." (SAA)

978. Stolz, M., 1972, *Leap Before You Look,* Harper & Row, New York
The young heroine lives with her mother and has difficulty adjusting to her father's remarriage. A friend helps her to reconcile her feelings. (DHHS)

979. Sueling, B., *What Kind of Family Is This?,* Golden Books, New York
One of the "Golden Book" series, this book is designed to be used by young children and parents as a springboard for discussion about the concerns and fears children have about living in a stepfamily.

980. Sullivan, M., 1975, *Blue Grass Iggy,* Nelson, New York
Iggy makes friends in the trailer camp where he lives with his father. (DHHS)

981. Surowiecki, S., 1972, *Joshua's Daddy,* Lollipop Power, Chapel Hill, N.C.
Little Joshua copes with living with his mother and attending a Day Care Center. (DHHS)

982. Thomas, I., 1976, *Eliza's Daddy,* Harcourt Brace Jovanovich, New York
This young heroine has feelings about her father's remarriage that are eased by revisiting his new family. Jealousy and fears are resolved in this "Let Me Read" book. (DHHS)

983. Thorval, K., 1974, *And Leffe Was Instead of a Dad,* Bradbury Press, New York
Magnus' mother lives with Leffe, who becomes the dad that Magnus always wanted. When Leffe begins drinking again, there is the chance that he will leave or break parole. An unusual story told with warmth and understanding, translated from the Swedish original. (DHHS)

984. Townsend, C.H., 1978, *The Single-Parent Family in Children's Books,* Scarecrow Press, Metuchen, NJ

A learned introduction focuses on the development and possible causes of the proliferation of single-parent families, an explanation of bibliography, and the author's reasons for writing this book. Previous authors are cited in a strong scholarly effort to unearth historical data on the subject. The major portion of the book concentrates on children's fiction: 215 books, 41 published in or before 1965; 59% were copyrighted between 1966 and 1976. The books are analyzed with respect to genre, characterization, style, and plot, and an evaluative coding chart is included. The annotated bibliography is classified by causes of single parenthood.

985. Troyer, W., 1979, *Divorced Kids,* Harcourt Brace Jovanovich, New York
The author, a divorced father himself, interviewed hundreds of children from age three on and uses their own words to tell their stories.

986. Turow, R., 1977, *Daddy Doesn't Live Here Anymore,* Greatlakes Living Press, Matteson, Ill.
A sensitive guide for divorced parents with many practical suggestions. It is useful for parents to read this book along with other literature for divorced parents. (DHHS)

987. Vigna, J., *Daddy's New Baby,* Albert Whitman & Co., New York
Book for children to read by themselves or with a parent. Tells the story of how a little girl changes her feelings toward her father's new baby through a near disaster.

988. Vigna, J., *She's Not My Real Mother,* Albert Whitman & Co., New York
Easy-reader for children tells how a young boy, after getting lost, must reevaluate his feelings about his stepmother when she rescues him.

989. Wagner, J., 1969, *J.T.,* Van Nostrand Reinhold, New York
A boy has a difficult time adapting to the changes and problems heightened by his father's absence. Outsiders, including a cat, help him to adjust. (DHHS)

990. Warren, M.P., 1976, *The Haunted Kitchen,* Westminster Press, New York
After the divorce, Dad decides to go back to school. He and his three children move to Oregon and live in what appears to be a

haunted house. Children are portrayed coping together and working cooperatively. (DHHS)

991. Wolitzer, H., 1976, *Out of Love,* Farrar Straus Giroux, New York
Two years after the divorce, Teddy is still scheming to reunite her parents, through illness and by crusading to better her mother's appearance. Acceptance of the divorce as final is a painful experience for her. (DHHS)

992. Zindel, P., 1975, *I Love My Mother,* Harper & Row, New York
The non-stereotyped story of a small boy living with his mother. (DHHS)

AUTHOR INDEX

Please note: The numerical listings after each name reflect the entry number for that author, *not* the page number on which it is located.

SUBJECT INDEX

Please note: The numerical listing(s) after each subject reflects the entry number for that subject, not the page number on which it is located.

ABOUT THE AUTHOR

GRETA W. STANTON (B.A. Hunter College, MSW, Columbia University, NASW Diplomate in Clinical Social Work) is Professor Emerita Rutgers University School of Social Work. She has also taught at Columbia School of Social Work, Hunter College School of Social Work, and Fordham University School of Social Services. Professor Stanton has taught Casework to graduate students, has instituted courses in Child Welfare and headed several national grants in Child Welfare and School Social Work. In more recent years, she has written and taught courses and workshops about stepfamilies. Since retirement she has continued to give workshops and family counseling to stepfamilies and their children, as well as some classroom and practice teaching to graduate students. She has also been active in community work.